The Triangle of Microfinance

**Other Books Published in Cooperation with
the International Food Policy Research Institute**

IFPRI

*Intrahousehold Resource Allocation in Developing Countries:
Models, Methods, and Policy*
Edited by Lawrence Haddad, John Hoddinott, and Harold Alderman

*Sustainability, Growth, and Poverty Alleviation: A Policy and
Agroecological Perspective*
Edited by Stephen A. Vosti and Thomas Reardon

Famine in Africa: Causes, Responses, and Prevention
By Joachim von Braun, Tesfaye Teklu, and Patrick Webb

Paying for Agricultural Productivity
Edited by Julian M. Alston, Philip G. Pardey, and Vincent H. Smith

*Out of the Shadow of Famine: Evolving Food Markets and Food Policy
in Bangladesh*
Edited by Raisuddin Ahmed, Steven Haggblade,
and Tawfiq-e-Elahi Chowdhury

Agricultural Science Policy: Changing Global Agendas
Edited by Julian M. Alston, Philip G. Pardey, and Michael J. Taylor

*The Politics of Precaution: Genetically Modified Crops
in Developing Countries*
By Robert L. Paarlberg

*Land Tenure and Natural Resource Management: A Comparative Study
of Agrarian Communities in Asia and Africa*
Edited by Keijiro Otsuka and Frank Place

*Seeds of Contention: World Hunger and the Global Controversy over
GM Crops*
By Per Pinstrup-Andersen and Ebbe Schiøler

*Innovation in Natural Resource Management: The Role of Property Rights
and Collective Action in Developing Countries*
Edited by Ruth Meinzen-Dick, Anna Knox, Frank Place, and Brent Swallow

Reforming Agricultural Markets in Africa
Mylène Kherallah, Christopher Delgado, Eleni Gabre-Madhin,
Nicholas Minot, and Michael Johnson

The Triangle of Microfinance

Financial Sustainability, Outreach, and Impact

EDITED BY MANFRED ZELLER AND RICHARD L. MEYER

Published for the International Food Policy Research Institute

The Johns Hopkins University Press
Baltimore and London

The Johns Hopkins University Press
2715 North Charles Street
Baltimore, Maryland 21218-4363
www.press.jhu.edu

International Food Policy Research Institute
2033 K Street, N.W.
Washington, D.C. 20006
(202) 862-5600
www.ifpri.org

LIBRARY OF CONGRESS CATALOGING-IN-PUBLICATION DATA
The triangle of microfinance : financial sustainability, outreach, and impact / edited by
Manfred Zeller and Richard L. Meyer.
    p.   cm.
    International Food Policy Research Institute.
    Includes bibliographical references and index.
    ISBN 0-8018-7148-4 (hardcover : alk. paper) — ISBN 0-8018-7226-X (pbk. : alk. paper)
    1. Microfinance.   I. Zeller, Manfred.   II. Meyer, Richard L., 1937– .
HG178.3 .T75   2002
332—dc21   2002005367

Contents

PART V   Summary and Implications for Policy and Research

Figures

Tables

Boxes

Foreword

The importance of financial intermediation in attacking poverty has long been recognized. Yet substantial challenges remain in providing affordable, useful, and sustainable financial services to the poor. Consequently, there remain instances in many developing countries in which financial constraints—rather than lack of skills, market opportunities, or supply bottlenecks—prevent poor families from making the key investments necessary to escape poverty. Economic returns to pro-poor public investments may often remain low because poor households lack access to financial services. For example, investments in irrigation might not be fully utilized when farmers are not able to afford seed or fertilizer during the cash-strapped planting season. Schools may remain less than fully attended when parents lack the saving services that make it easy for them to accumulate and pay fees in the lump-sum amounts that are often required. Examples like these abound, and they highlight the critical role of financial institutions in poverty reduction programs.

From the perspective of the International Food Policy Research Institute (IFPRI), particularly worrisome are the punishing consequences of inadequate financial support for the health, well-being, and earning capacity of the poor. In the uncertain world of rainfed agriculture, food availability and earnings vary widely from one season to the next, and the specter of harvest failure is ever present. In cities, market upheavals can produce unexpected swings in employment, especially in the informal economy in which the poorest tend to work. Without access to formal institutions offering savings, credit, or insurance services, the poor can have difficulty in maintaining essential food consumption during lean seasons, poor harvests, or periods of unemployment. This can cause temporary but acute nutritional deficiencies that affect the long-term physical and mental growth of small children. Further, the pressure of financing basic needs can force the poorest to take drastic actions, such as pulling children from school or selling productive assets. Disposed assets and forgone human capital investments cannot always be easily replaced, and permanent income losses can be substantial.

What are the main obstacles to providing adequate financial services to the poor, and how should policymakers tackle them? To be sure, significant headway has been made in reducing the transaction costs of serving the poor. With the explosion of microfinance in the 1990s, millions of poor people now have access to formal financial services for the first time. But much remains to be accomplished in reaching a wider population, improving product design, and reducing the cost of service delivery. This requires not only learning from recent experiences, but also gaining a deeper understanding of the nature of the financial constraints faced by the poor and their demand for financial services.

This book brings together critical empirical work done by IFPRI researchers and others from collaborating institutions. The editors introduce the concept of the triangle of microfinance, not only as the organizing framework for the volume but also as the analytic core of the microfinance challenge. This challenge lies in (1) reaching the poor in substantial numbers, (2) enabling them to move out of poverty, and (3) creating financial institutions that are sustainable. These objectives are not naturally conflicting; in fact, the editors conclude that the most successful innovations are those that are able to expand all sides of this triangle. But the book also points out situations in which a tradeoff has to be struck. When this happens, it is most important to make an accurate and transparent assessment of the tradeoffs involved. This book helps us make judicious decisions about difficult tradeoffs, with foremost attention given to the role finance can play in achieving long-term poverty alleviation and economic growth.

Joachim von Braun
Director General
International Food Policy Research Institute

Preface

Many chapters in this book are outcomes of the multicountry research program on rural financial policies for food security of the poor set up by the International Food Policy Research Institute (IFPRI). IFPRI undertook this research with collaborators at a number of research institutions to help policymakers reach informed decisions on issues concerning the microfinance sector and its role in poverty alleviation. An overview of IFPRI's research on microfinance provides background and clarifies the context in which various topics are discussed.

Poverty and food security considerations drove IFPRI's research on rural microfinance. By the early 1990s, an increasing number of IFPRI and other research studies revealed that borrowing and savings decisions were key coping mechanisms in maintaining household food security. Yet food security policies rarely considered this financial dimension. The multicountry research program was set up to fill this vacuum.

Three important research implications became obvious. First, policymakers and managers in the financial sector need to look beyond production-oriented credit and consider ways to finance consumption activities that have important short- and long-term effects on household welfare. This requires a clearer understanding of the nature and scale of the financial constraints that poor households face. However, in the early 1990s this essential client-related information was quite limited. Therefore, IFPRI's multicountry research program invested substantial resources in conducting household surveys that highlighted, empirically, the nature of financial transactions in nine Asian and African countries.

Second, the institutional design of microfinance institutions (MFIs) needs to respond to the struggle of poor people to live healthy, productive lives. Policies have to create conditions conducive to innovations that marry prudent financial management with pro-poor products and services. Hence, initial IFPRI research addressed institutional innovations in member- or group-based systems and gradually expanded to examine individual lending systems as well as larger issues related to the governance and regulation of MFIs.

Third, policymakers and researchers lacked an appropriate methodology to measure and evaluate impact. This made it difficult to conclude unambiguously whether transferring public resources from education, health, and nutrition to microfinance programs resulted in clear-cut social gains. The multicountry program therefore developed methodologies to clarify the basic conditions under which microfinance can be a cost-effective poverty alleviation tool. IFPRI conducted studies on this front in both Asia and Africa.

This book synthesizes diverse country-level research results in all the three areas outlined above. The editors encapsulate this synthesis in the concept of the "critical triangle of microfinance," the simultaneous management of outreach, sustainability, and impact. Policymakers can use this conceptual framework to derive broad working principles to formulate and evaluate decisions that affect the microfinance sector.

The list of contributors and their institutional affiliations indicates the extensive collaboration involved in the IFPRI multicountry research program. Research partnerships were established early on with the universities of Hohenheim, Kiel, and Bonn and the German Foundation for International Development (DSE)—all in Germany—and with the Bangladesh Institute of Development Studies, the Chinese Academy of Social Sciences, the Ministry of Research of the Government of Madagascar, and the University of Malawi. Additional collaborations were also established at conferences and workshops where much of the research in this volume was first presented. In 1997, for example, IFPRI and The Ohio State University organized mini-symposia on microfinance and poverty at the Conference of the International Association of Agricultural Economists in Sacramento, California. In 1998, the International Workshop on Innovations in Microfinance for the Rural Poor was held in Accra, Ghana, cosponsored by DSE, the Bank of Ghana, and the International Fund for Agricultural Development, and IFPRI. The editors of this volume gratefully acknowledge the useful feedback received at these workshops and the valuable comments of two anonymous reviewers.

IFPRI gratefully acknowledges the generous financial support of the Ministry of Economic Cooperation and Development (BMZ), Federal Republic of Germany, for funding conferences and institutional collaboration enabling the publication of the majority of the papers in this book. Other donors to IFPRI's multicountry research on rural finance presented in this book include the Consultative Group to Assist the Poorest; the German Agency for Technical Cooperation (GTZ); the Government of France; Ireland Aid; the Rockefeller Foundation; the United Nations Children's Fund; and the United States Agency for International Development. The conclusions in the book are, of course, our own and do not necessarily reflect those of the funding organizations.

The Triangle of Microfinance

1 Improving the Performance of Microfinance: Financial Sustainability, Outreach, and Impact

MANFRED ZELLER AND RICHARD L. MEYER

The founders of microfinance shared a vision. In the disparate settings of Bangladesh, Bolivia, and Indonesia, their vision was to supply formal financial services to poor people shunned by banks because their savings were tiny, their loan demand was small, and they lacked loan collateral. Professor Muhammad Yunus, a Bangladeshi, addressed the banking problem faced by poor villagers in southern Bangladesh through a program of action-research. With his graduate students at Chittagong University, he designed an experimental credit program to serve the villagers (Bornstein 1996). The program spread rapidly to hundreds of villages. Through a special experimental relationship with local commercial banks, he disbursed and recovered thousands of loans, but the bankers refused to take over the project at the end of the pilot phase. They feared it was too expensive and risky in spite of its success.

Similar stories are told by Pancho Otero, founder of Fundación para la Promoción y Desarrollo de la Microempresa (PRODEM), which gave rise to BancoSol, in Bolivia, and other microfinance pioneers. Poor people in developing nations lack access to formal financial services and the problem is especially serious in rural areas. This constrains their ability to acquire assets, start businesses, finance emergency needs, and insure themselves against illnesses and disasters. The pioneers believed that improved access to financial services would resolve these problems, at least to some extent. This vision motivated them to create successful village banking networks, such as the village banking system (*unit desas*, or UD) of the Indonesian Bank Rakyat Indonesia (BRI), as well as numerous nongovernmental organizations (NGOs) with programs for lending to the poor. The design of the programs varies with the circumstances of the country, and a great deal of experimentation and a multitude of institutional failures and setbacks usually led to revisions of their original designs.

Some microfinance institutions (MFIs) tie credit to education and nutrition programs. Others follow the minimalist approach of providing only loans. Some require their clients to show good faith by accumulating savings before seeking a loan, whereas others entirely neglect the importance of savings for the poor.

1

Some grant individual loans, but most use some type of group lending in the hopes of reducing transaction costs and achieving good loan recovery, particularly when lending to poorer segments of the population or in more sparsely populated areas. All these institutions stress serving clients outside the frontier of formal finance, although relatively few data are available to document the nature of the clientele actually served.

Much has been accomplished since the 1970s when the pioneer institutions began what is now being termed the microfinance revolution (Morduch 1999). Of course, poverty has not been solved, but millions of poor people have gained access to formal financial services for the first time. This is a remarkable achievement. A few flagship NGOs have even evolved into licensed specialized banks for the poor, and their institutional innovations have grown to a sustainable scale. Part of the vision has certainly been realized, but the reality is that much remains to be done before it can be claimed that the challenge of answering the demand for financial services by the poor, especially in rural areas, has been met. Most microfinance programs are small and vulnerable to resource constraints. Most operate in a few locations and serve specific clusters of clients, so they are exposed to the systemic risks of undiversified loan portfolios. Most mobilize few savings and are not financially self-sufficient, so they are dependent on the whims of donors and governments for their future existence. There is certainly a lot of waste and duplication in this sector, with many MFI start-ups collapsing after the pilot phase of a project. Reports of declining loan recovery in some of the mature programs suggest that the lending technology may not be able to cope well with long-term clients when they reach higher loan amounts. In a few countries, with support from government and donors, the microfinance industry has developed successful technologies that can be readily replicated. Therefore, competition is increasing from banks and finance companies entering microfinance, mostly by seeking out the wealthier clientele groups in urban areas. As a result, MFIs targeting the poor risk losing their better-off clients to competitors that offer more flexible products with larger loan sizes and better conditions. The typical microfinance loan products are best suited for borrowers who can make small, frequent loan payments. It is unclear how well they serve farmers and other clients who experience irregular cash flows.

Apart from some key articles and books, there is a dearth of sound empirical literature on microfinance, in particular on the demand side. There is thus limited understanding about the outreach, sustainability, and impact of the entire microfinance industry. Many microfinance documents are highly promotional, designed to disseminate the idea and to seek increased funding. Likewise, some publications that attempt to quantitatively evaluate the strongest claims made by its advocates have a weak empirical base.

This book is designed as a contribution to empirical knowledge and research methods for measuring households' access to and demand for financial services. The book features chapters that link these issues within the conceptual framework of the triangle of microfinance, which seeks a better understanding of the existing trade-offs and synergies between three overarching policy objectives in microfinance—namely financial sustainability, outreach to the poor, and the welfare impact. These objectives can be analyzed from the supply as well as the demand side. This book leans strongly toward the latter because many influential publications in recent years have focused on the supply side, such as those on best practices in the management of microfinance institutions and on methods for measuring and comparing financial sustainability across different types of MFIs (see, for example, Yaron 1992; Christen et al. 1995; Otero and Rhyne 1994; and Kimenyi, Wieland, and Von Pischke 1998). The chapters reflect attempts by the authors to employ unique data and robust techniques to analyze the access and demand patterns of the poor, and the outreach and welfare impact of formal and informal financial institutions.

The individual chapters were mainly selected from the papers presented at two mini-symposia on microfinance at the triennial meetings of the International Association of Agricultural Economists (IAAE) held in Sacramento in August 1997. These symposia were organized by the International Food Policy Research Institute (IFPRI) and Ohio State University (OSU). In addition, several chapters in this volume were presented at the International Workshop on Innovations in Microfinance for the Rural Poor held in November 1998 in Accra, Ghana. This workshop was jointly organized by the German Foundation for International Development (DSE), IFPRI, the International Fund for Agricultural Development (IFAD), and the Bank of Ghana.[1]

The Conceptual Framework: The Triangle of Microfinance

The organization of this volume was guided by a conceptual framework that summarizes recent shifts in paradigms, strategies, and development practices in the field of microfinance during the 1990s, leading to the recognition of the three overarching policy objectives: financial sustainability, outreach to the poor, and welfare impact.

There has been a paradigm shift in thinking about appropriate policies for financial sector development, and much of this can be traced to the failures of small farmer credit and the successes of a few microfinance institutions. Finance policy has traditionally been based on an assumed gap between the demand for

---

1. Earlier versions of Chapters 2, 3, and 16 (Zeller and Sharma, Nguyen et al., and Zhu et al.) were published in Zeller and Sharma (2000) and are included here with permission of the German Foundation for International Development (DSE). Chapters 11 and 14 (Sharma and Buchenrieder, and Lapenu) are substantial revisions of papers that originally appeared in Zeller and Sharma (2000).

credit and savings services and access to these services by specific population groups. Small farmers were the primary concern in the 1960s and 1970s; the poor emerged as the focus in the 1980s and 1990s. Matching access to or supply of financial services with demand has been a consistent challenge for financial institutions attempting to serve clientele groups outside the frontier of formal finance (Von Pischke 1991).

Policymakers have sought to narrow the gap between the access to and demand for financial services through various interventions during the past four decades, albeit with mixed success. These interventions, and the rationale for them, have changed over time. In the 1960s and 1970s, the state was at the center of action on the ground, and parastatal development banks and agricultural credit projects predominated. It is fair to say that this traditional approach to finance, as noted by Yaron and Benjamin (Chapter 15), has now been replaced by a new paradigm (Adams 1998). The new paradigm began to emerge in the second half of the 1980s because of the widespread failures of development banks and the encouraging results of some bold microfinance innovations to serve the poor. The most important included those implemented by the Grameen Bank, by the *unit desa* system of Bank Rakyat Indonesia, and by PRODEM, BancoSol's predecessor in Bolivia. It is important to note that these innovations, and related efforts to build new institutions, were not borne exclusively from market forces, but relied heavily on financial support from the state and donors. The focus was on building cost-efficient MFIs able to expand the financial frontier sustainably. The new paradigm recognizes that high transaction costs and risks, which partly result from information asymmetries and moral hazard (Stiglitz and Weiss 1981) for both financial intermediaries and clients, are root causes of the gap between demand and supply. Therefore, the new paradigm emphasizes institutional innovations to reduce costs and risks. Although the new paradigm is more market-oriented than the old approach and has greater potential to expand the financial frontier sustainably, it is more complex and challenging to implement.

The objectives of financial policy have changed along with the paradigm shift. Initially, the focus was on improving the outreach of microfinance institutions to the poor, that is, on serving more of the poor (breadth of outreach) and more of the poorest of the poor (depth of outreach). Eventually, the objective of sustainability of financial institutions took on great importance. Following the work of Ohio State University and other institutions in the 1980s, the view emerged that the building of lasting financial institutions requires that they become financially sustainable, that is, they cover their costs. Some analysts (for example, Otero and Rhyne 1994; Christen et al. 1995) argued that increasing the depth of outreach and sustainability are compatible objectives. However, Hulme and Mosley (1996), along with some authors in this volume, argue that there appears to be a trade-off between improving outreach, in particular reaching the poorest, and achieving financial sustainability. This trade-off stems from the fact that MFI transaction costs are high for obtaining information about the creditworthiness of poor clients (see Chapter 8 by Navajas et al.). Transaction costs have a large fixed-cost component, so unit costs for smaller savings deposits or smaller loans are high compared with those for larger financial transactions. This law of decreasing unit transaction costs with increasing transaction size generates the trade-off between improved outreach to the poor and financial sustainability, irrespective of the lending technology used.

However, financial sustainability of financial institutions and outreach to the poor are only two of the policy objectives characterizing recent developments in the field of microfinance. When policy intervention and direct support for institution building require public investments, the question arises as to the pay-off or impact, for example in terms of economic growth and the alleviation of poverty and food insecurity.

It is commonly believed that further institutional innovation and microfinance expansion will continue to rely on public intervention and financial support. In fact, most, if not all, MFIs that reach large numbers of female and male clients below the poverty line require state or donor transfers to subsidize their costs. At least, the most successful ones that have achieved financial sustainability have required investment by the state or donors in the past. Such public investments are justified from a public policy perspective only if the discounted social benefits of public investment in microfinance are expected to outweigh the social costs. These costs include the opportunity costs of forgoing the benefits of other public investments, such as in primary education, when scarce government or donor funds are used for microfinance (Zeller et al. 1997). The subsidy dependence index (see Yaron and Benjamin in Chapter 15) has become a widely accepted operational measure to quantify the amount of social costs involved in supporting the operations of a financial institution. Addressing the policy question of whether or not such public transfers are economically sustainable (as argued by Zeller and Sharma in Chapter 2) requires a comparison of social costs with social benefits. This consideration raises the third objective of finance: improving the welfare impact. This objective introduces the highly contentious and complicated issue of measuring the impacts of financial services.

The critical triangle of microfinance reflecting the three objectives of outreach, financial sustainability, and impact is represented in Figure 1.1. All MFIs attempt to contribute to these objectives, but many stress one particular objective over the other two. Some may produce large impacts but achieve limited outreach. Others may have smaller impacts but are highly sustainable. The potential trade-offs between depth of outreach and financial sustainability have been noted, but trade-offs may also exist between impact and financial sustainability. As Sharma and Buchenrieder (Chapter 11) suggest, the impact of finance can be enhanced through complementary services—such as business or marketing services or training of borrowers—that raise the profitability of loan-financed projects. Complementary services are sometimes offered by MFIs, but supplying them in-

FIGURE 1.1 The critical triangle in achieving economic sustainability of microfinance

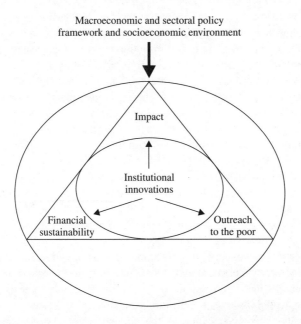

creases operating costs, thereby jeopardizing financial sustainability if the additional costs are not covered by borrowers or public transfers. There may also be trade-offs between impact and depth of outreach. The recent research reviewed by Sharma and Buchenrieder suggests that the very poor may benefit from microfinance largely by smoothing their consumption through borrowing or improved management of their savings. Those just above or just below the poverty line may be able to use loans more effectively for productive purposes, which ultimately raise their income and asset base. Thus, expanding financial services may improve the welfare of the very poor but not necessarily lift them out of poverty because of their lack of access to markets, technology, education, and other factors that raise incomes by expanding their production frontier.

These potential trade-offs must be addressed when MFIs develop their business plans and decide between marketing their services to only the very poor or to a mix of clients clustered around the poverty line. Clearly, to improve the prospects for achieving financial sustainability, MFIs may wish to target clients other than the very poor, as the Bolivian MFIs seem to do (see Chapter 8 by Navajas et al.). This raises the question of what outcome is considered most socially desirable or optimal. For example, is public support more desired for MFIs that specifically target the poor, such as those in Bangladesh that use specific wealth criteria in an attempt to screen out the nonpoor?

There are also potential synergies among the three objectives of microfinance policy. First, financial sustainability may be perceived by potential clients as a crucial indicator of MFI permanence and will influence their decision about whether it is worthwhile in the long run to become clients. Thus, greater financial sustainability can positively influence outreach. This synergy may be even more important for savers, who must have faith in the permanence of the institution to which they entrust their savings. Zeller and Sharma (Chapter 2) and Nguyen et al. (Chapter 3) stress the role that savings play, especially for the poor. No one will save with an institution that is thought to be only temporary. Second, striving for financial sustainability forces MFIs to be sensitive to client demand and induces them to improve products, operations, and outreach. Better financial products, in turn, generate greater economic benefits for clients, and thus greater impact.

The analytical framework points to the wide set of potential trade-offs and synergies that needs to be better understood by policymakers, microfinance practitioners, and researchers alike. The triangle in Figure 1.1 is drawn with an inner and an outer circle. The inner circle represents the many types of institutional innovations that contribute to improving financial sustainability (such as employment of cost-reducing information systems), impact (such as designing demand-oriented services for the poor and more effective training of clients), or outreach to the poor (such as more effective targeting mechanisms or introducing lending technologies that attract a particular group of clients). The outer circle represents the external socioeconomic environment as well as the macroeconomic and sectoral policies that directly or indirectly affect the performance of financial institutions. Innovations at the institutional level (the inner circle) and improvements in the policy environment (the outer circle) contribute to improving the overall performance of financial institutions.

Efficiency in the allocation of public resources to microfinance compared with alternative policy interventions requires that performance be evaluated by comparing the social benefits generated by the financial system with its social costs. In theory, a financial institution is economically sustainable if its social benefits outweigh its social costs. Economic sustainability of the financial system implies that it is possible to justify public transfers for MFIs to make them financially sustainable (Zeller et al. 1997).

The social benefit–cost ratio of public support for MFIs is affected by many factors, including the overall policy framework and socioeconomic environment. Some macro- and socioeconomic environments may be so hostile to financial sector development that public investments in MFIs may generate a dismal or negative social return, whereas in others the same investment may be highly profitable. Several chapters in this book highlight the importance of macroeconomic and financial sector policies as well as other conditions, such as infrastructure and education, and their role in influencing the social benefit–cost ratio of microfinance.

Organization of the Book

A brief summary of the highlights and major findings of the individual chapters is presented in this section. It serves as a guide to readers concerning the structure, content, and organization of the book.

Part I: Access to and Demand for Financial Services by the Poor

The first part of the book contains five chapters that explore the demand for and access to financial services by the poor. In Chapter 2, Zeller and Sharma focus on the linkages between household food security and access to formal credit, savings, and insurance services. They address several questions from both a conceptual and an empirical perspective. What is the role of microfinance in the overall mix of policy instruments for development and poverty alleviation? What types of financial services are demanded by and accessible to the poor? What are the gaps between demand and access, and what types of financial services need to be offered more by MFIs in order to improve outreach to poor women and men?

A conceptual framework is presented that distinguishes three pathways through which financial services potentially increase the household's income, consumption, and investments in human, social, and physical capital. The first pathway represents the traditional rationale for microfinance, that is, the provision of credit for income generation through expanded production. The second and third pathways focus on the demand for financial services for the efficient management of asset portfolios and for consumption smoothing. Then a synthesis is presented of the empirical results of IFPRI's multicountry research on rural finance. Patterns of demand and access by rural households, differentiated by poverty level, are stressed. The authors call for increased emphasis on innovations to diversify financial products and institutional arrangements aimed at improving the risk-bearing ability of the poor.

Along the same line of argument, Nguyen et al. (Chapter 3) provide empirical evidence from Burkina Faso that shows the potential for rural microfinance to go beyond loans and serve the broader demand for savings and insurance services. The rural poor in that country are exposed to strong seasonal income and demand patterns and to great uncertainty regarding crop yields and market conditions. Therefore, the poor demand not only credit but also savings and insurance services to smooth income and consumption. Most MFIs, however, provide only loans, and informal lenders are found not to fully satisfy the demand for financial services. The authors review four MFIs formed in recent years in Burkina Faso and highlight their potential and constraints. They conclude that a gap exists between access to and demand for financial services. To close this gap, MFIs will have to diversify their financial services to meet the diverse demands of small farmers, women, and micro-entrepreneurs.

Stanton (Chapter 4) looks at whether the socioeconomic characteristics of clients of Mexican rural lending institutions coincide with the declared target groups. Her results show that two state-owned lenders that target poorer clients actually serve a large number of wealthier nontarget clients, and private banks mainly serve larger commercial farmers. Informal lenders likewise provide more credit to wealthier clients, a result confirmed for Bangladesh by Zeller and Sharma (Chapter 5). Stanton points out that effective outreach requires that the target group voluntarily demands and seeks the services offered. The potential clients' demand for loans depends on their perceptions of the costs and benefits of getting a loan. This requires the client to assess the transaction costs of loan application and the probability of actually receiving the loan applied for. Hence, the author argues that the two state-owned MFIs should strive to offer credit services more adapted to and demanded by their target clientele, and they need to address the public perception that their programs are difficult for poorer clients to access. Thus, the results support the arguments in the preceding two chapters for greater innovation in financial products specifically demanded by the poor. The development of products designed for specific market segments would enhance self-targeting by clients and improve access to financial services by the poor.

Zeller and Sharma (Chapter 5) investigate the determinants of access to formal and informal credit. They introduce the concept of credit limits for measuring access to loans and argue that a potential borrower, irrespective of wealth and other characteristics, can obtain only a finite amount from lenders. For some, this amount is zero. A person is said to have access to credit if he or she is able to borrow a positive amount from the informal or formal market. Exercising the option to borrow is a decision made by the client. Hence, many nonborrowers may have access to credit, whereas other nonborrowers do not.

Both access to credit, measured by credit limits, and the amounts actually borrowed are empirically explored with data from 350 rural households in Bangladesh. At the time of the surveys some households were members of solidarity credit groups promoted by three MFIs, mainly the Association for Social Advancement (ASA),[2] the Bangladesh Rural Advancement Committee (BRAC), and the Grameen Bank. The results show that these group-based credit programs successfully reach poor people owning less than half an acre of land. Even households in the lowest expenditure decile of the rural households sampled have access to formal credit and borrow an average of US$75, which is more than household per capita income. Yet, among credit program members, those owning more land are found to have higher credit limits. Zeller

---

2. ASA has since ceased to provide group solidarity loans.

and Sharma conclude that formal and informal loans are imperfect substitutes. Formal credit, whenever available, marginally reduces, but does not completely eliminate, informal borrowing. Informal and formal lenders provide credit products that differ in interest rates, transaction costs, and loan term conditions. These products, therefore, fulfill different functions in the household's intertemporal transfer of resources. Once again, this result indicates that the design of financial products and their characteristics matter in determining borrowing patterns and credit market participation.

Most MFIs provide loans with only short-term maturities of one year or less. The lack of access to long-term credit for capital investments and housing is especially pronounced even where MFIs are active. The final chapter of Part I, by Lyne and Darroch, analyzes the role of long-term credit in the acquisition of agricultural land by poorer farmers in the Republic of South Africa. They first discuss the distribution of land and the objectives of the land reform program, which aims to increase access by black farmers. They show that market-based land transfers to smallholder farmers have been sluggish at best, and suggest that conventional mortgage loans were either inaccessible to or unsuitable for black farmers in financing the acquisition of land. They argue that innovative product design can alleviate these constraints. Based on the experience of a private sector mortgage scheme, they conclude that subsidized mortgage loans with graduated repayment schedules can address the cash-flow problem faced by medium-scale emergent commercial farmers. The authors conclude that the government could learn from the positive experiences of private sector programs and introduce mortgage loans with graduated repayment schedules as a component of the land redistribution programs.

Part II: Outreach and Financial Sustainability of Institutions

The chapters in Part II largely concern the two criteria that have dominated recent discussions about how to evaluate MFIs: outreach and sustainability (Yaron 1992; Christen et al. 1995). The number of total clients, the number of female clients, and the total number of loans made or outstanding are regularly reported as indicators of the breadth of outreach by most MFIs. Less information is provided about the depth of outreach, that is, the poverty level of the clients served, and loan sizes are used as admittedly imperfect substitutes for more precise data on poverty levels.

Paxton and Cuevas (Chapter 7) ask the question, "Does type of MFI influence outreach and sustainability?" A depth of outreach measure was constructed to represent the degree to which the MFIs reach rural, female, poor, and illiterate clients. They found that village banks in Latin America tend to have greater depth of outreach, whereas credit unions have higher levels of sustainability. They argue, however, that this does not necessarily reflect a trade-off between the two objectives, but rather is the result of the credit unions' greater breadth of outreach and more heterogeneous clientele. Village banks have made significant progress toward sustainability, but a strong correlation was noted between the depth of outreach and reliance on subsidies.

Navajas et al. (Chapter 8) constructed an absolute measure of poverty composed of variables that are used in the national poverty assessment in Bolivia. The authors evaluate the poverty level of clients of five competing MFIs, two operating in rural areas and three in urban areas. Two used individual lending technologies and three used peer group lending; all five are moving toward financial self-sufficiency. Although most clients were too poor to be served by commercial banks, none of the five reaches the poorest of the poor. In a competitive environment, matching occurs between clients and MFIs. Clients who are somewhat richer and are willing to offer collateral for loans tend to be served by individual lenders, whereas poorer clients without acceptable collateral are served by group lenders.

The lack of simple, low-cost methods for assessing in an operational context whether an MFI reaches the poor results at present either in no project monitoring, or in monitoring activities that use simple but crude descriptions of project beneficiaries (such as the share of women among clients, farm size, or the occupation of program beneficiaries), or in rapid or participatory appraisals that are not well suited for within- or between-country comparisons. Whereas Navajas et al. use several indicator variables to reconstruct an index of absolute poverty, as done by the government of Bolivia, Zeller et al. (Chapter 9) present a method to measure relative poverty, developed by the authors for the Consultative Group to Assist the Poorest (CGAP), now being promoted by CGAP to assess the depth of poverty outreach of MFIs. The method was designed to measure the poverty level of MFI clients in relation to the general population in the intervention area of the MFI to provide reliable information on poverty outreach. To be useful to policy analysts, donors, and development practitioners, the method must meet reasonable time as well as cost constraints. Zeller et al. present results from four case-study countries in Central America, eastern and southern Africa, and South Asia where the method was tested successfully. Whereas the group-based MFI in South Asia is successful in reaching poor people, MFIs with individual lending technologies tended to serve the better-off in their operational area.

The findings by Navajas et al. and Zeller et al. are consistent with the view that group lending, in particular when combined with poverty targeting, is preferred, and may even be necessary, for making small loans to the very poor because lender transaction costs are high for individual lending. However, few comparative studies of lender transaction costs have tested this hypothesis with empirical data from the same socioeconomic and agroecological setting. Heidhues, Belle-Sossoh, and Buchenrieder (Chapter 10) address this issue in a study of lender and borrower transaction costs in the Cameroon. They compare transaction costs for two state-supported rural lending schemes, Fonds d'Investissement des Micro-réalisations Agricoles et Communautaires (FIMAC) and

Crédit Agricole du Cameroun (CAC), and for the Cameroonian Cooperative Credit Union League. The first two use solidarity credit groups, whereas the credit union provides loans directly to individuals. The results show that credit unions lending directly to individuals had the lowest transaction costs, partly because the group lenders had to bear the costs of forming and training groups. Borrower transaction costs were also lower for credit union borrowers.

Part III: Measuring the Impact of Microfinance

The chapters in Part III focus on the problem of assessing the impact of micro-finance institutions at the household level. In Chapter 11, Sharma and Buchenrieder comprehensively review recent research aimed at measuring the impact on household income and welfare of access to credit. They first argue that impact assessment is important to evaluate the social benefits of public resources spent on promoting MFIs. They distinguish investment-led benefits, which conceptually correspond to the first pathway distinguished by Zeller and Sharma (Chapter 2), from insurance-led benefits, which relate to the second and third pathways. Then they discuss a range of methodological problems in impact analysis that recent research has not yet fully resolved. Concerning investment-led benefits, they identify impacts on income, assets, and production and their effect on food security and gender equity. Impact studies of insurance-led benefits have so far assessed the effects of credit access on consumption and income smoothing.

In Chapter 12, Diagne analyzes the impact of credit access on technical efficiency and productivity for smallholder maize and tobacco production in Malawi. A stochastic frontier production function is used to estimate maximum output for given fixed quantities of inputs, such as land, seed, fertilizer, and water. Once the household's fixed constraints are controlled for, any deviation from the potential maximum output is attributed to the farmer's technical inefficiency in production. The study tests whether various socioeconomic factors, such as access to credit, extension, infrastructure, and household demographics, could be determinants of technical inefficiency. A distinction is made between access to the credit market and participation in it through borrowing: access is measured by the credit limit, whereas participation is measured by the amount borrowed. This distinction is important for impact analysis because credit access influences household outcomes through two main channels. In the first channel, access can alleviate liquidity constraints, thereby enabling a farmer to acquire inputs and farm equipment to increase output. The second channel (equivalent to Zeller and Sharma's second and third pathways) works through the positive effect of access on household risk-bearing capacity, which affects the adoption of new, riskier technologies. Moreover, the option to borrow, even if not exercised, helps avoid risk-reducing, inefficient production practices such as mixed cropping, late planting, and poor timing of input applications. The econometric analysis finds no significant impact of credit access on technical efficiency and productivity, except for tobacco production in one survey region and for local maize. Although the drought during the two survey years partly explains this result, the analysis highlights that credit access may not have a positive impact on income and agricultural productivity if complementary inputs, especially improved agricultural technology, are not available to farmers.

In Chapter 13, Kochar examines the effects of adult male illness on the savings decisions of rural Pakistani households, in particular the effects on the composition of asset portfolios. Recent research has argued that the lack of insurance markets in developing economies, in conjunction with imperfectly functioning credit markets, forces households to accumulate assets primarily for consumption-smoothing purposes. Such behavior would favor investments in assets that are relatively liquid but low yielding, such as food stocks, cash, or animals. Thus, the liquidity of an asset is preferred over its return, thereby lowering lifetime wealth and increasing poverty. Kochar found that anticipated ill health, in particular of adult males, significantly influences the amount and type of assets the household saves. It causes households to reduce their productive assets, and this is a major determinant of poverty.

Part IV: Toward Economic Sustainability of Rural Financial Systems for the Poor: The Role of Public Action and the Private Sector

Both public and private institutions play a role in developing sustainable financial systems. During the 1960s and 1970s, governments and donors spent vast sums in direct efforts to expand rural finance in developing countries. Most of those efforts failed, however, prompting great debate in the 1980s and 1990s about the appropriate role of the public sector in supporting microfinance. Lapenu (Chapter 14) concludes that the state has relevant direct and indirect roles in strengthening microfinance. The direct role involves supporting the start-up costs of new MFIs where they do not exist, supporting state-owned institutions that serve the poor, and creating appropriate prudential supervisory and regulatory systems for financial institutions. The indirect role includes establishing policies for stable economic growth, removing the policy bias against agriculture and small businesses, and creating efficient legal systems to protect property rights and ensure contract enforcement. Although financial self-sufficiency should be the objective of MFIs, public subsidization may be justified if it is determined that this is the most cost-efficient method to reduce poverty.

Yaron and Benjamin (Chapter 15) also support an active role for government in establishing a favorable policy environment and a sound legal and regulatory framework, but only through limited and carefully justified direct intervention. They argue that interventions such as public works, rural infrastructure, and human resource development are more viable alternatives for reducing poverty than are targeted credit schemes for the poor. They report data on the *unit desa* system of Bank Rakyat Indonesia (BRI-UD), the Bank for

Agriculture and Agricultural Cooperatives (BAAC) in Thailand, and the Grameen Bank in Bangladesh to show major achievements in outreach and sustainability. The BRI-UD is an unusual example of a failed subsidized agricultural credit institution that was successfully rehabilitated and became exceptionally profitable by adopting a market-oriented strategy, using its flexibility to create and correctly price new savings and loan products, and enjoying sufficient autonomy to develop efficient management and staffing systems.

The transition economies of Europe and Asia have encountered great difficulties in creating market-oriented financial systems. Zhu, Zhongyi, and von Braun (Chapter 16) report on the efforts made by the Chinese government to create a sustainable financial system to serve the rural poor. These initiatives involved dissolving the mono-banking system, and several direct efforts to create and fund financial institutions, as well as to invest in social infrastructure and rural public works. In spite of these efforts, the rural financial system has not achieved great outreach, and bad debts undermine institutional sustainability. Although some programs reach the rural poor, the total outreach is small. The reasons for poor performance include heavy administrative interference and inadequate pricing of financial products to cover costs and risks. The country still has a long way to go in defining the appropriate role for the state in developing its rural financial system.

Part V: Summary and Implications for Policy and Research

The diverse topics covered in this volume reflect a cross section of papers on the current policy debates and research concerning the critical triangle of microfinance. The three elements of this triangle are the financial sustainability of the financial institution, outreach to the poor, and the welfare impact. The three policy objectives determine the overall economic sustainability of the microfinance system. The chapters in this book show that both the research on and practice of microfinance evolved quite rapidly during the 1990s. The implications for policy and research are summarized in the last chapter.

References

Adams, D. W. 1998. The decline in debt directing: An unfinished agenda. Paper presented at the Second Annual Seminar on New Development Finance, Goethe University of Frankfurt.

Bornstein, D. 1996. *The price of a dream*. New York: Simon & Schuster.

Christen, R. P., E. Rhyne, R. C. Vogel, and C. McKean. 1995. *Maximizing the outreach of microenterprise finance: An analysis of successful microfinance programs*. Program and Operations Assessment Report No. 10. Washington, D.C.: U.S. Agency for International Development.

Hulme, D., and P. Mosley. 1996. *Finance against poverty*. London: Routledge.

Kimenyi, M. S., R. C. Wieland, and J. D. Von Pischke. 1998. *Strategic issues in microfinance*. Brookfield, Vt., U.S.A.: Ashgate.

Morduch, J. 1999. The microfinance promise. *Journal of Economic Literature* 37 (4): 1569–1614.

Otero, M., and E. Rhyne, eds. 1994. *The new world of microenterprise finance.* West Hartford, Conn., U.S.A.: Kumarian Press.

Stiglitz, J., and A. Weiss. 1981. Credit rationing in markets with imperfect information. *American Economic Review* 71 (6): 393–410.

Von Pischke, J. D. 1991. *Finance at the frontier: Debt capacity and the role of credit in the private economy.* EDI Development Studies. Washington, D.C.: World Bank.

Yaron, J. 1992. *Successful rural finance institutions.* World Bank Discussion Paper No. 150. Washington, D.C.: World Bank.

Zeller, M., and M. Sharma, eds. 2000. *Innovations in rural microfinance for the rural poor: Exchange of knowledge and implications for policy.* Proceedings from an international conference organized by the German Foundation for International Development (DSE), the International Food Policy Research Institute (IFPRI), the International Fund for Agriculture (IFAD), and the Bank of Ghana. Feldafing, Germany: German Foundation for International Development (DSE).

Zeller, M., G. Schrieder, J. von Braun, and F. Heidhues. 1997. *Rural finance for food security for the poor: Implications for research and policy.* Food Policy Review No. 4. Washington, D.C.: International Food Policy Research Institute.

PART I

Access to and Demand for Financial Services by the Poor

2 Access to and Demand for Financial Services by the Rural Poor: A Multicountry Synthesis

MANFRED ZELLER AND MANOHAR SHARMA

Introduction

At first glance, many might say that the poor in developing countries, earning incomes of less than a dollar a day, are neither creditworthy nor able to save; nor can they pay for insurance against the severe risks they face. Empirical research on informal financial markets and the risk-coping behavior of households has demonstrated time and again that these common assumptions are wholly unfounded. Since the mid-1980s, these myths should also have been laid to rest by the increasing number of successful institutional innovations, which provide financial services to poor people in developing countries who were previously thought to be unbankable.

Yet much of rural financial policy until the end of the 1980s and even today has been based on these faulty premises, leading to well-meant but inefficient and costly policies for the development of rural financial institutions (RFIs) with negligible outreach to and impact on the poor. Past policy neglected to provide savings and insurance services. Much, if not all, of the emphasis was on "giving and forgiving" loans. Most, if not all, so-called credit projects quickly degenerated into transitory income transfer programs with doubtful coverage of the poor, but with a never-ending need for injections of public resources to keep rural state-driven, top-down banks and cooperatives from collapsing.[1] In recognition of these past failures and in conjunction with the structural adjustment policies implemented during the past two decades, donor and government support for development banks and parastatal agricultural credit institutions has largely dwindled. Today, many (but not all) developing countries lack a single functioning RFI operating on a widespread, if not national, scale. Credit for smallholder and tenant agriculture appears to have been especially hard hit. On

This chapter is a revised version of one that appeared in Zeller and Sharma (2000) and is reproduced with permission from the German Foundation for International Development (DSE).

1. For a comprehensive critique of past credit policy, see, for example, Adams (1988), and Adams, Graham, and Von Pischke (1984).

the other hand, new member-based institutional innovations have emerged with the support of government and donor organizations, such as solidarity credit groups, village banks, and member-managed savings and credit cooperatives.

Faulty perceptions about the clientele and its demand serve as excuses for inaction or lead to policy recipes promoting ill-adapted services, market structures, and institutions. The truth is that the poor are creditworthy, can save, and can pay for insurance: they have done it all along, as the myriad of informal contracts between friends, relatives, and other networks daily demonstrate. But it is also true that the financial institutions, the related knowledge and technology, and the enabling policy environment were not in place in the past (and still are not in many countries or areas within countries). Because such policies and institutions did not exist or were not acceptable to central, commercial, or parastatal banks, the poor were deemed to be unbankable. To put it positively, one thing that we can learn from the past two decades of the microfinance revolution, as Jonathan Murdoch (1997) terms it, is that institutional (not just technological) innovations and related changes in the legal and regulatory policy framework can make it possible to reach the poor with financial services on a sustainable basis. Although increasing numbers of people living on or below the poverty line are reached by innovations in financial institutions, outreach to the ultrapoor continues to be low. However, this does not mean the ultrapoor are not bankable. They may not be bankable in many circumstances, given current institutional knowledge in microfinance, but innovations will surely be generated in the future, motivated and helped by the ever faster development of new information technologies and our increasing understanding of how institutions form, behave, change, and collapse over time.

Why should policy matter at all in improving access to financial services for the rural poor? What is the role of financial sector development in the overall mix of policy instruments? And, if we agree for the moment on the role of financial market development in economic growth, in enhancing food security, and in reducing poverty,[2] what types of financial services are demanded by and accessible to the poor? What are the gaps between demand and access, and what types of financial services need to be offered by microfinance institutions (MFIs) to improve outreach to and participation by poor men and women in financial markets?

This chapter seeks to address these questions. We begin by briefly describing a conceptual framework (see Zeller et al. 1997 for more details), and then provide a synthesis of the empirical results of the multicountry research program on rural finance of the International Food Policy Research Institute (IFPRI). In particular, we look at patterns of demand and access of rural house-

---

2. The effects of improved access to financial services on welfare and development are dealt with in other chapters of this volume. See, for example, Chapter 11 by Sharma and Buchenrieder.

holds, differentiated by their poverty level. We conclude with a number of policy conclusions that call for an increased emphasis on developing financial products and related institutional arrangements that increase the ability of the poor to bear risks.

The Role of Microfinance for Food Security and Rural Poverty Alleviation

In most rural areas of developing countries, achieving household food security remains a critical objective of rural development. This can be done in principle by increasing agricultural productivity and off-farm income and by improving the ability of households to stabilize their income and food purchasing power.

The Contribution of Rural Finance within the Framework of Development Policy

Food security, at the household level, is defined in its most basic form as access by all people at all times to the food needed for a healthy life (von Braun et al. 1992). Many policy instruments have the potential to improve household food security. In general, packages combining a range of policy instruments are more effective in improving food security than reliance on a few sector-specific, single policy instruments.

Given the determinants of household food security, the available policy instruments can be systematized into policies that (1) aim to increase household income; (2) stabilize and/or lower food prices; or (3) improve the households' access to financial markets (Zeller et al. 1997). The first two policy sets are geared toward increasing household income and purchasing power, either in particular seasons or years or as part of long-term strategies. Key policy instruments for achieving long-term food security are the transfer of technology and investments in agriculture and rural infrastructure, combined with the provision of social services, such as health and education. These measures must be part of any development strategy. Policies to address problems of income and purchasing power directly in specific periods include the stabilization of key commodity prices and targeted interventions, such as income transfers, food subsidies, or public works projects for the food insecure. The third policy set aims to improve the household's ability to adjust its consumption and investment between periods through access to savings, credit, and insurance services. In contrast to the other two policy sets, the immediate goal is not to influence income directly in a particular period but to enable households to make intertemporal adjustments of disposable income.

Policy instruments that directly aim to diversify and increase incomes are necessary, but not sufficient, for ensuring household food security. Many poor households face the risk of transitory food insecurity, even if, on average and over several years, their incomes are sufficient to provide a sustainable standard of living. Thus, there is a potential demand for savings, credit, and insurance services that can more efficiently contribute to consumption stabilization while at the same time enhancing income generation and self-employment.

How Can Access to Financial Services Make a Difference for Food Security?

Zeller et al. (1997) distinguish three pathways through which access to financial services (or lack thereof) can increase the income and the food security of households and their individual members. These pathways provide a framework for identifying institutional arrangements that address the poor's diverse demand for savings, credit, and insurance services, for evaluating them, and for comparing their costs and benefits with alternative policy measures aimed at improving food security (see Figure 2.1). The pathways are

- Pathway 1: income generation,
- Pathway 2: asset (dis-)investment strategies to smooth disposable income over time at sufficient food consumption levels, and
- Pathway 3: direct use of credit to finance urgent consumption.

PATHWAY 1: IMPROVED INCOME GENERATION.   The hypothesized effects of access to credit are twofold. First, additional capital can be temporarily used to enhance the level of the household's or firm's productive human and physical capital. This is the traditional argument for the provision of credit. With the provision of credit, the costs of (capital-intensive) technology and assets will be reduced relative to family labor. For example, instead of growing low-yielding local crop varieties with a low level of mineral fertilizer, access to credit may allow an increased use of improved seeds and fertilizer and higher crop output per unit of labor and land (Feder, Just, and Zilberman 1985). Of course, savings services that enable the accumulation of assets serve the same purpose: they provide capital for future investment and income generation.

Second, apart from this direct effect on factor income and already related to the second pathway described below, access to credit (Eswaran and Kotwal 1990), but also to savings and insurance services, will increase the risk-bearing capacity of the household. Access to services that help to avoid severe shortfalls in food consumption will then indirectly allow the household to adopt riskier, but more profitable, income-generating activities, and will partially substitute for traditional risk-coping measures, such as crop diversification and field fragmentation.

PATHWAY 2: DECREASING INSURANCE COSTS THROUGH MORE COST-EFFICIENT ASSETS AND LIABILITIES.   Improved access to financial services is expected to reduce the holding of traditional forms of savings such as jewelry or staple food, and perhaps even livestock, which have lower risk-adjusted returns but are exposed to various risks (theft, loss, or disease). These assets are likely to be partially substituted for if savings opportunities with higher

FIGURE 2.1 How does access to finance influence household food security?

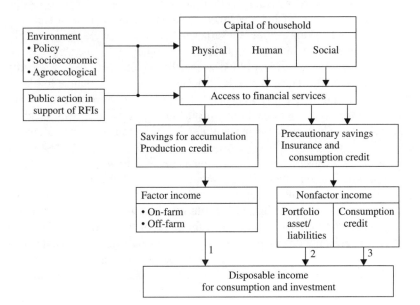

risk-adjusted returns arise. This demand response, however, is conditioned by the quality of households' access to labor, food, and other commodity markets. For example, if food markets during the hungry season are segmented and food prices are highly volatile, households may continue to save in the form of food, even if formal savings options with high liquidity and low transaction costs are accessible. Such conditions prevail in the rice market of Madagascar, where price differences reach up to 300 percent between regions or 100 percent between seasons (Minten, Randrianarisoa, and Zeller 2000). The imperfections in the food marketing system explain why member-managed rice banks in Madagascar, linked with a cash credit program, have grown and performed quite successfully since their implementation in the early 1990s. This example may highlight the importance of financial products that are adapted to the local socioeconomic and agroecological conditions.

Access to microfinance may also decrease the amount of credit obtained at high cost from informal sources and reduce the occurrence of distress sales of productive assets (land, livestock, and seeds) at low prices. Although the demand for high-interest informal consumption loans is well known, Rutherford (1998) points to the not-so-well-known fact that the poor often pay heavily for the opportunity to save. These costly informal savings could be substituted if MFIs offered diverse savings services meeting the demand of the poor.

PATHWAY 3: CONSUMPTION CREDIT.   Households attempt to stabilize their consumption by adjusting their disposable income. Total disposable income for consumption and investment is composed of both factor and nonfactor income. If factor income is insufficient because of shocks, various traditional consumption stabilization techniques are employed to generate nonfactor income, such as the depletion of food stocks, the sale of assets, requesting gifts from relatives and friends, borrowing, and so on. Nonfactor income for stabilizing consumption can also be generated by payments from insurance contracts with formal institutions, from informal insurance arrangements (such as state-contingent loan rescheduling or gift exchange), and from social safety-net schemes.

Another means of smoothing income is the withdrawal of precautionary savings, which is a particularly important method of self-insurance by the poor. Access to financial services thereby has the potential to substitute for some higher-cost traditional savings, other forms of self-insurance, and community-level coinsurance strategies, as well as for some of the higher-cost informal sources of consumption credit. These services may be much in demand where incomes fluctuate considerably from season to season and year to year, and therefore they may be particularly relevant for rural households that depend mainly on agriculture for their livelihoods.

Policy Implications Derived from the Conceptual Framework

It appears likely that financial policies will perform better in alleviating poverty and contributing to food security and rural development when they address all three pathways for food-insecure households and their members.

The vulnerability and low risk-bearing capacity of the poor, and particularly of women, mean that for these target groups the savings, credit, and insurance services addressed in the second and third pathways are especially important. These services could help the poor avoid serious shortfalls in their consumption and therefore increase their capacity to bear risks. This, in turn, could favor the adoption of new technology and enterprises. The latter two pathways have been by and large neglected by the microfinance industry (with a few notable exceptions, such as Rutherford 1998 for Bangladesh), although they are the raison d'être for most of the informal financial contracts in which the poor, and in particular the poorest, engage in practice.

With respect to developing savings products for the rural poor, it follows that more emphasis ought to be placed on liquidity and low transaction costs than on attractive interest rates. Financial services to enhance food security currently include traditional "production" credit, be it for agricultural or off-farm enterprises, as well as savings services that emphasize return over liquidity. However, rural finance policy—if it aims to become more relevant for the poor and the poorest—should seek to develop new financial products that are particularly useful for stabilizing the consumption of food, thereby increasing the ability of the poor to bear risks.

These policy recommendations are substantiated in the next section by a review of empirical findings by IFPRI and its collaborating institutions, based on their research in African and Asian countries.

Demand for and Access to Financial Services by Rural Households in Developing Countries: A Multicountry Synthesis

In general, access to a service, including financial ones, can be defined using various characteristics of its availability for a particular client and the client's transaction costs for accessing the service. Whether access to a service eventually leads to an articulated demand is an entirely different issue.

For example, household surveys usually focus on the number and type of households borrowing, from whom they borrow, for what they borrow, and so forth. These observations tell us only about the demand side (and then only the demand that was successfully voiced) and give us a truncated picture of households' access to credit. Many households may have chosen not to borrow even when they had access to credit, and others wanted to borrow but had no access. For these reasons, one cannot equate observed demand for credit with access to credit.

In the following three sections, we will highlight major findings with regard to the access to and demand for credit, savings, and insurance, respectively.[3]

Credit Services

The focus of the intercountry comparisons presented in this section is not so much on the nature of credit transactions themselves (because conditions among countries vary greatly), but on the differences between the poor and the nonpoor within countries. As a working definition, the poor are defined here as the bottom one-fourth of the sample households when ranked by per capita household income levels. In some of the sample countries, such as Malawi, Madagascar, Nepal, and Bangladesh, more than half of the sample households would easily fall below a statistical poverty line, that is, they do not have enough income to secure their basic needs for food and other essential nonfood goods and services.

In much of the analysis, a distinction is made between the informal and formal market or institutions. For the purposes of this chapter, formal lenders are defined as state and agricultural development banks and other banking institutions, as well as member-based MFIs. The last group includes credit unions

---

3. The section on credit services draws heavily from Zeller and Sharma (1998), and the section on savings services draws from Zeller et al. (1997).

TABLE 2.1 Selected household characteristics, by country

Indicator	Bangladesh P	Bangladesh NP	Cameroon P	Cameroon NP	China P	China NP	Egypt P	Egypt NP
Mean household size (number of people)	5.4	5.0	8.5	6.0	4.8	4.4	7.7	6.2
Years of education of household head (percent)[a]								
None	73.3	49.3	36.9	33.9	17.1	9.3	56.2	39.2
Under five years	21.3	20.4	52.8	58.8	42.4	42.0	15.0	13.6
Five to eight years	3.3	14.2	8.3	8.2	32.5	38.1	12.9	16.1
Nine or more	2.0	16.0	0.0	4.2	7.7	10.3	16.0	30.9
Household heads reporting self-employed farming as principal occupation (percent)[b]	16.0	44.6	69.4	62.0	91.1	81.2	23.4	27.3
Mean land ownership (hectares)	0.2	0.6	2.5	4.3	2.0	2.0	0.4	0.8
Mean annual income per household member (US$)	108.6	232.2	179.1	357.2	74.1	204.7	236.3	641.5

SOURCE: Zeller and Sharma (1998).

NOTES: P = poor—those in the lowest quartile of income (or consumption expenditure) in their respective countries. NP = nonpoor—those in the three other quartiles. The time periods of the surveys are Bangladesh, 1994; Cameroon, 1992; China, 1994; Egypt, 1997; Ghana, 1992–93; Madagascar, 1992; Malawi, 1995; Nepal, 1991–92; Pakistan, 1986–91; n.a. means "not available."

[a] "Household head" refers to the major family laborer. For years of education of household head, the category "none" refers to those who are illiterate; "under five years" to those who had at most some primary education; "five to eight years" to those who completed some junior-level school; and "nine or more" to those who completed some senior-level school.

[b] Household heads working principally as day laborers in agriculture account for an additional 37.6 percent for the poor and 10.1 percent for the nonpoor.

and cooperatives, group-based programs supported by government agencies or nongovernmental organizations (NGOs), village banks, and financial service associations. All other household financial transactions are within the informal sector—from friends and relatives; from socially distant informal agents, such as traders, moneylenders, or deposit-keepers; and from indigenous savings and credit associations.

Poverty has many dimensions, and the rural poor face many constraints in accessing markets, education, and other social services. These constraints have a negative impact on the role that microfinance can play in poverty alleviation.

Ghana		Madagascar		Malawi		Nepal		Pakistan	
P	NP	P	NP	P	NP	P	NP	P	NP
8.4	6.8	6.8	5.3	5.3	4.0	6.3	7.5	11.2	8.4
29.3	20.9	13.0	21.6	30.0	27.0	93.1	93.3	64.2	59.6
10.6	4.6	67.4	53.6	51.0	39.0	2.3	3.7	0.0	0.0
14.6	7.9	17.4	13.5	18.0	29.0	4.5	2.6	29.0	24.2
45.4	66.89	2.2	11.2	1.0	5.0	0.0	0.6	6.8	16.3
76.0	63.0	76.6	81.0	80.0	59.0	n.a.	n.a.	42.0	58.1
2.6	3.4	2.1	3.3	1.5	1.7	0.5	1.5	1.5	4.9
82.8	217.2	86.6	223.9	32.7	61.0	90.0	118.5	216.6	407.2

When comparing the socioeconomic characteristics of the poor and nonpoor in the IFPRI samples, as defined above, the majority of the poor lack basic education, are primarily dependent on agriculture for their livelihood, own extremely small amounts of land for cultivation, and support large families on low average per capita incomes (Table 2.1). Further, since rural areas are not as well serviced as urban centers by physical and social infrastructure such as roads, schools, telephones, radio, shops, and health clinics, their capacity to take advantage of market opportunities is severely curtailed.

Rural MFIs that seek to cater to the poor cannot and should not ignore the role that financial services can and do play in stabilizing food consumption. Households in the lowest income quartile spend as much as 91 percent of their consumption budget on food (Figure 2.2). Even so, because their earnings are so low, they sometimes go hungry. As a result, a drop in their earnings or the need to finance unexpected expenditures such as medical expenses could have quite serious consequences.

The cycle of borrowing during adverse times or during planting seasons and repaying loans after harvest is an integral part of the livelihood system of the poor. This is evident in IFPRI studies in Madagascar, Nepal, and Pakistan. In Nepal, an overwhelming majority of the poor, about 72 percent, engaged in

FIGURE 2.2 Proportion of consumption budget allocated to acquiring food

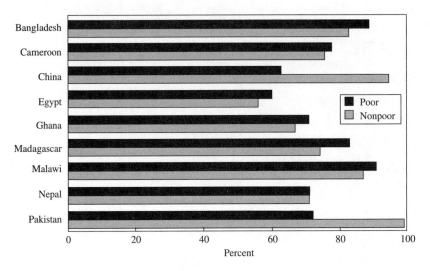

SOURCE: Zeller and Sharma (1998).

some form of financial transactions. In Madagascar, nearly half of the poor households reported that loans were used to cope with any household emergencies. In Pakistan, a 1985 rural credit survey conducted by the government of Pakistan indicated that nearly 40 percent of poor households engaged in credit transactions (Zeller and Sharma 1998). Given the importance of food in total consumption expenditure, and given the rural poor's apparent demand for financial services to smooth consumption, RFIs attempting to reach clients hovering around the poverty line or well below it cannot and should not ignore this demand.

Although, on average, fewer than half of households carry debt at any given point in time, borrowing from informal sources, and less frequently from formal sources, is an integral part of their economic strategy, irrespective of the level of poverty. On average for the 10 country case studies undertaken by IFPRI, between 50 and 70 percent of households borrowed at least once during the re- call period of one to two years. The average cumulative yearly amount borrowed by poor households from the formal and informal sectors ranges from about US$4 in Malawi, to US$80 in Bangladesh, to US$133 in Cameroon. In other words, the total amount of yearly loans taken represents between 50 and 100 per- cent of annual per capita income. In some countries, borrowing exceeds per capita income.

However, the samples drawn are not nationally representative; with the exception of China, Egypt, and Pakistan, they are concentrated in areas and in

FIGURE 2.3 Average amount borrowed from formal and informal rural financial sectors per household year

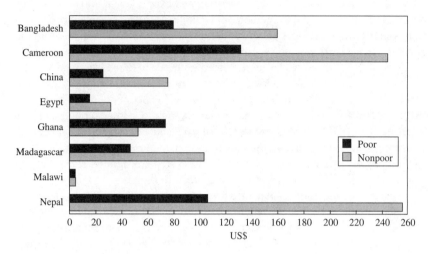

SOURCE: Zeller and Sharma (1998).

villages where formal financial institutions are located. For this reason, the amounts reported here for borrowing are certainly higher than the national average. Nevertheless, Figure 2.3 shows that, as expected, the nonpoor households (the upper three quartiles of household income) borrow much more than the poor, with the exception of Ghana.[4] Moreover, the loan amount shown in Figure 2.3 is not available to the borrower throughout the year but only for several weeks or months. This is because most informal loans are given for only a few days or weeks. Even many formal loans obtained by the sample households are seasonal loans for farm or nonfarm enterprises. The smallest amount borrowed is in Malawi, a very poor country with a relatively inactive informal credit market. On average, less than 5 percent of formal loans are given for a loan period longer than a year, and most seasonal agricultural loans are given for cash or export crops. In crop lending, many financial institutions seek to exploit marketing bottlenecks in order to secure loan repayment, for example tobacco in Malawi or cotton and brewery barley in Madagascar.

---

4. The household sample in Ghana was drawn from villages with credit programs that targeted relatively large loans to poor women. The survey sampled many of these program beneficiaries, and the results reported in the figure are the simple, unweighted sample means. All data from the other case countries are weighted averages, thus correcting for oversampling of program beneficiaries in the survey villages.

By far the biggest rural banks are the households themselves. Informal lenders—friends, relatives, neighbors, informal groups, or moneylenders—provide the lion's share of loans in every country except Ghana and Malawi (Figure 2.4). In Pakistan and Cameroon, for example, less than 5 percent of the total amount borrowed during a year by poor rural households was obtained from formal lenders. Figure 2.4 shows, however, that member-based microfinance institutions successfully reach the poorest income quartile in Bangladesh and Malawi.

There has been considerable progress in reaching the poor through new innovative member-based financial institutions. The poor obtain a smaller share of their loans from the formal sector than the nonpoor in six countries (Bangladesh, China, Egypt, Madagascar, Nepal, and Pakistan), about the same in one country (Cameroon), and a larger share in two countries (Ghana and Malawi) (Figure 2.4). In Bangladesh, member-based credit programs run by NGOs now play a significant role in providing credit to the poor. In Ghana, the villages selected for the survey benefited from the existence of rural banks and NGO-assisted credit programs, the latter targeting poor female-headed households.

Although progress has been made, outreach to the poor remains very limited. In many countries, including the ones sampled by IFPRI (with the exception of Bangladesh), significant improvements in outreach to the poor have been achieved only within geographically small areas covering a small fraction of all households in a nation. Even in a country such as Egypt, where formal RFIs have relatively dense coverage but few member-based MFIs have dispensed with requiring land as collateral, the role of informal lenders remains important, especially for the very poor.

Formal credit, so far, has not crowded out informal credit. Diagne (1999) shows that, in Malawi, informal and formal loans are far from perfect substitutes because of differences in product characteristics, such as restrictions on loan use, maturity of the loan, mode of repayment, and so forth. However, the informal sector, in particular the high-cost segment covered by moneylenders, is likely to lose market share if the characteristics of the formal loan products allow their use for stabilizing consumption.

Another observation that can be made from Figure 2.4 is that the ultra-poor can be reached through financial services, as the figures on market shares for the poorest quarter of households in the Bangladesh sample demonstrate. Results not reported here show that the NGO programs in Bangladesh seem to reach even the poorest income decile (people who are ultra-poor by any measure). The poorest decile in the IFPRI sample borrow an average cumulated amount of US$75 during a year (which is more than their per capita income). On average, 16.2 percent of their loans are obtained from member-based MFIs.[5]

---

5. The corresponding share for friends and relatives is 79.2 percent, for banks 0 percent, for moneylenders 3.3 percent, and for informal groups 1.2 percent.

FIGURE 2.4 Share of different sources of loans to poor and nonpoor, by country

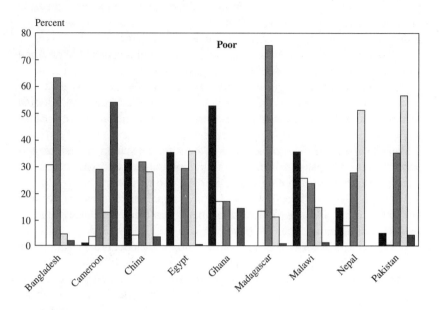

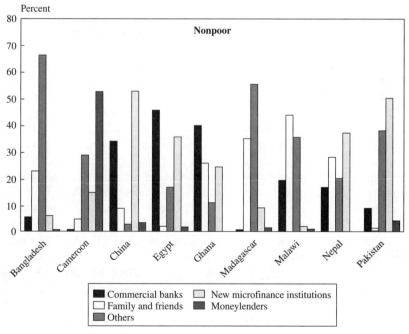

SOURCE: Zeller and Sharma (1998).

Thus, MFIs can reach even the ultra-poor if the services not only are well targeted, but also offer financial products that are in demand. Although not the topic of this chapter, it should be pointed out that there is a trade-off between transaction costs for the formal lender and outreach to the poor.

The poorer the household, the more it will spend on consumption (food and nonfood combined), financed either from its own sources or from loans. Figure 2.5 indicates how households spend their loan money. Between 50 percent and over 80 percent of the loans obtained from the formal and informal sectors combined went to consumption-related purchases. In Pakistan, more than 80 percent was spent on consumption. Moreover, in six out of eight countries—Malawi and Nepal being the exceptions—loans for consumption are more important for the poorest quartile than for the nonpoor. In every country, the share of loans used for consumption was higher for informal loans than for formal loans. In Malawi, only a small share of loans was used for consumption because the Malawi Rural Finance Company, the major rural lender, provides all loans in kind as fertilizer and seeds.

Why are most loans used for consumption instead of production? First, the main suppliers of credit—informal lenders—are generally ill equipped to finance substantial, long-term investments because they rely on their own personal funds. The average duration of an informal loan period was, for example, 86 days in Bangladesh and 65 days in Madagascar. The characteristics of informal loans make them more useful for financing short-term activities such as consumption stabilization and providing working capital for farm and off-farm enterprises, in particular those with a rapid rate of capital turnover, such as vegetable and poultry production, food processing, handicrafts, and petty trade. Formal loans, which are larger in amount and usually given as seasonal or one-year loans in rural areas, are more useful for financing seasonal agricultural and other inputs. However, on average, less than 5 percent of formal loans were given for more than one year, which would allow the borrower to use them for capital investments, such as farm equipment, dairy cows, oxen, irrigation, and trees.

Second, in poor households the spheres of consumption, production, and investment are not separable, in the sense that consumption and nutrition are important to a household's ability to earn income. Because of the unity of the household and its consumption and production activities, the fungibility of loans implies that their use is ultimately driven by the overall budgetary needs of the household. Thus, loans will be mixed with own resources, no matter how hard lenders try to keep this from happening.

Loans used for consumption can be seen as working capital loans for maintaining or enhancing the productivity of labor (or human capital). In general, family labor is by far the most important production factor, and the maintenance and enhancement of labor productivity are central for securing and increasing income. If a farmer does not have enough to eat during the planting season, he or she may be too weak to work. Whereas, for the poor, labor is the major fac-

FIGURE 2.5 Stated use of formal and informal loans by the poor and nonpoor, by country

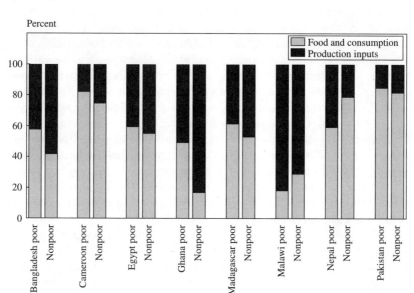

SOURCE: Zeller and Sharma (1998).

tor of production, for the ultra-poor it is generally the only one. Once minimum requirements for a healthy and adequate diet have been met, additional consumption does not generate further increases in labor productivity. Many view such excess consumption as a luxury and understandably see no social benefit in financing it through publicly supported programs. Yet, it is fair to say that luxurious or excessive consumption is extremely rare among the rural poor.

In conclusion, innovative MFIs would do better in reaching the poor and ultra-poor by considering policies and financial products that allow not only for production credit, but also for credit that could be used for consumption of foods and other basic necessities. The problems of moral hazard and information asymmetry, which are particularly severe for consumption loans (and also for insurance), call for services that are designed by and with the clients, and that are at least partially financed and controlled by the members of community-based MFIs. For example, the Caisses Villageoises (CVECAs)—promoted by the French NGO Centre International de Développement et de Recherche (CIDR) in the Gambia and in other African countries—allow their members to raise internal savings funds and to lend these funds for consumption (Zeller et al. 1994).

Yet economists and bankers frequently disagree on the merits of consumption credit. Although consumption loans do not constitute a controversial issue for economists, bankers frequently argue against consumption loans on the grounds that loans should finance activities that generate income for repaying the loan (although this argument seems to fade away quickly whenever the bank can secure its loan with good collateral). This argument has merit, but the linkage between food consumption and labor productivity is consistent with it.

Bankers cannot micromanage microloans. Moreover, lending only for narrowly defined productive activities seldom prevents rural households from diverting borrowed funds from production to consumption purposes because lenders rarely have the resources and time to supervise loan use (Von Pischke and Adams 1980). Only when loans are given in kind—in seeds or fertilizer, for example, instead of cash—do farmers have difficulty in diverting the loan to consumption uses, as the data from Malawi, for example, indicate. But just because a loan is used for consumption purposes does not imply that repayment will falter. Consumption loans in Cameroon and Madagascar were found to have repayment rates the same as or even higher than those for production loans (Schrieder and Heidhues 1995; Zeller 1995).

What about the access to credit services? In spite of the vibrant informal markets observed in many countries, financial services for the poor remain inadequate.[6] This is because informal financial services have various strengths, but also serious shortcomings that cannot be reviewed here (see, for example, literature cited in Zeller and Sharma 1998). In countries as diverse as Bangladesh, Ghana, Madagascar, Malawi, and Pakistan, access to credit is severely limited for small farmers, tenants, and entrepreneurs, and in particular for women.

In many rural areas, access to formal credit is a rare opportunity. A useful and innovative way of examining credit access is to enumerate the credit limits imposed by lenders (Diagne, Zeller, and Sharma 2000). Based on responses from female and male adult household members in Bangladesh about the estimated maximum they could borrow at any one time from formal and from informal sources, Diagne, Zeller, and Sharma (2000) found a median formal credit limit of US$50 and an informal limit of US$3. The ability to borrow was significantly more restricted in Malawi, where the median formal credit limit was found to be zero (that is, half of the households could not borrow anything) and the informal limit was US$3.

Credit constraints are frequently experienced by small farmers, forcing them to choose less rewarding income, investment, and consumption strategies. The low credit limits mean that while some households frequently are unable to borrow enough to meet their needs, others simply do not apply for loans be-

---

6. The Consultative Group to Assist the Poorest (CGAP 1996) estimates that fewer than 10 million of the few hundred million small businesses in urban and rural areas have access to financial services. The picture for rural and particularly agricultural entrepreneurs is likely to be worse than for those operating in urban areas, however, because banking services are mostly offered in urban and semi-urban locations.

FIGURE 2.6 Self-reported reason for households not borrowing, by country

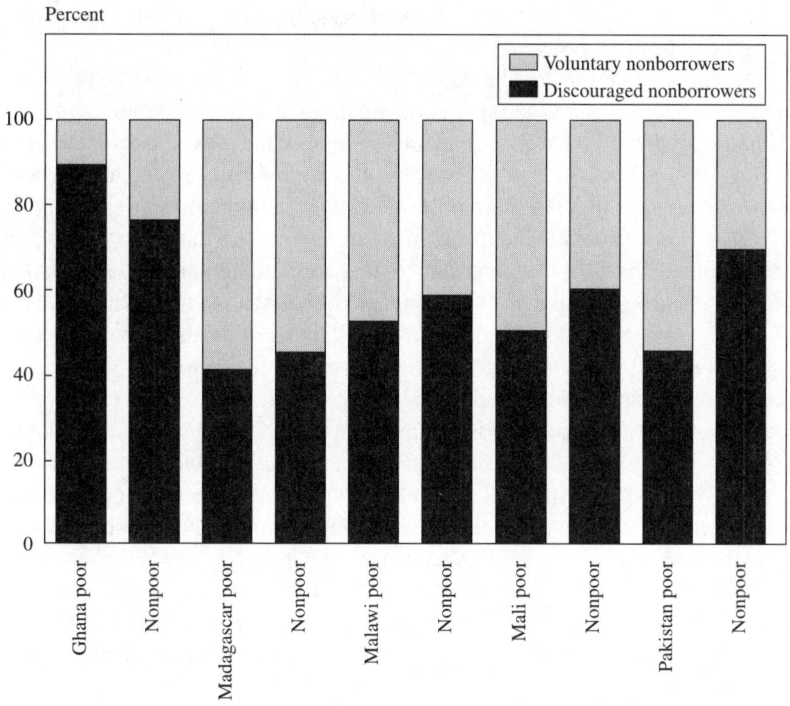

Percent

SOURCE: Zeller and Sharma (1998).

cause of the expectation that they will be turned down. In Madagascar, for example, about 50 percent of loan applicants received less than they asked for, or nothing, from formal and informal lenders alike (Zeller 1994). In Ghana, Madagascar, and Pakistan, IFPRI studies show that a significant proportion of the poor who do not apply for loans are discouraged from applying by the strict collateral requirements and high transaction costs frequently involved in doing business with formal institutions. There is some variation in the percentage of discouraged nonborrowers by country: it is highest in Ghana and lowest in Madagascar (Figure 2.6). Given such widespread credit rationing, it is entirely possible that even households with average annual incomes above the poverty line may not be able to avoid transitory food insecurity when faced with an adverse shock such as a bad harvest or serious illness of a family member.

Not every household is constrained in its access to credit; other limitations, such as low risk-bearing capacity and inadequate access to know-how, markets, and infrastructure, may often be more binding. Although these figures describe the extent of inadequate access to credit, one must not assume—as it is frequently implied—that all households that do not borrow lack access to credit. In fact, Figure 2.6 shows that the share of voluntary nonborrowers among the poor ranges from 11 percent in Ghana to 59 percent in Madagascar.

For the ultra-poor, savings and insurance services appear to be relatively more important than production credit, and credit may come into play once an adequate capacity to bear risks is attained. Three of the most important reasons given by the respondents for not having borrowed were (1) adequate liquidity within the household, (2) lack of profitable investment opportunities that could carry the cost of the loan, and (3) inability or unwillingness to bear the risks of indebtedness. The third reason points to the poor's vulnerability, which causes them to choose not to take any formal loans even when the financial institution actually targets them. If the necessary complementary infrastructure and markets, as well as health and other social services, are not in place, the impact of credit access on income generation may be negligible. The second reason mentioned above for not borrowing is an important one, too. Not being able to invest profitably may in many cases be caused by a lack of complementary services (such as business management training, agricultural extension, access to services for the prevention of diseases, and so forth) and by inadequate access to agricultural input and output markets and to rural infrastructure. Access to markets and infrastructure is particularly important to reduce the (farm) entrepreneur's transaction costs in buying inputs and selling produce. The higher the transaction costs, the lower the supply response and demand for viable production credit.

Savings Services

Much progress has been made over the past 10 years or so in recognizing the poor's demand for savings services. However, much more remains to be done, from the perspective both of institutional sustainability and of achieving customer satisfaction. Savings are particularly demanded by farmers who earn lumpy and risky incomes from crop production and livestock sales. Savings are equally important for the poorest of the poor, who rely largely on their own savings, on informal credit, and on their luck in the labor market to avoid food shortages and hunger (Wright, Hossain, and Rutherford 1997).

Although the need for savings mobilization is almost universally accepted, many rural finance institutions fail to satisfy the demand of their many potential clients. The default in rural finance is still to have no savings services (and instead to rely on grants and loans for on-lending) or to demand obligatory savings deposits from loan applicants, which are then linked as collateral to the loan. However, this kind of saving should not be called a service; it is a downpayment on a loan and a screening device. Checking accounts and term deposits with a variety of different maturity and interest rates are still a rarity among RFIs. In this section, we highlight features of the demand of the poor for savings services and discuss gaps between the services usually offered by rural MFIs and those demanded by the poor.

THE POOR CAN AND DO SAVE.   There is ample empirical evidence that the poor save, in terms of monetary and physical assets and certainly in the form of human capital (improved health and nutritional status, education, number of children, and so forth). In fact, among the three financial services, savings are used by most households or persons during at least some period of life. Household savings are usually the largest component of domestic savings in developing countries, especially in lower-income, predominantly agricultural countries.

WHY THE POOR SAVE.   Saving provides for the accumulation of capital that, in turn, can generate future disposable income and therefore enable future consumption. Two main motives for savings can be distinguished. The first is accumulation—the desire to build assets for the future, and usually for a particular purpose, such as financial security in old age, a dowry, or a house or a piece of land. The second motive is precautionary. It is driven by the desire to be able to afford a minimum level of consumption during future periods, even if income shocks or unexpected increases in expenditures occur, such as for medical needs or social obligations. When such shocks occur, savings must be in a form that enables them to be withdrawn at short notice and to be readily usable for financing the consumption expenditure. The basic distinction between the two motives for saving is that one is concerned with a planned and foreseeable expenditure, whereas the other relates to an expense of an unknown amount at an unknown future point in time.

Because the two principal motives are so different and because their importance changes with the level of poverty of the clients, they call for distinctly different types of savings products and forms of savings. Better-off and well-insured clients tend to save simply for accumulation. They therefore demand term deposits that offer an attractive and reliable return or, if they are really well off, high-risk bonds and stocks. On the other hand, the poorer, more risk averse, and more vulnerable a household or individual, the more important is the precautionary savings motive.

To emphasize the point: poor, food-insecure people want easy and quick access to their money at all times. The less people own, the more liquidity and accessibility they demand. For example, large cash holdings at home—earning zero nominal interest and negative real interest—representing up to one season's revenues for rural households, are reported for Cameroon by Schrieder and Heidhues (1995) and for Malawi by Diagne (1999). These empirical results indicate that the desire for liquidity can outweigh the desire for a positive return. The two diverging savings motives also explain why empirical studies, such as those reviewed in Deaton (1992), do not find a significant relationship between the level of interest rates and the volume of savings. The interest paid on savings deposits is just one characteristic of a savings product, and other characteristics, such as liquidity and low transaction costs for withdrawal or for depositing small amounts, become more important when clients put more emphasis on the precautionary motive.

HOW THE POOR SAVE.   In financial terms, savings are defined as the net change in equity between periods. This definition includes changes in monetary and nonmonetary assets, such as food, jewelry, and other consumption and production durables, and adjustments for changes in debt. When investigating food security and intertemporal behavior, this standard definition of household savings and investment, focusing on only monetary and physical capital, is too narrow. It neglects savings and investments in human capital, such as education and improved health status of family members.

Households save in the form of human, physical, and monetary capital. Expenditures for education and improved nutrition may not only increase available human capital and income in current periods, but could also have a beneficial effect on human capital and income available in future periods. A food-insecure individual or household faces decisions on how much to invest in human capital, compared with physical capital and monetary assets. In food-insecure, poor households, the distinction between consumption, on the one hand, and investment in human capital, on the other, is difficult to make. This is well expressed by Dasgupta (1993:247):

> At low levels of nutrition and health care, increases in current consumption improve future labor productivity: if nothing else, morbidity is reduced. . . . At the margin, consumption of basic needs amounts to investment. One may even go further and argue that consumption and investment at the margin are, over time, synergistic up to a point.

SAVINGS IN MONETARY AND NONMONETARY ASSETS.   Households evaluate different forms of savings in terms of security, liquidity, and economic returns net of the costs of making the savings transaction. The types of assets in which savings are held exhibit different degrees of liquidity, depending on the physical characteristics of the asset (divisibility versus lumpiness) and on the conditions and imperfections of the asset markets. The most liquid asset is money in the pocket. Putting money in a checking or savings account already incurs transaction costs for liquidating the savings. Holding cash reserves maintains flexibility in future use but is of course exposed to the risk of inflation and to demands from other household or community members. Apart from money, households hold savings in many other forms, such as food stocks, livestock, and jewelry. For these forms of savings, cultural norms, traditions, and the desire for prestige or to demonstrate economic or social status play an important role too.

A general systematization of forms of household savings according to their degree of liquidity, security, and rate of return is, of course, not feasible.

Physical characteristics of assets such as divisibility and lumpiness may be overridden by specific cultural, regional, or country market conditions. For instance, livestock can be a desired form of savings in some environments but not in others. One can conclude from this that formal savings services must be adapted to local environments too.

There are major gaps in savings products offered by RFIs. Most institutions still neglect the provision and marketing of different savings products to various groups of clientele among the rural population. Many state or donor-driven agencies do not offer savings at all; other RFIs are not allowed to do so. Some excuse themselves by pointing out that they offer obligatory savings linked with a loan product. However, such a service responds neither to the accumulation nor to the precautionary savings motive.

Innovative RFIs offer a range of savings products, differentiated in terms of their maturity and return (see Hannig and Wisniwski 2000). Products need to be developed to better satisfy the demand by poor clients, including checking accounts, savings deposits to finance consumption loans, and savings deposits to build emergency RFI funds to pool risk, as well as member-financed and member-controlled insurance products.

Insurance Services

Whereas savings were called the forgotten half of finance during the 1980s (Vogel 1984), one may consider insurance the forgotten third of finance during the 1990s (Zeller 1995). A formal insurance contract features the promise of a future payout by the insuring party to the insuree if the latter person experiences a certain risk that is covered by the insurance contract.

A large proportion of rural households borrow, and many more save, but all seek to insure against the vagaries of life. In view of the virtually complete absence of formal insurance markets and social security systems in rural areas of most developing countries (Haddad and Zeller 1997), farmers and other rural households use a number of measures to reduce the likelihood or impact of risks, through either ex ante or ex post measures. For example, farmers undertake mixed cropping and use multiple seed varieties. For these insurance substitutes, the farmer pays a premium in the form of additional work or lower yields but can reduce the downside risk of having crop failures. Households also enter into informal insurance arrangements with their neighbors, relatives, and market partners who help in difficult times. Among the poor, who may also lack access to informal insurance arrangements, self-insurance in the form of precautionary savings is important.

Personal or covariant weather risks are major causes of households sliding into or being trapped in poverty. In a household survey by IFPRI in Madagascar in 1997, 33 percent of rural households mentioned personal risk and 20 percent mentioned covariant risk as major factors causing a deterioration in living standards during the previous five years (Table 2.2). Among the poor, the

TABLE 2.2 Causes of changes in food insecurity over the previous five years in rural Madagascar (percent)

Item	Worsened ($N = 195$)	Improved ($N = 142$)
Covariant risks: natural disasters harming crop, animals, house (drought, locusts, flood)	20	. . .
Negative idiosyncratic risks: accident, human disease	33	. . .
Adverse changes in market access or price	30	. . .
Private transfer received: heritage, gift	. . .	3
Public transfer received: social assistance or farm/ business extension	. . .	2
Favorable changes in market access or prices	. . .	51
Increase in expenses for social events or schooling	3	. . .
Positive idiosyncratic events: mainly more household members of working age	. . .	31
Other adverse causal factors	14	. . .
Other positive causal factors	. . .	13

SOURCE: IFPRI/FOFIFA 1997 Household Survey in Rural Madagascar, cited in Minten, Zeller, and Lapenu (1998).

NOTES: The table lists the different types of responses given by the household head to the question "What was the primary cause for the change in quantity of food consumed in your opinion?" The sample size was 495 households, of which 195 experienced more food insecurity and 142 less food insecurity; the remainder reported no significant change.

incidence of personal risk was higher, whereas among the wealthier households the reverse was true. The poor are more affected by personal risk, which affects their labor—their main production factor. The wealthier households are relatively more affected by weather risks because these mainly affect crops and therefore the returns to land (Zeller, Minten, and Lapenu 2000). However, the poor are also negatively affected by crop failures due to natural calamities because these will have an effect on the price of food and the demand for paid labor.

Informal systems of insurance may be effective for covering personal risk to some extent, but not for protecting against weather and other covariant risks. Personal risk, such as illness, death, accident, theft of cattle, and old age, usually affects only a few persons in a village at the same time. Covariant risk, such as drought, hail, and locusts, affects everybody in the village who depends directly or indirectly on agriculture for their livelihoods. Unfortunately, in agrarian villages in the developing world, almost everybody is hit by weather risk. Because of these characteristics, personal risk can in principle be insured for within smaller informal groups, whereas covariant risk cannot. However, the existing economies of scale and scope in insurance also make it more economical to insure larger groups of individuals (at the extreme, all citizens of a state).

For example, in many countries of Western Europe it is mandatory for every person to enroll in the health and old-age insurance systems, if the individual is not already covered through private insurance.

The potential for innovation in sustainable insurance products remains by and large untapped by the MFIs, with the result that—among the three types of financial services—the largest gap between demand and access is for insurance. One should note, however, that this gap is not easy to close. Insurance is the most difficult financial service to offer because of the problems of information asymmetry and moral hazard among market partners, which are particularly severe in insurance contracts. When discussing the potential for innovation in microinsurance, one needs to distinguish between personal, or idiosyncratic, risk and covariant risk, because the institutional and policy responses will differ for the two categories of risk.

Member-based financial institutions can provide insurance services if local, member-based knowledge and monitoring systems are used to determine charges and possible payouts. Studies of informal credit and savings associations or semiformal credit groups show that members of the same group attempt to pool their risk and to support each other to some extent in times of difficulty (Sharma and Zeller 1997; Zeller 1998).

Innovative formal institutions have already made an entry in the business of insurance. For example, the Bangladesh Rural Advancement Committee offers life insurance contracts to women who live below the poverty line; the Indian self-help organization, the Self-Employed Women's Association (SEWA), allows pregnant borrowers to reschedule their loans; and the members of the Caisses Villageoises in Mali or Gambia allow the provision of consumption loans at a lower interest rate if financed through internal savings of the members.

Insurance contracts with the formal sector, as well as informal insurance substitutes such as credit explicitly given for consumption or precautionary savings, appear to become most cost-effective and therefore eventually sustainable if the services are controlled by and are at least partially—if not fully—financed by their members. Because of the problems of moral hazard and information asymmetry, it appears that the insurance of personal risk can be sustainably handled only if these services are financed largely or entirely by savings or premiums raised and controlled by the member-based institution itself. The same argument applies to the provision of consumption credit, which is frequently used by the poor as an insurance substitute. Because the retail financial institution at the community level is small, information asymmetries between members and costs of information acquisition are relatively low so that it could be relatively costless to detect those who try to cheat the system (Zeller 2000).

Government and donor support is required for research and pilot programs that experiment with member-financed and member-controlled insurance services, including consumption credit. Institutional innovation, just like new technology products or new seed varieties, often creates public goods that can be used by other countries, firms, households, and individuals. The private sector response to innovative institutions is often lacking (Zeller and Sharma 1998). On a more advanced segment of the institutional learning curve, grassroots institutions may form associations or federations, which may pool emergency funds across regions. For example, in 1992, the Grameen Bank rescheduled loans in flood-affected areas, and these were partially financed by emergency reserves.

The appropriate institutional and policy response to covariant risk remains an open but very important question, particularly for reviving agricultural credit. Weather risk poses major threats to farmers and rural banks alike. Private insurance companies usually shy away from insuring weather risk in agriculture. The major reason for this is the difficulty and the cost of assessing the damage and the amount to be paid. For an insurer, it is simply too costly to go out and check the fields of every smallholder to determine how much the yield of maize or cotton was reduced by drought. One of the major problems of microinsurance, which is also a problem for microcredit and microsavings, is the smallness of the transaction, leading to high unit transaction costs. While several proposals, such as insurance payouts linked to regional rainfall data or use of satellite images of crops, have recently been suggested to reduce the costs of information for the insurer, little progress has been made in practice.

Another possibility that is often suggested is to form associations of member-based financial institutions or networks of banks that raise monies from their clients for emergency funds, which are then matched in varying ratios by state funds. The emergency funds are used to finance disaster relief or insurance payouts. However, many issues need to be resolved before this proposition can be initiated.

Although the state is in a position to spread the fixed cost of establishing institutions that insure against covariant risks (Dasgupta 1993), many governments choose not to do so. They prefer instead to be the implicit insurer of last resort, designating disaster areas and giving handouts to affected areas and households, or coercing state-driven banks to forgive loans in drought years, perhaps for political motives.

Policy Implications for Future Innovations in Financial Products for the Poor

A large proportion of rural households borrow, many of them save, and all of them seek to insure against the vagaries of life. The poorer the household or individual, the more important (precautionary) savings products and insurance services become, including consumption credit. Unfortunately, many of the RFIs, including member-based MFIs, focus on credit, while downplaying the demand for savings services. Very few have ventured into the admittedly difficult business of providing insurance. Moreover, because of covariant weather risks, many RFIs shy away from lending to small-scale agricultural production.

To reverse this pattern of gaps between demand and access with respect to small-scale agricultural credit, savings, and insurance, bold pilot programs and experiments with alternative institutional designs and products in microfinancing will be essential. These innovations are crucial if microfinance is to increase its applicability and outreach to the poor and ultra-poor in rural areas and thus contribute more effectively to poverty alleviation. Further empirical research, some of it undertaken along with action-oriented field experimentation, is also needed. Concerted public action by governments, donors, civic organizations, community-based institutions, and the private sector is required to provide an enabling framework for this to happen. A useful premise for innovation in microinsurance, and thus privately funded safety nets, is to build upon local knowledge about the monitoring and enforcement of contracts.

Designing, experimenting with, and building financial institutions for the rural poor require economic resources and adequate consideration of longer-term social returns. Policy choices must weigh the social costs of supporting the formation of RFIs for the poor against their social benefits. This chapter has not focused on the benefits of microfinance for the poor, or on the private and social costs of providing financial services. A word of caution against overemphasizing the role and potential of microfinance in alleviating poverty is therefore in order.

Poor households face complex, multiple constraints on earning opportunities. They often lack education, markets, and other essential services. Hence, the impact of financial services on welfare is likely to vary with accessibility to complementary inputs such as irrigation, education, markets, and social services. In some environments or for some socioeconomic groups, access to microfinance in general and to credit in particular may do no good, whereas in other regions and for other groups it can make an important difference. It is essential for microfinance programs to identify the nonfinancial constraints that their target clientele face and to adjust the financial products accordingly. For the poor and ultra-poor who may choose not to borrow out of fear of failing to repay the loan, savings and insurance services that increase their risk-bearing capacity and integrate them into member-based financial institutions appear to be an important and promising point of departure for improving outreach to the poor.

References

Adams, D. W. 1988. The conundrum of successful credit projects in floundering rural financial markets. *Economic Development and Cultural Change* 36 (2): 355–367.

Adams, D. W, and J. D. Von Pischke, eds. 1984. *Undermining rural development with cheap credit*. Boulder, Colo., U.S.A.: Westview Press.

Braun, J. von, H. Bouis, S. Kumar, and R. Pandya-Lorch. 1992. *Improving food secu-rity of the poor: Concept, policy, and programs.* Washington, D.C.: International Food Policy Research Institute.

CGAP (Consultative Group to Assist the Poorest). 1996. *Microfinance programs.* CGAP Focus Note No. 1. Washington, D.C.: World Bank.

Dasgupta, P. 1993. *An inquiry into well-being and destitution.* Oxford: Clarendon Press.

Deaton, A. 1992. *Understanding consumption.* Oxford: Clarendon Press.

Diagne, A. 1999. Determinants of household access to and participation in formal and informal credit markets in Malawi. Discussion Paper No. 67. Food Consumption and Nutrition Division, International Food Policy Research Institute, Washington, D.C., April 1999.

Diagne, A., M. Zeller, and M. Sharma. 2000. Determinants of household access to and participation in formal and informal credit markets in Malawi and Bangladesh. Paper presented at the Annual Meeting of the American Economics Association, Chicago, January 3–5, 1998. Revised version published as Discussion Paper No. 90. Food Consumption and Nutrition Division, International Food Policy Research Institute, Washington, D.C. July 2000.

Eswaran, M., and A. Kotwal. 1990. *Implications of credit constraints for risk behaviour in less-developed countries.* Oxford Economic Papers No. 42. Oxford: Oxford University Press.

Feder, G., R. E. Just, and D. Zilberman. 1985. Adoption of agricultural innovations in developing countries. *Economic Development and Cultural Change* 22 (2): 255–296.

Haddad, L., and M. Zeller 1997. How can safety nets do more with less? General issues with some evidence from Southern Africa. *Development Southern Africa* 14 (April): 125–153.

Hannig, A., and S. Wisniwski. 2000. Successful mobilization of small and micro-savings. Experiences from seven deposit-taking institutions. In *Innovations in rural micro-finance for the rural poor: Exchange of knowledge and implications for policy*, ed. M. Zeller and M. Sharma. Proceedings from an international conference organized by the German Foundation for International Development (DSE), the International Food Policy Research Institute (IFPRI), the International Fund for Agriculture (IFAD), and the Bank of Ghana. Feldafing, Germany: German Foundation for International Development (DSE).

Minten, B., C. Randrianarisoa, and M. Zeller. 2000. Agricultural market surplus. In *Beyond market liberalization: Income generation, welfare and environmental sus-tainability in Madagascar*, ed. B. Minten and M. Zeller. Aldershot, U.K.: Ashgate Publishing Company.

Murdoch, J. 1997. The microfinance revolution. Harvard University, Cambridge, Mass., U.S.A. Photocopy.

Rutherford, S. 1998. The savings of the poor: Improving financial services in Bangla-desh. *Journal of International Development* 10 (1): 1–15.

Sharma, M., and M. Zeller. 1997. Repayment performance in group-based credit pro-grams in Bangladesh: An empirical analysis. *World Development* 25 (10): 1731–1742.

Schrieder, G., and F. Heidhues. 1995. Reaching the poor through financial innovations. *Quarterly Journal of International Agriculture* 34 (2): 132–148.

Vogel, R. C. 1984. Savings mobilization: The forgotten half of rural finance. In *Undermining rural development with cheap credit*, ed. D. W Adams, D. H. Graham, and J. D. Von Pischke. Boulder, Colo., U.S.A.: Westview Press.

Von Pischke, J. D., and D. W Adams. 1980. Fungibility and the design and evaluation of agricultural credit programs. *American Journal of Agricultural Economics* 62 (4): 719–726.

Wright, G., M. Hossain, and S. Rutherford. 1997. Savings: Flexible financial services for the poor. In *Who needs credit? Poverty and finance in Bangladesh*, ed. G. D. Wood and I. A. Sharif. London/New York: ZED Books.

Zeller, M. 1994. Determinants of credit rationing: A study of informal lenders and formal groups in Madagascar. *World Development* 22 (12): 1895–1907.

———. 1995. The demand for financial services for rural households: Conceptual framework and empirical findings. *Quarterly Journal of International Agriculture* 34 (2): 149–170.

———. 1998. Determinants of repayment performance in credit groups in Madagascar: The role of program design, intra-group risk pooling and social cohesion. *Economic Development and Cultural Change* 46 (1): 599–620.

———. 2000. On the safety net role of microfinance for income consumption smoothing. In *Shielding the poor: Social protection in developing countries,* ed. N. Lustig. Washington, D.C.: The Brookings Institution and the Inter American Development Bank.

Zeller, M., and M. Sharma. 1998. *Rural finance and poverty alleviation*. Food Policy Report. Washington, D.C.: International Food Policy Research Institute (also available in French and Spanish).

———, eds. 2000. *Innovations in rural microfinance for the rural poor: Exchange of knowledge and implications for policy*. Proceedings from an international conference organized by the German Foundation for International Development (DSE), the International Food Policy Research Institute (IFPRI), the International Fund for Agriculture (IFAD), and the Bank of Ghana. Feldafing, Germany: German Foundation for International Development (DSE).

Zeller, M., B. Minten, and C. Lapenu. 2000. Socioeconomic situation of rural households and changes in indicators of welfare. In *Beyond market liberalization: Income generation, welfare and environmental sustainability in Madagascar*, ed. B. Minten and M. Zeller. Aldershot, U.K.: Ashgate.

Zeller, M., J. von Braun, K. Johm, and D. Pütz. 1994. Sources and terms of credit of the rural poor in The Gambia. *African Review of Money, Finance and Banking* 1 (Supplementary Issue): 167–188.

Zeller, M., G. Schrieder, J. von Braun, and F. Heidhues. 1997. *Rural finance for food security for the poor: Implications for research and policy*. Food Policy Review No. 4. Washington, D.C.: International Food Policy Research Institute.

3 Characteristics of Household Demand for Financial Services in Highly Uncertain Economies: A Review of Evidence from Burkina Faso

GENEVIÈVE NGUYEN, BETTY WAMPFLER,
MICHEL BENOIT-CATTIN, AND KIMSEYINGA SAVADOGO

The conference "Finance and Rural Development in West Africa," held in Ouagadougou in 1991, unveiled an emerging consensus on the promotion of rural finance in the Sahel. The failures of financial institutions launched in the 1970s and 1980s to support the agricultural sector were discussed and analyzed. Conference attendees generally recognized that targeted and subsidized credit were among the principal causes of this crisis because these forms of credit were not adapted to the demand of rural households for financial services. A demand-led approach was, therefore, recommended.

Numerous studies on informal finance supported the demand-led approach. Based on analysis of indigenous savings and lending institutions, such as the tontines and informal lenders, these studies underscored the importance of household demand for credit and savings services, but no clear agreement was reached on the extent to which informal finance satisfied this demand (Christensen 1991; Reardon and Mercado-Peters 1991; Adams 1994). In other words, the question was whether market niches for microfinance innovations existed or not. Adams (1994) stated that household demand for credit was important, but that informal lending and self-financing capacity were sufficient to cover this demand. Reardon and Mercado-Peters (1991) hypothesized, on the contrary, that household demand for investment and consumption credit is far from being satisfied because many poor households do not have access to informal finance. According to Christensen (1991), informal finance showed substantial limits in the financial intermediation process.

Our main objective in this chapter is to review empirical evidence showing that, when an analysis of true household demand for financial services is conducted, important market niches for financial innovations can be identified that are not filled by existing financial institutions. Indeed, in a context of high uncertainty and poverty, true household demand for financial services is more

This chapter is a revised version of one that appeared in Zeller and Sharma (2000) and is reproduced with permission from the German Foundation for International Development (DSE).

diverse and complex than is observed demand. In the same context, because of their particular characteristics, informal financial institutions can satisfy only part of the true demand. Financial innovations could effectively lift many of the constraints faced by rural households in their access to financial services, given the appropriate regulatory and legal frameworks.

In the absence of formal contingent valuations,[1] this analysis of household demand for financial services was conducted on the basis of combined analysis of actual informal financial practices, the role of savings and credit for household economies, and the performances of microfinance projects launched in the late 1980s (in terms of outreach, services offered, and financial viability).

After reviewing the household socioeconomic environment, we summarize the major findings from studies conducted in Burkina Faso by the Centre de Coopération Internationale en Recherche Agronomique pour le Développement (CIRAD) on the characteristics of household demand for financial services (Box 3.1). We then discuss how these characteristics might shape the promotion and building process of microfinance institutions.

Characteristics of Uncertainty in Burkina Faso

In this section we review the socioeconomic context of Burkina Faso to show the effects of environmental factors on household economies and, in turn, on household demand for financial services. We show that, in Burkina Faso, uncertainty and poverty go hand in hand and, as a consequence, household demand for financial services exhibits particular characteristics.

Current Poor Economic Performance

With a per capita GNP of less than US$300 in 1995, Burkina Faso ranks among the poorest countries in the world. The economy is based principally on the agricultural sector, which represents 40 percent of GDP and offers employment to 85 percent of the total active population. Located in the semi-arid tropics southwest of the Sahara, most cropping systems are rainfed and are, therefore, very vulnerable to drought.

As in many other Sub-Saharan African countries, the population of Burkina Faso (8.8 million in 1995) is growing rapidly—at a rate of 3 percent per year. In 1994, 44 percent of the population lived below the poverty level of US$74 per adult per year, and 97 percent of the people living on less than US$50 per adult per year can be found in rural areas (Raffinot 1997).

---

1. Contingent valuation is a method used to estimate consumers' true demand for a commodity, as opposed to observed demand. It basically attempts to evaluate the consumer's willingness to pay on the basis of hypothetical markets designed by the researcher. This method has been applied to the estimation of the value of environmental goods, for which no direct market exists.

BOX 3.1 Description of the studies conducted by CIRAD on household economies and microfinance institutions

The demand analysis developed in this chapter is based for the most part on studies conducted by the Centre de Coopération Internationale en Recherche Agronomique pour le Développement (CIRAD) in Burkina Faso. We can identify four types of study depending on the research focus and the methodology used.

Analysis of Economic Strategies at the Household Level

The first type of study corresponds to the first step of the research-action approach of CIRAD, which consists in elaborating a diagnosis of a given context to identify the relevant development issues and context-specific constraints. This diagnosis theoretically results in one or several development projects. The methodology used in this type of study follows the French farming system approach, which underscores the diversity and the complexity of observed development contexts. For a given context—and going from the larger scale to the smaller scale— researchers using this approach try to identify the different agroecological regions, agrarian systems, farming systems, individual socioeconomic strategies, and cropping systems. This exercise yields one or several typologies and enables researchers to recommend development action adapted to each situation. Regarding the topic of interest, these studies were able to identify different types of households on the basis of their objectives (for example, food security, income maximization); the socioeconomic strategies they use to achieve these objectives (for example, income diversification, production specialization); the constraints they face (for example, high dependency ratio, capital constraints); and structural criteria.

Analysis of Local and Regional Markets

Surveys of local and regional markets for key products (cereals and livestock) have been conducted by CIRAD in the four provinces of Burkina Faso where the Projet de Promotion du Petit Crédit Rural (PPPCR) operates. The objective was to gain a better understanding of the role of saving and credit in village and regional economies. The analysis was therefore concentrated on studying the importance of market exchanges for households, and in general for economies in transition, and on studying the profitability of key economic activities in order to develop recommendations for new microfinance services. Data were collected at regular intervals (mostly weekly) and included information on the different types of economic agents involved in market exchanges, their motivations, the volume of products exchanged, and their prices.

Market Analysis of Specific Credit Products

The third type of study was motivated by the demand for specific credit products expressed by PPPCR's clientele. In line with the demand-led approach, PPPCR has tried to diversify its credit activities and to adapt them to the demand. Loan officers recorded credit demand from potential clients, and PPPCR launched market analyses on the basis of this demand. For each type of credit service demanded, the analysis identified the existing market, the different types of economic agents involved, the profitability of the economic activity, and existing problems. Basic simulations were done to test the profitability of new credit products.

Monitoring and Evaluation of Microfinance Institutions

Two types of monitoring and evaluation study were conducted: financial and impact evaluations. Financial evaluations were done on the basis of standard financial criteria. The impact assessments identified the effects of financial services from the points of view of the institution and the clientele. They therefore included institutional analyses of outreach and type of services offered. The impact analysis from the clients' point of view tried to overcome classic shortcomings of impact studies by focusing on the household's economic strategies and on the uses of saving and credit services with respect to these strategies. One of the studies used the Social Accounting Matrix to follow flows of money and to try to identify the impact of credit injections in village economies.

Burkina Faso's economy suffers from severe handicaps, including a difficult transition from a publicly to a privately run economy, a lack of competitiveness of its formal private sector, and a heavy dependence on external funding. Since its independence in 1961, no significant structural changes have been observed and most of the GDP growth has been offset by the population growth.

Limited resources and poor economic policies have always constrained the government's ability to secure adequate food and to meet the basic needs of its growing population. Food production is increasing slowly at a rate of 2.5 percent per year, and the country's food purchasing power remains limited. Life expectancy at birth is only 48 years, the infant mortality rate is 132 per thousand, and the adult literacy rate is 31 percent (World Bank 1995). Given poor performance based on these social indicators, it is not surprising that Burkina Faso is in 172nd place out of 175 countries for its index of human development (UNDP 1997).

The informal sector has always played an important role in maintaining a minimum level of welfare among the population. In 1985, the informal sector provided 74 percent of total urban employment (Charmes 1996), while, in rural areas, kinship networks of family and friends still represent the most cost-efficient social safety net (Raffinot 1997; Nguyen 1998). Despite the dynamism of this sector, its capacity to absorb the population growth and other major socio-economic changes on its own is questionable.

The Relationship between Uncertainty and Poverty

STRUCTURAL IMBALANCE BETWEEN PRODUCERS AND NATURAL RESOURCES. In Burkina Faso, institutionalized interaction patterns within an ethnic group or among different ethnic groups were traditionally based on production specialization and barter transactions. They were also set up in such a way that they were perfectly adapted to the prevailing cultural ecology. The mixture of agricultural and pastoral farming systems developed by the Fulani, who are cattle herders, and the Rimaaybe, who are cultivators, provides a good illustration of what can be described as a rational and ecologically stable relationship under the low density of population of precolonial time (Ford 1982).

In equilibrium and able to absorb any agricultural shocks, these symbiotic relationships were disrupted first by the arrival of Islam in the northern regions in the mid-eighteenth century, then by the French colonial regime in 1895 (Riesman 1974). The 1974 and 1984 droughts accelerated the transformation of the traditional agropastoral economies by exposing their fragility in an environment characterized by high covariant risks and increasing resource scarcity (Sheets and Morris 1976; Bonte 1986).

The population is increasing at a rapid pace in all regions of Burkina Faso. For example, in northern Burkina Faso, population density was up from 16.0 inhabitants per square kilometer in 1910 to 43.6 inhabitants per square kilometer in 1985 (Marchal 1983; INSD 1985). Under population pressure, production specializations adapted to the climate were progressively replaced by risk-management diversification strategies that do not necessarily take into account the availability of resources (Diop 1990; Ngobounan 1992; Rubrice 1995). As a result, 20–40 percent of rural households experience chronic food deficits (Colliot and Nguyen 1993; Ouedraogo 1993).

INCREASED MONETIZATION AND MARKET PENETRATION. Exchanges were traditionally based on the barter system. By imposing tax payments, French settlers introduced money as a medium of exchange along with the need for households to develop cash-earning activities.

Since that time, household demand for cash has dramatically increased. Successive droughts over the recent decades have increased households' dependence on the cereal markets (Colliot 1993). In the Province of Yatenga, for example, food consumption represents up to 80 percent of total household expenditures in years of bad harvests, such as 1990. In years of good harvests, the demand for cash remains high because of shifts in household expenditures from food to nonfood consumption and to spending on social events (Colliot and Nguyen 1993; Ouedraogo 1993). An important seasonal demand for cash for investment and production-related purchases also exists, because cash is needed to purchase inputs for both farm (cultivation and livestock breeding) and off-farm (handicrafts, petty trade, cottage industries) activities.

Markets have, therefore, emerged in Burkina Faso as a response to communities' increasing dependence on the rest of the world and on monetized exchanges for acquiring food and manufactured products. Markets for agricultural and manufactured products were established first, followed by the labor market, and, more recently, by the formal financial market.

The opening up of isolated communities and villages to the outside world indisputably increases household opportunities in the marketplace. However, the penetration of market economies into traditional societies arguably creates room for opportunistic and free-riding behavior within the domestic sphere. New and more individualized economic strategies can be developed outside of traditional kinship spheres. More important than the weakening and progressive disappearance of traditional kinship-based institutions are the effects of this disappearance on household welfare. In the absence of well-functioning markets and a public safety net, Zimmerman (1994) and Nguyen (1998) suggest that the disappearance of social risk-sharing institutions leads to an inverse relationship between individual risk exposure and resource endowments.

AMBIGUOUS EFFECTS OF MACROECONOMIC REFORMS ON HOUSE-HOLD WELFARE. In 1991, because of the poor economic performance caused by the inefficiencies of the public sector, the government of Burkina Faso decided to undertake major macroeconomic reforms and, in the same year, adopted a comprehensive structural adjustment program. Measures suggested by the International Monetary Fund to contain public spending and deficits and to boost the private sector and trade did not, however, permit the country to regain the relatively good economic growth of the early 1980s. The different formal sectors of the economy and, particularly, the agricultural and manufacturing sectors lack competitiveness because of structural factors, such as numerous trade barriers, high energy costs, and poor technical skills.

In January 1994, along with other countries of the Communauté Financière Africaine (CFA) zone, Burkina Faso devalued the CFA franc (CFAF) by 50 percent. The socioeconomic consequences of the devaluation are still under evaluation, but the World Bank (1995) reported that exports of livestock and other agricultural products definitely benefited from the devaluation. At the household level, however, the cost–benefit ratio was less evident. In most cases, the increase in income from production was barely sufficient to compensate for the increase in expenditure on imported inputs and consumption goods.

In general, most of the macroeconomic reforms adopted by Burkina Faso in the 1990s aimed to lessen the role of the state in the economy and to support the growth of the formal private sector. On the other hand, these corrective measures have not sufficiently emphasized the government's responsibilities as regards the failure of markets, such as the financial and insurance markets. Meanwhile, social programs launched by the government in the 1990s—along with the structural adjustment program to support health care, education, and employment—had ambiguous results. The provision of public goods is still too costly and ineffective (Raffinot 1997).

The Effects of Uncertainty and Poverty on Household Economies

The lack of extensive time-series data prevents us from formally documenting the decline in household welfare over time. However, factors we have discussed above indisputably suggest that uncertainty is an important component of economic and social poverty in Burkina Faso. Social poverty has increased particularly in rural areas, where agricultural risks have the highest impact, markets are either absent or function imperfectly, and the informal sector is the weakest.

In the presence of high uncertainty and in the absence of a public safety net, household economies are organized around the development of cost-efficient risk-management and risk-coping strategies, such as diversifying activities, migration, storage, borrowing, saving, and strengthening social ties. Most often, households combine several strategies according to their available economic opportunities and their own physical and human capital endowments. In addition, in recent years new patterns of family labor allocation have emerged with the involvement of women and young people in tasks traditionally performed by men (Diop 1990; Kuela 1996; Wampfler 1998b).

These new patterns of consumption and labor allocation have made the picture of household economies particularly complex.

Complexity in Household Demand for Financial Services: Major Findings from Studies of Household Economies

The challenge of evaluating true household demand for financial services lies in the fact that the complexity of household economies makes this demand highly diversified in its nature and magnitude. In this section, we review empirical evidence showing that household demand for financial services has been significantly underestimated. Moreover, the true household demand cannot be completely revealed because of imperfect financial markets. Uncertainty in all its forms and the resulting poverty repress both the demand for and the supply of financial services.

The Multiple Roles of Savings and Credit in Household Economies

In transition economies characterized by high uncertainty and poverty, credit and savings are used not only for investment purposes but also for smoothing the flow of consumption, managing cash on a daily basis, and strengthening social ties. A narrow view of financial services links these services to the promotion of income-generating activities only because it tends to separate household enterprises from household domestic activities. For example, it is a common practice for small traders with limited investment capital to demand credit in kind from wholesalers (Ali 1993; Rubrice 1995; Kuela 1996). On the other hand, it is also true that many informal credit contracts involving networks of friends and families are for consumption purposes.

In Burkina Faso, as in most Sub-Saharan African countries, a household is a complex entity where production and domestic spheres are closely interrelated. The fungible nature of credit is particularly pronounced because households tend to combine short-term consumption with long-term capital accumulation strategies (Diop 1990; Oppenheim 1998). The contingent nature of most informal credit contracts indicates, in addition, that credit includes a strong insurance component, enabling households to cope with risks and, consequently, to smooth both income and consumption.

Just as it tends to represent the household as a black box, conventional wisdom tends to stress the importance of credit over savings in household economies. Reardon and Mercado-Peters (1991) and Nguyen (1998) found that informal credit in fact represents a small part of household income compared with savings. As with credit, informal savings have multiple roles and can take many forms.

Nonfinancial savings, such as in livestock and stored grain, are by far the most important form of savings in transition economies. In addition to being stores of value, nonfinancial savings had a social value in traditional societies because they were accumulated to enlarge the domestic group and strengthen social ties within a community. In daily life, nonfinancial savings are used by households to manage daily cash needs and seasonal operating capital. In general, the first capital investment made by microenterprises rarely comes from credit, but rather comes from wealth accumulated after occasional employment opportunities, such as migration to Côte d'Ivoire (Oppenheim 1998).

With the increase of uncertainty, household savings nowadays play a major role in smoothing household consumption. Whereas savings through tontines and other rotating savings associations serve the purpose of financing expected investment or consumption, nonfinancial savings are in most cases allocated to unexpected consumption. In years of bad harvest, rural households in northern Burkina Faso can sell all their livestock to meet family food needs (Ngobounan 1992; Colliot and Nguyen 1993; Rubrice 1995).

Finally, most studies ignore one of the most important forms of savings—investment in human capital. More frequent in urban than in rural areas, this form of saving or investment does make a dramatic difference in terms of household welfare in an economy that lacks a highly skilled labor force.

Diversification and Substance of Demand

SPECIFICS OF DEMAND ACCORDING TO AGE, GENDER, AND SOCIAL RESPONSIBILITIES. Within a household, the complex allocation of labor across gender and age translates into a demand for financial services that varies according to age, gender, and responsibilities.

In traditional economies, household heads own family labor and common stores of assets. They are responsible in theory for major investments, such as agricultural inputs and working tools, and for housing, as well as for the supply of the household's basic needs, such as food, health care, education, and clothing. Their savings and credit strategies and access to sustainable financial services are, therefore, critical for ensuring the family's daily life, cohesion, and growth (Benoit-Cattin and Faye 1982; Binswanger, McIntire, and Udry 1989).

Independently of the household head, all economically active members of the household have their own specific demands for financial services depending on their consumption needs and the type of activities practiced. Households' expenditures become progressively individualized as markets penetrate traditional societies, bringing with them new, nontraditional consumption (Kuela 1996). The satisfaction of these personal needs requires members of the household to engage in individual income-generating activities and to manage their own budgets. Initially, young people do not have any wealth as long as they remain within the household. However, they still have a desire for goods, such as radios or nice clothes for social events, and they get these primarily through informal credit arrangements with family members and friends. Much informal credit demanded by young people is used to finance seasonal or long-term migration. Kuela (1996), Tassembedo (1996), and Oppenheim (1998) showed the importance of long-term migration in strengthening individuals' entrepreneurial capacity and accumulating substantial funds for starting highly profitable off-farm activities.

On the other hand, married women have to take care of daily purchases of ingredients for cooking. Even if they have inherited from their parents upon marrying, the majority of women are heavily constrained by lack of capital. Men have, on average, a financing capacity that is 10 times that of women (Kuela 1996). In general, women can develop income-generating activities only by using low-cost inputs or by getting some financial help from their husbands. Table 3.1 summarizes the different activities undertaken by men and women and, for each activity, the startup capital required. This table suggests that women's limited access to capital prevents them from engaging in capital-intensive or large-scale activities. As a consequence, women are often involved in activities that generate low income, such as handicrafts or small-scale food processing for the village or local market (Kuela 1996).

In addition, survey results reported in Table 3.2 show that a woman who has the financing capacity to invest in a substantial stock of inputs can earn up to five times more than a woman who is forced to buy inputs on a daily basis. Participation in a tontine represents an efficient means for these women to alleviate their capital constraints. Tontines are, however, more common and more dynamic in urban areas than in rural areas, where markets are less developed and covariant risks are higher.

In northern Burkina Faso, successive years of severe food deficits have also revealed the importance of the role of rural women in ensuring household food security—traditionally men's responsibility (Colliot and Nguyen 1993; Ouedraogo 1993). Women and men may now tend to shoulder the same responsibilities within a household, but their access to financial services is far from being equal.

THE CYCLE OF THE ANNUAL FOOD DEFICIT AND THE HOUSEHOLD'S SELF-FINANCING CAPACITY.   In rural areas, the household's production

TABLE 3.1 Activities traditionally undertaken by women and men and their operating costs

Activity	Operating Costs (CFA francs)
Women	
Food processing	7,000 to 16,000 per cycle of 7 days
Handicrafts (mats, hats, etc.)	1,500 to 3,000 per cycle of 7 to 15 days
Restaurant	20,000 per day
Beer processing	22,400 per cycle of 5 days
Sheep fattening	8,000 to 16,000 per cycle
Small trading activity (milk, ingredients)	10,000 per cycle of 7 days
Trading of manufactured goods	15,000 to 30,000 per cycle of 7 days
Trading with substantial storage capacity	60,000 to 100,000 per cycle of 7 days
Men	
Sale of labor for manual tasks (cultivation, construction)	500 per day plus food
Animal fattening (sheep and cattle)	10,000 to 70,000 per cycle
Livestock trading at the local level	20,000 to 50,000 per cycle
Livestock trading at the regional level	400,000 to 900,000 per cycle
Trading of manufactured goods	50,000 to 100,000 per cycle
Production of cash crops (potatoes, onions)	450,000 to 2,600,000 per hectare and per cycle (once a year)

SOURCES: Ngobounan (1992); Ali (1993); Barry (1994); Kongbo (1994); Naitormbaide (1994); Kuela (1996); Nguyen (1998).

NOTE: CFA = Communauté Financière Africaine.

and consumption activities exhibit a marked seasonality. During the rainy season, from June to September, the entire family labor force is exclusively allocated to agricultural activities. Activity diversification normally takes place only during the off-farm season. Peaks of income inflows, therefore, correspond to harvest time and the dry season. Similarly, household consumption has peaks at the beginning of the rainy season—when households have to invest in agricultural activities and most granaries are empty so the need for food is more important—and after the harvest—when households have to finance social events and amass the startup capital for dry-season activities.

Figure 3.1 shows theoretical outflows and inflows of income. Understanding the household's economic cycle is important because it enables identification of seasonal bottlenecks for the household's budget and, thus, the types of financial services required. According to the cycle shown in Figure 3.1, households tend to spend their savings or borrow money at the start and during the rainy season and save at harvest time and during the dry season if they are not capital constrained. In other words, a household can be a net saver during certain periods of the year and a net borrower during other periods.

TABLE 3.2 An example of the impact of self-financing capacity on the profitability of an activity

Operating Costs and Benefits of Processing Oil from Groundnuts	Woman Who Purchases a Substantial Stock of Groundnuts at Harvest Time	Woman Who Purchases Small Quantities of Groundnuts on a Daily Basis
Cost of groundnuts (CFA francs per bag)	4,500	7,000
Output in oil (liters per bag of groundnuts)	12	12
Output in edible (kilograms per bag of groundnuts)	24	24
Sale price of oil (CFA francs per liter)	600	600
Sale price of groundnut, edible (CFA francs per kilogram)	50	50
Total sale price (CFA francs per bag of groundnuts)	8,400	8,400
Extra operating costs (CFA francs per bag of groundnuts)	800	800
Profit margin (CFA francs per bag of groundnuts)	3,100	600

SOURCE: Wampfler (1998b).

The household economy varies greatly from one year to another depending on the food deficit. Household food security is strongly correlated to the household's ability to develop cash-earning activities (Tassembedo 1996). In years of bad harvests, better-off households are those that can easily mobilize a sufficient amount of cash; in other words, those that have a high capacity for self-financing and easy access to financial markets.

In years of bad harvests, most of the household's budget will clearly be allocated to food expenditure, thereby dramatically reducing the household's capacity to finance income-generating activities. For example, following the serious food deficit in 1990, more than half of the economically active people in rural areas reported difficulties in restarting a dry-season activity. Even in normal years, between 10 and 20 percent of households in rural areas have a chronic food deficit caused by several factors, including a large number of dependants as a proportion of economically active members. For these households, granaries are usually emptied during the dry season or at the start of the rainy season, and sometimes even before. Large food expenditures tend to coincide, therefore, with the period requiring major agricultural investments, when households need financing to increase their production.

FIGURE 3.1 Seasonal pattern of household income and expenditure in Burkina Faso

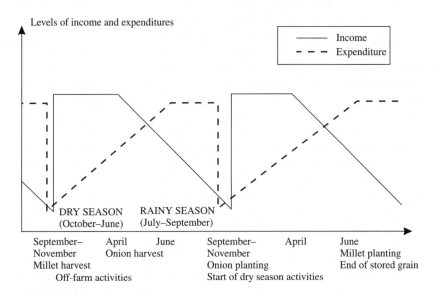

Levels of income and expenditures

——— Income
– – – Expenditure

DRY SEASON   RAINY SEASON
(October–June)   (July–September)

September– November Millet harvest	April Onion harvest	June	September– November Onion planting	April	June Millet planting End of stored grain
	Off-farm activities		Start of dry season activities		

SOURCE: Ouattara et al. (1997).

In northern Burkina Faso, the number of households entering into loan contracts in 1990, a year of severe harvest deficit, was twice the number in 1991, a year of relatively good harvests (Nguyen 1998). Similarly, the average rate of livestock sales was far greater in 1990 than in 1991 (Ngobounan 1992; Colliot 1993; Rubrice 1995). On the other hand, 67 percent of the households surveyed in the Province of Yatenga did try to accumulate wealth by buying livestock in 1991, compared with only 43 percent in 1990. However, following successive years of bad harvests and increased resource scarcity, dissaving rates tend to exceed average savings rates, further reducing the household's self-financing capacity. Wealth accumulation tends to be very low among rural households (Oppenheim 1998). Comparing the population of agropastoral households in northern Burkina Faso in 1984 and in 1992, Ngobounan (1992) reported the emergence of a new population of households without any livestock. In 1992, these poorest households with very limited self-financing capacity represented 23 percent of agropastoral households. Therefore, the importance of the food security dimension as a prerequisite for economic development cannot be overstressed.

THE DEGREE OF MONETIZATION AND OF MARKET PENETRATION. In the context of transition economies, the last, but not least, determinant of household demand for financial services is the social and economic environment of households. Studies conducted on household activity and economies, on the one hand, and on specific products, on the other hand, suggest that the diversity, number, and volume of households' savings and credit transactions are positively correlated with the dynamism of village institutions and local markets.

Financial intermediation has an indisputable role in economic growth. However, this process can take place only in an economy that is relatively dynamic in terms of the number and frequency of contractual exchanges and market transactions. In rural Burkina Faso, markets are expanding rapidly, but many do not function correctly and others that are essential to household welfare, such as the insurance market, have not emerged yet. Most villages in northern Burkina Faso are connected to major markets through small local markets, which are limited in size and scope mainly because of the lack of infrastructure— paved roads in particular.

Nowadays, more than two-thirds of households' total market transactions take place in local markets. Colliot (1993) and Wiest (1993) demonstrate that local markets provide households not only with essential goods such as food, but also with cash so that households can purchase other consumption goods as well as inputs for income-generating activities. The function of local markets as the household's main supplier of cash appears to be critical because households in rural areas in Burkina Faso have very little cash. Traditional savings through livestock and granaries remain the most predominant forms, although they are not always marketable—as is often the case with livestock.

Given the exclusive, monopolistic position of local markets with respect to the household's transactions, we can infer that the profitability of activities and opportunities for new market niches depend essentially on the degree of development of local markets and on their integration with the rest of the economy. Profitable market niches exist to a certain extent across the different types of activity but in most cases households are not able to take advantage of them because they have limited financing capacity or do not hold sufficient cash at the right time (Ali 1993; Mai Tanimoune 1993; Kongbo 1994; Naitormbaide 1994; Wampfler 1998a). On the other hand, credit contracts will be set up and credit will be repaid only if borrowers can have access, on a sustainable basis, to more than one repayment source; in other words, more than one cash-earning strategy. The pervasiveness of money keepers, of professional lenders, and especially of active and durable tontines in urban areas—compared with villages— is a good example of the importance of a dynamic market environment for financial deepening.

What Can We Learn from the Recently Launched Microfinance Institutions?

We base most of our discussion here on evaluation studies conducted on four major microfinance projects launched in the late 1980s and early 1990s in Burkina

Faso (Poulain 1995). These projects are the Projet de Promotion du Petit Crédit Rural (PPPCR), the Caisses Villageoises d'Epargne et de Crédits Autogérées (CVECAs) in the province of Sissili, the Association des Tontines of Nouna (ATN), and the Association pour le Développement de la Région de Kaya (ADRK), as shown in Box 3.2. These evaluation studies provided interesting results about household demand for financial services and complement results drawn from research studies of the household economy.

The objective of these microfinance projects was to provide savings and credit services to populations impoverished by successive years of severe harvest deficits so that these populations could engage in income-earning activities and start actively accumulating wealth. Despite PPPCR's problems associated with its institution-building process, numerous studies have reported the relative success of these four projects, which is largely attributed to their context-adaptive approach.

For our purposes, evaluation studies of the performances of microfinance projects represent a rich source of information for the following reasons:

- All of the projects offer a large range of savings and/or credit services more or less targeted at some specific activities through the terms of the contract (for example, duration or loan amount). Most of these products are not offered by the informal sector; therefore, analysis of demand for them by the different socioeconomic categories of households can reveal interesting information about characteristics of household demand that were previously hidden, and about the adaptability of the supply.
- In the specific cases of the CVECAs and ATN, because credit contracts are not limited to a certain number of products, we can push the analysis further and infer that households' observed demand for credit services corresponds to households' true demand, provided that no limits exist on the amount of the loan disbursed.
- Comparison of the projects' performance in terms of outreach with the information we have on the household economies can also provide information about households' behavior with respect to savings and credit. For example, wealthy households may not be members of any of the projects because they demand financial services that are offered neither by the projects nor by the informal sector.

Table 3.3 shows some of the most significant indicators for our analysis of true household demand for financial services.

Project Outreach and Potential Clientele

Results confirm the importance of women's demand for financial services. The significant difference in terms of female participation between projects that target women (PPPCR and ATN) and the other projects (CVECAs and ADRK) is

BOX 3.2 Brief description of the objectives and methodologies of four microfinance institutions launched in the late 1980s and early 1990s in Burkina Faso

Projet de Promotion du Petit Crédit Rural (PPPCR)

Launched in 1988, PPPCR's primary objective was to offer credit services to rural households, which lost much of their equity capital following successive years of drought. The project was inspired by the Grameen Bank model. It offers diversified credit products to its clientele, the majority of whom are women, organized into solidarity groups of five. Credit products are more or less targeted to specific income-generating activities. Only compulsory saving services exist. PPPCR now operates in four provinces of Burkina Faso (two in the north, one in the center–north, and one in the east), and has a pyramidal organization in which loan officers play a key role.

Association des Tontines of Nouna (ATN)

Launched in 1991 by CIDR, a French NGO, the objective of ATN was to support the existing tontines and to promote the emergence of more dynamic and sustainable indigenous microfinance institutions. Tontines are composed of groups of 15–40 people, who decide on the rotating organization. The main innovation introduced was that each tontine holds three different types of account. The money contributed by the members was used to finance a common pot that goes to one member at each rotation; a credit fund that offers short-term credit services with an interest rate of 2 to 3 percent per month; and term deposits, which are individual and earn interest. ATN operates in the center–west region of Burkina Faso.

Caisses Villageoises d'Epargne et de Crédits Autogérées (CVECAs)

Launched in 1992 by CIDR in the Province of Sissili (in the southeast of Burkina Faso), the objective of the village-based CVECAs was to provide the rural poor with access to sustainable financial institutions. CVECAs were designed to have complete financial and organizational autonomy. They offer several saving (one checking service, and two different deposit services that earn interest) and nontargeted credit products to villagers, who have to pay a fee to become members of the institution. CVECAs are managed by committees selected by the villagers, and the terms of the contracts are decided by the villagers (interest rates on loans and savings are about 40 and 20 percent, respectively).

Association pour le Développement de la Région de Kaya (ADRK)

ADRK was created in 1969 in the northeast region to promote agricultural innovation and help increase farmers' income. Started as an NGO, ADRK progressively turned into a farmers' mutual association. The credit system was introduced as recently as 1993 to alleviate farmers' capital constraints and to promote investment. Members of the credit system are organized into large groups managed by a village committee. The credit system offers, on the one hand, individual short-term and long-term loans with interest rates ranging from 8 to 15 percent and, on the other hand, collective short-term and long-term loans at an interest rate of 37 percent to finance collective projects, such as a cereal bank. A large proportion (37 percent) of credit is in kind (for example, agricultural machinery, carts, plows, bicycles, animals for fattening). The association also offers individual and collective saving services.

important. Female members represent two-thirds of total members in the first case and less than half in the second. Despite the fact that women are credit-worthy and could contribute significantly to the capital of microfinance institutions such as ATN, they continue to be excluded socially from most of the institutions.

In general, access to microfinance institutions concerns individuals from low- and medium-income households. The poorest households most often choose not to borrow because they are strongly averse to risky but potentially profitable enterprises. On the other hand, only a few wealthy households borrow from these microfinance institutions, and then mostly either to alleviate cash constraints or to take advantage of interest-earning deposit services. Loans offered by projects are too small and too costly for individuals. In the case of the CVECAs, a larger percentage of the savings collected come from village self-help groups and not from individuals (Poulain 1995).

Credit Use and Characteristics of Demand

THE COMPLEX ALLOCATION OF CREDIT AND HOUSEHOLD RISK-AVERSE BEHAVIOR. In general, loans borrowed from all four projects are rarely used to finance new activities because of people's risk-averse behavior. Fewer than half of the borrowers reported that credit was used to start a new activity. Most often, loans were used to supplement inadequate operating capital or to restart an activity after a break. This underscores once more the critical role of credit in daily cash management and in sustaining an activity over time in the context of transition economies.

In-depth studies of credit use by women who borrowed from PPPCR reveal that the allocation of credit can be quite complex. This allocation usually reflected a combination of women's short-term economic strategy of consumption smoothing (direct financing of the household's basic needs) and their long-term strategy of wealth accumulation (investments in more than one activity traditionally practiced and in the purchase of sheep). This allocation of funds is perfectly consistent with the household's risk-management strategies.

At this point, it is important to discuss the relevance of some of the loan products offered by projects such as PPPCR that were designed to induce women to capture a certain number of market niches considered as profitable (Ali 1993; Mai Tanimoune 1993; Kongbo 1994; Naitormbaide 1994). Examples are those designed for women who weave carpets. These credit products in fact corresponded to a demand formulated by women whose capital constraints prevented

TABLE 3.3 The performance of four microfinance institutions in Burkina Faso

	PPPCR	ATN	CVECAs	ADRK
Date of creation	1988	1991	1992	1993
Number of members	9,000	686	7,046	8,579
Percentage of women	98	60	30 to 47	21
Major funding source	External	Internal	Internal	External
Nature of credit	In cash and theoretically nontargeted	In cash and nontargeted	In cash and nontargeted	In cash and nontargeted and agricultural credit in kind
Total credit disbursed (million CFA francs)	105	8.4	50	100
Average credit (CFA francs)	25,000	4,000–7,000[a]	30,000	49,300
Minimum amount (CFA francs)	2,500	15,000	500	30,000
Maximum amount (CFA francs)	50,000	500,000	40,000	65,000
Repayment rate (percent)	98.5	100	100	95
Percentage of borrowers using credit to finance a new activity	44	20	32	43
Total savings collected (million CFA francs)	56.0 (compulsory)	1.97 (voluntary)	75.0 (voluntary)	63.0 (voluntary)
Percentage of members saving on a regular basis	0	80	100	71
Percentage of savers with a checking account	0	0	68	57
Percentage of savers with a term deposit	0	100	45	57

SOURCE: Poulain (1995).

NOTES: PPPCR = Projet de Promotion du Petit Crédit Rural; ATN = Association des Tontines of Nouna; CVECAs = Caisses Villageoises d'Epargne et de Crédits Autogérées; ADRK = Association pour le Développement de la Région de Kaya.

[a] Average amount depending on the amount of contributions accumulated by the group of women.

them from minimizing operating costs. Evaluations show positive results because women were able to build up substantial stocks of inputs to lower the overall production costs and to improve their profits. However, women also stated that the market could quickly reach saturation point and thus limit their benefits (Barry 1994). This single example suggests that knowledge about markets, and more precisely about supply and demand, constitutes an essential aspect of microfinance that was understated. In fact, the real problem is the issue of market saturation and can be formulated as follows: how much exogenous money can a transition economy absorb?

CREDIT DEMAND FOR AGRICULTURAL VERSUS RURAL ACTIVITIES. The failures of agricultural development banks in the 1960s have long obscured the issue of the financing of agricultural activities and, more generally, of rural activities. In the case of the CVECAs, which offer nontargeted credit services, 45 percent of loans were used partially or totally by villagers to finance the purchase of agricultural inputs, including seeds, chemicals, animal feed, and labor.

Agricultural activities still provide employment to a high percentage of the population and are completely integrated with rural households' activity diversification strategies. Rural households' demand for credit to finance agricultural activities remains substantial and very diverse. It includes the financing of input expenditures and major investments in livestock, machinery, and tree plantations (Ngobounan 1992; Lesueur and Torre 1993; Kongbo 1994; Wampfler 1998a). On the other hand, microfinance projects have recently been looking to diversify their credit portfolio and to attract both new and old clients.

However, in a context characterized by high covariant risks and imperfect markets, these types of agricultural investment tend to be costly, risky, and often not profitable in the short term. The complex allocation of nontargeted credit to both off-farm and farm activities, or to either one, demonstrates that households are perfectly aware of the limitations of agricultural credit. In fact, the question that needs to be formulated may be how both microfinance institutions and borrowers can lower the risk and cost associated with agricultural credit, given the micro- and macroeconomic characteristics of the economy.

The Use of and Potential Demand for Deposit Services

Important lessons can be learned from the experiences of the CVECAs, ATN, and ADRK with respect to the mobilization of household savings. In contrast to PPPCR, these three projects offer voluntary savings services to their clientele. Indicators of the projects' performance as regards savings services clearly indicate that individuals do have a savings capacity and, more importantly, households are interested in monetary savings instruments (Table 3.3). Researchers should, however, extend the analysis to characterize more precisely the nature of household savings behavior. Because of ATN's institutional design, which is based on existing tontines, it is usual for ATN's clients to use only long-term deposit services. Results from the CVECAs and ADRK reveal more interesting patterns in the sense that members of these projects use term deposits and the equivalent of checking accounts equally. An evaluation study of the CVECAs in the Pays Dogon (in Mali) actually shows that a majority of individuals use checking deposits, some of them use both savings services, while wealthy individuals and village self-help groups prefer term deposits exclusively (Ouattara et al. 1997).

Savings patterns observed at the level of microfinance institutions are, indeed, perfectly consistent with the fact that many households are cash constrained. In this specific case, checking account services enable households to smooth their monetary income in exactly the same way a professional money keeper would. Only better-off households demand term deposits. Having reached a certain degree of wealth accumulation, these households are searching for alternative savings instruments that earn interest and that are more secure than traditional forms of savings, such as livestock.

Conclusions, Policy Recommendations, and Research Agenda

With respect to the empirical results from studies of household economies (Box 3.1) and of the performance of selected microfinance institutions, we can point out three major findings:

- The household demand for financial services varies with age, gender, social responsibilities and status, income and food deficit levels, and the degree of monetization and market penetration. The diversity of demand simply reflects the complexity of households' organization in uncertain economies.
- In an uncertain environment, credit and savings services are needed less to finance investment than to smooth both consumption and income, and particularly monetary inflows.
- Because of internal and external limitations, existing informal finance and formal microfinance projects can satisfy only part of true demand. Improving the satisfaction of existing and future demand will require microfinance institutions to diversify their services further and to reach more potential clients.

Several market niches for financial innovations exist, which, because of their nature and magnitude, cannot necessarily be captured by existing informal financial institutions. The first of these market niches is related to the role of credit in household consumption smoothing. Supplying credit for direct consumption may not be the best solution considering the household's socioeconomic environment. Given that individuals do have a certain savings capacity at given periods, despite their low degree of overall wealth accumulation, supplying a broader spectrum of savings services—including checking accounts and different term deposits—and insurance services may be more effective.

The second market niche is associated with the financing of agriculture. The CVECA experience showed that agricultural activities could be success-fully financed. However, questions should be raised about the capacity of micro-finance institutions to identify and to manage covariant risks.

In trying to adapt supply to demand, microfinance institutions should also concentrate their attention on their outreach and on their clientele's demands. As clients' economic activities grow and their standard of living improves, they will be interested in a larger range of financial services. Their demand will shift from small and short-term to larger and medium-term credit and deposit ser-vices. Aspects of the so-called graduation process of clients are interrelated with outreach performance in the sense that it is in the institution's best inter-ests to satisfy the demand of as many socioeconomic categories of household as possible in order to increase the profitability of their services, to lower the portfolio's risk, and to induce their members to become regular customers. Creditworthy women and better-off households are still excluded from the system. Likewise, building a long-term relationship by taking into account the client's graduation process is, for an institution, the best protection against asymmetric information.

In this chapter, we have discussed the fact that, in a context characterized by rapid change and poverty, household demand for financial services is far more complex than one might imagine. The objective was not to analyze the microfinance institutional building process. Nevertheless, the satisfaction of this demand certainly affects the design of microfinance innovations. We have briefly discussed the performance of four existing microfinance institutions. All of them claim to have adopted a demand-led approach. However, they exhibit very different institutional designs and offer very diverse savings and credit services. We need to ask which of the institutions offers the best services in terms of quality and cost. Given the same environment, can two different in-stitutions achieve the same results in terms of the supply of services adapted to demand; in other words, is any comparative advantage attached to one institu-tional design?

It is a great challenge for many of the microfinance institutions to supply the best financial services at the lowest sustainable cost to everybody. Asking them to achieve a role in financial intermediation and in optimizing the allo-cation of resources represents an even greater challenge. The sustainability of microfinance institutions and their impact on the development of local economies depend on exogenous factors, such as the infrastructure and the development of well-functioning markets. To produce a positive impact on household wel-fare it is not sufficient to offer adapted credit services. Markets may quickly reach saturation point and leave microenterprises in debt. We found that little information on markets exists and nobody knows exactly to what extent an economy can absorb increasing monetary transactions.

This finding leads naturally to another relevant research question relating to the effects of market development on the performance of microfinance institutions in transition economies. Work remains to be done formally to identify the demand for financial services by the different socioeconomic categories of households. Such work can be done through formal contingent valuations combined with market studies.

References

Adams, D. 1994. Introductory presentation: Building durable financial markets. In *Finance and rural development in West Africa.* Proceedings of the Ohio State University/CIRAD International Seminar, October 21–25, 1991, Ouagadougou, Burkina Faso.

Ali, A. 1993. Diagnostic de l'existant en matière de diversification économique et perspectives de financement par un système de crédit décentralisé: Province de la Tapoa (Burkina Faso). Thesis. Ecole Supérieure d'Agronomie Tropicale, CIRAD, Montpellier, France.

Barry, A. 1994. *Suivi des crédits expérimentaux artisanats. Unité provinciale du Soum.* Ouagadougou, Burkina Faso: Projet de Promotion du Petit Crédit Rural.

Benoit-Cattin, M., and J. Faye. 1982. *L'exploitation agricole familiale en Afrique soudano-sahélienne.* Paris, France: ACCT-PUF.

Binswanger, H., J. McIntire, and C. Udry. 1989. Production relations in semi-arid African agriculture. In *The economic theory of agrarian institutions*, ed. P. Bardhan. Oxford: Oxford University Press.

Bonte, P. 1986. The Sahel: Transformation and drought. In *The roots of catastrophe, drought, and man: The 1972 case history*, vol. 3, ed. R.V. Garcia and P. Spitz. New York: Pergamon Press.

Charmes, J. 1996. *Le secteur informel au Burkina Faso: Evolution sur longue période et suivi conjoncturel.* Ouagadougou, Burkina Faso: MEF-FED-GTZ.

Christensen, G. 1991. Informal financial intermediation: Quest for the grail? In *Finance and rural development in West Africa.* Proceedings of the Ohio State University/ CIRAD International Seminar, October 21–25, 1991, Ouagadougou, Burkina Faso.

Colliot, E. 1993. Les interactions entre le marché des céréales, le marché du bétail, et le marché financier. Master's thesis. Ecole Supérieure d'Agronomie de Montpellier, France.

Colliot, E., and T. D. P. Nguyen. 1993. Le crédit rural et l'économie villageoise à Banh (Burkina Faso). *Les Cahiers de la Recherche-Développement* 34: 65–83.

Diop, M. 1990. Contribution à la mise en place d'un nouveau système de crédit rural. Banh, Burkina Faso. Thesis. Ecole Supérieure d'Agronomie Tropicale, CIRAD, Montpellier, France.

Ford. R. E. 1982. Subsistence farming systems in semi-arid Northern Yatenga (Upper Volta). Ph.D. dissertation. Geography Department, University of California– Riverside, U.S.A.

INSD (Institut National des Statistiques Démographiques). 1985. Analyse des résultats définitifs du recensement général de la population. Direction de la Démographie, Ouagadougou, Burkina Faso.

Kongbo, A. 1994. Diversification économique et crédit rural (Province du Soum–Burkina Faso). Thesis. Ecole Supérieure d'Agronomie Tropicale, CIRAD, Montpellier, France.

Kuela, N. 1996. Femmes, argent, pouvoir. Essai sur la problématique de l'accumulation en milieu rural. Master's thesis. FLASHS, University of Ouagadougou, Burkina Faso.

Lesueur, C., and C. Torre. 1993. Contribution à la mise en place d'un système expérimental de crédit à l'élevage dans le village de Sé (Province du Soum, Burkina Faso). Thesis. Ecole Supérieure d'Agronomie Tropicale, CIRAD, Montpellier, France.

Mai Tanimoune, M. 1993. Diagnostic de l'existant en matière de diversification économique et perspectives de financement par un système de crédit décentralisé: Province du Yatenga (Burkina Faso). Thesis. Ecole Supérieure d'Agronomie Tropicale, CIRAD, Montpellier, France.

Marchal, J. Y. 1983. Yatenga, Nord Haute-Volta: La dynamique d'un espace rural soudano-sahélien. Ph.D. dissertation, ORSTROM, Paris, France.

Naitormbaide, M. 1994. Crédit rural et diversification économique: Province du Yatenga (Burkina Faso). Thesis. Ecole Supérieure d'Agronomie Tropicale, CIRAD, Montpellier, France.

Ngobounan, F. 1992. Etude préalable à la mise en place de systèmes de financement aux activités d'élevage dans un espace sahélien (Province du Soum, Burkina Faso). Thesis. Ecole Supérieure d'Agronomie Tropicale, CIRAD, Montpellier, France.

Nguyen, T. D. P. 1998. Food insecurity and the evolution of indigenous risk-sharing institutions in the Sahel. Ph.D. dissertation. Department of Agricultural Economics, Ohio State University, Columbus, Ohio, U.S.A.

Oppenheim, M. 1998. Dynamique d'accumulation en milieu rural sahélien. Quel rôle pour les crédits décentralisés? Le cas du village de Gandaogo, Province du Ganzourgou, Burkina Faso. Master's thesis. Ecole Supérieure d'Agronomie de Montpellier, France.

Ouattara, K, T. D. P. Nguyen, C. Gonzalez-Vega, and D. H. Graham. 1997. The Caisses Villageoises d'Epargne et de Crédit Autogérées in the Dogon region of Mali: Elements of impact. Centre International de Développement et de Recherche, Autrèches, France, and Ohio State University, Columbus, Ohio, U.S.A.

Ouedraogo, C. 1993. Analyse et typologie des marmites de Madougou. Perspectives de l'impact du crédit. Master's thesis. FASEG, University of Ouagadougou, Burkina Faso.

Poulain, C. 1995. Systèmes financiers décentralisés au Burkina Faso. Thesis. Ecole Supérieure d'Agronomie de Montpellier, France.

Raffinot, M. 1997. Strategies nationales de réduction de la pauvreté. Etude de cas du Burkina Faso. Master's thesis. University of Paris XI, France.

Reardon, T., and M. Mercado-Peters. 1991. Self-financing of rural household cash expenditures in Burkina Faso: The case of net cereal buyers. In *Finance and rural development in West Africa*. Proceedings of the Ohio State University/CIRAD International Seminar, October 21–25, 1991, Ouagadougou, Burkina Faso.

68   *Geneviève Nguyen et al.*

Riesman, P. 1974. *Société et liberté chez les Peul Djelgobe de Haute Volta. Essai d'anthropologie introspective*. Paris: Cahiers de l'Homme Ethonologie-Géographie-Linguistique, EHESS.

Rubrice, E. 1995. Elevage, embouche et crédit rural dans la Province du Soum, Burkina Faso. Thesis. Ecole Supérieure d'Agronomie Tropicale, CIRAD, Montpellier, France.

Sheets, H., and R. Morris. 1976. Disaster in the desert. In *The politics of natural disaster: The case of the Sahel drought,* ed. M. H. Glantz. Oxford: Clarendon Press.

Tassembedo, M. 1996. *Etude de l'impact du crédit PPPCR dans les provinces du Soum et du Ganzourgou*. Ouagadougou, Burkina Faso: Projet de Promotion du Petit Crédit Rural.

UNDP (United Nations Development Programme). 1997. *Rapport mondial sur le développement*. Paris: Economica.

Wampfler, B. 1998a. *Diagnostic de la demande et de l'offre en matière de financement rural dans la zone de Gaya, Niger*. Study Report No. 21/98, CIRAD, Montpellier, France.

Wampfler, B. 1998b. Les innovations en matière de microfinance ouvrent-elles des perspectives pour le financement de l'agriculture? Communication presented at the International Symposium AOCA/RSP-GRN "Recherche-système et politiques agricole," September 21–25, 1998, Bamako, Mali.

Wiest, M. 1993. Les relations entre le marché du mil, le marché du bétail et le marché monétaires à Nogodoum, Yatenga, Burkina Faso. Master's thesis. University of Hohenheim, Germany.

World Bank. 1995. *Trends in developing economies: Burkina Faso*. Washington, D.C.: International Bank for Reconstruction and Development and World Bank.

Zeller, M., and M. Sharma, eds. 2000. *Innovations in rural microfinance for the rural poor: Exchange of knowledge and implications for policy*. Proceedings from an international conference organized by the German Foundation for International Development (DSE), the International Food Policy Research Institute (IFPRI), the International Fund for Agriculture (IFAD), and the Bank of Ghana. Feldafing, Germany: German Foundation for International Development (DSE).

Zimmerman, F. J. 1994. Structural change and evolving institutions in developing agrarian economies: A dynamic programming simulation analysis. Ph.D. dissertation. Department of Agricultural Economics, University of Wisconsin-Madison, U.S.A.

4 Wealth and Rural Credit among Farmers in Mexico: Is Market Participation Consistent with Targeting?

JULIE STANTON

Improving access to credit for smaller, less-endowed producers has been part of policy discussions for many years and in a variety of contexts (see Braverman and Guasch 1989; Yaron 1992; and Gonzalez-Vega 1998 for good overviews). Direct government provision of credit and subsidies to commercial lending have been the typical policies chosen. Unfortunately, it is generally agreed that intensive government involvement has not been successful in assuring access to credit for small farmers, although the experiences have produced valuable lessons (Yaron 1994; Gonzalez-Vega and Graham 1995).

One essential factor for successful rural finance initiatives is the voluntary participation of the producers. A combination of establishing institutional credibility and having potential borrowers invest in that institution via savings mobilization is often suggested as key to improving the long-term relationship between borrower and lender. However, one of the first hurdles encountered in these initiatives is the reluctance of some potential borrowers to request loans from institutions that do not have a reputation of serving similar clients. They may also be reluctant owing to their perceptions of a complicated loan process, riskiness associated with borrowing, high collateral requirements, and high interest rates and borrowing costs (Adams and Nehman 1979).

This chapter investigates the composition of participants in the rural financial market in Mexico with respect to four distinct lender types, and assesses the appropriateness of that composition given the target groups that the lenders wish to reach. Much has been written about how asymmetric information can lead to a bias in loan markets toward larger, richer borrowers (Stiglitz and Weiss 1981; Gonzalez-Vega 1984; Carter 1988). However, the focus is on the pool of applicants: are they, as a group, already inconsistent with the supposed target group of the lender? If so, then the decision to participate (or not) in the lender's market has as much to do with poor program results as do decisions taken by lenders.[1]

---

1. Although geographic targeting may be poor in some cases, it is difficult for a government lender to justify setting up shop in an area occupied solely by nontargeted producers. Even so, as

The Mexican Rural Finance Market

Historically, the Mexican government has been heavily involved in rural finance. It presents a typical example of development banks and financial institutions that have incurred huge deficits and contributed to national fiscal crises (Mansell Carstens 1995). Among the chief problems were a lack of emphasis on repayments and interest rate restrictions that were incompatible with inflation.

The four distinct lender types in Mexico are (1) the Banco Nacional de Crédito Rural (Banrural), the principal governmental agricultural lender; (2) the Programa Nacional de Solidaridad (Pronasol or Solidaridad), the Salinas administration's lending assistance program for the poorest farmers; (3) private banks, found in most medium-sized cities surrounded by farming regions; and (4) the informal lenders, primarily merchants involved in sales of inputs, traders of agricultural output, and the so-called pure moneylenders.[2]

Banrural

Banrural, established in 1975, has been the most prominent arm of the government's rural credit strategy. For nearly 20 years, it was the principal lender to smallholder agriculture, at subsidized interest rates and with very little demand for collateral. Unfortunately, repayment was not strongly emphasized and a pattern of default became increasingly accepted by both borrowers and Banrural loan officers. Maintaining Banrural in operation required significant government transfers. In 1992, the government announced changes in Banrural that would reduce interest rate subsidies and place more emphasis on loan collection. The lender was reorganized and downsized. Banrural was to be more tightly targeted on farmers who appeared to have viable projects but who lacked access to other sources of credit either because they were unable to offer collateral or because they had no credit history with private lenders.

Solidaridad

In 1990, the government of Mexico announced the Programa Nacional de Solidaridad, which created a new set of funds for lending. Also known as *crédito a la palabra*, this program was designed to provide credit to poorer producers who were excluded from coverage by Banrural. The relatively small loans were given at zero interest and had no collateral requirement; the producers were required to repay the loans into a community fund. In addition to this rather charity-like role, Solidaridad actually received part of Banrural's portfolio of bad loans as well. Hence, the target group for this lender is the smallest, least-endowed producer who is unable to obtain loans elsewhere.

---

the demographics change, for example through entry or exit, the lender's continued presence should be re-evaluated.

2. An additional governmental arm, Fideicomisos Instituidos en Relacion con la Agricultura (FIRA), which primarily discounts loans through other lenders, is not included in the analysis. Farmers in our survey rarely identified FIRA as a lender from whom they requested a loan.

Private Banks

Two principal aspects of private banking in Mexico limit its accessibility for small producers. First, like private banks everywhere, the motive of earning profits is not always consistent with lending to smallholders (Carter 1988). Second, the commercial banking system is relatively limited geographically. Although private banks are widely available in medium and large cities, less than a third of the country's municipalities have banking offices of any kind. The combined population of municipalities without banking offices was 20 percent of the national population in 1990.

Because of asymmetric information, high transaction costs, and the existence of governmental lenders, private bankers are expected to target larger landowners who have collateral and demand larger loans, thereby reducing the transaction costs per loan.

Informal Lenders

Three typical varieties of informal lender are the merchant, the trader, and the pure moneylender. Both the merchant specializing in the sale of inputs and the trader of agricultural outputs may extend credit to farmers either as a pure monetary transaction or linked to the input or output transaction. Interlinked transactions reflect the "deliberate intertwining" of transactions between two agents (Bell 1988). A merchant may allow a customer to purchase inputs "on credit" on the condition that the customer frequent only that merchant's store, at least while the loan is in effect. This arrangement makes it possible for the farmer to use chemical inputs without going through lengthy formal lending procedures. Traders may extend a cash or in-kind loan to the farmer on the condition that they are given first option to purchase the farmer's output, perhaps at a preset price. In contrast, pure moneylenders are likely to act much like a private bank, except that personal reputations may be more important and the lenders may be inclined to impose much higher collateral requirements. They also may charge rather high interest rates (Bottomley 1975).

Although these informal lenders vary considerably, they offer reasonable alternatives to farmers who are unable to obtain credit in the formal market. They have no official target group, but their clients are likely to be in the low-to-medium wealth groups if the moneylender has good knowledge about the borrower (reducing transaction costs), and perhaps also in the high wealth group if the farmer has had trouble with institutional sources (because of a previous default, for example).

Survey Data and Estimation of Wealth

The empirical work in this study is based on the results of a 1994 survey conducted in four states in Mexico. The regions surveyed were the Ciudad Obregón and Navojoa areas of the state of Sonora; the Bajio region near Irapuato and

Celaya in the state of Guanajuato; and the border region of the states of Puebla and Tlaxcala, near cities of the same name. The sample is not necessarily nationally representative, but the three regions chosen provide a wide range of farming conditions for comparison.[3] In the Puebla/Tlaxcala region, agriculture consists mostly of rainfed small farms with little use of mechanization and advanced inputs. In Guanajuato, although agriculture is more diversified, with some vegetable production and use of machinery, it still includes small-to-medium farms with no access to irrigation. In Sonora, farming is largely commercial, with canal irrigation and larger farms. Still, within each region, there is considerable variation.

For the 1994 survey, 567 interviews were completed, covering most aspects of production, household composition, off-farm income sources, and access to credit. The 1991 sample, which contained 973 farmers, was constructed by first randomly selecting *ejidos* within the region from a national directory of these communities.[4] Then, individual *ejidatarios* were randomly selected within the *ejido*, along with private farmers in the vicinity. In terms of numbers, Mexican farmers are predominantly *ejidatarios*, and the sample reflects this representation. For the 1994 survey, farmers were randomly selected from the 1991 sample, maintaining regional and tenure characteristics.

Table 4.1 describes the variables used in the survey, and Table 4.2 presents some of the results. A few points are worth mentioning. First, wealth is measured based on the value of all agricultural land, machinery, buildings, vehicles, and large animals owned by the farmer. Where possible, actual values given by the farmer were used. If these values were not available, they were estimated using regression analysis. Second, the value of assets on a per capita basis is used to classify the farmer into one of five quintiles, where group I refers to the lowest values and group V the highest. The calculations produce intuitive relationships between a farmer's wealth and other characteristics.[5]

---

3. The regions were chosen by the Instituto Tecnológico Autónomo de México, which conducted a survey in 1991 on this same sample. Unfortunately, the 1991 survey, which was intended for a study of differences in productivity by land tenure, did not collect sufficient detail about lender types to be useful in this analysis.

4. *Ejidos* are communities of farmers that were created at the time of the Mexican Constitution. Each *ejido* received a quantity of land to be used among its members, whose number varied. They were permitted to choose between operating the land in a communal way or distributing the land to the individuals (*ejidatarios*). Considerable restrictions were placed on the use of the land, although many were legally lifted in 1992.

5. The survey requested information on each of the five components of wealth, including their age, quality, and value as perceived by owner. When these values were not available, econometric prediction was used to approximate a value.

For land values, subregional dummies, existence of full documents, size of parcel, and a wide range of parcel characteristics (such as slope, irrigation, and erosion) were used to explain the value per hectare of the individual parcel. The resulting R^2 was .69. For machinery, tenure of the owner, type of machinery, whether repairs were needed, and whether fuel was used, plus regional dummies and age of the machine, were used as explanatory variables. The resulting R^2 was .69 for machinery

TABLE 4.1 Definition of variables

Variable	Definition
Wealth	Sum of value of all agricultural land, machinery, buildings, vehicles, and large animals owned by the farmer
Age of head	In years
Education of head	In years
Male	Dummy variable: takes value of 1 if head of household is male and 0 if female
Household size	In number of people
Works off-farm	Dummy variable: takes value of 1 if any member of the household holds a job off-farm, even if seasonal or temporary
Looked for job	Dummy variable: takes value of 1 if any member of the household looked for work during 1994, and was not immediately successful
Received remittances	Dummy variable: takes value of 1 if the household received money from a migrated relative
Distance to paved road	In kilometers
Have full documents	Dummy variable: takes value of 1 if the producer has private title or certificate of agrarian rights to at least one of his or her parcels
Crop diversity	Number of different crops produced by the farmer
Intercrop	Dummy variable: takes value of 1 if the producer intercrops at least two crops during the year
Corn/beans	Dummy variable: takes value of 1 if the farmer produces corn and/or beans
Field crops	Dummy variable: takes value of 1 if the farmer produces grains, etc.
Fruit/vegetables	Dummy variable: takes value of 1 if the farmer produces fruits and/or vegetables
Guanajuato	Dummy variable: takes value of 1 if farmer lives in state of Guanajuato
Sonora	Dummy variable: takes value of 1 if farmer lives in state of Sonora
Private farmer	Dummy variable: takes value of 1 if farmer has full and private ownership rights to his or her land (i.e. is not an *ejidatario*)
Mixto farmer	Dummy variable: takes value of 1 if farmer is both an *ejidatario* and a private farmer

as well. For buildings, state dummies, tenure status, age of building, type, whether own-built, and dummies for how it was paid for were used. The R^2 was .50. For vehicles, state dummies, age and type of vehicle, whether repairs were needed, whether fuel was used, and tenure of the owner were used, giving an R^2 of .80. For animals, there was insufficient information to run regression analysis. Local averages were used to fill in missing values.

TABLE 4.2 Distribution of selected indicators across asset groups

Variables	Sample Average (N = 567)	Group I (N = 113)	Group II (N = 114)	Group III (N = 113)	Group IV (N = 113)	Group V (N = 114)
Asset value in 1994						
Total agricultural assets (N$1000)	257.20	34.42	68.55	138.11	210.72	831.42
Average ratio of agricultural to total assets	0.741	0.679	0.691	0.762	0.768	0.807
Hectares owned	10.5	3.7	5.4	7.7	10.2	25.1
Characteristics of the household head						
Age	58.4	54.9	56.7	60.4	60.0	60.1
Gender (percentage female)	16.6	11.5	16.7	18.6	16.8	19.3
Works off-farm (percentage of all farmers)	33.7	46.9	38.6	25.7	31.9	25.4
Ejidatarios (percentage of all farmers)	76.5	78.8	76.5	82.1	77.9	67.5
Household characteristics						
Household size	6.0	7.9	6.7	6.3	5.3	4.3
Dependency ratio (ratio of family members under 16 to adults)	0.42	0.67	0.46	0.40	0.29	0.28
Household member(s) work off-farm (percentage of all farmers)	67.9	84.3	68.4	68.1	69.9	50.8
Household member(s) looked for work (percentage of all farmers)	21.0	42.5	24.6	15.0	15.9	7.0
Received remittances from someone migrated (percentage of all farmers)	15.3	20.4	16.5	12.5	15.0	12.3

Input usage (percentage of all farmers who produce crops)

Purchases seeds	63.2	45.7	43.5	66.7	79.8	83.1
Uses fertilizers	92.5	88.3	90.6	94.1	96.6	93.5
Uses pesticides	71.6	55.3	58.8	78.6	79.8	88.3
Irrigates	51.8	19.1	27.1	59.5	74.2	84.4
Uses machinery in harvest	48.3	19.2	29.4	57.1	62.9	77.9
Uses tractor in soil preparation	86.3	73.4	80.0	94.1	91.0	94.8
Uses mechanized fumigation	17.3	1.1	4.7	17.9	21.4	45.5
Uses technical assistance	20.9	15.9	16.5	20.2	21.4	27.3
Insures crops	12.4	1.8	3.5	16.8	17.7	21.9
Production						
Number of crops produced	2.2	2.0	2.0	2.0	2.2	2.4
Intercrops (percent)[a]	17.5	31.9	21.2	10.7	14.6	6.5
Value of crop production (N$1,000)	56.13	5.87	7.42	19.24	30.51	244.31
Produces corn and/or beans (percent)[a]	82.8	88.2	96.4	83.8	77.3	66.2
Produces field crops (grains, oilseeds, beans) (percent)[a]	55.7	28.0	32.5	68.8	71.6	83.8
Produces fruits and/or vegetables (percent)[a]	27.3	32.3	26.5	25.0	25.0	27.0

NOTE: N$ refers to "new pesos." At the time of the survey, the peso crisis was just under way, devaluing the currency from N$3.5 per U.S. dollar in December 1994 to approximately N$6 per dollar during fieldwork.

[a] Percentage of all farmers who produce crops.

TABLE 4.3 Distribution of requests for and success in obtaining loans, by asset group and lender

Lender	Group I (N = 113)	Group II (N = 114)	Group III (N = 113)	Group IV (N = 113)	Group V (N = 114)
Percentage of group requesting loan					
Banrural	7.1	16.5	28.8	24.8	25.7
Private banks	2.7	1.7	0.9	2.7	21.2
Solidaridad	21.2	19.1	18.0	18.8	10.6
Informal lenders	3.5	3.5	5.4	10.7	10.6
All others	22.1	25.2	21.6	27.4	33.6
Percentage of successful requests					
Banrural	75.0	89.5	100.0	89.3	93.1
Private banks	33.3	50.0	100.0	66.7	95.8
Solidaridad	95.8	95.5	100.0	100.0	100.0
Informal lenders	100.0	100.0	100.0	100.0	91.7
All others	100.0	96.5	100.0	93.5	100.0
Percentage of all requests to lender deriving from each group					
Banrural	6.9	16.4	27.6	24.1	25.0
Private banks	9.1	6.1	3.0	9.1	72.7
Solidaridad	24.2	22.2	20.2	21.2	12.1
Informal lenders[a]	11.4	9.1	13.6	36.4	29.5
All others[a]	16.4	20.8	15.7	20.1	27.0

[a] When dividing requests and successes among the groups, they are counted individually, not as a group. "Informal lenders" comprises three lenders; "All others" comprises six lenders.

Patterns of Access to Credit across Asset Groups

Using asset groups (quintiles), we can look at how farmers in each group participate in the market. Table 4.3 shows the distribution of requests for and success in obtaining loans, by group and by lender. Because of the focus on four lender types in Mexico—Banrural, private banks, Solidaridad, and informal lenders—the remaining lenders found in the survey are lumped together under "all others."[6]

---

6. The other lender types include credit unions, savings institutions, family members, and some regional organizations, as well as a few FIRA requests.

Proportion of Group Participating

The first set of figures in Table 4.3 shows the percentage of farmers in each group who requested a loan from a particular lender.[7] For example, 7.1 percent of the poorest group of farmers applied to Banrural, compared with 25.7 percent of the richest group. Participation in the Banrural "market" generally increases across the groups, with the exception of group III, which shows greater participation than does group V. Purely on face value, this may indeed be consistent with Banrural's target group. However, the otherwise increasing nature of participation with wealth raises the question of whether the targeting of relatively less fortunate producers can be accomplished.

Not surprisingly, we find considerable difference in participation in the private bank "market" between the wealthiest farmers and the less wealthy. Indeed, 21.2 percent of wealthy farmers requested loans from private banks, compared with only 2.7 percent for groups I and IV and 0.9 percent for group III. For Solidaridad, there is a generally decreasing participation rate as wealth rises. However, it is surprising that more than 10 percent of the wealthiest farmers made requests to a lender whose expressed target group is the poorest producers.

Participation rates in the informal credit market increase with wealth. In fact, group V participants ask for loans from informal lenders as frequently as they do from Solidaridad. This may be related to their greater participation in the input and sales markets as well, as shown in Table 4.2.

For all other lenders, the participation rates are quite high, outpacing those for almost every other lender. However, a closer examination of the components (not shown) of this group reveals that, for groups I to IV, the major part of all these requests is to family members, whereas for group V it is to credit unions. This heterogeneity precludes any general conclusions about participation.

Proportion of Groups Obtaining Loans

The next set of figures, showing the proportion of requests that are successful, indicates that a high proportion of loan requests are granted. For example, 75.0 percent of the requests made by group I to Banrural are granted and all group III applicants are successful.[8] The poorest producers appear to be most successful with the non-institutional lenders (informal moneylenders and family members). Groups IV and V show greater success rates with Solidaridad than do the poorest of the producers in the sample. In fact, Solidaridad and informal

---

7. "Participation" and "requesting a loan" are used synonymously with "completed appropriate application."

8. This raises a doubt about whether farmers who were actually rejected for a loan responded truthfully to our survey. However, because some did report rejections and because the problems with *cartera vencida* (defaults on loans from other government programs, which restricts access to new programs) are prevalent, we cannot reject the validity of the survey responses.

lenders are the most fruitful for group IV and Solidaridad and "all others" for group V. Neither Banrural nor private banks offer them the same success rate.

Requests to Lenders by Group

The third set of figures turns the picture around to ask what proportion of requests to the lender derive from each group. For example, 6.9 percent of all requests to Banrural came from producers in group I. Group III provides the most requests to Banrural, group V to private banks and to "all others," group I to Solidaridad, and group IV to informal lenders.

These rankings appear to be consistent with the objectives of the lenders. However, it is surprising that group V makes up a larger share of the applicant pool for Banrural than the poorest two groups do. Similarly, despite Solidaridad's stated purpose of serving the poorest producers, there appears to be little difference in the distribution of applicants to Solidaridad across the first four groups. Indeed, fewer than half of all participants in Solidaridad's market are in the two poorest groups. Since acceptance rates are high for most groups, these patterns apply to the distribution of actual borrowers across the groups as well.

These figures indicate that, although there is some success in reaching target groups, much participation and indeed lending appears to be outside of the intended group, especially for Banrural and Solidaridad. This finding demonstrates that participation and targeting are not wholly consistent with one another. The next section considers one case in more detail.

Wealthy Solidaridad Participants

The data in Table 4.4 permit an analysis of the wealthy farmers who requested and received loans from Solaridad. The wealthy participants in the Solidaridad market (V-SOL) are similar to other wealthy farmers—both in general (V) and those who participate in the private bank market (V-PRVT). But they also have much in common with the poorer farmers (I), particularly Solidaridad participants (I-SOL). Although the V-SOL farmers are about the same age and have the same incidence of productive input use and crop selection as the V-PRVT and V farmers, they fall at the lower end of the asset value range for the wealthy group (less than half the group average).

The V-SOL farmers are also less educated than their V-PRVT counterparts. They use off-farm income sources more frequently, and they are very likely to be *ejidatarios*. They have smaller parcels of land with less access to irrigation and at a greater distance from paved roads. They are largely located in Guanajuato, rather than in Sonora (compared with 41.7 percent of V-PRVT farmers), and they all grow corn. In many cases, the I-SOL farmers share these characteristics with their V-SOL counterparts.

Although the patterns of the wealth groups are generally understandable (Table 4.2), it is surprising that farmers who apparently have valuable assets

TABLE 4.4 Comparison of Solidaridad participants with other farmer groups

Indicator	I[a]	I-SOL[b]	V-SOL[c]	V-PRVT[d]	V[e]
Number of farmers	113	24	12	24	114
Agricultural assets (N$)	34,420	36,537	365,842	1,320,373	831,423
Farmer characteristics					
Age (years)	54.9	49.2	61.75	61.0	60.1
Education (years)	2.7	2.7	1.7	5.1	4.3
Works off-farm (percent)	46.9	33.3	41.7	20.8	25.4
Any household member works (percent)	82.3	62.5	58.3	37.5	50.9
Receives remittances (percent)	20.4	29.2	25.0	8.3	12.3
Land characteristics					
Ejidatario (percent)	78.8	91.7	83.3	33.3	67.5
Hectares owned	3.6	5.2	11.2	27.8	24.9
Access to irrigation (percent)	24.8	16.7	75.0	100.0	87.7
Kilometers to nearest paved road	3.4	4.3	3.2	1.7	3.0
Geographic characteristics (percent)					
In Sonora	11.5	4.1	0.0	41.7	51.8
In Guanajuato	26.5	33.3	83.3	58.3	41.2
Production characteristics					
Producers (percent)	84.1	100.0	91.7	91.7	67.5
Among producers (percent)					
Grow corn/beans	87.4	95.8	100.0	54.5	66.2
Grow field crops	28.4	29.2	100.0	100.0	83.1
Grow fruits/vegetables	32.6	37.5	18.2	27.3	26.0
Purchase seeds	46.3	41.7	90.9	95.5	83.1
Use pesticides	54.7	58.5	90.9	100.0	100.0
Use fertilizers	87.4	91.7	81.8	100.0	93.5
Intercrop	31.6	41.7	9.1	0.0	6.5

NOTES: N$ refers to "new pesos." At the time of the survey, the peso crisis was just under way, devaluing the currency from N$3.5 per U.S. dollar in December 1994 to approximately N$6 per dollar during fieldwork.

[a] Group I—poorest 20 percent of sample, based on assets per capita.

[b] Farmers in group I who participate in Solidaridad market.

[c] Farmers in group V who participate in Solidaridad market.

[d] Farmers in group V who participate in private bank market.

[e] Group V—wealthiest 20 percent of sample, based on assets per capita.

still participate in the off-farm labor market and receive a considerable amount of migrant remittances, both characteristics of agricultural households with low cash flow. These anomalies, combined with their status as *ejidatarios* and the high incidence of corn and bean production (traditional crops), may indicate that they have difficulty in obtaining loans through private lenders and thus must turn to the targeted sources.

Nonparticipants

Finally, we compare the farmers who participate in the rural lending market with those who do not. Table 4.5 provides statistics for a number of characteristics, with indications of results that are significantly different. On average, nonparticipants are older, less educated, further from paved roads, less diverse in their crop mix, more often intercropping, less often producing field crops, less often from Sonora, less wealthy, and own less land. They are not significantly different from participants in their tenure status and nonfarm income.

Nonparticipants' principal reason for not making loan requests to a lender is that the lender is not available to producers in the area. Given the local nature of informal markets, along with a wide network of Banrural offices, it would seem that "not available" does not refer to physical representation. More likely, this captures one of two possibilities: that the nonparticipants are ignorant of the rural credit market in general, or that they do not believe that the lenders would work with their type of farmer. The latter explanation has merit in that problems with default and *cartera vencida* have affected the climate between lenders and borrowers.

Econometric Analysis

The preceding analysis is limited because it suggests only a general relationship between the quintile into which farmers fall and their participation in the finance market. In order to control for other characteristics that might be influencing producer participation, and thereby legitimately attribute some of the influence to farmers' wealth, econometric analysis is conducted. As indicated earlier, the primary goal of this study is to see who is participating in the rural financial market, to which lenders they make their requests, and whether they fit the profile of the lenders' target group. Therefore, the underlying economic principle guiding this analysis is the demand for credit, but a demand that recognizes particular lender characteristics and hence the likelihood of receiving a loan.[9]

---

9. After all, a farmer with a quarter of a hectare of rainfed land does not go to a private bank and ask for a US$1,000,000 loan to install irrigation equipment, even if irrigation would produce greater profits.

TABLE 4.5 Comparison of nonparticipants with participants

Indicator	Nonparticipants	Participants	Significance
Number of farmers	243	322	
Agricultural assets (N$)	185,457	302,772	**
Farmer characteristics			
Age (years)	61.2	56.4	***
Education (years)	2.74	3.50	***
Household head works off-farm (percent)	32.1	35.1	
Household member works off-farm (percent)	65.4	69.6	
Receives remittances (percent)	15.6	15.2	
Land characteristics			
Ejidatario (percent)	75.7	77.6	
Hectares owned	8.07	11.90	***
Kilometers to nearest paved road	3.55	2.55	***
Geographic characteristics (percent)			
In Sonora	26.7	35.4	**
In Guanajuato	35.4	33.2	
Among producers			
Number of crops produced	1.55	1.89	***
Grow corn/beans (percent)	63.8	62.7	
Grow field crops (percent)	30.9	50.6	***
Grow fruits/vegetables (percent)	18.9	21.1	
Intercrop (percent)	16.9	10.6	**

NOTES: The means of the two groups of observations (nonparticipants contrasted with participants) are tested for being equal. Significance indicates the probability of a greater absolute value of the resulting t-statistic under the null hypothesis of equality of means, that is, ** indicates 5% and *** 1% probability of accepting the null.

N$ refers to "new pesos." At the time of the survey, the peso crisis was just under way, devaluing the currency from N$3.5 per U.S. dollar in December 1994 to approximately N$6 per dollar during fieldwork.

A number of authors have recognized (see, for example, Maddala and Trost 1982; Zeller 1994) that the decision to apply for a loan is one of the more important aspects of analyzing how a rural financial market functions. Many authors have looked into the question of credit rationing or discrimination in lending based on borrower characteristics,[10] but if self-selection by applicants changes the potential client pool significantly, as argued earlier, credit rationing could turn out to derive as much from producer decisions about applying as from the lender's decisionmaking.

---

10. See, for example, Sealey (1979); Eaton and Gersovitz (1981); Maddala and Trost (1982); Aguilera (1990); Aguilera and Graham (1990); Zeller (1994); and Stanton (1996).

Several theoretical models have been developed that illustrate the relationship between the decision to apply for a loan and characteristics of the borrower, lender, and market (for example, Aguilera 1990; Stanton 1996), and others more explicitly model the segmentation often found in rural financial markets (Nagarajan, Meyer, and Hushak 1995). A number of factors could influence the decision to apply for a loan, based in principle on the models referred to above.

Modeling Approach

Two scenarios are considered in the analysis. In the first, a range of lenders is available to each potential applicant. The ability to choose among them makes the farmer's decision process a two-stage one: the first stage is deciding whether or not to request a loan; the second is deciding which lender to patronize. This is the more general case. In the second scenario, potential applicants perceive only one real choice to meet borrowing needs. This implies that the decision to request a loan is the same as the decision to patronize that lender; hence there is only one step in the decision process. Which of these two scenarios applies depends on both local circumstances as well as the mindset of farmers. In Mexico, the second scenario is plausible because farmers tend to return repeatedly to the same lender. Indeed, they often deal exclusively with that lender—more than 80 percent of the applicants in the sample patronized just one lender.

THE GENERAL CASE.   The first scenario requires that we consider the factors that influence both the general decision to request a loan and the more specific question of which lender to patronize. Without formalizing these relationships further, we hypothesize the following. The decision to request a loan should be based on the need for more capital than the farmer currently has. Let K^* designate the optimal capital stock that results from profit maximization by the farmer. Since the farmer's profits are a function of production technology and crop choice, K^* will be a function of these factors. Let K_0 designate the capital stock owned by the farmer. Since we consider both physical capital and cash assets in the measure of capital, K_0 should reflect the farmer's agricultural assets (land and so forth) plus any cash on hand that could be converted to needed inputs.

Then the decision to request a loan is based on whether or not K^* is greater than K_0. That is,

$$D_1 = 1, \text{ if } K^* > K_0;$$
$$D_1 = 0 \text{ otherwise,}$$

where D_1 is the binary representation of the decision.

The decision about which lender to patronize, in contrast, should reflect which offers the greatest net benefit to the farmer, tempered by the farmer's expectations of being accepted for the loan by that lender. The benefits derive from the loan itself, and the costs from the complexity of the transaction and the loan terms imposed by the lender. So for lender i, compared with other lenders j, we have

$$D_2^i = 1, \text{ if } ENB^i > ENB^j \text{ for all other lenders } j;$$

$$D_2^i = 0 \text{ otherwise,}$$

where ENB is expected net benefits and D_2 is the binary representation of the decision. Farmers' expectations of being accepted for a loan will depend largely on their characteristics, in relation to those anticipated as preferred by the lender. Therefore, a farmer's age, education, ability to offer collateral, overall wealth, crop choice, and production methods could influence that expectation.

THE LIMITED CASE.   In the more restrictive case of a one-step decision process, farmers decide whether or not to request a loan (from the one anticipated source) based on (1) whether $K^* > K_0$ and (2) whether they expect to get the loan from that lender. The latter could reflect the same factors just discussed with respect to the general case. If $K^* > K_0$ but farmers have little expectation of receiving the loan, then they may forgo the request on the supposition that the expected net benefits would not be positive. Thus,

$$D = 1 \text{ if (a) } K^* > K_0 \text{ and (b) } ENB > 0$$

$$D = 0 \text{ if either (a) or (b) does not hold.}$$

Estimation Method

For the general case discussed above, we will use a set of probit models with selection. That is, the decision to patronize a particular lender is observed only when the decision in a prior step—to request a loan at all—is taken. To conduct a simple probit estimation on the decision to patronize that lender could introduce a selectivity bias in the estimates of the regression parameters, since some factors affecting the first decision could also influence the second. A simple probit model would confuse the two effects.[11]

The more limited case considers only one decision as relevant: the combined determination that borrowed funds would allow for optimal profit levels to be obtained, and that those funds can be obtained from the available lender. In this case, a simple probit model can be used.

Results of Estimation

Tables 4.6–4.9 report the results of the estimation. The data reported refer to the marginal effects or slopes of the explanatory variables and the t-statistics are calculated using the adjusted variance–covariance matrix.

---

11. The reader is referred to Greene (1997:chapter 20) and Maddala (1983:chapter 9) for more information on self-selection problems.

TABLE 4.6 Estimation results for Banrural

	Two-Stage Probit Estimation			Simple Probit Estimation	
Variable	Apply with Any Lender	(i)	(ii)	(i)	(ii)
Intercept	−.448	−.715	−.409	−.285	−.315
	(−2.67)***	(−1.66)*	(−1.21)	(−2.54)**	(−2.77)
Log assets	.066	.099	.044[a]	.038	.073
	(1.85)*	(1.15)	**(.55)**	(2.29)**	(1.66)*
(Log assets)^2	.012	−.010	**−.027**[b]		−.006
	(2.04)**	(−.76)	**(−.36)**		(−.88)
Age of head		−.000	.000	−.002	−.002
		(−.13)	(.15)	(−1.67)*	(−1.64)*
Education		−.012	−.011	−.011	−.010
		(−1.02)	(−.92)	(−1.80)*	(−1.57)
Male				.041	.038
				(.93)	(.88)
Household size	.010			.001	.001
	(.57)			(.26)	(.25)
Work off-farm	.254			.016	.016
	(2.03)**			(.45)	(.46)
Look for job	−.219				
	(−1.50)				
Receive	.026			.021	.018
remittances	(.17)			(.48)	(.43)
Distance to		−.014	−.016	−.012	−.011
road		(−1.37)	(−1.56)	(−2.24)**	(−2.22)**
Crop diversity	.069	−.011	−.016	−.002	−.002
	(1.00)	(−.31)	(−.46)	(−.11)	(−.11)
Intercrop	−.300	−.297	−.240	−.158	−.151
	(−1.65)*	(−2.05)**	(−1.70)*	(−2.67)**	(−2.23)**
Field crops	.296	.150	.118	.085	.081
	(1.82)*	(1.29)	(1.09)	(1.86)*	(1.82)*
Fruit/vegetables	.016	.159	.155	.066	.064
	(.09)	(1.76)*	(1.70)*	(1.37)	(1.38)
Guanajuato		.222	.285	.091	.081
		(2.28)**	(3.31)***	(1.67)*	(1.50)
Sonora		.497	.560	.254	.237
		(4.98)***	(6.32)***	(4.78)***	(4.27)***
Private farmer		−.258	−.267	−.138	−.120
		(−2.87)***	(−3.14)***	(−2.87)***	(−2.41)**
Mixto farmer				−.090	−.092
				(−.81)	(−.86)
Inverse Mills		.341	.023		
ratio		(.84)	(.08)		

(continued)

TABLE 4.6 *Continued*

Variable	Two-Stage Probit Estimation			Simple Probit Estimation	
	Apply with Any Lender	(i)	(ii)	(i)	(ii)
Log-likelihood	−365.64	−159.3	−160.7	−223.5	−223.1
Chi-squared test	40.89	94.78	92.01	118.5	119.2
Number of observations	565	315	315	553	553
Percentage predicted correctly	61.6	76.2	75.6	81.4	81.6

NOTES: * significant at 10 percent level; ** significant at 5 percent level; *** significant at 1 percent level.

[a] Indicates the coefficient on the dummy for wealth groups II and III (20th to 60th percentiles).

[b] Indicates the coefficient on the dummy for wealth groups IV and V (60th to 100th percentiles).

The tables are broken into two parts: the two-stage probit model and the simple probit model. The first column of figures in each table reports the result of the probit model of general participation in the rural credit market. As argued, the decision to participate should reflect the demand for credit, that is, $K^* > K_0$, and the production characteristics along with factors affecting the farmer's wealth and cash flow should be examined. The results show that farmers who produce field crops and do not intercrop are more likely to participate in the rural credit market, as are households with some nonfarm income. The latter finding is somewhat surprising but may reflect the households' general efforts to acquire additional funds and hedge against risks, rather than a substitute for borrowing funds, something often observed in poorly functioning credit markets.

In addition, wealth influences the probability of participation positively and at an increasing rate. Although not unexpected, this result does underline the general perception that poor producers—often considered to be the ones who could benefit most, relatively, from additional capital—may be too risk averse to demand credit from formal sources.

Banrural

The specific results for Banrural are shown in Table 4.6. A number of factors contribute significantly to farmers' application to Banrural in both models considered. Farmers in Guanajuato and Sonora are more likely to apply than are those in the Puebla/Tlaxcala region, while private farmers are less likely to apply. It is a bit disturbing how much more likely Sonoran farmers are to apply to Banrural given the advanced nature of agriculture in the state. However, since farmers in Sonora are more likely to be *ejidatarios* and *mixtos*, the result may not be inconsistent with Banrural's targeting. In addition, farmers who inter-crop are less likely to apply to Banrural.

Under the two-stage scenario, we also find that fruit and vegetable pro-ducers are more likely to participate in Banrural's market. Combined with the one-stage finding that field crop producers are more likely to apply, we can in-fer that producers of subsistence crops of corn and beans are not as likely to apply. In any case, most corn producers use traditional technologies, so they would not generally qualify under Banrural's new "viability" criteria for lending projects.

Under the one-stage scenario, we also find that younger, better-educated producers are more likely to apply, as are those located closer to paved roads. Since the formality of Banrural's application process requires a visit to its offices, transportation costs would be relevant in making a decision.

Finally, the results with respect to wealth are revealing, if not generally significant. The signs in the two-stage model imply that wealth contributes pos-itively to the decision to apply to Banrural, but at a decreasing rate. Indeed, in the second equation shown, the coefficient on the wealth group covering the 20th to 60th percentiles is positive, whereas that on the 60th to 100th percen-tiles is negative. Admittedly, these breakdowns are somewhat arbitrary, but they also reflect roughly what Banrural's target group should be (the 20th to 60th percentiles). Together, the results imply that there is a good chance that the middle range of producers is indeed more likely to receive loans from Ban-rural than are producers in other wealth categories.

However, the one-stage probit estimation is unequivocal in the significant and increasing relationship between wealth and the probability of applying to Banrural. The two equations are identical except that the second considers a quadratic form for wealth. Hence, if the decision to apply to Banrural can in-deed not be separated from the decision to apply for a loan, the evidence is that wealthier producers are more likely to apply. This raised the question of why wealthier farmers rely on Banrural for their credit demands. To the extent that Banrural interest rates are still low relative to those of other sources, collateral requirements are low, and transaction costs are reasonable, wealthier clients may still find Banrural attractive compared with other sources. Moreover, they may be able to use their influence to delay repaying the loans they receive.

Solidaridad

As in the case of Banrural, certain results are robust across the two models for Solidaridad (Table 4.7). Farmers in both Guanajuato and Sonora are less likely to apply to Solidaridad, as are private farmers (farmers who do not belong to *ejidos*). Generally speaking, both results are consistent with targeting, given the kind of agriculture found in the two states. Further, farmers with more educa-tion and those producing fruits and vegetables are less likely to apply to Solidaridad. Since the program is meant to target the least viable producers, the crop distinction is reasonable.

In the two-stage scenario, the results show in addition that farmers who are further from paved roads will apply, which is consistent with the expectation that those farmers also probably have less market integration and more traditional agriculture. Moreover, since Solidaridad primarily operates via the *ejido* itself, thus not requiring that the farmer visit a Solidaridad office, this lender would be relatively more convenient to those located away from population centers (and paved roads).

In the one-stage scenario, two results are unexpected: older farmers are less likely to apply, whereas those who grow multiple crops are more likely to apply. Generally, older farmers are more traditional in their production practices and hence would seem better candidates for Solidaridad. However, perhaps they also "know the ropes" of rural finance better than their younger counterparts and seek loans elsewhere. Multiple cropping is generally a sign of diversification of agricultural risks, and it is anticipated that it will improve the farmers' expected returns, making these farmers less consistent with Solidaridad's target group.

Finally, there is little evidence of a significant relationship between wealth and participation in Solidaridad's market. In the two-stage scenario, the signs indicate that wealth has a positive influence, but at a decreasing rate, and no significant difference is found between the groupings (20th to 60th percentile, etc.). Indeed, the reader is reminded of the distribution of Solidaridad participants in Table 4.3, which showed little difference across the five groups. It does not appear from this estimation that poorer producers have a greater likelihood of participating in the Solidaridad market. Further, the results of the one-stage analysis show an increasing and significant relationship between wealth and the probability of participating in Solidaridad's market. To support the targeting intentions, we should see a declining relationship. Therefore, the results are not encouraging regarding the success of Solidaridad in reaching poorer producers.

Private Banks

Table 4.8 shows the results of estimation for the private bank market. It is clear that private farmers are significantly more likely to participate than are *ejidatarios*. Commercial banks tend to require collateral, particularly land, so it is not surprising that those with titles to private land are more likely to apply for loans. Other results demonstrate reasonable signs, although little significance is found in the two-stage estimation. For example, field crops and fruits and vegetables show positive signs and intercropping is negatively related. Unlike for other lenders, little difference is found in this sample between farmers from different states. In the specification using wealth groups, we also find that older,

TABLE 4.7 Estimation results for Solidaridad

Variable	Two-Stage Probit Estimation			Simple Probit Estimation	
	Apply with Any Lender	(i)	(ii)	(i)	(ii)
Intercept	−.448	.119	.202	−.014	−.030
	(−2.67)***	(.34)	(.66)	(−1.10)	(−.36)
Log assets	.066	.069	**.009**[a]	.017	.054
	(1.85)*	(1.26)	**(.15)**	(1.26)	(1.89)*
(Log assets)^2	.012	−.017	**.028**[b]		−.009
	(2.04)**	(−1.52)	**(.43)**		(−1.34)
Age of head		−.001	−.002	−.002	−.002
		(−.58)	(−.67)	(−2.18)**	(−2.30)**
Education		−.023	−.026	−.012	−.012
		(−2.08)**	(−2.32)**	(−2.20)**	(−2.12)**
Household size	.010			.004	
	(.57)			(1.07)	
Work off-farm	.254			.031	.032
	(2.03)**			(1.11)	(1.19)
Look for job	−.219			−.057	−.054
	(−1.50)			(−1.73)*	(−1.72)*
Receive remittances	.026			−.008	−.008
	(.17)			(−.23)	(−.26)
Distance to road		.014	.017	.001	.001
		(1.70)*	(2.04)**	(.31)	(.29)
Have full documents				.084	
				(1.90)*	
Crop diversity	.069	.038	.036	.030	.032
	(1.00)	(1.33)	(1.27)	(2.42)**	(2.57)***
Intercrop	−.300	.111	.123		
	(−1.65)*	(1.19)	(1.37)		
Corn/beans				.024	.019
				(.64)	(.52)
Field crops	.296	.082	.084		
	(1.82)*	(.87)	(.89)		
Fruit/vegetables	.016	−.161	−.165	−.076	−.074
	(.09)	(−2.23)**	(−2.21)**	(−2.19)**	(−2.20)**
Guanajuato		−.144	−.161	−.068	−.066
		(−2.00)**	(−2.54)**	(−1.86)*	(−1.84)*
Sonora		−.564	−.600	−.289	−.280
		(−6.37)***	(−7.55)***	(−5.78)***	(−5.45)***
Private farmer		−.201	−.235	−.120	−.102
		(−2.780***	(−3.34)***	(−3.22)***	(−2.69)***
Mixto farmer				−.038	−.039
				(−.68)	(−.73)

(continued)

TABLE 4.7 *Continued*

	Two-Stage Probit Estimation			Simple Probit Estimation	
Variable	Apply with Any Lender	(i)	(ii)	(i)	(ii)
Inverse Mills ratio		−.117 (−.36)	−.142 (−.54)		
Log-likelihood	−365.64	−127.23	−128.61	−200.4	−202.2
Chi-squared test	40.89	132.16	129.41	109.3	105.79
Number of observations	565	314	314	552	552
Percentage predicted correctly	61.6	78.3	79.0	82.8	82.8

NOTES: * significant at 10 percent level; ** significant at 5 percent level; *** significant at 1 percent level.
a Indicates the coefficient on the dummy for wealth groups II and III (20th to 60th percentiles).
b Indicates the coefficient on the dummy for wealth groups IV and V (60th to 100th percentiles).

better-educated farmers are more likely to participate in the private bank market. In the one-stage model, we see that farmers with a more diversified crop base, those who do not produce corn and beans, and those with smaller households are more likely to apply to private banks. These results make sense.

With respect to wealth, we find a significant positive association between the 80–100th quintile and participation, a result supported by Table 4.3. Recall that some 73 percent of all private bank requests came from this group. Moreover, in the one-stage estimation, the farmer's level of wealth is positively and significantly related to participation. Although not significant, the quadratic forms indicate that this positive relationship is increasing as well. Thus, while noting the lack of significance for many of the estimates, the results are about what we can expect. Applicants to private banks appear to be consistent with the profit goals of that lender.

Informal Lenders

The final set of estimations, for informal lenders, is presented in Table 4.9, and the results are generally robust across the two models. Farmers in Guanajuato and those producing fruits and vegetables are more likely to participate in this market. Since many of the borrowing opportunities from merchants and traders arise with respect to horticultural crops, this result makes sense. Moreover, agriculture in Guanajuato is more diversified than in either of the other two regions; it lies between the two in terms of wealth and general level of technology. This can be attractive to traders who like to contract with growers to reduce their supply risks. We also find that farmers who are further from paved roads are

TABLE 4.8 Estimation results for private banks

	Two-Stage Probit Estimation			Simple Probit Estimation	
Variable	Apply with Any Lender	(i)	(ii)	(i)	(ii)
Intercept	−.448	−.696	−.450	−.094	−.110
	(−2.67)***	(−3.28)***	(−2.88)***	(−1.86)*	(−2.15)**
Log assets	.066	.035	−.036[a]	.014	.014
	(1.85)*	(.89)	(−.81)	(2.33)**	(1.01)
(Log assets)^2	.012	.002	.107[b]		.000
	(2.04)**	(.33)	(3.12)***		(.02)
Age of head		.002	.002	.000	.000
		(1.62)	(1.85)*	(.27)	(.25)
Education		.006	.007	−.000	−.000
		(1.18)	(1.72)*	(−.22)	(−.11)
Household size	.010			−.006	−.006
	(.57)			(−2.500**	(−2.35)**
Work off-farm	.254			−.00	−.004
	(2.03)**			(−.43)	(−.35)
Look for job	−.219				
	(−1.50)				
Receive	.026			−.031	−.030
remittances	(.17)			(−1.51)	(−1.43)
Distance to road		.001	.002	.000	.000
		(.25)	(.68)	(.16)	(.16)
Have full				−.017	
documents				(−1.10)	
Crop diversity	.069	.012	.008	.013	.013
	(1.00)	(.87)	(.64)	(2.12)**	(1.96)**
Intercrop	−.300	−.003	.025	.001	.002
	(−1.65)*	(−.05)	(.52)	(.08)	(.09)
Corn/beans				−.030	−.032
				(−1.81)*	(−1.79)*
Field crops	.296	.071	.030		
	(1.82)*	(1.26)	(.66)		
Fruit/vegetables	.016	.018	.021	−.003	−.003
	(.09)	(.47)	(.63)	(−.18)	(−.18)
Guanajuato		.011	.020	.000	.003
		(.24)	(.56)	(.00)	(.15)
Sonora		.001	.055	−.007	−.006
		(.01)	(.15)	(−.32)	(−.27)
Private farmer		.104	.076	.038	.038
		(3.16)***	(2.54)**	(2.61)***	(2.53)**
Inverse Mills		.269	.075		
ratio		(1.35)	(.60)		

(continued)

TABLE 4.8 *Continued*

	Two-Stage Probit Estimation			Simple Probit Estimation	
Variable	Apply with Any Lender	(i)	(ii)	(i)	(ii)
Log-likelihood	−365.64	−75.66	−69.41	−84.1	−84.73
Chi-squared test	40.89	51.08	63.58	70.5	69.30
Number of observations	565	314	314	552	552
Percentage predicted correctly	61.6	92.0	92.0	95.1	95.1

NOTES: * significant at 10 percent level; ** significant at 5 percent level; *** significant at 1 percent level.
a Indicates the coefficient on the dummy for wealth groups III and IV (40th to 80th percentiles).
b Indicates the coefficient on the dummy for wealth group V (80th to 100th percentile).

more likely to participate in this market. Whereas transactions with merchants would imply that producers need to go to the place of business, it is plausible to expect that both traders and informal moneylenders would go to their clients and in some cases might even be neighbors or friends. These lenders may have more information about prospective borrowers, through observation and knowledge about the farms.

We find no significant relationship between wealth and participation. This is reasonable since we have no preconceived idea about who can borrow from informal lenders. The signs suggest that, if anything, wealthier farmers would be more likely to participate. This too would be reasonable since traders, in particular, would probably prefer to lower transaction costs by dealing with fewer farmers, each with some minimum production capacity. On the whole, the participants in the informal lending market are consistent with expectations.

Conclusions

As indicated earlier, efforts to improve access to credit for smaller, less-endowed farmers require voluntary participation in the lending markets by those producers. To the extent that farmers choose not to patronize even the government lenders who aim to serve them, any evidence of poor targeting by public lending programs cannot be blamed solely on the lenders' decisions.

This study examined the composition of participants in the markets of four different lenders in Mexico's agricultural sector: Banrural, Solidaridad, private commercial banks, and informal lenders. We have seen that, by and large, the participants in each of these markets exhibit characteristics that are consistent with the objectives of those lenders. Nevertheless, with respect to farmers'

TABLE 4.9 Estimation results for informal lenders

Variable	Two-Stage Probit Estimation			Simple Probit Estimation	
	Apply with Any Lender	(i)	(ii)	(i)	(ii)
Intercept	−.448	−.337	−.259	−.245	−.235
	(−2.67)***	(−1.57)	(−1.41)	(−4.10)***	(−3.94)***
Log assets	.066	.000	.041[a]	.007	.004
	(1.85)*	(.01)	**(1.18)**	(.90)	(.66)
(Log assets)^2	.012	.003			.001
	(2.04)**	(1.13)			(1.43)
Age of head		.001	.001	.001	.000
		(.81)	(.82)	(.85)	(.67)
Education		.003	.004	.003	.002
		(.54)	(.78)	(1.08)	(.77)
Household size	.010			.004	.004
	(.57)			(1.83)*	(1.81)*
Work off-farm	.254			−.009	−.009
	(2.03)**			(−.55)	(−.54)
Look for job	−.219				
	(−1.50)				
Receive remittances	.026			.004	.006
	(.17)			(.21)	(.29)
Distance to road		−.011	−.011	−.007	−.007
		(−1.81)*	(−1.80)*	(−2.37)**	(−2.26)**
Crop diversity	.069	.009	.006	.003	.003
	(1.00)	(.51)	(.36)	(.46)	(.43)
Intercrop	−.300	−.046	−.034		
	(−1.65)*	(−.66)	(−.52)		
Field crops	.296	.019	−.002	.032	.031
	(1.82)*	(.31)	(−.03)	(1.59)	(1.53)
Fruit/vegetables	.016	.088	.090	.040	.040
	(.09)	(2.07)**	(2.16)**	(2.00)**	(1.98)**
Guanajuato		.111	.119	.050	.045
		(2.18)**	(2.63)***	(2.02)**	(1.82)*
Sonora		−.034	−.030	−.005	−.009
		(−.62)	(−.60)	(−.20)	(−.36)
Private farmer		−.004	.011	.003	−.002
		(−.09)	(.28)	(.14)	(−.11)
Inverse Mills ratio		−.015	−.105		
		(−.07)	(−.63)		
Log-likelihood	−365.64	−93.44	−93.32	−111.51	−110.75
Chi-squared test	40.89	45.07	45.33	54.11	55.62
Number of observations	565	315	315	555	555

(continued)

TABLE 4.9 *Continued*

	Two-Stage Probit Estimation			Simple Probit Estimation	
Variable	Apply with Any Lender	(i)	(ii)	(i)	(ii)
Percentage predicted correctly	61.6	88.9	88.9	93.3	93.3

NOTES: * significant at 10 percent level; ** significant at 5 percent level; *** significant at 1 percent level.
ª Indicates the coefficient on the dummy for wealth groups IV and V (60th to 100th percentiles).

wealth, a great deal of participation and lending occurs outside of the intended group.

In the case of Banrural, about half of all requests come from the wealthiest 40 percent of the sample and less than half from the 20th to 60th percentiles, which, as anticipated, would better satisfy Banrural's targeting objectives. Moreover, estimation results showed a positive relationship between wealth and participation in Banrural's market, even controlling for farmers' other characteristics. Part of the reason for refocusing lending operations toward a target group was because too great a share of the lending portfolio was going to the richer agricultural producers. With Banrural's new focus on "viable" operations, especially where access to other services is negligible, we should see a shift toward more middle-wealth groups. The data do not show an adequate shift occurring in the few years since reforms, implying that loan sizes and interest rate subsidies are still attracting wealthier borrowers despite the redesign of the program.

In the case of Solidaridad, the main objective was to fill the gap between the poorest farmers and those served by the reformed Banrural. Simple statistics demonstrated that, in fact, less than half of the loan applications and the loans granted are from the poorest 40 percent of the sample, whereas more than 10 percent are in the wealthiest quintile. The rather flat distribution of participation and loans across the wealth spectrum is also seen in the econometric results, which mostly failed to detect a significant relationship between participation and wealth. This case, even more than that of Banrural, raises the question of how lending decisions are made: why not lend to the applicants that fit the target group and reject the rest? Loan sizes are quite small and should not be attractive to larger farmers. Moreover, unlike other lenders, Solidaridad does not have an emphasis on profit or cost recovery nor does it receive payments directly, so there is little about the program's design that should encourage lending to nontarget farmers based on risk perceptions. The evidence that Solidaridad loans are being granted to wealthier producers is thus troublesome.

For private banks and informal lenders, clearly there are no preset guidelines for target groups other than the motives of profit-maximization. In the case of private banks, it is not surprising that their client base is concentrated among richer producers, and that, if anything, participation in this market increases with wealth. However, the high concentration of participation in the richest quintile of the sample raises the question of how soon the other 80 percent will realistically be able to access private sources rather than continue to be dependent on public lending programs.

For informal lenders, the wide range of reasons for establishing an informal loan contract is sufficient cause to accept that farmers' wealth may not play a major role in this cross-section analysis. Simple statistics demonstrated that nearly two-thirds of all informal market participants are from the wealthiest 40 percent of the sample. This probably reflects a greater degree of market integration by those producers, a factor that would contribute to more contacts with merchants and traders. Furthermore, other characteristics that were shown to affect participation indicate that the market functions roughly as expected.

Together, these results are generally encouraging in that target groups are at least represented in the applicant pool of all lenders and in fact receive loans. Nevertheless, there appears to be considerable leakage of public program funds to groups that do not appear to qualify, which is consistent with observations made about such programs in many countries. It is important to remember that, particularly for poorer producers and first-time borrowers, the perception of whether one is likely to receive a loan from a particular lender will affect the decision to participate in that market. If it is generally perceived that public program funds are largely channeled to wealthier producers, there will be little hope for voluntary participation by poorer producers. The results reported here support such a conclusion, although additional research is needed. Nevertheless, it is clear that government lenders such as Banrural and Solidaridad need to address the public perception of their programs if they are to reach their target groups more efficiently.

References

Adams, D. W, and G. I. Nehman. 1979. Borrowing costs and the demand for rural credit. *Journal of Development Studies* 15: 165–176.

Aguilera, N. A. 1990. Credit rationing and loan default in formal rural credit markets. Ph.D. dissertation. Ohio State University, Department of Agricultural Economics and Rural Sociology, Columbus, Ohio, U.S.A.

Aguilera, N. A., and D. Graham. 1990. Measuring credit rationing in rural financial markets: A Portuguese case study. Economics and Sociology Occasional Paper No. 1742. Ohio State University, Columbus, Ohio, U.S.A.

Bell, C. 1988. Credit markets and interlinked transactions. In *Handbook of development economics*, ed. H. Chenery and T. N. Srinivasan. New York: North Holland.

Bottomley, A. 1975. Interest rate determination in underdeveloped rural areas. *American Journal of Agricultural Economics* 57 (May): 279–291.

Braverman, A., and J. L. Guasch. 1989. Rural credit reforms in LDCs: Issues and evidence. *Journal of Economic Development* 14 (1): 7–34.

Carter, M. R. 1988. Equilibrium credit rationing of small farm agriculture. *Journal of Development Economics* 28: 83–103.

Eaton, J., and M. Gersovitz. 1981. Debt with potential repudiation: Theoretical and empirical analysis. *Review of Economic Studies* 48: 289–309.

Gonzalez-Vega, C. 1984. Credit-rationing behavior of agricultural lenders: The iron law of interest-rate restrictions. In *Undermining rural development with cheap credit,* ed. D. W Adams, D. H. Graham, and J. D. Von Pischke. Boulder, Colo., U.S.A.: Westview Press.

—————. 1994. Do financial institutions have a role in assisting the poor? In *Strategic issues in microfinance,* ed. M. S. Kimenyi, R. C. Wieland, and J. D. Von Pishke. Brookfield, Vt., U.S.A.: Ashgate, pp. 11–26.

Gonzalez-Vega, C., and D. Graham. 1995. State-owned agricultural development banks: Lessons and opportunities for microfinance. Economics and Sociology Occasional Paper No. 2245. Ohio State University, Columbus, Ohio, U.S.A.

Greene, W. H. 1997. *Econometric analysis,* 3rd ed. Englewood Cliffs, N.J., U.S.A.: Prentice-Hall.

Maddala, G. S. 1983. *Limited dependent and qualitative variables in econometrics.* Econometric Society Monographs. Cambridge, U.K.: Cambridge University Press.

Maddala, G. S., and R. P. Trost. 1982. On measuring discrimination in loan markets. *Housing Finance Review* 11: 245–268.

Mansell Carstens, C. 1995. *Las finanzas populares en Mexico: El redescubrimiento de un sistema financiero olvidado.* Mexico City: Centro de Estudios Monetarios Latinoamericanos, Instituto Tecnológico Autónomo de México.

Nagarajan, G., R. L. Meyer, and L. J. Hushak. 1995. Segmentation in the informal credit markets: The case of the Philippines. *Agricultural Economics* 12: 171–181.

Sealey, C. W., Jr. 1979. Credit rationing in the commercial loan market: Estimates of a structural model under conditions of disequilibrium. *Journal of Finance* 34 (3): 689–702.

Stanton, J. 1996. Access to credit among farmers in Mexico: Evidence of quantity rationing and links between credit access and farm characteristics. Ph.D. dissertation. University of Maryland, Department of Agricultural and Resource Economics, College Park, Md., U.S.A.

Stiglitz, J., and A. Weiss. 1981. Credit rationing in markets with imperfect information. *American Economic Review* 71 (3): 393–410.

Yaron, J. 1992. *Successful rural finance institutions.* World Bank Discussion Paper No. 150. Washington, D.C.: World Bank.

—————. 1994. What makes rural financial institutions successful? *The World Bank Research Observer* 9 (1): 49–70.

Zeller, M. 1994. Determinants of credit rationing: A study of informal lenders and formal credit groups in Madagascar. *World Development* 22 (12): 1895–1907.

5   Credit Constraints and Loan Demand in Rural Bangladesh

MANFRED ZELLER AND MANOHAR SHARMA

The past widespread failure of government-supported financial institutions throughout the developing world has been well documented (Adams, Graham, and Von Pischke 1984; Adams and Vogel 1985; Braverman and Guasch 1986). Both in response to these failures and in recognition of the critical role that credit can play in alleviating poverty, innovative credit delivery systems are being experimented with in many developing countries. A common characteristic of these institutional innovations is that they are based on the participation of their members and communities. Successes leading to sustainable institutions are few so far. However, institutional development is not a short-term undertaking; it may take decades, as demonstrated by the experience of the cooperative movement in Germany in the nineteenth century or by group-based financial institutions such as the Grameen Bank and the Bangladesh Rural Advancement Committee (BRAC) in Bangladesh over the past 25 years.

The dismal past experience with rural credit programs has motivated recent research on how poor households in lesser developed countries, often living in highly risky environments, insure against risk and conduct their intertemporal trade in the absence of well-functioning financial markets (see, for example, Deaton 1992; Fafchamps 1992; Coate and Ravallion 1993; Townsend 1994; Udry 1994, 1995; Kochar 1997). This and other research has substantially increased our understanding of the workings of informal financial institutions in developing countries (see, for example, recent literature surveys by Gersovitz 1988; Adams and Fitchett 1992; Alderman and Paxson 1992; Besley

An earlier version of this chapter, featuring a comparative analysis between Bangladesh and Malawi, and co-authored by Aliou Diagne, was presented at the mini-symposium "Risk Sharing, Consumption Smoothing, and Financial Intermediation" of the Annual Meeting of the American Economics Association, Chicago, January 3–5, 1998 (a revised version was published as Diagne, Zeller, and Sharma 2000). This version benefited from a discussion of the paper by Andrew Foster, and from comments by Alain de Janvry, Elizabeth Sadoulet, and other participants at the mini-symposium. For brevity, this chapter focuses on Bangladesh and provides a shorter discussion of the conceptual and econometric model.

1995; Zeller et al. 1997). These studies have shed light on the complex strategies used by poor households in developing countries to increase their productive capacity, share risk, and smooth consumption over the life cycle. These strategies generally work through informal contracts among friends, neighbors, and members of the extended family, and are arranged within networks of informal institutions of diverse natures. These nonmarket informal institutions, whose economic rationales have long eluded the attention of researchers and policymakers, have often been found to outperform the credit and other financial institutions set up by developing countries' governments to provide financial services to the rural population.

An important strand of the recent literature focuses on credit rationing because this is widely observed in economies irrespective of their stage in development. The theoretical work by Stiglitz and Weiss (1981) motivated a number of studies that have attempted to measure empirically the occurrence of credit rationing and its underlying determinants. Two methods for measuring household access to credit and credit constraints have been empirically exemplified in the recent literature. The first method infers the presence of credit constraints from violations of the assumptions of the life cycle or permanent income hypothesis. More precisely, the method uses household consumption and income data to look for a significant dependence (or excess sensitivity) of consumption on transitory income. Empirical evidence of a significant dependence is taken as indicating borrowing or liquidity constraint (see, for example, the surveys by Besley 1995 and by Browning and Lusardi 1996). The second method uses survey information on households' experiences with loan applications and related rejection or rationing to classify them as credit constrained or not. This classification is then used in reduced form regression equations to analyze the determinants of the likelihood of a household being credit constrained (see, for example, Feder et al. 1990; Jappelli 1990; Zeller 1994; Barham, Boucher, and Carter 1996).

Although both methods have enriched our empirical understanding of credit constraints in developing countries, certain limitations nevertheless exist. With respect to the first method, Deaton (1992) points out that, if uncertainty is negatively correlated with income, current income will be negatively correlated with consumption growth, even in the absence of borrowing constraints. Moreover, the effect of negative income shocks on consumption also depends on the initial asset position of households (Deaton 1992). Another problem with the first method is that it identifies not particular households or individuals as being credit constrained, but only groups, for example landless laborers. Thus, the measurement of credit or liquidity constraints remains imprecise, and cannot be used in subsequent policy analysis of the welfare impacts of the lack of access to credit. The second method enables such identification and econometric estimates of households or individuals being credit constrained, but falls short of saying by how much they are rationed. Yet, for at least two reasons, it is important from a policy perspective to know by how much households or individuals are unable to meet their credit demand. First, policy can influence the amount available for lending to target groups, and thereby ease particularly severe credit constraints. Second, because such policy intervention is not costless, one would need to know the welfare impact of improving credit access, that is, relaxing credit constraints. An analysis of the welfare impact of credit access (or the lack of it) requires the measurement of the extent of credit rationing, not just of its occurrence.

The shortcomings of the two methods motivate the analysis in this chapter. To analyze the determinants of both access to credit and participation in formal credit programs satisfactorily, we make the distinction between access to credit (formal or informal) and participation (in formal credit programs or in the informal credit market). A household has access to a particular source of credit if it is able to borrow from that source, even if for some reason it may choose not to borrow. We measure the extent of access to credit by the maximum amount a household can borrow (credit limit).

The next section briefly presents a methodology based on the credit limit concept that allows the determinants of the extent of household access to credit and household demand for formal and informal loans to be analyzed more satisfactorily. Our empirical part of the study is based on a 1994 three-round survey of 350 households in seven villages randomly drawn from each of the four divisions of Bangladesh. After briefly describing the structure of the formal and informal credit markets in Bangladesh and the data used in this chapter, we present the results of the econometric analysis of the determinants of the extent of households' access to informal and formal credit markets, as well as their demands for formal and informal credits. We conclude the chapter with some remarks on the policy implications of our findings.

Measurement and Determinants of Access to Credit

Analyzing Access to Credit with the Credit Limit Variable

In general, lenders are constrained by factors outside their control on the maximum amount they can possibly lend to any potential borrower.[1] Consequently, all borrowers, however creditworthy, face a limit on the overall amount they can borrow from any given source of credit, regardless of how high an interest rate they are willing to pay or how much collateral they are willing and able to put up to back the loan. However, in many developing countries, land as collateral might not even provide sufficient security to the lender because of cul-

---

1. This section and the following section draw heavily on papers by Diagne (1996, 1999) and by Diagne, Zeller, and Sharma (2000).

tural constraints or weaknesses in the legal framework that hinder effective transfer of the land from the defaulter to the lender. Furthermore, owing to the possibility of default and the lack of effective contract enforcement mechanisms, lenders have the incentive to restrict the supply of credit further, even if they have more than enough to meet a given demand and borrowers are willing to pay a high enough interest rate (Avery 1981; Stiglitz and Weiss 1981). Lenders are well advised to ration the loan amount if borrowers' demand exceeds their debt repayment capacity. Therefore, from the borrowers' view, the relevant limit on supply is not the maximum lenders are able to lend but rather the maximum lenders are willing to lend. This perceived maximum limit or credit limit that cannot be exceeded when borrowing, regardless of how much interest one is willing to pay, is the focus of the methodology used in this chapter for quantifying the extent of household access to credit.

To motivate the reduced form equations estimated in the empirical section of the chapter, a conceptual framework focusing explicitly on the maximum credit limit variable is presented next. The conceptual framework follows from a contract theory view of loan transactions. It is based on the fact that the credit limit variable, b_{max}, facing potential borrowers and the amount potential lenders want to be repaid are the variables that lenders can choose. On the other hand, the optimal amount, b^*, to be borrowed within the range set by lenders remains the sole choice of borrowers, who also choose ex post (that is, once the loan is disbursed) whether and when to pay back the loan.

Lenders' optimal choice of b_{max}, which is interpreted here as the supply of credit, is a function of the maximum they are able to lend, b^a_{max}. It is also a function of lenders' subjective assessment of the likelihood of default and of other borrowers' characteristics. However, this function is not a supply-for-credit function in the traditional meaning of the term where, under the assumption of price-taking behavior, the function represents the schedule of what lenders are willing to lend as the market interest rate varies. This traditional supply function for credit is not defined in this context where lenders themselves choose the interest rate. Similarly, the optimal interest rate r chosen by lenders is a function of b^a_{max}, the lenders' subjective assessment of the likelihood of default, and of other borrowers' characteristics.[2] On the other hand, the function defining borrowers' optimal choice of loan size b^* is a demand-for-credit function in the traditional meaning of the term (that is, the schedule of what borrowers are willing to borrow when the interest rate varies). The fact that b^* is a function of b_{max} in addition to being a function of the interest rate is a mere reflection of the borrowing constraint and the imperfect substitutability of the

---

2. The reader is referred to Avery (1981) and Stiglitz and Weiss (1981) for an analysis of how the lender's assessment of the likelihood of default affects the optimal choice of both b_{max} and r.

different sources of loans. However, because of imperfections in the enforcement of the loan contract and the resulting adverse selection, the demand for credit need not be a downward-sloping function of the interest rate. Hence, as pointed out by Stiglitz and Weiss, lenders cannot use the interest rate as a way of rationing credit.

Access to Credit and Participation in Credit Programs

Access to credit is often confused with credit market participation or, more precisely, borrowing. Indeed, the two concepts are used interchangeably in many credit studies. The crucial difference between the two concepts lies in the fact that participation in a formal credit program, for example, is something that households choose to do freely, whereas access to the credit program is a limiting constraint put upon them (credit programs' availability and eligibility criteria, for example). In other words, participation is more of a demand-side issue related to potential borrowers' choice of the optimal loan size b^*, whereas access is more of a supply-side issue related to potential lenders' choice of the maximum credit limit, b_{max}.

The lack of access to credit from a given source can be defined as the maximum credit limit, b_{max}, for that source of credit being zero. That is, one has access to a certain type of credit when its maximum credit limit, b_{max}, for that type is strictly positive; and access to that type of credit is improved by increasing b_{max} for that type of credit.

Expectations, Observability of the Credit Limit, and the Demand for Credit

The observations above suggest that the maximum credit limit a borrower faces depends on both the lender and the borrower's characteristics and actions. However, it also depends on random events that affect the fortune of lenders and other potential borrowers (who may compete with the borrower for the same possible credit). For example, one would expect a covariant shock, such as flood or drought, in a rural agriculture-based economy to reduce the supply of informal credit, while also increasing the number of people looking for loans. This is because the lenders' asset base for lending might decrease as a result of the covariant shock, and because the loan demand by borrowers increases whereas their creditworthiness decreases, owing to the loss of assets or income-earning opportunities. Hence, the maximum credit limit, b_{max}, available to a potential borrower is a random variable whose value is determined by events—some of which are under the borrower's control, others under the lender's control, and still others outside the control of both.

The fact that b_{max} depends on random events also implies that its realized value at the times when borrowing actually takes place cannot be known exactly in advance by either the lender or the borrower. The fact that the borrower cannot know it in advance is clear since it will ultimately be the result of the lender's choice (although, as explained above, the borrower can influence that choice to some extent). The borrower can form only expectations about the likely value of b_{max}. But formal lenders usually provide enough information about their loan policy (eligibility criteria, types of project funded, collateral and down-payment requirements, and so on) to enable potential borrowers to have reasonably accurate expectations about their b_{max} from each source of formal credit. In some credit programs supported by nongovernmental organizations (NGOs) or government, fixed credit limits are set for borrowers, for example in relation to their years of membership or their area cultivated. Past credit transactions and applications by the borrower, or by neighbors and friends, in informal market segments will also allow borrowers to form expectations about the maximum amount of credit that they might be able to obtain from the informal market.

It is precisely borrowers' prior expectations about the likely value of b_{max} and its variability that influences their behavior and makes them decide in particular whether or not to seek a loan from that particular source of credit. For example, in the direct method of detecting credit constraint discussed above, the classification of borrowers usually includes a class of discouraged borrowers (see Jappelli 1990, for example). These discouraged borrowers did not seek any loan because either they expected to face zero or very low b_{max}, or they expected a relatively high cost (including transaction costs) for getting loans. The discouraged borrowers may have been wrong in their expectations and could perhaps obtain worthwhile loans at reasonable costs. But, whether they are wrong or right, at the end it is those expectations about their b_{max} that have determined their behavior, not the realized values of their b_{max}, which will remain unknown to them. Even when borrowers seek a loan from a given source of credit, the realized value of the optimal loan size is largely determined by their expectations about their b_{max}.

The arguments in the previous paragraphs imply that, in the analysis of the demand for credit, borrowers' expectations about b_{max} are much more important in determining the actually demanded amounts of credit than the realized values of b_{max}. However, from a policy point of view, what is of interest a priori is not borrowers' response to changes in their expectations about b_{max}, but their response to change in b_{max} itself, since it is the variable under the lenders' control and can be altered by policy.

Data were therefore collected on borrowers' expected b_{max} from different sources of credit. The survey did not collect the realized values of b_{max}, which only lenders could provide with some reasonable accuracy. The survey was focused on the demand side of the credit market and, for a relatively large survey, it is not feasible to interview the lender for each loan transaction. Moreover, borrowers may not be willing to identify their informal lenders or may refuse to be interviewed if they know that the latter are going to be interviewed too.

Specification of the Empirical Model

The reduced form equations for the determination of the maximum credit limits and the demands for credit presented below can be rationalized by a household utility maximization model in which the contractual relationships between the household and its lenders and the (imperfect) substitutability between formal and informal credit are explicitly recognized (see Diagne 1996). The following reduced form linear equations are postulated:

$$b^F_{max} = a_1 x_1 + \beta^F_2 z^F_1 + \varepsilon^F, \tag{5.1}$$

$$b^I_{max} = a_2 x_2 + \beta^I_1 z^I_1 + \varepsilon^I, \tag{5.2}$$

$$b^F = a_3 x_3 + \beta^F_2 z^F_2 + \delta^F r + \gamma^F_1 b^F_{max} + \gamma^I_1 b^I_{max} + u^F, \tag{5.3}$$

$$b^I = a_4 x_4 + \beta^I_2 z^I_2 + \delta^I r + \gamma^F_2 b^F_{max} + \gamma^I_2 b^I_{max} + u^I, \tag{5.4}$$

where b^F_{max}, b^I_{max}, b^F, and b^I are the maximum credit limits and amounts borrowed for formal and informal credits, respectively. The x_is, $i = 1, 2, \ldots, 4$, represent for each i a vector of household demographics and assets, community characteristics, and prices. The z^F and z^Is are vectors of formal and informal lenders' characteristics and r is the (transaction cost adjusted) formal interest rate. Finally, the as, βs, γs, and δs are the parameters to be estimated, and ε, u, and v are error terms.

Identification of the Model

Equations (5.1) to (5.4) make up a recursive system of simultaneous equations with the exogenous variables constituted by the household demographics and assets, community characteristics, and lenders' characteristics appearing in all equations. Hence, exclusion restrictions on these variables are needed for the system to be identified. The simultaneity of the maximum credit limit variables (which are choice variables for lenders but not for borrowers) results from the fact that they are likely to be correlated with unobservable household characteristics (its likelihood to default, for example) absorbed in the error terms, u and v.

The main argument used for identifying (5.3) and (5.4) is that not *all* the lender's characteristics variables enter directly in the determination of the amount borrowed. That is, some of the lender's characteristics influence the amounts borrowed *only through* the effects they have in determining how much the lender is willing to lend. For informal credit, the data collected on the lender's characteristics are relative wealth compared with the borrower, professional occupation, relation to the borrower, place of residence, and whether he or she is a member of a credit program. It is argued here that all these characteristics influence the amounts borrowed only through the informal maximum credit limit. Identification of the formal credit limit is straightforward and based on the exogenous eligibility condition, which group-based NGO programs impose on applicants. To be eligible, most programs require that a household not possess more than 0.5 acre of land. Because most of the formal credit available in the survey villages is provided by NGO programs and not by commercial or state-owned banks, the possession of land is a useful instrument in identifying the supply equation of the formal credit. The specific variable that is used is a dummy variable, which reflects eligibility based on the most important criterion: landownership below the specified cutoff point of 0.5 acres. The Bangladesh sample contains villages served by three major NGOs: the Association for Social Advancement (ASA), the Bangladesh Rural Advancement Committee (BRAC), and the Rangpur-Dinajpur Rural Services (RDRS). In the BRAC and ASA villages, the landownership cutoff point used is 0.5 acres (the cutoff used by both the NGOs). In the RDRS villages, the cutoff used is 1.5 acres.

Sampling and Estimation Methodologies

The study included 350 rural households, repeatedly visited during three rounds in 1994, covering the *boro* and *aman* harvest and the pre-*aman* hungry season. The sample covers seven villages in rural Bangladesh (see Zeller et al. 2001 for further details). In order to increase the cost-efficiency of the survey, households in each of the villages were first stratified according to the amount of land owned. The number of sample households owning land of 1 acre or more was randomly drawn in proportion to their distribution in the village, irrespective of their membership in NGO programs. For households owning less than 1 acre of land, participant households were over-sampled, so that about 55 percent were members of BRAC, ASA, or RDRS.

The information collected in the survey includes household demographics; land tenure; agricultural production; livestock ownership; asset ownership and transactions; food and nonfood consumption; credit, savings, and gift transactions; wage, self-employment income, and time allocation; and anthropometric status of preschoolers and their mothers.

Because this chapter focuses on credit limits and credit demand, details will be given next on the way these variables were collected in the survey. The questionnaire on credit demand and savings was administered to all adult household members (over 17 years old) in the sample. In each round, each adult household member was asked the maximum amount he or she *could* borrow during the recall period from informal and formal sources of credit separately. If respondents were involved in a loan transaction as a borrower, the question was asked for each loan transaction (for both granted and rejected loan demands). In this case the maximum credit limit refers to the time of borrowing and to the lender involved in that particular loan transaction. If respondents did not ask for any loan during the recall period of the survey, the question was asked separately for formal and informal sources of credit with no reference to particular formal or informal lenders. Respondents who were granted loans were also asked the same general question (that is, with no reference to particular formal or informal lenders) in a way that elicited the maximum credit limit they would face if they wanted more loans not just from the same lender, but from the same sector of the credit market (formal or informal) in which they have already borrowed. Consequently, for both formal and informal credit, the maximum formal and informal credit limits of each adult household member were obtained in each round, even if the member was not involved in any loan transaction.

Equations (5.1) to (5.4) are estimated with a standard two-stage simultaneous equation method that corrected for the choice-based sampling method.[3] The credit limit in the formal sector is estimated by instrumenting actual participation status with predicted probability of participation from the estimated logit model.

Empirical Findings

Empirical Distribution of Credit Limits

Table 5.1 presents the average informal and formal credit limits with the corresponding average amounts of unused credit lines (that is, the average of the differences between the respective credit limits and the amounts borrowed).[4] These averages refer to the household and are obtained by summing the observations for all individual adult household members and by computing a simple average over all three rounds. In the sample population as a whole, the average informal and formal credit limits for a household are, respectively, US$40 and US$71. To put these figures somewhat in perspective, the 1995 per capita gross national product in Bangladesh was US$240. In relation to per capita income, these figures appear reasonable. Although the majority of adult males and females in our samples had borrowed at least once during the recall period of almost two years, most of the loans were given by the informal sector for consumption needs. Moreover, because of the truncated nature of the credit limit distributions, these average figures are not good indicators of the levels of access to credit. We therefore also show the median formal and informal credit limits in Table 5.1, which are, respectively, US$50 and US$13. Moreover, further inspection of data not reported here shows that 50 percent of the population can

---

3. As indicated in the previous section, participation in a credit program was the criterion for stratifying the sample. In order to arrive at results representative of the village population as a whole, conditional probabilities were computed from an estimated binomial logit equation where the dependent variable took the value 1 if the household was a member of any of the three programs. Because the sample was choice based, the likelihood function was weighted and an appropriate covariance matrix was computed following Manski and McFadden (1981).

4. To correct for the over-sampling of credit program participants, the summary statistics in the tables have been weighted using the strata population weights from the village census.

TABLE 5.1 Credit limits, by financial sector and gender of household member (US$)

Credit Limits	Formal			Informal		
	Male	Female	All	Male	Female	All
Mean	71	71	71	53	11	40
Median	0	75	50	13	5	13
Standard deviation	139	59	118	174	22	143
Minimum	0	0	0	0	0	0
Maximum	1,250	300	1,250	2,500	150	2,500

borrow, at most, US$100 from the formal sector and US$35 from the informal sector. Formal sector borrowers were also found to have a higher median informal credit limit than households that did not borrow from formal lenders. This positive correlation between borrowing from the formal sector and informal credit limit suggests that informal lenders are willing to lend significantly more to those who are participating in the formal credit market than to the rest of the population. One plausible explanation is that formal sector borrowers—mostly longstanding members of NGO credit programs—are perceived as good credit risks by informal lenders because they appear to be able to negotiate and manage quite large loans from formal sources and because they could resort to repaying informal loans with a future formal loan. The latter reason is confirmed by the survey.

With respect to gender differences in access to credit, Table 5.1 further shows that women have higher median formal credit limits but lower median informal credit limits compared with men. This result is driven by the fact that most formal group-based programs in Bangladesh aggressively target women, and often exclude men from membership. However, when the comparison is restricted to formal sector borrowers (results not shown here), men have higher median credit limits in both sectors of the credit market. In other words, if Bangladeshi men become members in credit programs and then become eligible to borrow from the formal sector, the group-based programs seem to grant them higher credit limits than those obtained by women.

Determinants of Access to and Participation in Credit Markets

The estimation results for the conditional probability of participating in a credit program and the estimation of the credit limit and loan demand equations are presented in Tables 5.3–5.7. Table 5.2 contains the descriptive statistics of all the variables used in the regression analysis.

DETERMINANTS OF PARTICIPATION IN CREDIT PROGRAMS. Table 5.3 presents the estimated logit equation describing participation in NGO programs. The dependent variable is a dummy variable with a value of 1 if at least one adult household member is a member of an NGO-promoted credit

TABLE 5.2 Definition and summary statistics of variables used in regression analysis

Variable	Description	Mean	Standard Deviation	Minimum	Maximum
FLNMAX	Credit limit formal sector	2,269.6	4,231.4	0	40,000
ILNMAX	Credit limit informal sector	5,201.5	12,913.7	0	151,100
ELIGIB	Eligibility status (1 = eligible)	0.7	0.4	0	1
FLOANVAL	Amount borrowed formal	2,303.9	4,418.5	0	32,500
ILOANVAL	Amount borrowed informal	4,963.2	8,180.7	0	86,787
AGEHH	Age of household head	42.5	13.1	14	92
AGEHHSQ	Age of household head squared	1,985.8	1,236.7	196	8,464
TMEM	Household size	5.1	2.3	1	16
HIGHEDUM	Highest educational level: male	0.8	2.2	0	14
HIGHEDUF	Highest educational level: female	0.3	1.3	0	10
ADMALE	Number of adult males	1.3	0.8	0	7
ADFEMAL	Number of adult females	1.3	0.6	0	4
DEPRATIO	Dependency ratio	0.3	0.2	0	1
LENGTH	Number of years in NGO program	1.9	5.8	0	9
SEXH	Sex of household head (male = 1)	0.9	0.2	0	1
LRATIO	Ratio of land owned 1995:1984	1.5	2.6	0	26
LENDRES	= 1 if lender in village of residence	0.9	0.1	0	1
NGOLNDER	= 1 if lender is NGO member	0.4	0.5	0	1
RICH	= 1 if lender is richer	0.9	0.2	0	1

program. Apart from the eligibility status of a household (ELIGIB2), a dummy with a value of 1 if a household owns less than 0.5 acres, the other explanatory variables are age of the household head in years and its square (AGEHH and AGEHHSQ), highest level of formal education achieved among males and females in the household (HIGHEDUM and HIGHEDUF), number of adult males and females in the household (ADMALE and ADFEMAL), household size (TMEM1), and the sex of the household head (SEXH), a dummy variable with a value of 1 for a male head. In addition, two variables that capture some attributes of the social capital of the households are used. These are the distances (in kilometers) from the household to the homes of the parents of the household head (HDIST) and of the parents of the spouse of the household head (SDIST). Whenever the parents lived in the same village as the household, the distance was recorded as zero. In the cultural context of rural Bangladesh, proximity to parental homes is assumed to be indicative of length of residency in the vicinity and, hence, ceteris paribus, of a greater level of social interaction. It could also imply less costly access to a wider kin network. Finally, district dummies (NDIST1, NDIST2, and NDIST3) are used to capture unobserved district-level effects in participation. These district dummies are also used in the subsequent credit limit and loan demand equations, but their coefficients will not be discussed.

As expected, a household's eligibility status based on landownership is important in determining participation: the coefficient of the variable ELIGIB2 is significant at the 5 percent level. The other statistically significant variables are the level of female education in the household (HIGHEDUF) and the sex of the household head (SEXH). The coefficient of SEXH is negative and significant, indicating that female-headed households are more likely to become members of NGO programs. The positive and significant coefficient of HIGHEDUF appears to be the result of two factors. First, it may be the case that better-educated females not only have better knowledge about the existence of NGO programs, but also, because of their better education, are in a position to derive greater benefits from program membership. Second, level of female education in the household may serve as a proxy for other important unobserved characteristics of the household. For example, it may be the case that households with a higher level of female education are precisely those that allow their women greater autonomy or freedom to join public programs. For these reasons, demand for membership may be higher for such households. On the other hand, all three programs in the sample villages put special emphasis on targeting poor women. None of the other variables, except household size (TMEM1), is statistically significant.

DETERMINANTS OF THE EXTENT OF HOUSEHOLD ACCESS TO CREDIT. Tables 5.4 and 5.5 present the results of the determinants of the extent of household access to formal and informal credits, as measured by household credit limits per capita in the two market segments.

TABLE 5.3 Participation in NGO credit programs

Variable	Coefficient	Standard Error	t-Value
ELIGIB2	1.2024	0.37368	3.218
AGEHH	−0.032524	0.36137E-01	−0.900
AGEHHSQ	0.00017214	0.42748E-03	0.403
HIGHEDUM	−0.12695	0.11125	−1.141
HIGHEDUF	0.27951	0.11569	2.416
ADMALE	0.042191	0.21096	0.200
ADFEMAL	−0.77343E-01	0.22983	−0.337
TMEM1	0.20662	0.84209E-01	2.454
SEXH	−0.76572	0.46710	−1.639
HDIST	0.42107E-01	0.36397	0.116
SDIST	0.10755	0.28707	0.375
NDIST1	0.33807E-03	0.30910	0.001
NDIST2	−2.1519	0.45294	−4.751
NDIST3	−1.4859	0.37651	−3.946

Log-likelihood function = −191.7340
Restricted log-likelihood = −235.2615
Chi-squared = 87.05499
Degrees of freedom = 13
Significance level = 0.0000000

NOTES: Corrected for choice-based sampling; multinomial logit model; maximum likelihood estimates.

Several variables are statistically significant in determining credit limits in the formal sector (Table 5.4). Predicted membership in an NGO program that provides credit (NEWNGO) importantly affects formal sector credit limits. This is intuitively obvious. In rural Bangladesh, group-based NGOs are often the only institutions that provide credit in the rural hinterland. Hence, members of these organizations are indeed likely to have greater credit limits compared with the rest. The gender focus of the programs continues to be apparent: as in the membership status equation, female-headed households (SEXH = 0) have, ceteris paribus, higher credit limits. In contrast, the level of female education (HIGHEDUF) loses its significance. Unlike in the membership status equation, the amount of land owned (LAND) has a significant positive effect on formal sector credit limits. This is likely to be the result of two factors: first, among members of NGO programs, those with a relatively greater amount of land are likely to present themselves as more creditworthy; second, among nonmembers, those who own more land are also more likely to access credit from other formal services.

The coefficient of HDIST is negative and significant, indicating that those families living further away from the parental village of the household head

TABLE 5.4 Determinants of household credit limits in formal sector: Two-stage least squares regression

Variable	Coefficient	Standard Error	t-Value
AGEHH	21.272**	10.876	1.956
AGEHHSQ	−0.17905*	0.10647	−1.682
HIGHEDUM	8.0708	24.645	0.327
HIGHEDUF	36.555	39.043	0.936
ADMALE	21.945	68.670	0.320
ADFEMAL	−11.157	58.458	−0.191
TMEM1	−72.651***	22.096	−3.288
LENGTH	−20.792	26.134	−0.796
SEXH	−367.12	179.30	−2.048
LAND	0.49304	0.28632	1.722
HDIST	−150.94**	80.004	−1.887
SDIST	0.14083	67.488	0.002
NDIST1	−6.1611	95.535	−0.064
NDIST2	137.39	124.58	1.103
NDIST3	185.38*	107.97	1.717
NEWNGO	1594.8***	364.75	4.372

Adjusted R^2 = .38822
F = 5.76
Probability value = .00000
Log-likelihood = −2774.6788

NOTES: N = 350. Weighted two-stage least squares regression. Results corrected for heteroskedasticity.
* significant at 10 percent level; ** significant at 5 percent level; *** significant at 1 percent level.

have a lower formal credit limit. As suggested previously, those living closer to parental villages may be expected to possess a higher degree of social capital and social collateral and hence are able to lay stronger claims to an improved access to credit. It is interesting to note that the distance to the spouse's parental village is highly insignificant. In other words, it is the husband's social network that seems to count in obtaining higher credit limits, not that of the wife, who is most frequently the member of the NGO program. The coefficient of household size (TMEM1) is negative and significant. Normally, microfinance NGOs allow only one membership per household (although households may be able to evade this); hence, all else remaining the same, formal credit limit per capita is likely to be lower for larger households.

Table 5.5 presents the estimated informal credit limit equation. Unlike in the formal sector equations, ADMALE—the number of adult males in the family—is positive and significant. In the informal sector, land and labor power (especially male labor power) are the principal indicators of future income

TABLE 5.5 Determinants of household credit limits in informal sector: Two-stage least squares regression

Variable	Coefficient	Standard Error	t-Value
AGEHH	−16.375	16.920	−0.968
AGEHHSQ	0.092346	0.20527	0.450
HIGHEDUM	41.770	61.170	0.683
HIGHEDUF	157.00	135.79	1.156
ADMALE	282.07	114.58	2.462
ADFEMAL	−76.638	106.28	−0.721
TMEM1	−102.98	43.513	−2.367
LENGTH	−3.7767	14.224	−0.266
SEXH	−233.43	202.16	−1.155
LENDRES	1302.8	284.60	4.577
NGOLNDER	254.30	139.43	1.824
HDIST	−61.148	210.56	−0.290
SDIST	68.560	158.55	0.432
LAND	3.4913	1.6568	2.107
NDIST1	105.51	193.25	0.546
NDIST2	−77.362	178.34	−0.434
NDIST3	−290.58	197.84	−1.469
FLNMAX2	0.083731	0.21701	0.386

Adjusted R^2 = .23298
F = 7.24
Probability value = .00000
Log-likelihood = −3015.2411

NOTES: N = 350. Weighted two-stage least squares regression. Results corrected for heteroscedasticity.

potential of the household. Hence it is not surprising that ownership of both these assets significantly affects credit access. What is surprising is that the social capital and collateral variables (HDIST and SDIST) are not significant. Note that those households that transact with village-resident lenders (LENDERES) have greater limits, as do those that transact with lenders who are NGO members (NGOLNDER). The latter result indicates that NGO members contribute to the size of the informal credit market. As in the formal credit limit equation, household size (TMEM1) has a negative impact on credit limit per capita. Lastly, the formal sector credit limit (FLNMAX2) does not appear to affect the credit limit in the informal sector.

DETERMINANTS OF DEMANDS FOR FORMAL AND INFORMAL LOANS.   In the formal sector borrowing equation (Table 5.6), the regression coefficient for the predicted formal sector credit limit (FLNMAX2) is highly significant and very close to one. The null hypothesis that the coefficient is equal

TABLE 5.6 Determinants of household borrowing in formal sector: Two-stage least squares regression

Variable	Coefficient	Standard Error	t-Value
AGEHH	−10.799*	6.3303	−1.706
AGEHHSQ	0.10831	0.072882	1.486
HIGHEDUM	25.970	24.087	1.078
HIGHEDUF	−30.592	54.412	−0.562
ADMALE	0.89395	51.168	0.017
ADFEMAL	−70.592	43.717	−1.615
TMEM1	22.826	17.695	1.290
SEXH	126.59	126.26	1.003
HDIST	136.44**	65.160	2.094
SDIST	−8.4049	57.382	−0.146
LAND	0.45786	0.54060	0.847
NDIST1	43.847	64.240	0.683
NDIST2	60.286	54.393	1.108
NDIST3	−18.501	97.916	−0.189
FLNMAX2	1.0846***	0.072881	14.881
ILNMAX2	−0.16893	0.13505	−1.251

Adjusted R^2 = .57544
F = 32.53
Probability value = .00000
Log-likelihood = −2700.2175

NOTES: N = 350. Weighted two-stage least squares regression. Results corrected for heteroscedasticity.
* significant at 10 percent level; ** significant at 5 percent level; *** significant at 1 percent level.

to 1 is not rejected at the 5 percent level, indicating that households are likely to increase borrowing to the full extent of the increase in the formal credit limit. In other words, if the NGO programs choose to increase credit limits and related loan sizes, their members are likely to take up all of such increases.

The coefficient of ILNMAX2, the predicted informal sector credit limit, is negative as expected. Yet, it is not statistically significant, indicating that formal and informal loans are not good substitutes. HDIST has a positive and significant effect on formal borrowing, suggesting that households that have relatively lower levels of social capital and collateral (and therefore might have less access to informal sector credit)[5] borrow more from formal sector sources despite their lower formal credit lines. The number of adult females (ADFEMAL)

---

5. The coefficient of HDIST in the informal sector credit limit equation was negative but not significant.

TABLE 5.7 Determinants of household borrowing in informal sector: Two-stage least squares regression

Variable	Coefficient	Standard Error	t-Value
AGEHH	3.8569	14.855	0.260
AGEHHSQ	−0.057199	0.18375	−0.31
HIGHEDUM	−9.6340	60.819	−0.158
HIGHEDUF	106.03	88.943	1.192
ADMALE	−36.841	107.22	−0.344
ADFEMAL	90.036	110.35	0.816
TMEM1	−2.2702	51.983	−0.044
SEXH	−85.332	161.76	−0.528
HDIST	111.37	209.68	0.531
SDIST	59.484	177.46	0.335
LAND	−0.68266	2.2980	−0.297
NDIST1	22.731	169.12	0.134
NDIST2	−52.277	159.53	−0.328
NDIST3	2.4194	172.78	0.014
FLNMAX2	−0.31657	0.20217	−1.566
ILNMAX2	1.1361***	0.18279	6.215

Adjusted R^2 = .25611
F = 9.01
Probability value = .00000
Log-likelihood = −2994.5665

NOTES: N = 350. Weighted two-stage least squares regression. Results corrected for hetero-skedasticity.
*** significant at 1 percent level.

has a negative impact on formal sector borrowing. If cultural constraints on female labor supply or demand outside the households are strong, then the marginal return to credit use is indeed likely to be lower for such households when family size and availability of adult male labor are controlled for. This may lead to less demand for credit even when credit limits are high. Additionally, the equation does not suggest any significant evidence that female-headed households borrow less (or more) from formal sector sources once their superior access is controlled. Note also that the coefficient of land, significant in the credit limit equations, is no longer significant in the borrowing equations.

The informal sector borrowing equation (Table 5.7) indicates that the level of informal sector borrowing depends primarily on the informal sector credit limit. As in the case of the formal sector borrower, the coefficient for predicted informal borrowing (ILNMAX2) is positive and not different from unity, indicating that the Bangladeshi sample households borrow to the full extent of the increase in credit limit even in the informal sector.[6] Also, although the coefficient of FLNMAX2 is negative, it just falls short of being significant at the 10 percent level, suggesting once again that formal and informal credit may not be adequately substitutable. Note that none of the other household's characteristics is significant. If informal credit is indeed mainly used to finance unexpected spurts in expenditures (for example, those due to temporary illness or unexpected social events) or to uphold consumption during temporary or unexpected downturns in household income, this result is as expected.

Conclusions

To help design credit programs targeted to the poor that offer services that expand and complement rather than substitute for the ones offered by the existing informal credit market, it is important to understand the socioeconomic factors influencing household access to formal and informal credit. It is also necessary to know how formal and informal credit interact and serve households' demands for financial services, when they are both available (Zeller et al. 1996). This chapter implemented the concept of credit limits to analyze the determinants of households' extent of access to and participation in informal and formal credit markets in Bangladesh. Several conclusions can be drawn from the analysis.

There is strong evidence that NGOs in Bangladesh are successful in targeting the functionally landless. But there also is evidence that, among program members, those with more land have greater access to credit in the formal market, mainly consisting of NGO group-based programs targeting the poor. Our finding that the informal credit limit increases with possession of land is not surprising. We further find that loan demand does not depend on the amount of land owned. This perhaps indicates that a lack of complementary inputs among landholders may be a principal factor suppressing credit demand, or that many landholders are, in fact, landlords who do not demand agricultural loans because they rent out their land. In fact, the nonsignificance of the other household characteristics in the borrowing equations, in general, strongly suggests that the characteristics of the NGO programs themselves determine credit demand. This may indeed be the case if the NGO programs provide crucial complementary services (marketing, basic education, skill development, and so on) in addition to credit, as they do in Bangladesh.

---

6. Similar analysis by Diagne (1999) shows that Malawian rural households choose to borrow significantly less than their credit limits in the informal market. As most informal loans are used for consumption smoothing in Malawi, this result shows that households choose to hold unused credit lines, probably for similar motives as holding liquid assets for precautionary savings.

A second conclusion relates to the nature of credit constraints. At households' present levels of access to credit, they are, on average, credit constrained in both the formal and the informal sectors. Households appear to increase their borrowing by the full amount of the increase in credit limits in both sectors, and seem not to be interested in leaving some credit lines unused for precautionary purposes (as Diagne 1999 and Diagne and Zeller 2001 have shown with household data from Malawi). The choice to preserve some credit limit for future use (instead of using it all up as the Bangladeshi households appear to do) is a decision under uncertainty, basically valuing present and future returns from credit access. Everything else equal, the value of unused credit limits (or of precautionary savings) rises with higher uncertainty. The drought-prone rainfed agriculture of Malawi appears in many ways much more risky than Bangladesh's mostly irrigated cropping sector, which delivers a more predictable grain harvest despite the risk of flood.

Apart from credit access, other household characteristics had little impact on the decision to borrow. These findings provide a strong case for financial market policies to expand access for poor households by charging cost-recovering interest rates and by creating an enabling rural development framework (through complementary policies such as ensuring households' access to technology, input and output markets, information, and health services), which will raise the marginal returns to credit use in farm and off-farm enterprises.

Another important finding from this analysis is the limited substitutability between formal and informal credit. This suggests that the forms of credit fulfill different functions in the household's intertemporal transfer of resources, and that credit market intervention—at least of the type undertaken by the NGO programs in Bangladesh—does not crowd out informal lending, although it might alter the terms of intertemporal trade in favor of the borrower. Despite the fact that capital is fungible, informal loan products differ from formal ones not only in their interest rate and transaction costs but also with respect to loan maturity and conditions governing collateral and loan use and regulating repayment. Informal loans in Bangladesh, as has been observed in other developing countries, are often used for consumption-smoothing purposes and for investment in human capital (that is, education), whereas formal credit is not only sought and used for agricultural or off-farm enterprises, but also almost exclusively offered for such purposes. The imperfect substitutability between informal and formal credit services is therefore mainly rooted in the differences in loan characteristics.

References

Adams, D. W, and D. A. Fitchett, eds. 1992. *Informal finance in low-income countries*. Boulder, Colo., U.S.A.: Westview Press.

Adams, D. W., and R. C. Vogel. 1985. Rural financial markets in low-income countries: Recent controversies and lessons. *World Development* 14 (4): 477–487.

Adams, D. W., D. H. Graham, and J. D. Von Pischke, eds. 1984. *Undermining rural development with cheap credit.* Boulder, Colo., U.S.A.: Westview Press.

Alderman, A., and C. Paxson. 1992. *Do the poor insure? A synthesis of the literature on risk sharing institutions in developing countries.* Discussion Paper No. 169. Princeton, N.J., U.S.A.: Woodrow Wilson School of Public and International Affairs, Princeton University.

Avery, R. B. 1981. Estimating credit constraints by switching regression. In *Structural analysis of discrete data with econometric applications*, ed. C. F. Manski and D. McFadden. Cambridge, Mass., U.S.A.: Massachusetts Institute of Technology Press.

Barham, B., S. Boucher, and M. R. Carter. 1996. Credit constraints, credit unions, and small-scale producers in Guatemala. *World Development* 24 (5): 793–806.

Besley, T. 1995. Savings, credit, and insurance. In *Handbook of development economics*, vol. III, ed. J. Behrman and T. N. Srinivasan. Amsterdam: Elsevier.

Braverman, A., and J. L. Guasch. 1986. Rural credit markets and institutions in developing countries: Lessons for policy analysis from practice and modern theory. *World Development* 14 (10/11): 1253–1267.

Browning, M., and A. Lusardi. 1996. Household saving: Micro theories and micro facts. *Journal of Economic Literature* 4: 1797–1855.

Coate, S., and M. Ravallion. 1993. Reciprocity without commitment: Characterization and performance of informal insurance arrangements. *Journal of Development Economics* 40 (1): 1–24.

Deaton, A. 1992. *Understanding consumption.* Oxford: Clarendon Press.

Diagne, A. 1996. Measuring access to credit and its impacts on household food security: Some methodological notes. Paper presented at 1996 annual meeting of the American Agricultural Economic Association (AAEA), San Antonio, Texas.

———. 1999. Determinants of household access to and participation in formal and informal credit markets in Malawi. Food Consumption and Nutrition Division Discussion Paper No. 67. International Food Policy Research Institute, Washington, D.C.

Diagne, A., and M. Zeller. 2001. *Access to credit and its impact on welfare in Malawi.* Research Report No. 116. Washington, D.C.: International Food Policy Research Institute.

Diagne, A., M. Zeller, and M. Sharma. 2000. Determinants of household access to and participation in formal and informal credit markets in Malawi and Bangladesh. Food Consumption and Nutrition Division Discussion Paper No. 90. International Food Policy Research Institute, Washington, D.C.

Fafchamps, M. 1992. Solidarity networks in pre-industrial societies: Rational peasants with a moral economy. *Economic Development and Cultural Change* 41 (1): 147–174.

Feder G., L. J. Lau, J. Y. Lin, and X. Luo. 1990. The relationship between credit and productivity in Chinese agriculture: A microeconomic model of disequilibrium. *American Journal of Agricultural Economics* 72 (5): 1151–1157.

Gersovitz, M. 1988. Savings and development. In *Handbook of development economics*, vol. 1, ed. H. Chenery and T. N. Srinivasan. Amsterdam: Elsevier.

Jappelli, T. 1990. Who is credit constrained in the U.S.? *Quarterly Journal of Economics* 105 (2): 219–234.

Kochar, A. 1997. Explaining poverty: An empirical analysis of the effects of ill-health and uncertainty on the savings of rural Pakistani households. Unpublished paper. Department of Economics, Stanford University, Calif., U.S.A.

Manski, C. F., and D. McFadden. 1981. Alternative estimators and sample designs for discrete choice analysis. In *Structural analysis of discrete data with econometric applications*, ed. C. F. Manski and D. McFadden. Cambridge, Mass., U.S.A.: Massachusetts Institute of Technology Press.

Stiglitz, J. E., and A. Weiss. 1981. Credit rationing in markets with imperfect information. *American Economic Review* 71 (3): 393–410.

Townsend, R. M. 1994. Risk and insurance in village India. *Econometrica* 62 (3): 539–591.

Udry, C. 1994. Risk and insurance in a rural credit market. *Review of Economic Studies* 61 (3): 495–526.

———. 1995. Risk and saving in northern Nigeria. *American Economic Review* 85 (5): 1287–1300.

Zeller, M. 1994. Determinants of credit rationing: A study of informal lenders and formal groups in Madagascar. *World Development* 22 (12): 1895–1907.

Zeller, M., G. Schrieder, J. von Braun, and F. Heidhues. 1997. *Rural finance for food security for the poor: Implications for research and policy.* Food Policy Review No. 4. Washington, D.C.: International Food Policy Research Institute.

Zeller, M., M. Sharma, A. Ahmed, and S. Rashid. 2001. *Group-based financial institutions for the rural poor in Bangladesh: An institutional- and household-level analysis.* Research Report No. 120. Washington, D.C.: International Food Policy Research Institute.

Zeller, M., A. Ahmed, S. Babu, S. Broca, A. Diagne, and M. Sharma. 1996. Rural financial policies for food security of the poor: Methodologies for a multicountry research project. Food Consumption and Nutrition Division Discussion Paper No. 11. International Food Policy Research Institute, Washington, D.C.

6 Improving Access to Land Markets: Evidence from Emerging Farmers in KwaZulu-Natal, South Africa

MICHAEL LYNE AND MARK DARROCH

Improving access to land is often seen as an important method to alleviate poverty in rural areas. However, emerging farmers with limited equity and off-farm income face liquidity challenges in servicing standard mortgages to finance land acquisition. Successful land reform involves complex legal and financial issues, and market-oriented land reforms require innovative financial strategies to facilitate private transfers of land to the poor, who lack the resources to pay for them.

Land reform has been accorded high priority in South Africa. Policy-makers believe that political stability and economic growth require rapid and substantial land transfers. Broadly speaking, government policy recommends two methods of redistributing land to achieve this. First, the Land Reform Pilot Program helps groups of landless people purchase and settle on land. Groups can apply for state grants to finance planning, land acquisition, and basic services. According to the Program Overview of 1994, this redistribution policy is not intended to establish farmers. Beneficiaries wanting to farm will need to augment the land allocated to them through the program with land acquired through the market. The Rural Financial Services Enquiry will remove obstacles to market-based acquisition (Department of Land Affairs 1994:10).

The Program's emphasis on group participation raises important questions about collective management and land tenure institutions. Perhaps the most significant lesson from international experience with land reform is that productive use of agricultural land requires efficient land markets (AID 1986). Although land markets often function well in regions where land is privately owned, private tenure is neither a necessary nor a sufficient condition for a land market to operate. Nevertheless, efficient land markets do require institutional arrangements that provide tenure security and reduce transaction costs (Johnson 1972). In a worst-case scenario in which commercial farms are purchased by groups of beneficiaries with no effective management or tenure institutions, land will become an open access resource devoid of economic rent and market value.

The second method for redistributing land accelerates private market transactions by restructuring financial services in rural areas, reducing transaction costs in land purchase, amending or scrapping the Subdivision of Agricultural Land Act, 70 of 1970, and (possibly) introducing a land tax. Free market champions in South Africa welcomed the acceptance of voluntary market transfers. In Kenya, market transfers redistributed much more land than all of the other government-sponsored schemes, and at much lower cost (World Bank 1993: 24). However, private market transfers do not guarantee the continued health of the land market. In practice, private land transactions may favor group purchase (to reduce transaction and subdivision costs) and, like the Land Reform Pilot Program, could produce institutional arrangements that are not conducive to an efficient land market.

To date, the government has concentrated its resources on implementing the Pilot Program in KwaZulu-Natal and other provinces in South Africa. Private market transactions are still constrained by the Subdivision Act (which imposes an "economic" farm size that most prospective buyers cannot afford, including those who qualify for the meager grant) and by a lack of financial products to alleviate cash-flow stress faced by the majority of new entrants into the land market. The KwaZulu Finance and Investment Corporation (KFC) and local sugar-milling companies have initiated an experiment that involves financing land purchases with graduated or increasing debt repayments over time to counter cash-flow stress. The experiment has shown promise (see below). Land is also transferring to privately financed companies in which equity is shared between commercial farmers and their (disadvantaged) employees. At present, most of these ventures involve capital-intensive fruit and wine operations in the Western Cape, and there are no such schemes in KwaZulu-Natal.

This chapter has two objectives. The first is to test a method of collecting data suitable for (1) estimating the overall rate of land redistribution in the province of KwaZulu-Natal (redistribution is defined as the transfer of title from the state and white owners to nonwhites, from Asians to other nonwhites, and, within nonwhite groups, from men to women); (2) analyzing methods used by emerging farmers to finance land purchase; and (3) gathering information about the nature of property rights, managerial arrangements, and land use patterns on farms acquired by disadvantaged people. These data are intended to show how quickly, and how much, farmland has been redistributed, how land purchases are being financed, and what institutions have developed on transferred land. The second objective is to identify ways of resolving the financial and other problems faced in improving access to land by emerging farmers in KwaZulu-Natal and other areas in South Africa. This is done by analyzing the survey method results and describing experience with the innovative KFC financing scheme since 1996.

The first section describes the pilot survey of land transactions, and extrapolates the results to give an estimate of land transfers in KwaZulu-Natal. We then present some descriptive statistics computed for a survey of farms acquired by disadvantaged owners. These statistics provide data about the methods used to finance land purchase and preliminary information about de facto property rights and managerial arrangements on redistributed land (Lyne and Graham 2001). The latter topics were explored more fully in a survey of households that occupied and used redistributed land, and this aspect of the study is not reported here. Instead, the chapter focuses on the issue of improving access to land markets. The third section discusses the mechanics of the innovative KFC land financing scheme, and some of its pros and cons; and the final section offers conclusions.

The Rate of Land Redistribution in KwaZulu-Natal

To generate estimates of land transfers for KwaZulu-Natal, the farmland available for redistribution in the province was stratified into three reasonably homogeneous farming regions, each comprising a number of census districts representing primary stage sampling units (PSUs). A complete census was made of every land transaction recorded during 1995 in two PSUs sampled from each region (stratum). PSUs were sampled with probability proportionate to an estimate of their size.

Table 6.1 summarizes information relating to land transfers observed in each of the PSUs sampled. Transfers to disadvantaged people were identified by contacting the new owners. Table 6.2 shows corresponding estimates for the province, which were extrapolated from the sample statistics with due regard for the multistage sampling technique employed.

The estimates show that, at the provincial level, 5.69 percent (302,243 hectares) of the farmland available for redistribution was transferred to new owners in 1995. Transfers to disadvantaged entrants accounted for 1.61 percent (4,879 hectares) of the area transferred, or 0.09 percent of the total area available for redistribution. This sample estimate for disadvantaged entrants compares favorably with Kirsten, van Rooyen, and Ngqangweni's (1996) estimates for the Northern Province in South Africa during 1994 and 1995 of 0.14 and 0.05 percent, respectively.

Characteristics of the Farms Acquired by Disadvantaged Entrants

Interviews were conducted with the registered owners of all farms acquired by disadvantaged people within the selected PSUs. There were seven transactions in 1995 (Table 6.1), but two of the new entrants acquired two properties each. In other words, a total of five farms were registered to disadvantaged owners. Although clearly unreliable as population estimators, the summary statistics presented in Tables 6.3, 6.4, and 6.5 highlight variables that provide useful information about the methods used by the poor to finance land and about the changes in de facto property rights that are expected to influence investment incentives and access to credit.

TABLE 6.1 Land transfers observed in a sample of properties drawn from the farmland available for redistribution, 1995

Stratum/PSUs	Registered Properties[a]	Properties Transferred		Transfers to Disadvantaged Owners		Hectares Transferred	
		Number	Percent	Number	Percent	Total	To the Disadvantaged
Coastal Region							
Lower Umfolozi A	577	38	6.59	0	0.00	8,542	0
Richmond A	1,209	92	7.61	0	0.00	8,650	0
Midlands Region							
Estcourt B	2,371	118	4.98	5	0.21	18,189	332
Richmond B	631	42	6.66	0	0.00	3,655	0
Lowveld Region							
Lower Umfolozi C	132	9	6.82	2	1.52	868	202
Weenen C	160	7	4.38	0	0.00	2,350	0
Total	5,080	306	6.02	7	0.14	42,254	534

a Commercial farms are composed of a number of registered properties (about six on average).

TABLE 6.2 Land transfers estimated for KwaZulu-Natal, 1995

Stratum	Registered Properties	Area (thousand hectares)	Properties Transferred		Area Transferred		Transfers to Disadvantaged Owners		Area Transferred to Disadvantaged Owners	
			Number	Percent	Hectares (thousand)	Percent	Number	Percent	Hectares (thousand)	Percent
Coastal	5,288	842.9	375	7.09	58.1	6.89	0	0	0	0
Midlands	30,634	3,694.2	1,782	5.82	206.2	5.58	32	0.11	2.14	0.06
Lowveld	3,569	771.3	200	5.60	37.9	4.92	27	0.76	2.74	0.35
Province	39,491	5,308.4	2,357	5.97	302.2	5.69	59	0.15	4.88	0.09

TABLE 6.3 Transaction details for farms acquired by disadvantaged respondents, 1995

Transaction Details	Mean
Previous owner was a corporate entity (percent)	20
Previous owner was the state (percent)	0
Transactions that involved subdivision (percent)	40
Transactions that involved land purchase (percent)	80
Area transferred (hectares)	107
New owner is a corporate entity (percent)	20

NOTE: $N = 5$.

Despite overrepresentation of the Land Reform Pilot Program in the PSUs sampled, none of the redistributed land was previously owned by the state, nor were any of the transactions supported by government grants (Table 6.3). Most (80 percent) of the sellers were owner-operators, but one farm had previously been registered to a corporate entity. Four of the five farms were purchased (the remaining farm was inherited). The average area transferred was 107 hectares and the average purchase price exceeded R211,000 (or about US$63,940 at the 1995 exchange rate of 3.30 rands to US$1). Although two of the farms were subdivisions (parts of larger farms), the lowest price paid was R130,000 (some US$39,394). Given our experience that most emerging farmers have equity capital considerably less than R130,000, these figures are evidence, albeit limited, of the adverse effect that the farm size provisions in the Subdivision Act have on land affordability.

Only one of the five new owners was registered as a corporate entity (a closed corporation), and the business had a single shareholder. There was no evidence in this small sample of purchase by legally constituted groups of disadvantaged people. However, as Table 6.4 shows, this does not imply that the sample farms were occupied and operated by just one household, or that other households had not acquired de facto rights to the land.

Although cropland was used exclusively by the individual new owners, other households had been permitted to use grazing and residential land on two of the farms. In one of these cases (the inherited farm), grazing land was used as an open access resource. In addition, two of the five owners reported that some land had been occupied for residential purposes without their consent. Illegal occupants and inclusive use rights tend to withdraw land from the market because potential buyers and lessees face additional transaction costs and risks (Feder et al. 1988:45). This lowers both the market and the collateral value of land, reducing the owner's incentive and ability to finance investments (Feder et al. 1988:49; Barrows and Roth 1990; Pasour 1990:204).

Taken together, the 5 sample farms were used by 10 households (excluding hired labor and managers): 3 farms were operated by individuals; 2 were

TABLE 6.4 Land use and de facto property rights observed on farms acquired by disadvantaged respondents, 1995

Land Use	Owner Uses Land Exclusively	Owner Leases Land to Tenants	Owner Allocated Land to Individuals	Owner Allocated Land to a Group	Land Used without Consent	Total Area (hectares)
Cropland						
Hectares	30.6	...	...	...	...	30.6
Cases ($n = 2$)	100%	...	...	...	...	...
Grazing						
Hectares	15.8	...	...	50.8	...	66.6
Cases ($n = 5$)	60%	...	...	40%	...	...
Forest						
Hectares	3.0	...	...	...	...	3.0
Cases ($n = 1$)	100%	...	...	...	...	...
Residential (hectares)	0.8	0.2	1.0	...	1.7	3.7
Waste (hectares)	...	...	...	...	...	2.9
Total (hectares)	50.2	0.2	1.0	50.8	1.7	106.8

NOTE: $N = 5$.

TABLE 6.5 Property rights to land and tenure security

Households' Property Rights Regimes	No Tenure Security	Low Tenure Security	High Tenure Security
Exclusive land rights (percent)	0	0	100
Common property rights (percent)	100	0	0
Open access rights (percent)	75	25	0

NOTES: $N = 8$. Likelihood ratio chi-square = 11.09 with 4 degrees of freedom (significant at the 3 percent level of probability).

used by more than one household. All of the users were contacted but only eight agreed to provide information. None of the sample households had invested in fixed improvements to agricultural land. However, four (50 percent) had built homes on the residential parts of the farms. The average value of residential improvements was R16,263 (US$4,928) and two of the four investors used loans to finance construction of their homes. This pattern of investment was not unexpected, because only a short period had elapsed since the land acquisition.

Table 6.5 draws a comparison between individual property rights to land and tenure security, where tenure security is measured by an index of transfer rights. Households that did not have rights to sell, lease out, or bequeath their farmland, and that did not possess a current title deed or rental contract scored a value of 0 on the index (no tenure security). Households that claimed all of these transfer rights scored the maximum value of 4 (high tenure security) if their rights were supported by a current title deed.

The index measuring tenure security is positively correlated with the value of fixed improvements made to land during 1995 (partial correlation coefficient, $r = .42$) and with the use of loans to finance investment ($r = .59$). This is consistent with the view that tenure security improves both the incentive and the ability to invest. Obviously a much larger sample is needed to explore the relationships between tenure security and investment in fixed improvements more fully.

Table 6.6 summarizes information about loans used to finance the land bought by respondents. Financing the purchase of land represents a formidable challenge for the poor. In this sample, all the purchases were partially financed with long-term mortgage loans. Two of the four loans were granted by sources other than financial institutions. Nevertheless, all of the loan agreements were formal contracts and the borrowers received regular statements.

On average, the buyers were relatively wealthy compared with most of the rural poor and were able to finance 70 percent of the purchase price from equity capital. Even so, the loan installments (based on a current nominal annual interest rate of about 16 percent) are high relative to current earnings from farming. In South Africa, the annual rent earned by farmland is roughly 5 percent of its market value (Nieuwoudt 1987). Not surprisingly, all four borrowers in the

TABLE 6.6 Loan details for farms purchased by disadvantaged respondents in 1995

Loan Details	Mean
Farms purchased with a mortgage loan (percent)	100.0
Mortgage loans provided by a financial institution (percent)	50.0
Mortgage loans provided by employers and moneylenders (percent)	50.0
Average purchase price (rand)	211,250
Average loan amount requested (rand)	65,833
Average loan amount received (rand)	62,500
Current interest rate (percent per annum)	16.0
Average loan term (years)	22.5
Average monthly installments (rand)	783
Borrowers who signed a formal loan agreement (percent)	100.0
Borrowers who received regular statements (percent)	100.0

NOTES: $N = 4$. For US\$ equivalent values, assume current exchange rate of R3.30 to US\$1.

sample were able to draw on off-farm incomes to supplement their cash flow during the critical early years after purchase.

Mortgage payments can create serious repayment problems for emerging farmers with limited equity capital and off-farm income. During periods of inflation, when nominal interest rates rise, conventional mortgage loans amortized with constant annual repayments (which consist of increasing principal portions and decreasing interest portions) create formidable liquidity problems over time. The reason is that these farmers are unable to make a substantial downpayment on the purchase price of land and so become heavily leveraged by borrowing most of the funds needed for purchase. Mortgage loan repayments at a high nominal annual interest rate (such as the 16 percent reported in Table 6.6) that is well above the current annual rate of return to farmland (roughly 5 percent) then create a cash-flow shortfall, particularly in the early years after purchase. This shortfall diminishes over time if inflation raises the nominal value of annual returns to farmland relative to the annual nominal debt repayments. A possible solution to the liquidity problem, therefore, is to allow borrowers to make graduated annual repayments that increase in size over time as their ability to repay increases. One way of facilitating graduated payments is to subsidize nominal interest charges at a decreasing rate over a finite period of time, while maintaining nominal principal payments (Nieuwoudt and Vink 1995). The experience of the KFC and two major local sugar-milling companies in using this method is described in the next section.

Experience with an Innovative Financing Scheme to Purchase Farmland

An innovative financing scheme was developed in KwaZulu-Natal when local sugar millers, who hold and farm relatively large areas of land, decided to sell

commercial sugarcane land in order to invest in higher-value downstream activities, help redistribute land, and promote the small business sector. Other
motives for this apparently benevolent decision might have been to reduce exposure to labor disputes and to safeguard against a perceived threat of land
expropriation. The intention was to sell a number of "medium-scale" sugarcane
farms to emerging black farmers, conditional on long-term cane supply agreements (25 years). The scheme thus provided a means to sell off land without
markedly reducing the supply of sugarcane to capital-intensive mills. Applicants with the potential expertise to run a farm business were selected in consultation with the communities in which the farmers lived.

When one of the millers invited applications for the first 20 farms (ranging from 55 hectares to 105 hectares) in 1996, none of the more than 100 applicants could afford to make a down-payment large enough to reduce the size of
a conventional mortgage loan to a level that could be serviced from current farm
income. To mitigate this problem, the miller agreed to sell the land at market-
related prices to the applicants but to invest 18.0 percent of the proceeds with
Ithala Bank (owned by the KwaZulu Finance and Investment Corporation).
This capital, and the interest accrued, would then fund a finite, decreasing annual interest rate subsidy for the first 6 years of the 20-year mortgage loans that
the borrowers obtained from the KFC. The rationale was that this would reduce
the buyers' cash-flow stress in the early years of land purchase, because the
resulting gradual rise in annual interest charges would be offset by higher nominal annual farm incomes driven by expected inflation and expected improvements in productivity over time (Simms 1997a). In effect, the miller discounted
the price of the land by 18.0 percent and the KFC used part of these (private
sector) funds to reduce (subsidize) its nominal mortgage loan rate in 1996 from
16.5 percent to 10.0 percent for the first year of the loan scheme. Over years two
to six, the borrowers would pay interest at an annual loan rate that increased
at the same rate as the expected annual rate of inflation—namely 10.0 percent—
based on Consumer Price Index (CPI) trends and the expectations of KFC
personnel. That is, the borrowers would be charged 11.0 percent in year two (a
10.0 percent increase on 10.0 percent), 12.1 percent in year three (a 10.0 percent increase on 11.0 percent), and so on until year six when the rate would be
16.1 percent. Over these six years, the remaining capital and interest accrued
with Ithala Bank would fund the gradually decreasing annual difference (subsidy) between 16.5 percent and the adjusted interest rate. Thereafter, the buyers
pay the full nominal mortgage interest rate of 16.5 percent per annum for the
remaining 14 years of the 20-year loan.

The scheme thus provides the borrowers and the KFC with a known, graduated schedule of loan repayments. This financing scheme was also adopted by
the second miller in cooperation with the KFC. The nominal mortgage rate of
16.5 percent reflects the KFC's costs of capital and administration costs in
1996, and is higher than the 16.0 percent loan interest rate reported in Table 6.6

because interest rates in South Africa rose after the farm surveys were conducted in 1995. The nominal mortgage rate will change only if the KFC's costs of capital change; this is unlikely in the medium term because the KFC has used long-term fixed interest rate loans to fund its contribution to the scheme. Although there is no prescribed ceiling interest rate, the KFC is reluctant to exceed 17.0 percent at the time of writing, as this would create liquidity problems for many of its clients (Simms 1997b).

Since 1996, the scheme has financed 90 "medium-scale" beneficiaries in KwaZulu-Natal, redistributing 10,461 hectares of commercial farmland with a market value of R81 million (about US$25 million). These figures reflect an average market price of a medium-scale sugarcane farm of some R900,000. To illustrate the mechanics of the scheme, 18.0 percent of this market price, or R162,000, would be invested by the KFC to finance a diminishing interest rate subsidy on the mortgage loan. The buyer would face the full purchase price, on which a down-payment of at least 10.0 percent (R90,000) is required. The KFC then provides a mortgage loan for the balance of R810,000 and the seller (miller) receives a net amount of R738,000 (R900,000 less R162,000) for the land.

For a conventional equally amortized mortgage loan of R810,000 with a nominal annual interest rate of 16.5 percent over 20 years, the equal annual amortization payment is R140,180. In year one, R133,650 of this payment would be nominal interest (16.5 percent on R810,000) and R6,530 would be nominal principal repayment. However, with the interest subsidy financed out of the R162,000 investment, the buyer actually pays R81,000 interest (10.0 percent on R810,000), a reduction of R52,650, while the nominal principal payment remains R6,530. By year four, when the buyer would usually pay R129,855 nominal interest on an outstanding nominal loan principal of R787,000, the actual nominal interest payment is R104,671, reflecting an annual interest rate of about 13.3 percent and a subsidy of R25,184. The balance of the required R140,180 installment is again used to repay (unsubsidized) nominal principal as per the conventional schedule. By year six, the annual nominal interest due is R126,167, compared with an actual payment of some R123,108—the rest of the R140,180 installment being nominal principal repaid.

From year seven onward, the buyer is scheduled to pay the nominal interest amount calculated at the original 16.5 percent annual interest rate, and there is no interest subsidy. Each year of the 20-year loan, the nominal principal portion of the equal annual amortization payment increases as per the conventional equally amortized mortgage schedule, and no part of the principal is subsidized. If the original capital amount of R162,000 invested to finance the subsidy, plus the interest thereon, is not exhausted after year six, the surplus funds are added to the final interest subsidy payment, unless the client is meeting scheduled payments well. In this case, the surplus funds remain in the Ithala Bank account to supplement future debt repayments in years when cash flows deteriorate.

Clearly, the transaction described above would be confined to relatively wealthier buyers who could make a R90,000 down-payment and use farm earnings to finance annual (subsidized) interest payments starting around R81,000 and rising to about R123,000 over six years, plus principal. The scheme has focused on buyers with these characteristics because the millers insisted that land be sold to full-time farmers and that the farm sizes represent the minimum area needed to service debt and sustain a family based on expected earnings. In addition, farms of this size would increase the potential for economies of size in spreading the largely fixed subdivision and transaction costs associated with transferring ownership. Rural finance personnel at KFC estimate annual earnings for these farms using expected yield, sugarcane prices forecast by the South African Sugar Association, and production cost estimates obtained from grower surveys made by the South African Cane Growers' Association (SACGA). Established and emerging farmers receive the same annual price for their sugarcane crops. This price is set according to a complex "division of proceeds" formula that is used to allocate the revenue from industry product sales between growers and millers.

Buyers have a number of incentives to participate in the scheme. First, they can purchase farmland with debt capital that they probably would otherwise not qualify for in terms of conventional mortgage loans. Second, they acquire freehold title to land (full, exclusive, and transferable rights), and are therefore able to realize capital gains by selling the property (in which case the unused portion of the interest subsidy would benefit the next disadvantaged buyer). Third, they have good reason to feel confident about future prospects because the KFC—which is exposed to the risks of their operations—has helped them to develop business plans. Finally, the new entrants can rely on financial monitoring and advice from the KFC and other support services funded by the South African sugar industry. Technical advice is supplied by the millers, by mentors (successful neighboring commercial farmers), and by the South African Sugar Extension Service; training is offered by the Small Grower Trust; and the SACGA provides a bookkeeping service.

The scheme offers the KFC four major financial advantages. First, the subsidy provided by the millers reduces the risk exposure because it helps to alleviate client cash-flow stress. Second, the KFC finances individual owner-operators rather than groups of co-owners, thereby avoiding the costs of registering and organizing creditworthy groups. Third, the mortgage loan is secured by the collateral value of land. Finally, loan repayments can be recovered directly from the millers before the farmers are paid for their sugarcane.

One major drawback of the scheme is that the graduated payments are fixed and make no formal allowance for random variations in borrower cash flows. These disruptions have not yet been experienced because the first three years of the scheme were characterized by good rains and favorable growing conditions. The KFC has attempted to reduce its exposure to this problem by insisting that farmers use private crop insurance to insure their sugarcane crops against damages caused by fire and acts of God. In addition, the KFC will consider extending loan maturities and rescheduling payments for clients with legitimate cash-flow problems. Farmers who appear to have no hope of financial success will be encouraged to sell their farms to other medium-scale farmers (preferably their more successful neighbors, or other disadvantaged buyers) to avoid repossession. If the farm sale price exceeds the outstanding loan balance, the seller receives the difference. Any unused (subsidy) balance in the Ithala Bank account is applied to the new mortgage loan unless the new buyer can make a substantial equity contribution, in which case the unused funds go to the seller. A second problem is that the interest rate subsidies may be capitalized into higher land values, making it more difficult for later emerging farmers to purchase land. This distortion may be less serious than first perceived because the scheme ensures that the subsidies are finite and do not become entrenched.

Another early problem was the protracted process of subdividing 3 large farms into the first 20 medium-sized operations financed by the scheme. Instead of delaying occupation until this had been achieved and transfer took place, the new farmers took occupation under contract to the miller, which enabled them to build up some working capital. After three years, albeit of relatively good rains and favorable growing conditions, only 3 out of 90 farmers were in arrears on graduated payments. The major problems with the project have been facilitative, in terms of difficulties in setting up financial information systems, training, and contractor services for harvesting and cane haulage (Simms 1997a). Similar future projects should not, therefore, underestimate the time taken by "new" entrants to adapt to the demands of managing viable commercial farms. Economists at the SACGA are also concerned that several farmers are meeting their debt obligations at the expense of reinvestment in fertilizer and seedcane (Chadwick 1997). This may indicate that the debt burden under inflationary conditions remains relatively high for these full-time, medium-scale farmers, and that the scheme could be amended to enable part-time farmers with off-farm income to participate. The financing of part-time emerging farmers on smaller farms than currently required by the scheme is another option to reduce initial capital demands and cash-flow stress.

Conclusions

The sampling techniques tested in the pilot survey produced useful information about the rate of land redistribution in KwaZulu-Natal and its implications for land use. Preliminary findings emphasize the relative importance of private market transactions as a means of redistributing commercial farmland, and suggest that meaningful redistribution will not occur unless much more is done to broaden access to the land market. In particular, the government should expedite the subdivision of agricultural land, and consider including innovative financial products in its own range of land redistribution programs in KwaZulu-Natal and other parts of South Africa.

Experience in KwaZulu-Natal with a mortgage loan scheme involving graduated (increasing) repayments and finite interest subsidies (financed by private companies) over time suggests that the scheme successfully improved access to land by emerging farmers who would not qualify for more conventional types of loan finance. Given the incentives for sugar millers and the KwaZulu Finance and Investment Corporation to participate in the scheme, and the South African sugar industry's capacity to support emerging farmers, it is not surprising that the scheme was initiated with emerging sugarcane farmers. Although relatively wealthier emerging farmers have benefited to date, the scheme could be extended by selling smaller farms to poorer part-time farmers with adequate off-farm income to fund debt repayments (particularly in the early years after purchase). In addition, the government could replicate the basic principles of the scheme by redirecting some cash grant funds into a (finite) diminishing interest rate subsidy scheme for emerging farmers. This could leverage substantial financial and human resources from private lending institutions and other private sector companies in KwaZulu-Natal and other parts of South Africa. The problems of managing variability in farm income, the impact on land values and land access if interest subsidies become entrenched, and the provision of services and training for emerging farmers would need to be addressed.

Lender involvement would also guard against (weak) institutional arrangements that might compromise the collateral value of redistributed land by withdrawing it from the market. It is significant that the open access conditions reported in this study were encountered only on the farm that was not debt financed. More research is needed to evaluate whether equity share schemes in the Western Cape have been successful, and whether these types of schemes could improve access to land by emerging farmers in KwaZulu-Natal and other areas in South Africa.

References

AID (Agency for International Development). 1986. *Land tenure policy determination*. Policy Determination No. 13. Washington, D.C.: Agency for International Development.

Barrows, R., and M. Roth. 1990. Land tenure and investment in African agriculture: Theory and evidence. *Journal of Modern African Studies* 28: 265–297.

Chadwick, J. 1997. Personal communication. Director, Grower Services, South African Cane Growers' Association, Durban, Republic of South Africa.

Department of Land Affairs. 1994. *Land reform pilot program: Program overview*. Pretoria, Republic of South Africa.

Feder, G., T. Onchan, Y. Chalamuong, and C. Hongladaron. 1988. *Land policies and farm productivity in Thailand*. Baltimore, Md., U.S.A.: Johns Hopkins University Press.

Johnson, O. E. G. 1972. Economic analysis: The legal framework and land tenure. *Journal of Law and Economics* 15: 259–276.

Kirsten, J. F., J. van Rooyen, and S. Ngqangweni. 1996. Progress with different land reform options in South Africa. *Agrekon* 35 (4): 218–223.

Lyne, M. C., and D. H. Graham. 2001. The impact of land redistribution on tenure security and agricultural performance in KwaZulu-Natal. *Agrekon* 40 (4): 656–668.

Nieuwoudt, W. L. 1987. Taxing agricultural land. *Agrekon* 26 (1): 10–14.

Nieuwoudt, W. L., and N. Vink. 1995. Financing of land purchase by small-scale farmers. *Development Southern Africa* 12 (4): 509–517.

Pasour, E. C. 1990. *Agriculture and the state: Market processes and bureaucracy.* New York: Holmes & Meier.

Simms, P. 1997a. Land redistribution in South Africa—some practical lessons. In *Proceedings of the 11th International Farm Management Congress*, Vol. 1, July 14–19, Calgary, Canada, ed. L. Bauer. Olds, Alberta, Canada: International Farm Management Association and the Canadian Farm Business Management Council.

Simms, P. 1997b. Personal communication. Manager, Rural Development, KwaZulu Finance and Investment Corporation, Durban, Republic of South Africa.

World Bank. 1993. Options for land reform and rural restructuring in South Africa. Unpublished report. Southern Africa Department, Washington, D.C.

PART II

Outreach and Financial Sustainability of Institutions

7 Outreach and Sustainability of Member-Based Rural Financial Intermediaries

JULIA PAXTON AND CARLOS E. CUEVAS

Scholars, donors, and practitioners have increasingly recognized that the sustainable provision of formal or semi-formal financial services to the poor and other sectors of the population is a useful tool in poverty alleviation, enterprise development, and financial-sector deepening. Although the majority of clients served by the formal financial sector in developing countries tend to be upper-class, urban, educated males, some financial intermediaries have attempted to encompass a wider clientele by operating in more isolated, rural areas. As a result of the information asymmetries and high transaction costs associated with financial intermediation in rural areas, member-based institutions such as credit unions and village banks have evolved as a mechanism to transfer the high costs of screening, monitoring, and evaluation from an external financial intermediary to the village level.

This chapter analyzes the degree to which member-based institutions reach a segment of the population that does not traditionally participate in the formal or semi-formal financial system (including low-income, illiterate, rural clients, and women) and the degree to which their depth of outreach is correlated with institutional dependence on external subsidies. The analysis focuses on measures of sustainability and outreach, as well as their interrelatedness, in relation to three credit unions and two village banking programs in Latin America.[1] The credit unions in the study are Unión Popular in Guatemala, Cupocrédito in Colombia, and the Workers' Center of the Education Credit Union (OSCUS) in Ecuador. The village banking programs are FINCA (Foundation for International Community Assistance) Costa Rica and CARE Guatemala. The contrast between the two member-based approaches is highlighted throughout the analysis.

---

1. The five case studies were prepared for the World Bank's "Sustainable Banking with the Poor" (SBP) project.

Background

In order to examine the outreach and performance of these member-based institutions, a brief description of the context in which they operate is useful. Three of the institutions are in Central America (two in Guatemala and one in Costa Rica), and the other two are in South America (Colombia and Ecuador). Although similar in some respects, several notable contrasts become evident when examining the country contexts and when the rural environments in which the institutions operate are explained.

The Country Context

The countries of Colombia, Costa Rica, Ecuador, and Guatemala differ from one another as well as from other regions of the world in several ways. Table 7.1 compares the general socioeconomic conditions of these countries with those in East Asia and the Pacific, South Asia, and Sub-Saharan Africa.

On average, these countries are wealthier than many countries in other parts of the developing world. Their annual per capita growth of gross national product (0.9 to 2.8 percent) is not as impressive as that in some Asian and Pacific countries, but is far superior to the average for Sub-Saharan Africa. With the exception of Guatemala, the adult illiteracy rates of these Latin American countries are below the other regional averages. However, these Latin American countries experienced high average inflation rates for the period 1984 to 1994. Inflation rates were particularly high during the 1980s but decreased significantly in the 1990s.

Costa Rica stands out among these four countries. Not only is its GNP per capita of US$2,400 significantly higher than that of the other three countries, but it has the highest growth rate, lowest inflation rate, and lowest adult illiteracy rate. The economy of Guatemala performed the worst of the countries studied. Its GNP per capita and GNP growth rate are the lowest of the four Latin American countries, while its adult illiteracy rate is more than four times that of the other countries.

The Gini index provides an indicator of income inequality within a country. Guatemala stands out as having a highly unequal income distribution, with a Gini coefficient of 0.59. Colombia also has a high measure of 0.51. Both Costa Rica and Ecuador have somewhat more equitable income distributions, averaging 0.46.

The Rural Context

Table 7.1 shows that the population density per hectare for Colombia, Costa Rica, Ecuador, and Guatemala is lower than the averages for the Asian and Pacific regions of the world. Colombia and Ecuador have especially low population densities (31.9 and 39.4, respectively), while Costa Rica has a population density of 64.7 and Guatemala has a population density of 94.5. In addition,

TABLE 7.1 Comparison of socioeconomic characteristics of case-study countries and other developing regions

Characteristic	Costa Rica	Guatemala	Colombia	Ecuador	East Asia and Pacific	South Asia	Sub-Saharan Africa
1994 GNP per capita (US$)	2,400	1,200	1,670	1,280	460	860	320
Gini index	46.1	59.6	51.3	46.6	n.a.	n.a.	n.a.
Average annual GNP / capita growth, 1985–94 (percent)	2.8	0.9	2.4	0.9	6.9	2.7	–1.2
Average annual inflation, 1984–94 (percent)	18.2	19.5	25.6	47.5	n.a.	n.a.	n.a.
Adult illiteracy, 1995 (percent)	5	44	9	10	17	50	43
Population density per hectare	64.7	94.5	31.9	39.4	106.0	237.7	23.6
Share of population that is rural (percent)	51	59	38	43	68	74	69

SOURCE: World Bank (1996).

NOTE: n.a. means not available.

each of these countries is mountainous (with Costa Rica being the least mountainous), and the rugged terrain makes it difficult and time-consuming to reach rural areas because, often, the access roads are not well maintained.

The rural infrastructure is underdeveloped in Latin America, with a lower incidence of clean water, health services, education, and formal financial services than in urban centers. Most of the rural people work in agriculture-related industries that are inherently risky because of variations in climate and international prices. It is not surprising that a marked rural exodus to the large cities has occurred. In 1970, 43 percent of the Latin American population lived in rural areas; by 1999 the figure was only 25 percent. The countries in this study have a greater rural population than the Latin American average. Colombia is the most urban (only 38 percent of its population live in rural areas), followed by Ecuador (43 percent) and Costa Rica (51 percent). The majority of the Guatemalan population (59 percent) live in rural areas.

Formal financial services, especially from commercial banks, often are not well developed in the rural areas of Latin America, and those that exist largely target an upper-income clientele. The financial services offered to low- and middle-income clients tend to come from informal sources such as commercial credit, moneylenders, rotating savings and credit associations (ROSCAs), and friends and family. However, member-based institutions, including credit unions and village banks, have had some success in reaching marginalized rural clients.

Rural Member-Based Financial Intermediaries: Village Banking versus Credit Unions

Both village banking and credit unions have a member-based structure, which has several advantages. A large urban-based bank may not possess sufficient information regarding the creditworthiness of rural clients to make good financial decisions. Member-based institutions often can overcome these information asymmetries through a greater understanding of the local context and its residents. The use of village-level knowledge about potential members helps to reduce screening, monitoring, and evaluation costs.

Although membership is a key component of both village banking and credit unions, they differ in several ways. Credit unions are owned by members through the holding of equity shares. All members have savings in some form, resulting in a "savings-first" focus, a characteristic that differentiates credit unions from the growing number of "credit-first" (Graham 1994) programs throughout the world that do not emphasize or offer savings facilities. A large volume of internally generated funds is on-lent to members through individual loans. Typically, the legal status of credit unions is as nonprofit institutions operating as cooperative financial organizations that may or may not be regulated by the banking superintendency. Decisions regarding leadership, rules, and conditions are made by the members on the basis of one-person, one-vote, although in some cases (such as Cupocrédito) not all members are voting members. Ultimate control of the credit union is left to the member-owners who form the General Assembly, but the daily operations are run by a management staff.

Village banking was developed in the 1980s by a number of international nongovernmental organizations (NGOs) such as FINCA International, CARE, and ActionAid. The original method called for the formation of self-managed peer lending groups that would receive external loans at first and then gradually mobilize internal savings to self-capitalize operations so that autonomy would be reached in three years. This concept of graduation, however, was replaced in the 1990s in favor of an ongoing relationship between the village banks and the external source of funding (for example, FINCA). Some of the general characteristics of village banking include mandatory savings in order to receive loans, blockage of credit to the entire village bank if even one person does not repay, the possibility of on-lending the savings held in an internal account, and standardized and simultaneous loan terms.

The village banking method has been adapted in many different ways. The heterogeneity of the approach is evident in the contrast between CARE Guatemala and FINCA Costa Rica. In general, FINCA Costa Rica follows a minimalist approach that focuses solely on the provision of financial services, whereas CARE Guatemala has a more comprehensive approach, including a greater emphasis on training and enterprise development. FINCA Costa Rica serves a rural clientele that is largely educated and male, and with prior experience with agricultural loans. In addition, a more developed legal system has allowed for legal recourse in the case of default. These conditions have allowed FINCA Costa Rica to offer strictly individual loans. In contrast, CARE Guatemala serves less-educated rural women without prior experience with formal finance. No legal remedies are available to pursue delinquent loans in rural Guatemala. In order to serve this market niche, CARE Guatemala has found it necessary to provide more training and to block additional credit to the village if even one woman defaults, thus relying on peer pressure and solidarity as enforcement mechanisms.

Table 7.2 compares some of the basic characteristics of the five member-based institutions studied. The credit unions have been in operation for several decades, in contrast to the village banks, which were founded in the 1980s. In addition, both of the village banking programs serve fewer than 10,000 clients, whereas the credit unions serve between 10,000 and 388,000 clients. The village banking programs have a lower average loan size as a percentage of per capita GDP, with CARE Guatemala standing out as offering the smallest loans, averaging only US$171 or 14 percent of per capita GDP. The provision of micro-level financial services by village banks is not surprising, given that the original village banking method was developed to provide financial services to the very poor. In contrast, the credit unions serve a wider range of socioeconomic levels within a community—the poor, the middle class, and the relatively wealthy.

TABLE 7.2 Basic characteristics of case-study institutions

	Village Banks		Credit Unions		
Characteristic	FINCA Costa Rica	CARE Guatemala	Unión Popular	Cupocrédito	OSCUS
Year founded	1984	1989	1972	1960	1963
Country	Costa Rica	Guatemala	Guatemala	Colombia	Ecuador
Number of clients	7,253	4,090	10,732	387,846	55,457
Average loan size (US$)	1,006	171	1,079	2,199	954
Average loan term (months)	24	6	36	15	24
Average loan as share of per capita GDP	0.42	0.14	0.90	1.32	0.75
Average deposit size (US$)	25	53	204	217	149
Average savings as share of per capita GDP	0.01	0.04	0.17	0.13	0.12
Average equity shares (US$)	150	0	53	226	59
Growth of loan portfolio (percent per year)	16	71	43	27	36

SOURCES: SBP case studies; 1995 data for FINCA, CARE, and Cupocrédito; 1996 data for Unión Popular and OSCUS.

Not only do the village banks offer smaller loans, but their loans have shorter terms, on average, than those of the credit unions. In many respects, FINCA Costa Rica is an anomaly among village banking programs in that it offers larger loans with longer terms than do other village banking institutions. In addition, some of the village banks formed by FINCA Costa Rica offer the option of purchasing equity shares, a feature more characteristic of credit unions.

On the deposit side, village banks typically require savings before a loan can be attained. Although voluntary saving is a growing phenomenon in village banking, most of the deposits are linked to access to credit and few members are solely depositors. Therefore, it is not surprising that the average deposit size for the village banking programs is quite small. In credit unions, it is more common for members to choose to save without requesting credit.

Outreach

Von Pischke (1991) describes a frontier between the formal and informal financial sectors. Those outside the frontier do not have regular access to formal financial services. They comprise a heterogeneous population, whose degree of exclusion from financial services may vary and whose distance from the poverty line (in either direction) in their respective countries may differ (Hulme and Mosely 1996). In measuring institutional outreach, it is important to distinguish between the *extent* (or breadth) and the *depth* of outreach. The extent of outreach is represented by the absolute number of households or enterprises (or relative market penetration) in the target population reached by the institution; the depth of outreach indicates how deep into the pool of the underserved the institution or program has been able to reach.

Depth of Outreach Index (DOI)

In developing countries, most formal and semi-formal financial institutions consistently do not serve several categories of people. These categories, which are usually positively correlated to some degree, include (but are not restricted to) the poor, women, rural inhabitants, and the uneducated.

THE POOR. Formal financial intermediaries experience relatively high transaction costs when dealing with very poor people because of the tiny size of each financial transaction. For instance, the cost of offering savings facilities to clients who make frequent small deposits can be quite high. The same applies for very small loans, which require as much administrative support as larger loans in formal financial institutions but generate little revenue, resulting in losses.

WOMEN. Women have been excluded from formal financial services for a variety of reasons. Perhaps foremost is a cultural bias against women. At the household level, most financial decisions have been made by male heads of household, although this cultural norm is shifting gradually. In addition, many of the poorest people in developing countries are women, and their microenterprises and petty trade are too small scale to interest formal financial intermediaries. Finally, literacy requirements have barred some illiterate women from obtaining formal financial services. Microfinance institutions have targeted women not only because of their exclusion from formal finance, but also because they spend a greater percentage of their share of household income on food, children's clothes, education, and health than men do, as several studies have demonstrated (Hopkins, Levin, and Haddad 1994).

RURAL INHABITANTS. Formal financial intermediaries have avoided rural areas because of the high transaction costs associated with serving a predominantly dispersed population and the high risk associated with agriculture. Government-sponsored programs that offer rural credit have had disappointing results because of their reliance on subsidized interest rates, inappropriate terms and conditions, a lack of repayment enforcement, and corruption.

THE UNEDUCATED. People who cannot read and write face an obvious obstacle in obtaining financial services that require any type of written application or paperwork. Microfinance institutions have served the illiterate by adopting innovative techniques, including oral training and screening, pictorial training, group guarantees, and use of thumbprint signatures.

We use these categories (poor, female, rural, and illiterate) to define and measure a *depth of outreach indicator* (DOI) for the institutions under analysis. The categories were chosen not only for their association with the degree of exclusion from financial services, but also for their relative ease of measurement in simple, rapid-appraisal surveys of program clienteles. Other variables (such as ethnicity or national origin) could be used in different scenarios, depending upon the factors perceived as determining exclusion. Given the likely correlation between the variables in the DOI, many people fall into several or all of the categories.

To analyze the degree to which financial institutions serve rural, female, poor, and illiterate clients, depth of outreach diamonds can be constructed. These diamonds provide a simple graphic representation of the four outreach indicators for the clients of microfinance institutions and compare them with overall country averages. Three of the variables (urban, male, and literate) are percentages calculated on a 0 to 1 scale. Rather than using GDP per capita as a measure of country-level income, the more appropriate measure of GDP divided by the economically active (EA) population was used. This measure was normalized to 1.00 for the country average. The income of the clients was put on the same scale by dividing the average income of the clients by the country-level income. Using this approach, smaller diamonds reflect a greater depth of outreach.

The DOI sums the differences between the institutional outreach average and the country averages for each category of people frequently excluded from formal finance. A positive number indicates that the institution serves a clientele that is more rural, poor, female, and illiterate than the country average. Although not a perfect measure of outreach, the DOI improves on traditional outreach proxies such as loan size because it incorporates several outreach indicators and takes country averages into account. In addition, its simple graphic nature and use of easily available data make it a practical, intuitive measure for cross-institutional analysis.

Depth of Outreach in the Five Case Studies

The DOI is used to examine the outreach of the village banks compared with the credit unions in this study. Measures of the degree to which these institutions serve poor, female, rural, illiterate clients were compared with the percentage share of these categories in the general population of the country (Figure 7.1). The most important finding from this analysis is that the village banking clients are more rural, female, poor, and illiterate than the country average, whereas credit unions tend to serve more literate, urban males. In terms of reaching underserved portions of the population, village banking appears to have a deeper outreach when examining the average clients of the institutions. This point is illustrated in Figure 7.1: the outreach diamond for village banks falls inside the corresponding country average diamond, whereas the credit union

FIGURE 7.1 Average outreach of village banks and credit unions

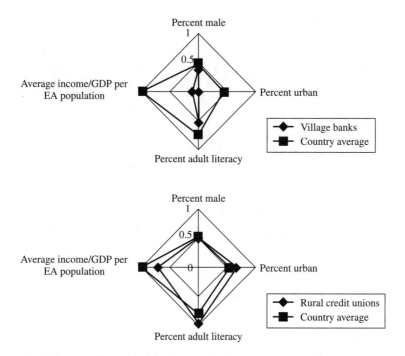

SOURCE: SBP case studies; original data from institutions.

outreach is largely outside the country average, with the exception that credit unions serve clients with incomes slightly below the GDP per economically active person. Table 7.3 provides the outreach data used to construct the depth of outreach diamonds and the DOI.

Sustainability

Although it is clear that the average clients served by village banks are further beyond the traditional financial frontier than are credit union clients, it is important to examine the extent to which these institutions are sustainable. Table 7.4 provides various measures of sustainability and efficiency for each of the five institutions.

Perhaps one of the most comprehensive indicators of sustainability is the Subsidy Dependence Index (SDI) (Yaron 1992). The SDI measures the percentage by which interest rates charged to clients would have to be increased hypothetically in order to cover program costs and eliminate subsidies. The SDI measures for credit unions are close to zero, indicating self-sufficiency without

TABLE 7.3 Outreach indicators

Measure	Costa Rica		Guatemala				Colombia		Ecuador	
	FINCA	Country Average	CARE	Country Average	Unión Popular	Country Average	Cupocrédito	Country Average	OSCUS	Country Average
Percentage male (0–1 scale)	0.74	0.50	0.00	0.50	0.60	0.50	0.59	0.50	0.50	0.50
Percentage urban (0–1 scale)	0.00	0.49	0.00	0.41	0.25	0.41	0.49	0.72	0.60	0.57
Adult literacy rate, 1995 (0–1 scale)	0.84	0.95	0.22	0.56	0.85	0.56	0.95	0.91	0.95	1.00
Income / GNP per economically active population[a]	0.17	1.00	0.06	1.00	1.1	1.00	0.88	1.00	0.59	1.00
Depth of Outreach Indicator[b]	1.19	...	2.19	...	−0.33	...	0.22	...	0.43	...

[a] Population aged 15–64.

[b] DOI – $(rur_i - rur_c) + (inc_i - inc_c) + (fem_i - fem_c) + (illit_i - illit_c)$, where i = institutional average and c = country average.

TABLE 7.4 Sustainability indicators

Indicator	Village Banks		Credit Unions		
	FINCA Costa Rica	CARE Guatemala[a]	Unión Popular	Cupocrédito	OSCUS
Subsidy Dependence Index	1.39	4.77	0.03	0.12	−0.03
Operational self-sufficiency[b]	1.44	0.29	2.12	2.35	2.75
Financial self-sufficiency[c]	1.08	...	1.11	1.14	1.19
Arrears rate (percent)	7.59	0.00	5.00	2.37	n.a.
Portfolio at risk (percent)	18.31	0.00	6.50	22.00	12.00
Real effective interest rates (percent)	55.00	38.25	19.51	12.88	11.04
Volume savings / volume of loans outstanding	0.05	0.09	1.37	1.18	0.91
Loan officer salary / per capita GNP	2.30	3.10	2.70	3.23	2.05

SOURCES: SBP case studies; 1995 data for FINCA, CARE, and Cupocrédito; 1996 data for Unión Popular and OSCUS.

NOTES: The leader dots indicate a nil or negligible amount; n.a. means not available.

[a] All funds used by CARE are grants.

[b] Operational income divided by operational costs.

[c] Operational income divided by operational costs + financial costs.

a dependence on external subsidies. The village banking programs, in contrast, would have to more than double interest rates in order to operate without subsidies. In the case of CARE Guatemala, a heavy reliance on subsidies results in an SDI measure of 477 percent. It is not surprising that CARE Guatemala also shows operational and financial self-sufficiency ratios of less than 1.[2] Across the board, credit unions have higher ratios of operational and financial self-sufficiency.

One of the most interesting findings in the comparison of credit unions and village banks is that the village banks charge higher real effective interest rates. The nominal interest rates charged by village banks are sometimes misleading, because they are quoted as flat rates. Membership and application fees, as well as the requirement of mandatory savings, contribute to an elevated effective interest rate. The higher real effective interest rates charged by village banks reflect the high cost of reaching a marginalized clientele. In spite of these higher interest rates, the village banks still depend on subsidization.

---

2. Operational self-sufficiency is defined as operating income divided by operating expenses. Financial self-sufficiency is defined as operating income divided by operating and financial expenses.

Another key contrast between the village banks and credit unions is related to savings mobilization. The volume of savings as a percentage of the total outstanding loan portfolio is relatively insignificant for village banking compared with credit unions. The volume of savings in two of the three credit unions exceeds the loan portfolio, whereas the savings to loan ratio for the village banks is less than 10 percent. This contrast underscores the importance of savings mobilization in credit unions. In many rural finance institutions, savings have been overlooked despite the fact that a deposit facility is a highly valued service to the rural poor, who often lack reliable places to store their money with a positive return. In fact, many experts agree that savings facilities are the more commonly demanded financial service and represent a critical element of poverty alleviation (USAID 1991). The small average deposit size of these credit unions (US$190) illustrates an important role of credit unions in rural finance.

No conclusions can be drawn about repayment performance since both the arrears rates and portfolios at risk vary from institution to institution regardless of institutional type. In addition, the salaries paid to loan officers as a percentage of GNP per capita are similar for each institutional type.

Outreach versus Sustainability

On the surface, the data show that credit unions have the advantage in sustainability whereas village banking programs have a deeper outreach. However, the extent to which these two desirable characteristics are mutually exclusive remains an important research and empirical question. In order to analyze their relationship, it is first necessary to examine outreach and sustainability together.

The two village banks achieved greater depth of outreach than the three credit unions, but had the highest level of subsidies. Figure 7.2 illustrates this relationship, showing a notable trend between the DOI and the SDI measures: the deeper the outreach to marginalized clients, the more reliant is the institution on subsidies in order to cover program costs. The Pearson product moment correlation between the two measures is 0.93. Although this sample comprises only five institutions, a more recent study of 17 institutions confirms this positive relationship between DOI and SDI, with a correlation of 0.85 (Paxton 2002).

Despite the correlation between outreach and dependence on subsidies, one cannot conclude that outreach and sustainability are mutually exclusive goals. Two main arguments offer hope about the feasibility of providing financial services to the rural poor in a sustainable manner. First, credit unions can and do serve the poor. Second, village banks may approach sustainability as they gain experience and scale.

Credit Unions Reach the Poor and Other Clients

One of the problems of examining institutional averages of outreach is that the degree of heterogeneity of clients is missing. Whereas the village banks studied

FIGURE 7.2 Outreach versus sustainability of the five case-study institutions

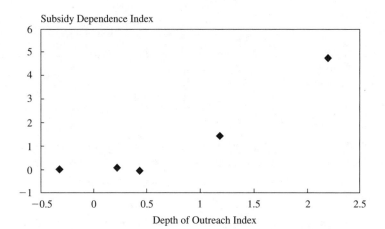

serve a somewhat homogeneous clientele (the rural poor and, in the case of CARE, only women), the credit unions serve a cross section of the rural population including lower-, middle-, and occasionally upper-income classes. Members include farmers, housewives, bakers, shoemakers, micro-entrepreneurs, laborers, teachers, and public employees. Given the credit unions' larger clientele, many rural credit unions serve as many marginalized clients as the village banks do. Rather than specifically targeting the poor, credit unions seek a diversified clientele. This heterogeneity facilitates the financial intermediation process by matching surplus and deficit units and hedges against risk through portfolio diversification. Table 7.5 illustrates the wide range of household income levels of the members of six Guatemalan credit unions.

The average household monthly income for members of Unión Popular in Guatemala is US$429. This average is skewed upward as a result of the presence of a few relatively wealthy members. Table 7.5 shows that only 17 percent of Unión Popular members have monthly incomes in excess of US$400. At the other end of the income spectrum, 16 percent of Unión Popular's members have household incomes of less than US$120 per month. This low level of income is comparable to that of the village bank members. The other credit unions in Table 7.5 have an even higher percentage of clients in the low-income ranges. In many cases, the number of members within the low-income bracket served by credit unions may exceed the total number of clients of a village banking program owing to the relatively larger size of credit unions.

The range of loan sizes provided by credit unions reflects the variation in income levels to some extent. For example, the average loan provided by OSCUS in Ecuador is US$954 (Table 7.2), which is roughly 75 percent of the

TABLE 7.5 Distribution of income by credit union, Guatemala, 1991

Credit Union	<20	21–60	61–120	121–200	201–400	>400	N.A.
			Percentage of Members per Category of Average Monthly Income (US$)				
Santa Maria Asunción	8	35	32	14	8	2	1
Parroquial Guadalupana	0	9	30	18	25	11	7
Guayacán	9	8	26	25	21	8	4
Teculutan	2	3	26	32	21	15	1
UPA	5	3	25	22	14	8	22
Unión Popular	2	1	13	22	27	17	18

SOURCE: Boucher, Barham, and Branch (1992).
NOTE: N.A. means not available.

average per capita GDP. However, nearly 1,800 loans (15 percent of the total loans granted) are for sums of less than US$300 (Table 7.6). Average loans of US$150 are only 12 percent of GDP per capita; this ratio is even lower than the average loan to GDP per capita ratio of 14 percent for the micro village banking program of CARE Guatemala.

Table 7.6 also shows that half of OSCUS borrowers are women. The number of OSCUS members who have savings accounts far exceeds the number with credit. Whereas only 5,737 women have loans, 26,501 women have savings accounts and shares. The average savings account size for women is US$142; however, 50 percent of the deposits are for less than US$30. Thus, the number of poor, rural women being served by microfinancial services in OSCUS is greater than the number served by the entire village banking program of CARE Guatemala, a program that exclusively serves poor rural women. If one were to map out the outreach diamond for this segment of OSCUS clients, it would be similar to the village banking outreach diamonds, although the literacy rate for credit unions would be higher because village banking avoids the requirement of literacy through the use of oral communication, fingerprint signatures, and pictorial training.

Village Banks Can Gradually Approach Sustainability

A second reason outreach and sustainability do not have to be mutually exclusive is that village banks may become more sustainable. Although the two case-study village banks have not severed their dependence on subsidized interest rates and donor grants, they are much younger institutions using a relatively new approach that is constantly being adapted with each year of experience. Because the programs are relatively young, their client base is not as developed as that of the credit unions, and economies of scale have not been reached. Looking at time series data, the general trend toward sustainability has been

TABLE 7.6 Distribution of loans by size and gender for OSCUS credit union, Ecuador, 1997

Loan Size (US$)	Women			Men		
	Percentage of Total Loans in Size Range	Number of Loans	Volume of Loans (US$)	Percentage of Total Loans in Size Range	Number of Loans	Volume of Loans (US$)
1–150	51	403	46,501	49	388	27,264
151–300	50	495	164,908	50	492	56,389
301–900	49	2,215	1,107,077	51	2,303	1,204,244
901–1,500	50	1,076	1,341,545	50	1,066	1,326,310
1,501–3,000	49	1,364	2,743,302	51	1,398	2,690,762
3,001–4,500	48	92	335,262	52	99	328,625
4,501–6,000	50	89	447,077	50	90	438,110
6,000+	50	3	18,645	50	3	18,238
Total	50	5,737	6,204,318	50	5,839	6,089,944

SOURCE: Almeyda and Branch (1998).

FIGURE 7.3 Village banking Subsidy Dependence Index measures, 1991–95

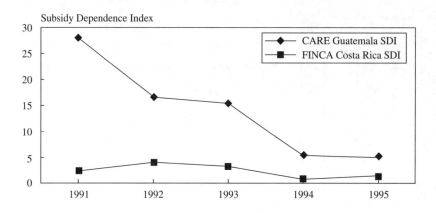

positive. Nevertheless, even after several years of operation, the SDI measures for village banks are much higher than those for the credit unions.

Figure 7.3 shows how the SDIs for CARE Guatemala and FINCA Costa Rica have evolved over the years. CARE Guatemala, a younger, more comprehensive program, has a much higher SDI, in part because of the depth of its outreach, but also because it is experiencing a marked decline. The SDI for FINCA Costa Rica remained somewhat stagnant in the 1990s after declining dramatically in the 1980s. The ability of these institutions to lower their SDI measures to levels comparable to those of credit unions is still an open question, one that may be answered as new cost-reducing innovations are implemented and economies of scale are reached.

Conclusions

In any context, sustainable financial institutions are desirable in that permanency creates confidence among clients and financial viability allows institutions to reach wider markets without relying on subsidies to target one small sector of the population. In rural Latin America, a wide range of market niches exists for financial intermediation. Village banking and credit unions are two member-based approaches to serving the rural financial market. They offer different financial products to different target groups: village banking targets the very poor (often women), whereas rural credit unions have a lower- and middle-class clientele.

In examining data from three rural credit unions and two rural village banking programs in Latin America, a strong correlation was found between depth of outreach and reliance on subsidies. The village banking programs, which target more poor people, more rural inhabitants, more uneducated people, and more women than are found in the general population, tend to be less sustainable in spite of charging higher interest rates than the credit unions, which do not have the same depth of outreach.

Despite the relationship between outreach and sustainability, this chapter does not suggest that the two are mutually exclusive. Although, on average, credit unions serve a wealthier clientele than village banks do, they also offer financial services to a much more heterogeneous population. The poorest 15 percent of their members are similar in socioeconomic characteristics to the clients of village banking. In addition, the credit unions have had success in providing these clients with voluntary microdeposit instruments, which are in great demand. This financial intermediation is being performed in a sustainable fashion without significant external subsidies. Based on this study, rural credit unions offer the most interesting model of financial intermediation in that they reach a larger number of marginalized clients than the village banks, while doing so in a sustainable fashion. Although the village programs have had a disappointing performance regarding institutional sustainability, they may become more financially viable through experience, innovations, and economies of scale, and as they continue to strive toward sustainability. In sum, it is possible for both these methodologies to coexist; their different institutional objectives and financial services can strengthen the rural financial landscape.

References

Almeyda, G., and B. Branch. 1998. *Case study of two Ecuadorian credit unions: OSCUS and Progreso.* Sustainable Banking with the Poor. Washington, D.C.: World Bank.

Boucher, S., B. Barham, and B. Branch. 1992. *Credit unions in Guatemala 1987–1992. Report No. 2—Financial market niche: Member behavior profile.* Madison, Wis.: World Council of Credit Unions.

Graham, D. 1994. *Reflections on savings-first and credit-first institutional designs in the Sahel.* Washington, D.C.: United States Agency for International Development.

Hopkins, J., C. Levin, and L. Haddad. 1994. Women's income and household expenditure patterns: Gender or flow? Evidence from Niger. *American Journal of Agricultural Economics* 76 (5): 1219–1225.

Hulme, D., and P. Mosley. 1996. *Finance against poverty.* London and New York: Routledge.

Paxton, J. 2002. Depth of outreach and its relation to the sustainability of microfinance institutions. *Savings and Development,* Giordano Dell 'Amore Foundation 26(1).

USAID (United States Agency for International Development). 1991. *Mobilizing savings and rural finance: The AID experience.* Science and Technology in Development Series. Washington, D.C.

Von Pischke, J. D. 1991. *Finance at the frontier: Debt capacity and the role of credit in the private economy.* EDI Development Studies. Washington, D.C.: World Bank.

World Bank. 1996. *World development report.* New York: Oxford University Press.

Yaron, J. 1992. *Assessing development finance institutions. A public interest analysis.* Policy Research Working Paper No. 174. Washington, D.C.: World Bank.

8 Microcredit and the Poorest of the Poor: Theory and Evidence from Bolivia

SERGIO NAVAJAS, MARK SCHREINER,
RICHARD L. MEYER, CLAUDIO GONZALEZ-VEGA, AND
JORGE RODRIGUEZ-MEZA

The professed goal of public support for microcredit is to improve the welfare of poor households through better access to small loans. Often public funds for microfinance organizations carry a mandate to serve the poorest (Consultative Group to Assist the Poorest 1995). For example, the Microcredit Summit in February 1997 rallied support to seek more than US$20 billion to provide microcredit to 100 million of the poorest households in the next 10 years (Microcredit Summit 1996).

Microcredit is the newest favorite of the aid community. In Latin America, most of the excitement is based on the fame of a few of the best microfinance organizations. These include BancoSol, Caja de Ahorro y Préstamo Los Andes, Fundación para la Promoción y Desarrollo de la Microempresa, Centro de Fomento a Iniciativas Económicas, and Fundación Sartawi in Bolivia; Caja Social in Colombia; Asociacion para el Desarrollo de Microempresos, Inc. (ADEMI) in the Dominican Republic; Financiera Calpiá in El Salvador; Compartamos in Mexico; and ACP/MiBanco in Peru. Worldwide, the best-known microfinance organizations are the Grameen Bank of Bangladesh and the *unit desa* system of Bank Rakyat Indonesia (BRI) (Yaron, Benjamin, and Piprek 1997). The Grameen Bank and BRI reach millions of depositors and borrowers, and many if not most are poor women. A survey of 200 of the thousands of microfinance organizations worldwide found 13 million loans worth US$7 billion outstanding as of September 1995 (Paxton 1996).

Although microcredit has claimed more and more of the aid budget, it may not always be the best way to help the poorest (Rogaly 1996; Buckley 1997). The fervor for microcredit may siphon funds from other projects that might help the poor more. Governments and donors should know whether the poor gain

This chapter was previously published as Navajas et al. (2000) and is reproduced with permission from Elsevier Science.

more from more small loans than from, for example, more health care, food aid, or cash gifts.

Is public support for microcredit wasted or worthwhile? No one knows. Most measures of the impact of microfinance organizations fail to control for what would have happened in their absence (Von Pischke and Adams 1980; Sebstad et al. 1995). If users borrow more than once, then they must get benefits. The question, however, is not whether microfinance is better than nothing for its users. The question is whether microfinance is better than some other development project for the poor as a whole.

We construct a theoretical framework for rigorous thought about the social worth of the output of a microfinance organization. The framework puts the standard theory of project analysis in terms of the jargon of microcredit. By precisely defining the social worth of service to the poorest, the framework helps to judge the trade-offs between service to the poorest and service to others. The goal is to render more explicit the judgments used to allot public funds.

We also address three empirical questions with evidence from a comparison of the poverty of a treatment group (borrowers of five microfinance organizations in La Paz, Bolivia) with the poverty of a control group (the population of La Paz). The first empirical question is whether microfinance organizations reach the poorest of the poor (Hulme and Mosley 1996; Gulli 1998). We find that the five microfinance organizations in Bolivia most often reached not the poorest of the poor but rather those just above and just below the poverty line. The theoretical framework lays out the conditions under which these microfinance organizations may still have been a good use of public funds meant to help the poor.

The second question is whether group loans or individual loans reach the poorest better. Although the theory is well developed (Conning 1997; Sadoulet 1997), less is known about when the assumptions of theory hold in practice. We find that group lenders in Bolivia reached the poorest better than individual lenders do.

The third question is whether rural lenders or urban lenders reach the poorest better. Rural poverty is both wide and deep, but, compared with urban lenders, rural lenders must deal with more seasonality, worse information, greater risks, less smooth cash flows, longer distances, more diversity, and sparser populations. We find that the share of the poorest in the portfolio was highest for rural lenders. We also find that, because the urban lenders had more borrowers, the share of the urban poorest who were borrowers exceeded the share of the rural poorest who were borrowers.

The chapter is organized as follows. After defining outreach, we briefly describe the empirical methods. We then compare the distribution of an index of the fulfillment of basic needs for borrowers with the distribution of a similar measure for the population. The final section presents our summary and conclusions.

A Theoretical Framework for Outreach

Judgments of the performance of microfinance organizations have been based on the concepts of outreach and sustainability (Yaron 1994). Here, we express outreach and sustainability in terms of the theory of social welfare. The purpose is to reconcile the jargon of microcredit with the standard tools of project analysis.

Outreach is the social value of the output of a microfinance organization in terms of depth, worth to users, cost to users, breadth, length, and scope.[1] Outreach is commonly proxied by the sex or poverty of borrowers, the size or the terms of loan contracts, the price and transaction costs borne by users, the number of users, the financial and organizational strength of the lender, and the number of products offered, including deposits.

Sustainability is permanence. The social goal is not to have sustainable microfinance organizations but rather to maximize expected social value minus social cost discounted through time, including the net gain of users from loans and deposits, the profits or losses of the microfinance organization, and the social opportunity cost of the resources used. In principle, sustainability is not necessary or sufficient for social optimality. In practice, however, sustainable organizations tend to improve welfare the most. Unsustainable microfinance organizations tend to inflict costs on the poor in the future in excess of the gains enjoyed by the poor now. Sustainability is not an end in itself but rather a means to the end of improved social welfare (Rhyne 1998). Sustainability affects outreach because permanency tends to lead to structures of incentives and constraints that prompt all the groups of stakeholders in a lender to act in ways that increase the difference between social value and social cost.

In principle, a complete evaluation would use cost–benefit analysis or cost-effectiveness analysis to compare social value with social cost in general equilibrium. In practice, it is so expensive to measure social value and social cost that almost all evaluation proceeds in terms of outreach and sustainability in partial equilibrium.

Six Aspects of Outreach

DEPTH.   Depth of outreach is the value that society attaches to the net gain from the use of microcredit by a given borrower. Since society places more weight on the poor than on the rich, poverty is a good proxy for depth. For example, society likely values the net gain from a small loan for a street kid or for a widow more than the same gains for a richer person.

Deeper outreach usually increases not only social value but also social cost. As income and wealth decrease, it costs more for a lender to judge the risk

---

1. This framework for outreach was first presented by Schreiner (1998) and has since been used by Gonzalez-Vega (1998).

of a loan. This happens because, compared with the rich, the poor are more heterogeneous and less able to signal their ability and willingness to repay (Conning 1999). Fixed costs also matter more for the poor since their loans are shorter and smaller and have more frequent installments, renewals, and disbursements.

Deeper outreach increases social value but not social cost when a lender finds better ways to judge risk at a cost less than the savings from the better judgment. Such progress increases *access*, the ability and willingness to borrow and to repay at a price that covers the long-run cost of an efficient producer. Access is the nexus of creditworthiness—demand based on ability and willingness to repay—and the lending technology—supply based on an efficient way to judge creditworthiness. More access is progress because loans depend more on the creditworthiness of the borrower and less on the constraints of the lender to judge creditworthiness. For example, a lender that does not need physical collateral to judge creditworthiness could serve poorer users and thus have deeper outreach, all else constant, than a lender that requires physical collateral.

WORTH TO USERS.   The worth of outreach to users is how much a borrower is willing to pay for a loan. Worth depends on the loan contract and on the tastes, constraints, and opportunities of the user. With the cost to the user constant, more worth means more net gain.

COST TO USERS.   The cost of outreach to users is the cost of a loan to a borrower. This is distinct from the cost of a loan to society or from the cost of a loan to a lender. Cost to users includes both price and transaction costs. Price includes interest and fees. Prices paid by the user are revenues for the lender. Transaction costs are nonprice costs, and include both noncash opportunity costs—such as the value of the time to get and to repay a loan—and loan-related cash expenses such as transport, documents, food, and taxes. Transaction costs borne by the user are not revenues for the lender.

The three aspects of depth, worth to users, and cost to users are tightly linked but still distinct. *Net gain* is the difference between worth to a user and cost to a user. It is the highest cost that the borrower would agree to bear to get the loan, less the cost that the borrower does in fact bear. In turn, depth of outreach reflects the social value attached to the net gain of a specific person. For example, US$100 of net gain for a poor person may be worth more to society than US$500 of net gain for a rich person.

Costs to users can be measured as the present value of the cash flows and transaction costs associated with a loan. Worth to users is more difficult to measure. Still, the relative worth of two or more loan contracts can be compared through their costs. If a borrower has alternative sources of loans, then net gain can be measured as the cost savings of a switch to a microfinance lender.

BREADTH.   The breadth of outreach is the number of users. Breadth matters because the poor are many but the aid dollars are few.

LENGTH.   The length of outreach is the time frame in which a microfinance organization produces loans. Length matters because society cares about the welfare of the poor both now and in the future. Without length of outreach, a microfinance organization might improve social welfare in the short term but wreck its ability to do so in the long term.

In theory, a perpetual source of support can allow a microfinance organization to achieve length of outreach without sustainability (Morduch 1998a; Woller, Dunford, and Woodworth 1999). In principle, such an organization could live a long time. In practice, however, longer outreach through sustainability usually strengthens the structures of incentives that serve to maximize expected social value less social cost discounted through time. Without length, borrowers have few selfish reasons to repay because the lender cannot promise to lend again in the future. Loan losses shorten length of outreach in a downward spiral. Likewise, lack of profits prompts employees to strip the lender bare and to bask in perks before the chance is gone.

SCOPE.   The scope of outreach is the number of types of financial contracts offered by a microfinance organization. In practice, the microfinance organizations with the best outreach produce both small loans and small deposits. Deposits matter for two reasons. First, all poor people are depositworthy and save to smooth consumption, to finance investment, and to buffer risk. In contrast, not all poor people are creditworthy. Second, deposits strengthen the incentives for sustainability and length of outreach. Depositors shun microfinance organizations if they do not expect them to live to return their deposits. To attract and to keep deposits, a microfinance organization must please not donors and government but rather users and regulators.

Trade-Offs and Feedback among the Six Aspects

Outreach is thus worth minus cost, weighted by depth, summed across breadth of users and scope of contracts, and discounted through length of time. These six aspects of outreach are useful because direct measures of the social value of microfinance are expensive.

Social welfare depends on all six aspects, but the most important of these is length. In particular, greater length in the short term requires more profit. This means higher prices, more cost to users, and less net gain per user. In the long term, however, the trade-off may vanish if the push for length leads to innovations in technology and organization that increase profits and/or increase worth to users without parallel increases in social cost or in cost to users. Increased length feeds back to decrease social cost because length gives users more selfish reasons to repay. Greater scope also increases worth to users and strengthens the incentives that boost length.

The debate over the social value of sustainability hinges on the effect of length. Microfinance organizations that do not aim for sustainability believe that the short-term increase in net gain caused by low prices swamps the effects of reduced length from low profits. Lenders that aim for sustainability believe the converse.

The rest of this chapter looks at evidence of depth of outreach for five microfinance organizations in Bolivia. Even if society cares only for the poorest, however, the theoretical framework highlights that social welfare depends on more than depth alone. Breadth affects the number of the poorest served, and cost and worth to users affect the net gain. The poorest can use not only loans but also deposits, not only now but also in the future.

The Poverty of Borrowers from Five Bolivian Lenders

The Organizations

By Latin American standards, Bolivia is a poor country. GNP per capita in 1997 was about US$950 (World Bank 1999). The income distribution was highly skewed, and rural households in particular were very poor (UNDP 1996). Still, Bolivia is a flagship for microcredit in Latin America and in the world (Gonzalez-Vega et al. 1997a).

At the end of 1995, two of the five Bolivian microfinance organizations were regulated, and three were nongovernmental organizations (NGOs). The three NGOs were Centro de Fomento a Iniciativas Económicas (FIE), Fundación para la Promoción y Desarrollo de la Microempresa (PRODEM), and Fundación Sartawi. BancoSol, the best-known microfinance organization in Latin America, is a bank that was split off from PRODEM (Mosley 1996; Gonzalez-Vega et al. 1997b; Schreiner 1997). Caja de Ahorro y Préstamo Los Andes is a regulated nonbank (Rock 1997).

The five lenders can be grouped by their lending technology and by their geographic market niche. In lending technology, BancoSol and PRODEM largely lend to groups, and FIE and Caja Los Andes lend to individuals. Sartawi works through communities to lend to both groups and individuals. In geographic market niche, PRODEM and Sartawi are mostly rural, while BancoSol, FIE, and Caja Los Andes are mostly urban. Thus BancoSol lends to urban groups, PRODEM lends to rural groups, and Caja Los Andes and FIE lend to urban individuals. Sartawi lends to rural groups and rural individuals.

The differences in technology and in market niche among the five lenders reflect their history of external support and the forces that spawned their creation. PRODEM lends to groups because, when founded in 1987, it followed the model of the Grameen Bank of Bangladesh. Although PRODEM worked at first in an urban market niche, it later shifted to a rural focus so as not to compete with BancoSol, which inherited most of PRODEM's urban borrowers when it was split off in 1992. BancoSol was created in part to mobilize large deposits from rich households and firms in order to relieve the constraints on funds that had limited the growth PRODEM, in part to test whether an NGO could become a commercial bank, and in part to mobilize small deposits from poor households and firms. The development of both PRODEM and BancoSol was heavily shaped by technical assistance from the Calmeadow Foundation of Canada and from Acción International, a U.S.-based NGO with links to group lenders in many countries in Latin America.

Caja Los Andes was founded in 1992 and has received funds from the Inter-American Development Bank, the German Agency for Technical Cooperation (GTZ), and the Swiss government. Its individual loans reflect the influence of extensive technical assistance from the German consulting firm Internationale Projekt Consult. At first, Caja Los Andes lent mostly for manufacturing in the belief that industry had the greatest effects on employment, but it soon added loans for commerce.

When FIE started to make loans in 1988, its clients were urban artisans who had completed classes with a training branch of the NGO. FIE made loans only for manufacturing until 1993, when, like Caja Los Andes, it started to lend for commerce. By 1995, the lending and training arms of FIE were separated. FIE is unique among the lenders studied here because it has not had a single dominant donor or a major source of technical assistance.

Sartawi started to lend to rural communities in part because it already worked with rural communities in nonfinancial development projects. The bulk of its funds came from Plan Internacional, a rural development NGO, and from the German Lutheran Church. Like FIE, Sartawi has had little external technical assistance. It separated lending from other activities in 1995. In Aymara, *sartawi* means "to progress."

The five lenders have several traits in common. They all work in niches untouched by traditional banks. All five make small loans to first-time borrowers and bigger loans to repeat borrowers. All five charge high prices, and all five keep arrears and loan losses low with various mixes of screening, monitoring, and contract enforcement. All five have received grants, technical assistance, and low-priced loans from the United States Agency for International Development (USAID) and other donors. Still, very little of their success has been due to access to funds from second-tier lenders in Bolivia. Compared with peers, all five have high outreach and sustainability (*Microbanking Bulletin* 1998). They all aim to reduce poverty, but none explicitly targets the poor.

Bolivia, although sparsely peopled, may have the densest microcredit in the world. The five microfinance organizations studied here are the most important of a total of about 30 in Bolivia, accounting for more than half of both clients and portfolio outstanding (*La Razón* 1997).

The Data

In November and December of 1995, we surveyed a random sample of 622 of the more than 52,000 borrowers active with the five lenders at the end of September in the urban areas in and near La Paz and in the rural Altiplano near Lake

Titicaca. Of the 588 cases with complete data, 221 came from BancoSol, 124 from Caja Los Andes, 91 from FIE, 83 from Sartawi, and 69 from PRODEM (Gonzalez-Vega et al. 1996).

An Index of Fulfillment of Basic Needs

CONCEPTUAL ISSUES. A vast literature explores the measurement of poverty (Lipton and Ravallion 1995). Here, we matched some questions in our survey of borrowers with questions in the 1992 Bolivian national poverty assessment (Ministerio de Desarrollo Humano 1995). The questions measured household use of goods and services thought to be linked with the fulfillment of basic needs.

The answers were condensed into an Index of Fulfillment of Basic Needs (IFBN). This approach is common in Latin America. It requires (Boltvinik 1994)

- theoretical definitions of basic needs and ways to satisfy them;
- choices of observable proxies that indicate degrees of fulfillment;
- norms that define the point where a need is considered unsatisfied;
- aggregation of indicators to construct an index; and
- choice of the poverty line for the index.

EMPIRICAL ISSUES. The nationwide assessment picked the indicators, their norms, and the poverty line. In most cases, the norm was the median of an indicator, but some cases had more complex norms. Like all measures of absolute poverty, the poverty line and the norms were at least somewhat arbitrary. The index was computed not for individuals but for households. It had four parts:

1. *Housing*
   - Type of materials used for floors, walls, and roof
   - Number of people per room
2. *Access to public services*
   - Source of water
   - Presence of an indoor toilet
   - Access to electricity
   - Type of fuel used to cook food
3. *Education*
   - Years of school completed
   - Current attendance in school
   - Literacy
4. *Access to health services*
   - Use of formal health care
   - Use of informal health care

Except for indoor toilets, the urban and rural norms were the same. The Index of Fulfillment of Basic Needs was the simple average of the ratios of the four observed indicators x_j to their norms $x_{j\text{norm}}$:

$$IFBN = \left(\frac{1}{4}\right) \sum_{j=1}^{4} \frac{x_j}{x_{j\text{norm}}}.\qquad(9.1)$$

The range of the ratio of x_j to $x_{j\text{norm}}$ depended on the range of answers in the nationwide assessment. The indicator for education was the average of indices for individual members of a household:

$$IE = \left(\frac{1}{N}\right) \sum_{i=1}^{N} \left(\frac{y_i + s_i}{y_{i\text{norm}} + s_{i\text{norm}}}\right) L_i,\qquad(9.2)$$

where

IE = index of education of the household
N = number of members of the household
y_i = years of schooling for person i
s_i = school attendance dummy for the age of person i
$y_{i\text{norm}}$ = norm for years of schooling for the age of person i
$s_{i\text{norm}}$ = norm for attendance for the age of person i
L_i = literacy dummy for person i.

The nationwide assessment set the poverty line at an IFBN of 0.9. Households below this were *poor*, and the rest were *nonpoor*. The nonpoor were subclassified as *fulfilled* or *threshold*. The poor were subclassified as *moderate* or *poorest*.

Our survey of borrowers included 56 percent of the indicators in the nationwide IFBN. Most of what was omitted had to do with access to health care. We believe this is highly correlated with the other indicators, so the comparison should not be biased.

Evidence of Depth of Outreach

The Population of La Paz

Two features stand out about the shares of the population of urban and rural La Paz in each of the four poverty classes (Table 8.1). The first is the extent of poverty. In 1992, more than half the urban households were poor, and almost all rural households were poor. The second is the depth of rural poverty. Not only were 96 percent of rural households poor, but 74 percent were among the poorest. In contrast, 17 percent of the urban households were in the poorest class. Poverty in Bolivia, especially rural poverty, was broad and deep.

TABLE 8.1 Distribution of the Index of Fulfillment of Basic Needs among poverty classes for borrowers from five microfinance organizations in La Paz, Bolivia, and for all households in urban and rural La Paz (point estimates and bootstrapped nonparametric 90 percent confidence intervals)

| Range of Index | N | Nonpoor | | | Moderate | Poor | |
| | | Fulfilled | Threshold | Subtotal | | Poorest | Subtotal |
		2.0 to 1.1	1.1 to 0.9	2.0 to 0.9	0.9 to 0.6	0.6 to 0.0	0.9 to 0.0
Urban La Paz	*436*	*28*	*17*	*45*	*38*	*17*	*55*
FIE	91	26–35–44	25–34–43	62–69–77	21–29–36	0–2–5	23–31–38
Caja Los Andes	124	14–19–25	40–48–55	60–67–73	23–29–35	2–4–7	27–33–40
BancoSol	221	12–16–20	27–33–38	43–48–54	42–47–52	2–5–7	46–52–57
Rural La Paz	*152*	*2*	*3*	*5*	*22*	*74*	*96*
PRODEM	69	0–0–0	6–13–20	6–13–20	43–54–64	24–33–43	80–87–94
Sartawi	83	0–2–5	7–12–18	8–14–20	40–49–58	28–36–45	80–86–92

NOTES: All figures are percentages. Point estimates and census parameters are in italics, and 90 percent confidence bounds for the point estimates are in regular typeface. The figures for the population of urban and rural La Paz do not have confidence intervals because they are not estimates but rather parameters from a census (Ministerio de Desarrollo Humano 1995). The figures for the lenders were computed from the survey by the authors. Rows may not sum to 100 owing to rounding.

FIGURE 8.1 Box-and-whisker plot of the distribution of the IFBN for sampled borrowers from the five microfinance organizations in La Paz, Bolivia

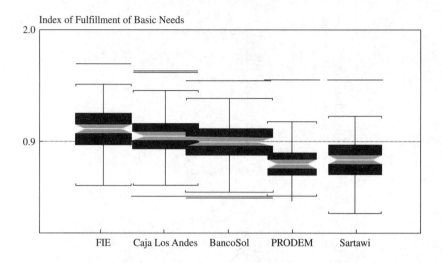

Borrowers of the Five Lenders

DISTRIBUTION OF THE IFBN.   A box-and-whisker plot (Tukey 1977) depicts the distribution of the IFBN for borrowers of the five lenders (Figure 8.1). We do not have data for a similar picture for the rural and urban populations. The IFBN is on the vertical axis; the poverty line is at 0.9; and the microfinance organizations are ordered from shallowest to deepest outreach.

The width of each box reflects the sample size for each lender. For example, the box for BancoSol ($N = 221$) is wider than the box for PRODEM ($N = 69$). The height of the boxes marks the interquartile distance, the range between the second and third quartiles of the distribution. Less-dispersed distributions have shorter boxes. For example, the box for PRODEM is shorter than the box for Sartawi because the distribution of PRODEM is more clustered near the median. The whiskers beyond the boxes bracket either the extreme points in the data or 1.5 times the interquartile distance from the median, whichever is less. In a Gaussian distribution, more than 99 percent of the data are inside the whiskers. The horizontal lines beyond the whiskers mark outliers.

The gray trapezoids in the center of each box bound a 95 percent confidence interval for the estimated median. FIE had the highest median. Half the sample of FIE had an IFBN of more than 1.02, and the other half had an IFBN of less than 1.02. A Kolmogorov–Smirnov test rejected the hypothesis that any of the distributions were Gaussian, so differences in medians were tested nonparametrically with Wilcoxon rank-sums (Hollander and Wolfe 1973). The median of FIE (1.02) is greater than that of Caja Los Andes (0.97) with more than 95 percent confidence. The borrowers of these two urban individual lenders clustered just above the poverty line in the threshold class. The median for BancoSol, the urban group lender, was at the poverty line (0.90). This is less than the other two urban medians with more than 99 percent confidence. The median rural borrowers in Sartawi (0.71) and in PRODEM (0.67) were moderately poor. The rural medians were statistically smaller than the urban medians, but they were not statistically different from each other.

The same pattern of three depths of outreach is suggested both by the Wilcoxon rank-sum tests for differences in medians and by the nonparametric Kolmogorov–Smirnov tests for differences in the distributions of the IFBN:

- threshold group (FIE and Caja Los Andes);
- poverty-line group (BancoSol); and
- moderately poor group (PRODEM and Sartawi).

DISTRIBUTION OF THE IFBN FOR BORROWERS VERSUS THE POPU-LATION.   We compare the estimated distribution of the IFBN among the poverty classes for the sample of borrowers from the five lenders with the known distribution of a similar measure for all urban and rural households in La Paz (Table 8.1). Because the estimated share of borrowers in a poverty class is a random variable, we report nonparametric bootstrapped 90 percent confidence intervals (Efron and Tibshirani 1993).

We do not expect the sample and population distributions to match because creditworthiness and demand for microcredit depend in part on income and assets. All else constant, lenders can more readily judge the creditworthiness of rich people than that of poor people. Suppose a lender drew borrowers at random from the subset of the population that, given its lending technology, had demand and was creditworthy. Then the profile of borrowers, compared with the population, would be skewed toward the rich.

We do not know the exact profile of demand and creditworthiness in Bolivia. However, we can answer three useful questions. The first asks about the depth of outreach to the poorest of the poor (whether the poorest had the same share in the portfolio as they had in the population, and how many of the poorest were reached). The second and third questions ask how depth compared between group and individual loan technologies and between rural and urban market niches.

Depth of Outreach to the Poorest of the Poor

THE SHARE OF THE POOREST IN THE PORTFOLIO AND IN THE POP-ULATION.   Of all households in urban La Paz, 45 percent were nonpoor (Table 8.1). For all three urban lenders, the point estimate of the share of nonpoor households exceeded the population parameter: 69 percent for FIE, 67 percent for Caja Los Andes, and 48 percent for BancoSol. The population parameter is within the 90 percent confidence interval for BancoSol but not for FIE and Caja Los Andes. In rough terms, this means we can reject the hypothesis that FIE and Caja Los Andes reached nonpoor borrowers in proportion to their population share, but we cannot reject this hypothesis for BancoSol. For threshold borrowers, all three urban lenders had a statistically bigger share than the population. Caja Los Andes and BancoSol had a smaller share of borrowers in the fulfilled class than did the population, and FIE had a bigger share.

For the moderately poor, the share was lower in FIE and in Caja Los Andes (both 29 percent) than in the population (38 percent). The share for Banco-Sol was higher than in the population (47 percent). For the poorest, the shares of all three urban lenders (2 to 5 percent) were smaller than in the population (17 percent). Thus, compared with the population, the urban lenders lent less to the fulfilled and to the poorest and more to the richest of the poor (threshold) and, in the case of BancoSol, to the poorest of the rich (moderate).

The same pattern holds in rural La Paz. The nonpoor were 5 percent of all rural households but 13 percent of PRODEM and 14 percent of Sartawi. In all rural households, 22 percent were moderately poor, and 74 percent were among the poorest. For PRODEM, 54 percent were moderately poor and 33 percent were among the poorest. For Sartawi, 49 percent were moderately poor and 36 percent were among the poorest. All of the differences are statistically significant.

Except for the fulfilled class and for the moderately poor in BancoSol, the profile of borrowers of each of the five lenders is, compared with the profile of the population, skewed toward the threshold class. This does not prove much, however, about depth of outreach. What matters is not whether the microfinance organizations reached the poorest of the poor but whether they reached the poorest of those who demanded loans and who were creditworthy. Our data cannot answer this question.

THE NUMBER OF THE POOREST IN THE PORTFOLIO.   If a lender has broad outreach, then it might reach many of the poorest even though they are not a big share of the portfolio (Rosenberg 1996). Table 8.2 contains point estimates of the share of the portfolio in a poverty class multiplied by the total number borrowers from these lenders in La Paz.

The five lenders reached about 4,500 of the poorest—1,900 urban and 2,600 rural. This number is derived from the relative share of the poorest in a portfolio and from the absolute size of the portfolio. For example, the share of the poorest was about 4 percent in Caja Los Andes and about 5 percent in BancoSol. With about 30,000 total borrowers, BancoSol served about 1,400 of the poorest, while Caja Los Andes, with 9,200 total borrowers, served about 370. FIE, with the lowest share of the poorest (2 percent) and the smallest urban portfolio, had about 120 borrowers among the poorest.

The rural lenders were smaller than the urban lenders, but the share of the poorest in their portfolios was higher. The effect of the greater share swamped

TABLE 8.2 Estimated breadth of outreach, by number of clients in a poverty class, for borrowers from five microfinance organizations in urban and rural La Paz

	Nonpoor			Poor			
	Fulfilled	Threshold	Subtotal	Moderate	Poorest	Subtotal	Total
Urban La Paz	8,500	16,000	25,000	18,000	1,900	20,000	45,000
FIE	1,900	1,900	3,900	1,500	120	1,600	5,500
Caja Los Andes	1,800	4,400	6,200	2,700	370	3,000	9,200
BancoSol	4,800	9,800	15,000	14,000	1,400	15,000	30,000
Rural La Paz	120	1,000	1,100	3,700	2,600	6,300	7,400
PRODEM	0	360	360	1,300	800	2,100	2,500
Sartawi	120	650	770	2,400	1,800	4,200	4,900
Total La Paz	8,600	17,000	26,000	22,000	4,500	26,000	52,000

SOURCES: Survey by the authors and Table 8.1.

NOTES: Rows and columns may not sum to totals owing to rounding.

the effect of the smaller portfolio. PRODEM, with about 2,500 borrowers in rural La Paz, served about 800 of the poorest, more than twice as many as Caja Los Andes. Sartawi, with about 4,900 borrowers, had about 1,800 among the poorest. This is 400 more than BancoSol and almost as many as for all three urban lenders combined.

About 4,500 of the poorest households in La Paz had debt from the five lenders in late 1995. Is this deep outreach? One way to check is *market penetration*, the ratio of borrowers from a given lender in a given class to the number of households in that class in the population (Table 8.3). In 1992, La Paz had about 260,000 urban households and about 160,000 rural households (Ministerio de Desarrollo Humano 1995). Of all urban households, FIE reached about 2 percent, Caja Los Andes 4 percent, and BancoSol 12 percent. Of all rural households, PRODEM reached about 1 percent and Sartawi reached about 2 percent.

Penetration in the market as a whole matters less than penetration in the part of the market with demand and creditworthiness. As before, we lack these data. Still, we know that urban lenders reached 38 percent of threshold households, 19 percent of moderately poor households, and 18 percent of all households. Given that not all households want debt at all times, that not all households are creditworthy, and that there are other microfinance organizations in urban Bolivia, this suggests scant room for more market penetration in urban areas. The amount of slack in rural areas is less certain. There, 12 percent of the nonpoor and 4 percent of the poor had debt when surveyed. This is much less than the urban penetration, but we do not know how much is possible because rural microcredit is more difficult than urban microcredit.

TABLE 8.3 Market penetration, by poverty class, for five microfinance organizations in urban and rural La Paz

	Nonpoor			Poor			
	Fulfilled	Threshold	Subtotal	Moderate	Poorest	Subtotal	Total
Urban La Paz	12.0	38.0	22.0	19.0	4.0	14.0	18.0
FIE	3.0	5.0	3.0	2.0	0.3	1.0	2.0
Caja Los Andes	3.0	10.0	5.0	3.0	0.8	2.0	4.0
BancoSol	7.0	23.0	13.0	15.0	3.0	11.0	12.0
Rural La Paz	5.0	15.0	12.0	11.0	2.0	4.0	5.0
PRODEM	0.0	0.2	0.1	1.0	2.0	2.0	1.0
Sartawi	0.2	2.0	0.7	2.0	4.0	3.0	2.0

SOURCES: Computed from Tables 8.1 and 8.2 and from Ministerio de Desarrollo Humano (1995).

NOTES: The figures for urban and rural La Paz are not population parameters from a census but rather totals for all the microfinance lenders in an area combined. Numbers may not sum to totals owing to rounding.

The five Bolivian lenders reached the richest of the poor and the poorest of the rich much more than they reached the poorest of the poor. This does not necessarily mean that they did a bad job. A loan that is not repaid is a gift. Although there is nothing wrong with a gift, a gift in loans' clothing may backfire (Adams, Graham, and Von Pischke 1984; Krahnen and Schmidt 1994). Also, outreach depends not only on depth for the poorest but also on breadth, worth to users, cost to users, length, and scope for all users. These lenders have uncommon breadth, worth, cost, and length. Furthermore, BancoSol and Caja Los Andes take deposits and so have an especially wide scope.

Depth by Loan Technology

Because both rural lenders use group loans, we look at technology only for the urban lenders so as not to confound the effects of technology with the effects of market niche. Compared with the individual lenders FIE and Caja Los Andes, the group lender BancoSol had the smallest shares in the fulfilled and threshold classes and the biggest shares in the moderate and poorest classes (Figure 8.1 and Table 8.1). BancoSol also had the most market penetration, reaching almost one-fourth of the households in the threshold class and 15 percent of the moderately poor (Table 8.3).

As a rule, the group-lending technology has more potential for deep outreach because it can substitute joint liability for physical collateral. Joint liability has high transaction costs, and it can also have high cash costs if borrowers must repay the debts of their comrades. Still, group loans attract those who cannot or will not post physical collateral. In contrast, individual loans appeal to richer borrowers who can post physical collateral and who want to avoid the costs of joint liability.

TABLE 8.4 The IFBN for clients of the five microfinance organizations as a ratio of the IFBN for the urban and rural population of La Paz

	Nonpoor			Poor		
	Fulfilled	Threshold	Subtotal	Moderate	Poorest	Subtotal
Urban La Paz						
FIE	1.2	2.1	1.6	0.7	0.1	0.5
Caja Los Andes	0.7	2.9	1.5	0.8	0.2	0.6
BancoSol	0.6	2.0	1.1	1.2	0.3	0.9
Rural La Paz						
PRODEM	0.0	4.8	3.2	2.4	0.5	0.9
Sartawi	1.6	4.4	3.5	2.2	0.5	0.9

SOURCE: Computed from Table 8.1 as described in the text.

BancoSol had both the deepest and the broadest outreach of the urban lenders. This does not necessarily mean that BancoSol had the best outreach overall, because the comparison ignores cost to users, worth to users, length, and scope.

Depth by Geographic Market Niche

At first glance, rural lenders seem to have deeper outreach than urban lenders (Table 8.1). About 86–87 percent of the rural borrowers were among the poor, compared with 31–52 percent for urban borrowers. In fact, this comparison is not valid because it does not control for the different distributions of poverty in urban and rural areas.

Table 8.4 does control for this. Each cell is the share of the portfolio in a given poverty class for a given lender divided by the share of the population in the poverty class from Table 8.1. A ratio of more than 1.0 means that the share of clients in that class was greater than the share of the population in that class. A ratio of less than 1.0 means the opposite.

If the poor were more concentrated in a microfinance organization than in the population, then the ratios in Table 8.4 would increase from less than 1.0 in the leftmost columns to more than 1.0 in the rightmost columns. In fact, the pattern is the opposite. For all five lenders, the ratios start near or above 1.0 in the leftmost column for the fulfilled and exceed 2.0 for the threshold class. The ratios decrease for the moderately poor and then decrease still more for the poorest. As seen before, the profile of borrowers is skewed, not toward the poorest but toward those near the poverty line.

The details of the broad pattern differ, however, for rural and urban lenders. For example, in the threshold class, no urban lender had a ratio above 3.0, whereas the ratios for the rural lenders were well over 4.0. The rural lenders mined the few nonpoor households more intensely than the many poor households.

Among the moderately poor and the poorest, the rural lenders had higher ratios and thus deeper outreach than the urban lenders did. This is a puzzle. If rural lending is more difficult than urban lending, then why did rural lenders have more depth? The answer is probably that the urban lenders had not yet exhausted their nonpoor niches. In contrast, the lack of a large number of nonpoor rural borrowers pushed the rural lenders to the poorest. For rural lenders, the ratios of the share of the threshold class to the population share is 4.8 and 4.4, and the ratios for the moderately poor class are 2.4 and 2.2. For urban lenders, the threshold ratios are between 2.0 and 3.0, and the moderate ratios are near 1.0. The rural lenders serve the niches of the richest of the poor and the poorest of the rich much more intensely than do the urban lenders. The greater depth of the rural lenders suggests that the urban lenders may not yet reach all of the urban poorest who are creditworthy and who want loans.

In terms of market penetration (Table 8.3), the two urban individual lenders, FIE and Caja Los Andes, had less than 1 percent of the poorest households in their portfolios. The urban group lender, BancoSol, served about 3 percent of the poorest. In rural La Paz, PRODEM reached about 2 percent, and Sartawi reached about 4 percent, of the poorest. Overall, about 4 percent of the urban poorest and about 2 percent of the rural poorest borrowed from microfinance organizations. Thus the average rural borrower was more likely to be a member of the poorest class than was the average urban borrower, but the average urban household among the poorest was more likely to be a borrower than was the average rural household among the poorest.

Summary and Conclusions

We analyzed the depth of outreach of five microfinance organizations in La Paz, Bolivia. The first step was to construct a theoretical framework in which depth is one of six aspects of outreach. The second step was to compare the poverty of a sample of the borrowers from the five lenders with the poverty of all households in La Paz.

We found five main results. First, improved social welfare from microcredit depends not only on depth of outreach but also on worth, cost, breadth, length, and scope. Length matters most because the drive for length leads to incentives that prompt improvements in the other aspects. Second, the lenders in La Paz tended to serve not the poorest but rather those near the poverty line. Most microfinance organizations will probably serve this same niche. The poorest are less likely to be creditworthy and to demand loans, and many of the nonpoor can borrow elsewhere. Third, because the distribution of demand and creditworthiness unconditional on supply is unknown, we cannot say whether the Bolivian lenders had deep outreach in an absolute sense. Fourth, group lenders in La Paz had deeper outreach than individual lenders did. In general, group technologies have more potential for deep outreach because they substitute joint liability for physical collateral. Fifth, the rural lenders in La Paz had deeper outreach than did the urban lenders in that the typical rural borrower was more likely to be among the poorest. At the same time, the urban lenders had more market penetration among the poorest owing to their bigger portfolios.

These results on depth of outreach do not tell us whether the five microfinance organizations did well in terms of all six aspects of outreach. On the one hand, perhaps the drive for length and breadth is what prompted these lenders to grow and to have some depth. On the other hand, perhaps these lenders would have reached more of the poorest had they stayed small and unprofitable with a single-minded focus on depth. The theoretical framework described here can help to improve social welfare by making more explicit the judgments that back the choice of which focus to take.

The empirical results sketch some of the limits of microcredit for the poorest of the poor. They highlight the need for more scrutiny of the flood of funds budgeted in the name of access to loans for the poorest. Even when microcredit does reach the poorest, it may not increase incomes as much as smooth consumption and diversify income (Morduch 1998b; Mosley and Hulme 1998). Even if it turns out that microfinance organizations do not reach relatively or even absolutely many of the poorest, this shallow depth may be more than balanced by net gains that accrue to those near the poverty line.

Microcredit may or may not be a good development gamble. If donors and governments have social welfare in mind, then they should check whether microcredit is the best way to spend public funds earmarked for development. Is microcredit worthwhile or worthless? The theoretical framework here is a better way to judge this than are simple measures of the number of the poorest served by a lender.

References

Adams, D. W, D. Graham, and J. D. Von Pischke. 1984. *Undermining rural development with cheap credit*. Boulder, Colo., U.S.A.: Westview Press.

Boltvinik, J. 1994. Poverty measurement and alternative indicators. In *Poverty monitoring: An international concern*, ed. R. van der Hoeven and R. Anker, pp. 57–83. New York: St. Martin's Press.

Buckley, G. 1997. Microfinance in Africa: Is it either the problem or the solution? *World Development* 25 (7): 1081–1093.

Conning, J. 1997. Joint liability, peer monitoring, and the creation of social capital. Williams College, Williamstown, Mass., U.S.A.

———. 1999. Outreach, sustainability and leverage in monitored and peer-monitored lending. *Journal of Development Economics* 60: 51–77.

Consultative Group to Assist the Poorest. 1995. A policy framework for the Consultative Group to Assist the Poorest (CGAP)—A microfinance program. World Bank, Washington, D.C.

Efron, B., and R. J. Tibshirani. 1993. *An introduction to the bootstrap.* Monographs on Statistics and Applied Probability Vol. 57. New York and London: Chapman & Hall.

Gonzalez-Vega, C. 1998. *Microfinance: Broader achievements and new challenges.* Economics and Sociology Occasional Paper No. 2518. Columbus, Ohio, U.S.A.: Ohio State University.

Gonzalez-Vega, C., M. Schreiner, R. Meyer, J. Rodriguez-Meza, and S. Navajas. 1997a. *An Ohio State primer on microfinance in Bolivia.* Columbus, Ohio, U.S.A.: Ohio State University.

————. 1997b. BancoSol: The challenge of growth for microfinance organizations. In *Microfinance for the poor?* ed. H. Schneider, pp. 129–170. Paris: Organisation for Economic Co-operation and Development.

Gonzalez-Vega, C., R. Meyer, S. Navajas, M. Schreiner, J. Rodriguez-Meza, and G. F. Monje. 1996. *Microfinance market niches and client profiles in Bolivia.* Economics and Sociology Occasional Paper No. 2346. Columbus, Ohio, U.S.A.: Ohio State University.

Gulli, H. 1998. *Microfinance and poverty: Questioning the conventional wisdom.* Washington, D.C.: Inter-American Development Bank.

Hollander, M., and D. A. Wolfe. 1973. *Nonparametric statistical methods.* New York: John Wiley.

Hulme, D., and P. Mosley. 1996. *Finance against poverty*, Vols. I and II. London: Routledge.

Krahnen, J. P., and R. H. Schmidt. 1994. *Development finance as institution building.* Boulder, Colo., U.S.A.: Westview Press.

La Razón. 1997. The power of NGOs: In 1 year they lent US$100 million. September 29, p. 8A, La Paz.

Lipton, M., and M. Ravallion. 1995. Poverty and policy. In *Handbook of development economics*, vol. IIIB, ed. J. Behrman and T. N. Srinivasan, pp. 2553–2657. Amsterdam: Elsevier.

Microbanking Bulletin. 1998. No. 2. Available at <http://www.colorado.edu/Economics Institute/bfmft/mbbdown.htm>.

Microcredit Summit. 1996. The Microcredit Summit Declaration and Plan of Action. *Journal of Developmental Entrepreneurship* 1 (2): 131–176.

Ministerio de Desarrollo Humano. 1995. *Mapa de Pobreza: Una Guía para la Acción Social, Segunda Edición.* La Paz.

Morduch, J. 1998a. The microfinance schism. *World Development* 28 (4): 617–629.

————. 1998b. *Does microfinance really help the poor? New evidence from flagship programs in Bangladesh.* Stanford, Calif., U.S.A.: Hoover Institution.

Mosley, P. 1996. Metamorphosis from NGO to commercial bank: The case of Banco-Sol in Bolivia. In *Finance against poverty*, Vol. II, ed. D. Hulme and P. Mosley, pp. 1–31. London: Routledge.

Mosley, P., and D. Hulme. 1998. Microenterprise finance: Is there a conflict between growth and poverty alleviation? *World Development* 26 (5): 783–790.

Navajas, S., M. Schreiner, R. I. Meyer, C. Gonzalez-Vega, and J. Rodriguez-Meza. 2000. Microcredit and the poorest of the poor: Theory and evidence from Bolivia. *World Development* 28 (2): 333–346.

Paxton, J. 1996. *A worldwide inventory of microfinance institutions.* Washington, D.C.: World Bank.

Rhyne, E. 1998. The yin and yang of microfinance: Reaching the poor and sustainability. *Microbanking Bulletin* 2: 6–8.

Rock, R. 1997. Other microfinance institution experiences with regulation. In *From margin to mainstream: The regulation and supervision of microfinance*, ed. R. Rock and M. Otero, pp. 87–106. Monograph Series No. 11. Boston, Mass., U.S.A.: Acción International.

Rogaly, B. 1996. Microfinance evangelism, "destitute women," and the hard selling of a new anti-poverty formula. *Development in Practice* 6 (2): 100–112.

Rosenberg, R. 1996. *Microcredit interest rates.* Consultative Group to Assist the Poorest Occasional Paper No. 1. Washington, D.C.: World Bank.

Sadoulet, L. 1997. The role of mutual insurance in group lending. Princeton University, Princeton, N.J., U.S.A.

Schreiner, M. 1997. A framework for the analysis of the performance and sustainability of subsidized microfinance organizations with application to BancoSol of Bolivia and Grameen Bank of Bangladesh. Ph.D. Dissertation. Ohio State University, Columbus, Ohio, U.S.A. Available at <http://www.microfinance.com>.

———. 1998. Aspects of outreach: A framework for the discussion of the social benefits of microfinance. *Journal of International Development* 14: 1–13.

Sebstad, J., C. Neill, C. Barnes, and G. Chen. 1995. Assessing the impacts of microenterprise interventions: A framework for analysis. Report to USAID, DOCID No. PN-ABS-523. Available at <http://www.dec.org/search/dexs/docs-1987-present>.

Tukey, J. W. 1977. *Exploratory data analysis.* Reading, Mass., U.S.A.: Addison Wesley.

UNDP (United Nations Development Programme). 1996. *Human development report 1996.* New York.

Von Pischke, J. D., and D. W Adams. 1980. Fungibility and the design and evaluation of agricultural credit projects. *American Journal of Agricultural Economics* 62: 719–724.

Woller, G. M., C. Dunford, and W. Woodworth. 1999. Where to microfinance? *International Journal of Economic Development* 1 (1): 29–64.

World Bank. 1999. *World development report 1998/99: From plan to market.* Washington, D.C.

Yaron, J. 1994. What makes rural finance institutions successful? *World Bank Research Observer* 9 (9): 49–70.

Yaron, J., M. Benjamin, Jr., and G. Piprek. 1997. *Rural finance: Issues, design, and best practices.* Environmentally Sustainable Development Studies and Monographs No. 14. Washington, D.C.: World Bank.

9 An Operational Tool for Evaluating the Poverty Outreach of Development Policies and Projects

MANFRED ZELLER, MANOHAR SHARMA,
CARLA HENRY, AND CÉCILE LAPENU

The reduction of poverty is an explicit or implicit objective of most development policies and projects; the targeting of policies and project services to the poor is therefore important in development practice. However, the lack of simple, low-cost tools for assessing whether a project reaches the poor results in either no project monitoring or monitoring activities that use simple but crude descriptions of project beneficiaries (such as the share of women, farm size, or occupation of program beneficiaries), or in rapid or participatory assessments that are not well suited for within- or between-country comparisons.

This chapter describes an operational tool developed by the International Food Policy Research Institute (IFPRI) with the technical and financial support of the Consultative Group to Assist the Poorest (CGAP). The tool was designed to assess the poverty level of beneficiaries of microfinance institutions in relation to the general population in the intervention area. The method constructs a poverty index based on a range of indicators that describe different dimensions of poverty and for which credible information can be quickly and inexpensively obtained. The statistical method of principle component analysis determines the mix of indicators that effectively describes a household's relative poverty status.

To ensure the tool's widespread usefulness to a broad range of institutions and programs, specific design parameters for its development were defined. First, the tool should be implementable by national research organizations, consultants, and universities in developing countries that have prior experience with socioeconomic surveys and statistical analysis. Second, to be useful to policy analysts, donors, and development practitioners, the tool must meet reasonable

We thank the Policy Advisory Committee of Consultative Group to Assist the Poorest (CGAP) and participants in a virtual meeting, who provided useful and critical comments. We also thank the managers and staff of the four participating microfinance institutions. Brigit Helms of CGAP deserves special thanks for valuable comments and critical questions that greatly improved the tool and its presentation. A manual (Henry et al. 2001) describing each analysis step in implementing the tool can be downloaded at CGAP's website: http://www.cgap.org/publications/other.

time as well as cost constraints; that is, the evaluation procedure must be completed in a few months, with the average cost per assessment not exceeding US$10,000. Third, the tool should be flexible and general enough for use in both urban and rural areas and results should be interpretable across programs within countries and, if possible, also between countries.

The tool was tested in collaboration with microfinance institutions (MFIs) in four case studies: one in Latin America, two in Sub-Saharan Africa, and one in Asia. The tool has a potential for broader application, however, not only in the field of microfinance but for other development interventions with clearly defined target groups such as various types of income transfer and public work programs as well as other interventions related to food and social security. However, it is recommended that future research studies validate the tool through comparison with established national poverty benchmarks.[1]

Choice of Methodology

The characteristics of poverty are multidimensional, encompassing several aspects of a household's economic and social status. Capturing these dimensions requires both qualitative and quantitative indicators. In development practice, three major types of poverty assessment method are generally used:

- Construction of a poverty line and computation of various poverty measures that take into account the way in which actual household expenditures fall short of the poverty line (Foster, Greer, and Thorbecke 1984; Ravallion 1994; Streeten 1994).
- Rapid appraisal and participatory appraisal methods, in which households are ranked with respect to their wealth by community members themselves (Bilsborrow 1994).
- Construction of a poverty index using a range of qualitative and quantitative indicators (Chung et al. 1997; Hatch and Frederick 1998).

Within the context of specific design constraints set for the tool's development, the advantages and disadvantages of the three methods can be assessed.

---

1. Among the different development interventions, microfinance is increasingly viewed as a way to enable the poor to carry out profitable self-employment activities. The need to reach out to the poor through microcredit was re-emphasized at the Microcredit Summit in 1997, but many practitioners, donors, and researchers perceive a trade-off between financial sustainability and depth of outreach, although the exact nature of the trade-off is not well understood (see, for example, Hulme and Mosley 1996 and other chapters in this volume). At present, no operational, low-cost tool exists for measuring the depth of poverty outreach of MFIs in a way that allows for within- or between-country comparisons. The lack of a practical poverty assessment tool was the motivation for this collaboration.

Computation of a Poverty Line Based on Household Expenditures

The standard practice in poverty analysis has been to use household total expenditure as the primary measure to evaluate the standard of living of households (Grootaert 1983, 1986). Nationally representative household surveys such as the Living Standard Measurement Survey conducted by the World Bank are typically used to estimate a poverty line and to measure the incidence of poverty.

The criteria used in assessing whether a household is poor are based on an evaluation of whether household income is sufficient to meet the food and other basic needs of all household members. To make the assessment, a basket of goods and services corresponding with local consumption patterns and satisfying a pre-set level of basic needs for one person is constructed and valued at local consumer prices to compute its minimum cost. The value of this basket is called the "poverty line," and is most commonly expressed in per capita terms. If the per capita income of household members is below the poverty line, the household and its members are considered poor. If this does not hold, the household is categorized as nonpoor (Lipton and Ravallion 1995; Aho, Larivière, and Martin 1998).

A poverty line based on household expenditures is a widely accepted measure of poverty—as far as its *economic* dimension is concerned. However, the data requirements of this method are very steep, and extremely comprehensive questionnaires are required to collect the data needed. The standard practice is to record food expenditures using a recall period of one week, and to collect information on various nonfood expenditures using a combination of monthly or yearly recall periods. Even though poor households in developing countries consume a small number of goods, accuracy in reporting is a valid concern given the long recall periods. Even if consumption items can be accurately recalled, ways have to be found to value home-produced foods when market prices are lacking; irregular weights and measures cause problems in the computation of quantities; and information on a number of high-value items (for example, the rental value of housing) is likely to be seriously deficient. Of course, the scale of these problems can be substantially minimized through extensive training of interviewers, multiple household visits, and cataloging of informal weights and measures. However, the resulting survey cost and the time required to address these problems are likely to be prohibitive. Moreover, the analysis of expenditure data necessitates advanced skills in statistical data analysis, which translates into high costs for data analysis as well.

The costs of the survey could potentially be reduced if evaluators have access to data on a national benchmark poverty indicator established in a previous national household survey on poverty. They could then choose to undertake a similar household survey only for MFI clients and to compare these results with the national poverty benchmark for the general population. This kind of comparison has recently been done by Navajas et al. (2000) in Bolivia. One of the major strengths of this approach is that a nationally accepted poverty measure is used and the issue of how to measure poverty is avoided. In the case of Bolivia, the national poverty benchmark is the Index of Fulfillment of Basic Needs (IFBN), an index based on a basket of indicators. This index comprises about 10 indicators capturing housing quality, access to public services, education, and access to informal and formal health services; the indicators are combined using weights determined by a form of consultative process among national poverty experts and policy analysts. Navajas et al. (2000) obtained information on these indicators in their survey of MFI clients (with the exception of access to health services) and computed the index so as to be comparable to the already available national benchmark. This is a useful approach when a relatively simple poverty index has been established at the national level.

However, the approach of comparing information on MFI clients with a national poverty benchmark for the general population is not universally applicable.

1. The method is applicable only in developing countries that have already undertaken a national poverty study on the basis of which a poverty benchmark index or a poverty line has been established.
2. The national poverty measure is usually based on expenditure data rather than on a range of qualitative indicators (as indeed is the case in Bolivia). When this is so, a very detailed and time-consuming expenditure survey of MFI clients is required, usually violating the design parameters for a low-cost operational tool for assessing the poverty outreach of a development institution. Moreover, whenever a substantial time lapse occurs between the national survey that established the accepted poverty measure and the assessment exercise, factors such as inflation and changes in relative prices are likely to make comparisons difficult or even plainly inadvisable. Tackling such issues usually requires advanced analytical skills and access to the source data from the national survey.
3. In many countries, access to the national data may be restricted or the government may be reluctant to release it. Other countries (for example, China) sell the data at costs that exceed the field research budget envisaged for this tool.
4. The data may be poorly documented so that considerable time is needed for a skilled poverty analyst to make the data comparable and to resolve the issues of inflation and changes in relative prices.
5. To assure valid comparison, the data collection methodology used in the program assessment exercise must closely replicate the method used in the national poverty assessment. This requires a level of collaboration with the national agency that implemented the national poverty assessment that may either not be feasible or be too expensive.

6. Because MFIs are expected to operate in less poor regions or cities of a country, there may well be selection bias in program placement, which an assessment should be able to account for (Sharma and Zeller 1999).

In summary, although comparison with existing national benchmarks may provide a valid assessment of the poverty outreach of an MFI, it is, in practice, often unfeasible. We conclude that the tool, to be universally applicable, must collect poverty data for nonclients as well in order to assess the relative poverty of MFI clients.

Rapid Appraisal and Participatory Appraisal

Rapid appraisal (RA) and participatory appraisal (PA) are grouped together as the second method. The two approaches are often thought to be the same, since they seek input from community members using similar techniques, for example, wealth ranking and community mapping. There are differences, however (Bergeron, Morris, and Banegas 1998). The ultimate goal of PA is empowerment of the target group. This necessitates extensive participation by the community and assumes an open research and development agenda. This can hardly be done within one or two days. RA methods, on the other hand, are meant to provide evaluators with data on the community in a very short time. RA requires the participation of the community, but the time frame is usually a one-day visit to the community and the agenda of the inquiry is predetermined.

RA and PA methods are widely used and accepted tools for identifying vulnerable groups in a community (Bilsborrow 1994; Boltvinik 1994; Hatch and Frederick 1998). Development programs and institutions, including MFIs, use them extensively for targeting services to poorer clients. The RA method, in particular, has relatively low time requirements for data collection. Although these methods can be well suited for targeting and for the participatory design of development projects and services, a number of disadvantages exist for assessing poverty for purposes of regional, national, or international comparisons (see also Chung et al. 1997).

1. The results are difficult to verify because they stem from the subjective ratings of community members. Thus, the results are difficult to compare across geographic locations or programs in a country (Chung et al. 1997).
2. The approach is likely to find poor people in any community, and the percentages of poor people may not vary much across villages. In other words, the method may be consistent in finding the poorest third in one village, but it may not be consistent in finding in which communities the poorest third of an entire region reside.
3. Because the results are hard to verify—a problem with household expenditure as well—strategic responses that make all or certain groups of the community poorer cannot be ruled out: the respondents may expect to receive benefits, such as access to financial services, after the completion of

the poverty assessment. To avoid this kind of bias or strategic response, verifiable indicators should be used as much as possible.
4. The PA method requires skillful and experienced communicators, who will command higher salaries than will enumerators who are required only to apply a structured and formalized questionnaire.
5. For national and international comparisons, there could be concern about the bias introduced by the way that PA is implemented.

Thus, although we agree with Chung et al. (1997) that these methods are useful and operational for targeting services by specific development programs, including MFIs, they considerably violate the design constraints spelled out above.

Constructing a Poverty Index Based on a Range of Indicators

A third method of assessment is to identify a range of household indicators that describe different dimensions of poverty and for which credible information can be quickly and inexpensively obtained. Once information on the range of indicators has been collected, the indicators may be aggregated into a single index of poverty by using some weighting scheme. One well-known application of this method is the Human Development Index (HDI) (Annand and Sen 1994; UNDP 1999), which is based on three components: educational attainment, life expectancy at birth, and per capita income adjusted for purchasing power parity. The national poverty index for Bolivia, mentioned above, also follows this method. Another popular indicator method is the housing index used by many MFIs (in particular, in South and Southeast Asia) for targeting financial services to poorer clients (Hatch and Frederick 1998). The method has shown considerable potential within South Asia but appears less appropriate in Africa, where housing characteristics are not as variable. The method also depends upon a predetermined list of indicators and weights for each indicator.

In principle, the time and cost requirements for data collection and analysis using the indicator method can be relatively low. In addition, the method supports the inclusion of several dimensions of poverty and permits the mix and weighting of indicators to be adjusted according to their relevance within a local context. For these reasons, the indicator method was chosen as the basis for the poverty assessment tool. The tool seeks to build on the many strengths of the housing index but allows for a rigorous and standardized procedure for determining the weights and including alternative, location-specific indicators through the application of principal component analysis.

Multiple Dimensions of Poverty and the Choice of Indicators for the Case Studies

Because of the multifaceted nature of poverty, reliance on any one poverty dimension such as housing, food security, or access to education was deemed inappropriate. Rather, to capture different dimensions of poverty, two groups of indicators were developed and tested with a generic questionnaire with four MFIs, one in Latin America, two in Sub-Saharan Africa, and one in Asia.

The first group of indicators expresses the means to achieve welfare. These reflect the income potential of households and their members and relate to the household's human capital (family size, education, occupation, and so on), physical capital (type and value of assets owned), and social capital (for indicators on social capital, see, for example, Grootaert 1998). The second group includes indicators related to achievements in consumption in order to fulfill present and future basic needs (namely access to health services, food, electricity, energy, water, shelter and clothing, human security, and environmental quality). Studies comparing different indicators based on income and consumption conclude that recommending one measure over another is difficult (Skoufias, Davis, and Soto 2000). However, consumption over time (seasons or years) is more stable than income, and households provide information more easily on what they consume than on what they earn. For this reason, our method heavily relies on consumption indicators, although the first group of indicators expressing the means available to the household to increase its standard of living is also included.

In coming up with reliable indicators, the key challenge is to identify key components of consumption that either are unambiguous measures of poverty (such as incidence of hunger) or correlate well with total household expenditures. Hence, it is not necessary to compile all the food and nonfood expenditures of a household, because some types of expense are closely related to the level of poverty of a household, and others are not. For example, studies have shown that the proportion of clothing expenditure in the household budget is stable, at 5–10 percent of total expenses (Aho, Larivière, and Martin 1998; Minten and Zeller 2000). Morris et al. (1999) found clothing expenditure to be one of the expenditure components that increased proportionally with total household expenditures. Since clothing, unlike food commodities, usually requires the purchase of either the finished garment or materials to make a garment, it does not pose the valuation problem associated with imputing costs for home-produced goods.

The initial compilation of poverty indicators for field testing was based on a detailed review of results from large, in-depth surveys on household economics as well as of indicators and methods used by MFIs, famine early warning systems, and national monitoring systems for food security, nutrition, and vulnerability (see, for example, Radimer et al. 1992; Wratten 1995; Microcredit Summit Campaign 1999). The preselection of over 300 indicators was guided by an extensive literature review and expert consultation as well as an eight-point set of criteria to evaluate the indicator's suitability based on suitability for rural and urban contexts, the sensitivity of the question, the time and cost requirements to obtain an answer, the quality of the indicator in discriminating between different poverty levels, reliability (including the possibility to verify the answer in a recheck), simplicity, and universality in an international context. In each test case, local insight was drawn upon to adapt the questionnaire for local-level specificities. It is, of course, not surprising that many of the preselected indicators are used by national poverty and vulnerability monitoring systems as well as by development programs, including MFIs. For example, all of the indicators used to construct the housing index and the indicators of the net worth test used by the Grameen Bank were included.

The questionnaire was field tested in four countries with large differences in poverty level and socioeconomic and cultural contexts, and with MFIs that worked in urban, or rural, or mixed areas with different target clientele and financial products. The selection of the case-study countries was guided by the desire to have as much heterogeneity as possible.

Indicators in the Final Recommended Questionnaire

The selection of the final list of indicators (Table 9.1) for a recommended questionnaire was based on a number of criteria, including the ease and accuracy with which information on the indicators could be elicited in the household survey and the significance of the correlation of the indicator with per capita expenditure on clothing and footwear (the poverty benchmark indicator).[2] Other important aspects were the suitability of indicators in all four case studies, the estimated cost and difficulty associated with each indicator, and the indicator's ability to meet data analysis requirements of being applicable to all households and transformable into an ordinal or scaled variable. Finally, local panels of researchers provided feedback on the validity of indicator results. The indicators that were selected for the final recommended questionnaire are listed in Table 9.1.[3]

Estimation of the Poverty Index with Principal Component Analysis

The use of multiple indicators enables a more complete description of poverty, but it also complicates the task of drawing comparisons. The wide arrays of indicators have to be summarized in a logical way, which underlines the importance of combining information from the different indicators into a single index. The creation of an index requires the difficult undertaking of finding a set of weights that can be meaningfully applied to different indicators so as to come to an overall conclusion.

---

2. Per capita clothing expenditure was chosen as the benchmark indicator because it bears a stable and highly linear relationship with total consumption expenditure, a comprehensive and widely accepted measure of poverty.

3. See Henry et al. (2001) for the full version of the recommended questionnaire.

TABLE 9.1 Indicators in the final recommended questionnaire

Human Resources	Dwelling	Food Security and Vulnerability	Assets	Others
• Age and sex of adult household members • Level of education of adult household members • Occupation of adult household members • Number of children below 15 years of age in household • Annual clothing/ footwear expenditure for all household members	• Number of rooms • Type of roofing • Type of exterior walls • Type of flooring • Observed structural condition of dwelling • Type of electric connection • Type of cooking fuel used • Source of drinking water • Type of latrine	• Number of meals served in last two days • Serving frequency (weekly) of three luxury foods • Serving frequency (weekly) of one inferior food • Hunger episodes in last one month • Hunger episodes in last 12 months • Frequency of purchase of staple goods • Size of stock of local staple in dwelling	• Area and value of land owned • Number and value of selected livestock resources • Value of transportation-related assets • Value of selected electric appliances	• Nonclient's assessment of poverty outreach of MFI

The usual practice is for evaluators to set the weights themselves, taking account of local conditions but otherwise involving a significant degree of arbitrariness. However, in order to allow comparisons between MFIs within and across countries, an aggregation method was required that would evaluate each indicator and determine the weights in a standardized and rigorous way. However, because the relative strengths of different indicators in predicting poverty are very likely to vary across regions and countries, a method was called for that allows weights for each situation to be adjusted based on the specific poverty context. For example, for the case of nutritional indicators, Habicht and Pelletier (1990) show that context matters in the choice of appropriate nutrition-related indicators. Moreover, the aggregation method should allow the testing and eventual inclusion of indicators that are location specific and are recommended by national experts. Thus, although the indicators in Table 9.1 are recommended, the poverty assessment tool allows the inclusion and testing of additional local indicators. For example, in Nicaragua, a large proportion of rural households had members who worked abroad and improved the living standard of the family through remittances. Hence, a remittance-related indicator was deemed important.

The method of principal component (PC) analysis, when used as an aggregation procedure, addresses most of the concerns raised above in an objective and rigorous way (see, for example, Temple and Johnson 1998; and Filmer and Pritchett 1998, 2000).[4] Specifically, PC analysis isolates and measures the poverty component embedded in the various poverty indicators and creates a household-specific poverty score or index. This index is then used to compare client and nonclient households' relative poverty. Basically, the principal component technique slices the information contained in the set of indicators into several components. Each component is constructed as a unique index based on the values of all the indicators. The main idea is to formulate a new variable, X^*, which is the linear combination of the original indicators such that it accounts for the maximum of the total variance in the original indicators. That is, X^* is computed as

$$X^* = w_1 X_1 + w_2 X_2 + w_3 X_3,$$

where the weights (the ws) are specified such that X^* accounts for the maximum variances in X_1, X_2, and X_3. This index has a zero mean and a standard deviation equal to one (Basilevsky 1994; Sharma 1996).

The PC analysis therefore extracts the underlying components from a set of information provided by summary indicators. In the case of this poverty assessment tool, information collected from the questionnaires makes up the "indicators," and the underlying component that is isolated and measured is "poverty." The first principal component accounts for the largest proportion of the total variability in the set of indicators used. The second component accounts for the next largest amount of variability not accounted for by the first component, and so on for the higher-order components.

---

4. Because of lack of income and expenditure data, Filmer and Pritchett (1998) and Sahn and Stifel (2000) apply the principal component method to national household data for India and to data from the Demographic and Health Surveys of various African countries, respectively. Filmer and Pritchett (1998) estimate the relationship between household wealth and the probability that a child is enrolled in school. As a proxy for household wealth, they constructed a linear asset index from a set of asset indicators, using the principal component technique. They conclude that this index is robust, produces internally coherent results, and provides a close correspondence with available economic data at higher aggregation levels. They then validate this method with other data sets from Nepal, Indonesia, and Pakistan that contain asset indicators and consumption expenditures as well. They find that the asset index has reasonable coherence with current consumption expenditures and works as well as—or better than—traditional expenditure measures in predicting enrollment status.

FIGURE 9.1 Poverty indicators and underlying components

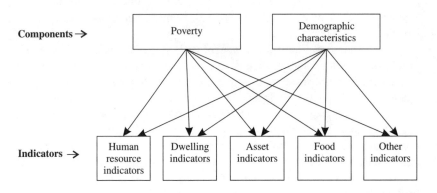

In the example presented in Figure 9.1, PC analysis uses the information on co-movement among the indicators to isolate and quantify the underlying common components, which are poverty and demography. The poverty component is expected to account for most of the movement in the indicators and will be the "strongest" of the components. The poverty component can be easily identified by analyzing the signs and size of the indicators in relation to the new component variable. For example, according to theory, education level should contribute positively—not negatively—to wealth.

PC analysis can thus be used to compute a series of weights that mark each indicator's relative contribution to the overall poverty component. Using these weights, a household-specific poverty index (or score) can be computed based on each household's indicator values.

In the test cases, the indicators contributing to the index were selected in two stages of statistical analysis. First, the strength and significance of the correlation of each of the initial 300 indicators used in the test studies with the poverty benchmark indicator (per capita clothing expenditure) were tested. Only those that were significantly correlated (with a probability of error of less than 10 percent) with the benchmark indicator were submitted to the second stage involving principal component analysis. In each of the four case-study countries, 40–50 indicators passed the first stage. In the second stage, various criteria and cutoff values concerning the results[5] of the PC analysis were used

---

5. The criteria or levels for accepting an indicator recommended in the manual (Henry et al. 2001) are that (1) the component loading has the expected sign following theory; (2) the values for communality for an indicator should be above 0.2 and the overall PC model should have a Kaiser–Meyer–Olkin (KMO) index above 0.6. These criteria were followed in all four case studies, and led—after prescreening them by their correlation with the poverty benchmark—to the selection of about 20 indicators to contribute to the country-specific poverty index.

across all case studies to accept or reject indicators. Table 9.2 lists the indicators for the four country studies (MFI-A, MFI-B, MFI-C, and MFI-D) that were selected by the standard two-stage selection procedure.

The four case studies use between 14 and 20 indicators each that combine different dimensions of poverty concerning human resources, housing conditions, assets, and food security and vulnerability. It is noteworthy that 9 indicators (out of a potential 300) were commonly used in three of the four cases studies.

HUMAN RESOURCES.   Eight indicators related to human resources were used in the four case studies. These indicators reflect the level of education in the household and the presence of unskilled labor force. The percentage of wage laborers in the household seems to be particularly important in the relatively poorer countries of southern Africa and South Asia (MFI-C and MFI-D). The indicator expressing the level of education of the household head was used in two out of four countries.

DWELLING.   Dwelling indicators discriminated between relative poverty levels well. In the case of MFI-D in South Asia, 8 of 20 indicators related to housing quality. This supports the use of the housing index as an important indicator of poverty in South Asia. However, in the African cases (MFI-B and MFI-C), where housing is relatively homogeneous, only four or five housing indicators were used, respectively. The quality of latrines appeared in all the case studies. House size (rooms per person) was used in three countries.

ASSETS.   A total of 15 indicators on the number or value of assets is included in the four case studies. They were particularly important (5 out of 16 indicators) in the Central American country (MFI-A), the most well-off country in the sample. The amount of land possessed is important only for MFIs serving rural and agricultural areas, as is the case for MFI-D.

FOOD SECURITY AND VULNERABILITY.   These indicators turned out to be very important in explaining differences in relative poverty in all four studies, particularly in the southern African country (MFI-C), which is the poorest. The indicator of chronic hunger (episodes of hunger in the last 12 months) appears in all four cases. Indicators of short-term hunger (episodes of hunger in the last 30 days) and frequency of luxury food consumption during the week appeared in three cases.

Interpretation of Results

As indicated above, principal component analysis produces a household-level poverty index. Figure 9.2 gives an example of the distribution of the poverty index across households using MFI-B data.

In each case study, a random sample of 300 nonclient households and 200 client households was chosen. To use the poverty index for making comparisons, the nonclient sample was first sorted in an ascending order according to its in-

TABLE 9.2 Indicators selected to represent the poverty index, by country

Poverty Indicator	MFI-A	MFI-B	MFI-C	MFI-D	Number of Indicators
Human resources	**1**	**1**	**2**	**3**	**7**
1. Maximum level of education in household			x	x	2
2. Percentage of adults who are wage laborers			x	x	2
3. Education level of household head	x			x	2
4. Percentage of literate adults in household		x			1
Dwelling	**5**	**4**	**5**	**8**	**22**
1. Value of dwelling	x			x	2
2. Roof made of permanent material			x	x	2
3. Walls made of permanent material		x		x	2
4. Quality of flooring material				x	1
5. Electric connection		x	x	x	3
6. Source of cooking fuel	x			x	2
7. Latrines in the house	x	x	x	x	4
8. Number of rooms per person	x		x	x	3
9. Access to water		x	x		2
10. Structure of the house	x				1
Assets	**5**	**4**	**3**	**3**	**15**
1. Irrigated land owned				x	1
2. Number of TVs	x	x			2
3. Number of radios				x	1
4. Number of fans			x	x	2
5. Number of VCRs	x				1
6. Value of radio	x				1
7. Value of electrical devices	x	x	x		3
8. Value of vehicles	x				1
9. Value of assets per person/adult	x	x	x		3
Food security and vulnerability	**4**	**4**	**7**	**6**	**21**
1. Number of meals served in last two days				x	1
2. Episodes of hunger during last 30 days	x	x		x	3
3. Episodes of hunger in last 12 months	x	x	x	x	4
4. Number of days with luxury food 1		x	x	x	3
5. Number of days with luxury food 2		x	x	x	3
6. Number of days with inferior food			x	x	2
7. Frequency of purchase of basic good (Type 1)	x		x		2

continued

TABLE 9.2 *Continued*

Poverty Indicator	MFI-A	MFI-B	MFI-C	MFI-D	Number of Indicators
8. Frequency of purchase of basic good (Type 2)			x		1
9. Food stock in house	x				1
10. Use of cooking oil			x		1
Miscellaneous indicators	**1**	**1**	**0**	**0**	**2**
1. Per person expenditure on clothing	x	x			2
Total number of indicators	**16**	**14**	**17**	**20**	

dex score. Once sorted, the 300 nonclient households were divided into terciles of 100 households each, based on their index score: the top third of the nonclient households were grouped in the "higher" group, the middle third in the "middle" group, and the bottom third in the "lowest" group (Figure 9.3). The cutoff scores for each tercile define the limits of each poverty group. Client households are then categorized in the three groups based on their household scores.

If the pattern of the client households' poverty matches that of the nonclient households, client households would divide equally among the three

FIGURE 9.2 Histogram of the standardized poverty index (MFI-B)

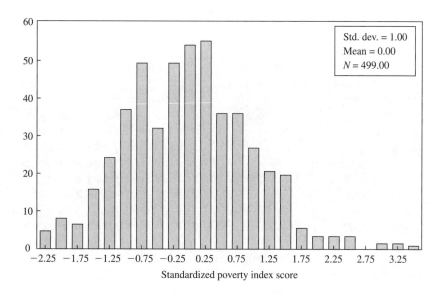

Std. dev. = 1.00
Mean = 0.00
$N = 499.00$

FIGURE 9.3 Constructing poverty groups

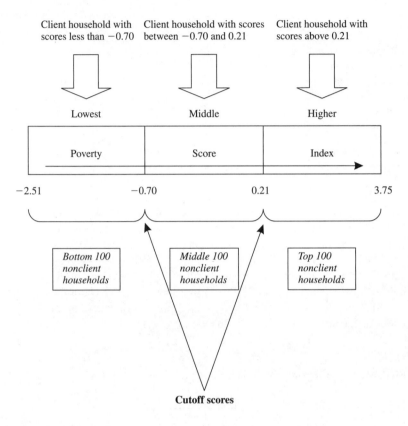

poverty groupings in the same way as the nonclient households, with 33 percent falling in each group. Any deviation from this equal proportion would signal a difference between the client and the nonclient populations. For instance, if 60 percent of the client households fall into the first tercile, or poorest category, the MFI is reaching a disproportionate number of very poor clients relative to the general population. We suggest two ratios for measuring poverty outreach within the operational area of the MFI. The first ratio is the share of clients in the poorest tercile divided by 33 percent. Ratios with values above 1 indicate disproportionately high MFI outreach within the tercile, while values below 1 indicate disproportionately low MFI outreach. In the above example, ratio 1 (see Henry et al. 2001) would have a value of 1.81. Ratio 2 is the share of clients in the least poor tercile divided by 33 percent, and it similarly assesses the MFI outreach for that tercile. Illustrative examples from the four case studies are provided below.

FIGURE 9.4 MFI-A: Distribution of client and nonclient households across poverty groups

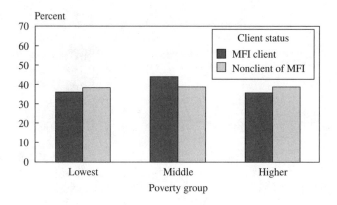

Microfinance Institution A

Figure 9.4 presents the poverty groups by client and nonclient households. The distribution of MFI-A's clients across the poverty groups closely mirrors the distribution of nonclients, indicating that MFI-A serves a clientele that is quite similar to the general population in its operational area. This result is consistent with MFI-A's stated objective of reaching micro, small, and medium enterprises and the diversity in the financial products that it offers.

Microfinance Institution B

Figure 9.5 shows that the poorest households are underrepresented among MFI-B clients. However, about one-half of the clients fall into the "lowest" and "middle" categories, which is remarkable considering the mission of the institution (to reach all women in business), the focus of the product (to finance businesses after submitting a business plan), and the lack of overt targeting.

Microfinance Institution C

About half of MFI-C's clients belong to the "higher" group, while they are underrepresented in the poorest group (Figure 9.6). This result reflects the fact that MFI-C's membership is share based and open to all individuals. However, poverty outreach is significantly higher when considering only clients belonging to the new program for women. Nearly one-half (45.2 percent) of these clients belonged to the "lowest" group and only 19 percent belonged to the "higher" group.

FIGURE 9.5 MFI-B: Distribution of client and nonclient households across poverty groups

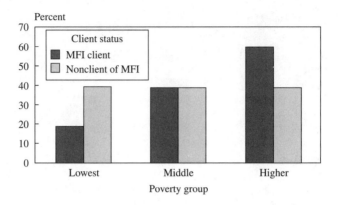

Microfinance Institution D

Figure 9.7 indicates quite clearly that the poorest groups are strongly over-represented and that less poor households are underrepresented among MFI-D's clients. This result not only is consistent with MFI-D's explicit aim to serve the poorest households in its operational area, but also indicates considerable success in its targeting practices.

Comparisons within and across Countries

Although the comparative percentage breakdowns of clients and nonclients can provide relative poverty comparisons in the operational area of the MFI (which

FIGURE 9.6 MFI-C: Distribution of client and nonclient households across poverty groups

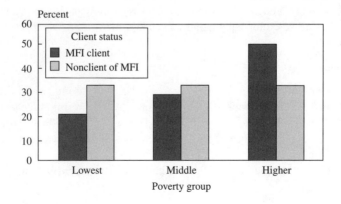

FIGURE 9.7 MFI-D: Distribution of client and nonclient households across poverty groups

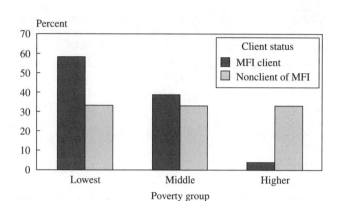

can be alternatively expressed as two ratios covering the outreach to households belonging to either the first or the third tercile), this information must be supplemented by country-level information when making comparisons within and across countries. This is because the index uses relative, and not absolute, poverty; thus, it may well be that the "poorest" clients in a relatively rich region or country have higher standards of living than the "least poor" clients in a poorer region or country.

For within-country comparisons we suggest a third ratio, based on either expert knowledge or national poverty assessments (Henry et al. 2001), that compares the poverty level of the operational area (province, counties, and so on) of the MFI with the national average to determine whether the MFI operates in above- or below-average areas.

A particularly simple way to account for between-country poverty levels using an indicator-based framework like ours is to use the human development index (HDI) computed by the United Nations Development Programme (UNDP). In all the case studies reported here, for example, countries had HDI indices that fell below the "developing country average" (see Table 9.3). To take a more specific example, the HDI for the southern African country where MFI-C is located is less than 60 percent of the average for all developing countries taken together. Therefore, even the "less poor" clients of MFI-C are likely to be very poor according to international standards. With these additional ratios, the poverty outreach of an MFI can be assessed within and across countries. Clearly an MFI operating in a better-off area of a country with a high HDI, a low ratio 1, and a high ratio 2 will receive low ranks for poverty outreach.

To give an example for a regional assessment based on secondary data, we refer to recent studies in Mexico (Wollni 2001; Zeller, Wollni, and Shaban 2002),

TABLE 9.3 Relative poverty ranking of clients versus nonclients

Percentage/Ratio	MFI-A	MFI-B	MFI-C	MFI-D
Percentage of client households that are as poor as the poorest one-third of the nonclient population	30.90	16.00	20.30	58.00
Percentage of client households that are as well off as the least poor one-third of the nonclient population	31.40	51.00	50.80	3.50
Ratio of country HDI to HDI for all developing countries taken together	0.98	0.79	0.75	0.79

which use the poverty assessment tool presented in this chapter to evaluate the poverty level of clients of Compartamos, an MFI working in several states of Mexico. The regional assessment of poverty outreach of Compartamos is based on secondary data provided by INEGI (the National Institute of Statistics, Geography and Informatics. INEGI had realized a classification of the Mexican regions according to their level of well-being at two geographic levels: states and municipalities, the latter being a smaller administrative division. The methodology applied for categorizing the different regions is an indicator-based approach encompassing different aspects of life such as housing, human capital, demography, and so on, thus being consistent with our poverty assessment tool. The state-level classification by level of well-being is presented in the map in Figure 9.8.

On the basis of these poverty categories (summarized for the purpose of this study from the original seven classes into three categories), the operational area of the MFI is compared with the remaining Mexican regions. Interestingly, the results of the state-level assessment, on one hand, and of the municipality-level assessment, on the other, diverge significantly. State-level results indicate that most clients of Compartamos are served in states that have a low living standard. The placement of branches seems to have been guided by the objective of reaching the poorest states in the country. But a state-level comparison does not account for major disparities within these areas. Equally relevant in evaluating the level of well-being of the operational area are the municipality-level results. Compared with states, municipalities are smaller and thus more homogeneous regions providing more accurate data on the level of well-being of the resident population. The comparison at this disaggregated level reveals that most branches of the studied MFI are located in municipalities with a high living standard. It is likely that this decision of branch placement has been guided by the availability of infrastructure and other facilities, economic opportunities, and density of population (Sharma and Zeller 1999). All these factors tend to favor areas with high living standards. Figure 9.9 shows the distribution

FIGURE 9.8 Classification of the Mexican states according to the level of well-being

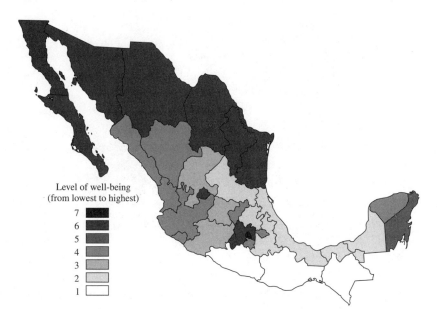

of clients and national population across municipalities with different levels of well-being. We can observe that the vast majority (60.7 percent) of MFI clients live in high living standard areas, whereas only a minute proportion is served by a branch located in a low living standard municipality.

Yet, considering the distribution of the national population, a slightly different picture emerges. As most Mexicans live in high living standard municipalities, clients are not overrepresented in that category. Even taking into account this distribution of the national population, it is evident that the MFI's market penetration is higher in the better-off areas, while the poor areas are clearly underserved. Thus, it can be concluded that the Mexican MFI operates mainly in above-average areas. For the household level this implies that it should be relatively easy for the MFI to reach the poorest parts of the population within its operational area. The percentages shown in Figure 9.9 can also be expressed as ratios, for example computed as the percentage of clients living in areas with a low living standard divided by the percentage of the national population living in those areas.

Finally, a comprehensive assessment of an MFI must include an evaluation of how its poverty outreach record reconciles with its mission and program objectives (Henry et al. 2001). In our case studies, the MFIs differ in terms of geography, their stated mission, the type of market niche they seek, their preference for a specific type of institutional culture, and a host of other factors.

FIGURE 9.9   Distribution of clients and of the national population across levels of well-being

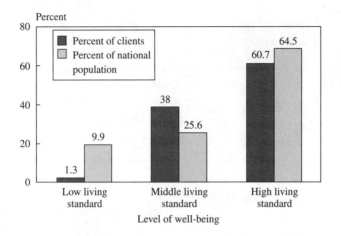

Ignoring these considerations or providing incomplete information on institutional details fails to tell a complete story, and the method can be easily misused. In all of the case studies reported here, the managers of the MFIs considered the results to be credible. The results, as discussed above, are also consistent with the mission, priorities, and targeting practices of the case-study MFIs.

Concluding Remarks

The case studies presented in this chapter contribute to the development and testing of a relatively simple tool that can be used to assess the poverty level of clients of development projects in relation to nonclients. The main features of this new tool are that (1) it identifies and/or constructs a small set of indicators that are powerful descriptors of poverty and are applicable across relatively diverse socioeconomic settings; (2) the chosen indicators are such that reliable information on them can be collected quickly and inexpensively; (3) the tool offers an objective method for summarizing overall poverty information and unambiguously ranking households by their relative poverty level; and (4) it recommends computation of three simple ratios that facilitate quick comparison of the poverty outreach of microfinance institutions even across international boundaries. The method is equally applicable for assessing the poverty outreach of other development policies and projects such as safety net and rural development programs (Zeller et al. 2001; Zeller, Wollni, and Shaban 2002). However, as with any new method, we recommend its additional testing and validation.

In particular, there is a need to compare rankings produced by this method with rankings produced by other methods and using other benchmarks (for example, total household income or expenditure).

A disadvantage of the method presented here is that it does not provide information on the absolute level of poverty. In many cases, however, it is relative rather than absolute poverty that is of concern to the policymakers or evaluators. Further, many summary measures used in development policy to measure absolute poverty, such as the cutoff of US$1–2 per day used by the World Bank and other international organizations, are essentially quite arbitrary (because purchasing power varies widely across countries), and the merits of using such measures are not clear in many cases. More precise measures of absolute poverty based on the poverty line and the basic needs concept are riddled with problems relating to the definition of the representative basket of basic needs in a country. Poverty is an inherently relative concept, and the tool developed in this chapter is indeed aiming to measure relative poverty. Therefore, the tool, and the poverty outreach ratios it generates, allow the poverty-targeting efficiency of development projects to be evaluated at low cost.

References

Aho, G., S. Larivière, and F. Martin. 1998. *Poverty analysis manual: Applications in Benin*. Benin: UNDP, Université Nationale du Bénin, Université Laval.

Annand, S., and A. Sen. 1994. *Human development index: Methodology and measurement*. Human Development Report Office Occasional Paper No 12. New York: United Nations Development Program.

Basilevsky, A. 1994. *Statistical factor analysis and related methods*. New York: John Wiley.

Bergeron, G., S. S. Morris, and J.-M. M. Banegas. 1998. How reliable are group informant ratings? A test of food security rating in Honduras. Food Consumption and Nutrition Division Discussion Paper 43. International Food Policy Research Institute, Washington, D.C., April.

Bilsborrow, R. 1994. Towards a rapid assessment of poverty. In *Poverty monitoring: An international concern*, ed. R. van der Hoeven and R. Anker. New York: St. Martin's Press.

Boltvinik, J. 1994. Poverty measurement and alternative indicators of development. In *Poverty monitoring: An international concern*, ed. R. van der Hoeven and R. Anker, pp. 57–83. New York: St. Martin's Press.

Chung, K., L. Haddad, J. Ramakrishna, and F. Riely. 1997. Identifying the food insecure: The application of mixed-method approaches in India. International Food Policy Research Institute, Washington, D.C.

Filmer, D., and L. Pritchett. 1998. Estimating wealth effects without expenditure data or tears: With an application to educational enrollments in states of India. Working Paper No. 1994, Poverty and Human Resources, Development Research Group. World Bank, Washington, D.C. Available at <http://www.worldbank.org/research/projects/edattain/edworld.htm>.

―――. 2000. The effect of household wealth on educational attainment around the world: Demographic and health survey evidence. *Population and Development Review* 25 (1). Appeared as World Bank Policy Research Working Paper No. 1980 in September 1998. Available at <http://www.worldbank.org/research/projects/edattain/edworld.htm>.

Foster, J., J. Greer, and E. Thorbecke. 1984. A class of decomposable poverty measures. *Econometrica* 52 (3): 761–765.

Gibbons, D., and J. DeWit. 1998. Targeting the poorest and covering costs. Paper No. 1, Microcredit Summit Poverty Measurement Discussion Group. Available at <http://www.microcreditsummit.org>.

Grootaert, C. 1983. The conceptual basis of measures of household welfare and their implied survey data requirements. *Review of Income and Wealth Series* 29 (1): 1–21.

―――. 1986. *Measuring and analyzing levels of living in developing countries: An annotated questionnaire.* Living Standards Measurement Study, Working Paper No. 24. Washington, D.C: World Bank.

―――. 1998. Social capital, household welfare, and poverty in Indonesia. Social Development Department, Environmentally and Socially Sustainable Development Network. World Bank, Washington, D.C.

Habicht, J. P., and D. L. Pelletier. 1990. The importance of context in choosing nutritional indicators. *Journal of Nutrition* 120 (11) (Supplement): 1519–1524.

Hatch, J., and L. Frederick. 1998. Poverty assessment by micro-finance institutions: A review of current practice. Micro-enterprise best practices. Bethesda, Md., U.S.A.

Henry, C., M. Sharma, C. Lapenu, and M. Zeller. 2001. Assessing the relative poverty of microfinance clients: A CGAP operational tool. Consultative Group to Assist the Poorest (CGAP), World Bank, Washington, D.C. (available at http://www.cgap.org/publications/other); first version published July 2000.

Hulme, D., and P. Mosley. 1996. *Finance against poverty.* London and New York: Routledge.

Lipton, M., and M. Ravallion. 1995. Poverty and policy. In *Handbook of development economics*, Vol. III, ed. B. J. Behrman and T. Srinivasan. Amsterdam: Elsevier.

Microcredit Summit campaign establishes poverty measurement tool kit. 1999. *Countdown 2005* 2 (3).

Minten, B., and M. Zeller, eds. 2000. *Beyond market liberalization: Income generation, welfare and environmental sustainability in Madagascar.* Aldershot, U.K.: Ashgate.

Morris, S. S., C. Carletto, J. Hoddinott, and L. Christiaensen. 1999. *Validity of rapid estimates of household wealth and income for health surveys in rural Africa.* Food Consumption and Nutrition Division Discussion Paper No. 72. International Food Policy Research Institute, Washington, D.C.

Moser, C., M. Gatehouse, and H. Garcia. 1996. *Urban poverty research sourcebook. Module I: Sub-city level household survey.* UNDP/UNCHS/World Bank Urban Management Programme, UMP Working Paper Series No. 5. Washington, D.C: World Bank.

Navajas, S., M. Schreiner, R. Meyer, C. Gonzalez-Vega, and J. Rodriguez-Meza. 2000. Microcredit and the poorest of the poor: Theory and evidence from Bolivia. *World Development* 28 (2): 333–346.

Radimer, K., C. Olson, J. Greene, C. Campbell, and J. P. Habicht. 1992. Understanding hunger and developing indicators to assess it in women and children. *Journal of Nutritional Education* 24 (1): 36–44.

Ravallion, M. 1994. *Poverty comparisons*. Chur, Switzerland: Harwood Academic Publishers.

Sahn, D. E., and D. C. Stifel. 2000. Poverty comparisons over time and across countries in Africa. *World Development* 28 (12): 2123–2155.

Sharma, M., and M. Zeller. 1999. Placement and outreach of group-based credit organizations: The cases of ASA, BRAC, and PROSHIKA in Bangladesh. *World Development* 27 (12): 2123–2136.

Sharma, S. 1996. *Applied multivariate techniques*. New York: John Wiley.

Skoufias, E., B. Davis, and H. Soto. 2000. Practical alternatives to consumption-based welfare measures. Mimeo. International Food Policy Research Institute, Washington, D.C.

Streeten, P. 1994. Poverty concept and measurement. In *Poverty monitoring: An international concern*, ed. R. van der Hoeven and R. Anker, pp. 15–30. New York: St. Martin's Press.

Temple, J., and P. Johnson. 1998. Social capability and economic growth. *Quarterly Journal of Economic Growth* 113 (3): 965–990.

UNDP (United Nations Development Program). 1999. *Human development report*. New York: Oxford University Press.

Wollni, M. 2001. Assessing the poverty outreach of microfinance institutions at household and institutional level. Unpublished Diploma thesis, Institute of Rural Development and Institute of Geography, University of Göttingen, Germany.

Wratten, E. 1995. Conceptualizing urban poverty. *Environment and Urbanization* 7 (1): 11–36.

Zeller, M., M. Wollni, and A. Shaban. 2002. Do safety net and microfinance programs reach the poor? Empirical evidence from Indonesia and Mexico. Paper presented at the International Symposium on Sustaining Food Security and Managing Natural Resources in Southeast Asia: Challenges for the 21st Century, January 8–11, Chiang Mai, Thailand.

Zeller, M., M. Sharma, C. Henry, and C. Lapenu. 2001. An operational tool for evaluating poverty outreach of development policies and projects. Food Consumption and Nutrition Division Discussion Paper No. 111. International Food Policy Research Institute, Washington, D.C., June.

10 Transaction Costs of Group and Individual Lending and Rural Financial Market Access: The Case of Poverty-Oriented Microfinance in Cameroon

FRANZ HEIDHUES, DIEUDONNE BELLE-SOSSOH,
AND GERTRUD BUCHENRIEDER

Rural finance plays an important role in capital formation, agricultural productivity increases, and economic development in rural areas. An accessible and adapted rural financial market offers the rural poor improved financing for production and other priority expenses, such as education, health, food, durable consumption goods, and social obligations (Heidhues 1990, 1995). For this reason, access to financial services can play a particularly important role in improving food security for the poor (Schrieder 1996a, 1996b; Zeller et al. 1997).

The critical role of rural finance in developing economies had been recognized by the 1950s. At that time, however, governments and bilateral and international donors tried to promote rural financial development by implementing approaches led by credit supply rather than savings. Farmers were considered too poor to be able to save. They were supplied targeted credit through specialized agricultural development banks for predefined production purposes. The credit was expected to increase their agricultural productivity, but these agricultural credit programs often failed owing to a lack of outreach, poor repayment performance, inefficiencies, operating losses, and increasing government dependence, all closely related to subsidized interest rates.

This approach to rural credit provision was a response to informal finance, which was widely considered exploitative by donors and governments. The general suspicion about informal financial intermediaries was ubiquitous among financial experts and policymakers. However, the resilience of informal lenders enabled them to continue and expand their activities despite the attempts to replace them with formal institutions (Adams and Fitchett 1992). Since the early 1980s, researchers and policymakers have increasingly recognized that informal financial intermediaries are key providers of financial services to the poorer segments of the urban and rural population in developing countries (African Studies Center 1978). Recognizing their important role in providing innovative financial services to the poor, planners made significant efforts to incorporate informal financial structures in formal financial institutions. These efforts were often built around group lending schemes. The underlying assumption in group lending schemes is that they entail lower transaction costs per unit lent than individual lending when dealing with small-scale debtors (Adams 1979; Desai 1980; Krahnen and Schmidt 1994; Schmidt and Zeitinger 1994). This chapter empirically tests the widely accepted hypothesis that transaction costs in group lending are lower than those in individual lending.

Methodology and Data

In the credit extension process, transaction costs are incurred at the level of both the financial organization and the borrower. If a group functions as an intermediary between the organization and the ultimate borrower, transaction costs occur also at the group level. This study therefore estimates transaction costs at three levels:

- The financial organization.
- The intermediating credit group.
- The individual borrower, whether individual client or member of a credit group.

At the level of the financial organization, data collected on transaction costs include all costs related to financial service extension. These transaction costs comprise costs of staff, buildings, office, travel, audits, training, and related maintenance costs. If a financial organization works with credit groups to reach small-scale financial clients, the transaction costs also include the costs of forming, training, and monitoring groups. To make these costs comparable across financial organizations, they must be defined in unit or percentage terms (Desai and Mellor 1993). As Cuevas (1984) and, later, Desai and Mellor (1993) rightly point out, the convention is to express these costs as a percentage of loanable resources because the liability side is an output of every rural financial intermediary (RFI). They suggest, however, that the output of an RFI should be defined as all assets plus all liabilities for two reasons. First, asset items such as loans and capital market assets are obvious outputs of an RFI. Second, liabilities are also an output because of the joint nature of the assets and liabilities of an RFI. Following the suggestion of Cuevas (1984) and Desai and Mellor (1993), unit transaction costs are defined here as a percentage of all liabilities plus assets. In the case of the specialized credit program in Cameroon, Fonds d'Investissement des Micro-réalisations Agricoles et Communautaires (FIMAC), the unit costs are based on the volume of activity, which comprises the total value of loans and recoveries, because it is a program based on a revolving fund and not on savings.

At the group and individual levels, transaction costs include all explicit and implicit expenses that occur in the process of obtaining a loan. Those costs are, for example, associated with transportation, paperwork, lodging and meals, gifts, and the opportunity costs of time. For this analysis, the opportunity costs of time were considered to be the going agricultural wage rate, around 1,500 CFA francs per day.[1]

Based on the work of Desai and Mellor (1993), the double-log cost function and the Cobb–Douglas specification are used to analyze economies of scale with respect to the transaction costs of the RFIs under consideration. At the level of the individual borrower, the analysis of variance (ANOVA) was applied to compare the transaction costs of individuals affiliated with a credit group with those of individuals not affiliated with a group.

The empirical data for the comparison of transaction costs in group and individual lending were collected from two rural financial organizations and one financial program during two survey rounds in several provinces of Cameroon.[2] The first survey round took place in 1994 and the second in 1995. The group lending data came from FIMAC, which is supported by the World Bank, and the agricultural bank Crédit Agricole du Cameroun (CAC).[3] Data concerning transaction costs associated with individual lending came from the Cameroonian Cooperative Credit Union League (CamCCUL). Figure 10.1 illustrates the transaction cost components that were calculated for FIMAC, CAC, and CamCCUL.

The survey included comparable finance organizations in one region that cater to the same target group but apply different extension approaches. Data on the group lending program at FIMAC were collected at the program level. Interviews with group executives and affiliated members were conducted in four provinces of the country: Center, East, Adamaoua, and North. In these provinces 40 FIMAC groups and 30 group members were interviewed in order to obtain data on their transaction costs in getting a FIMAC loan. For CAC, 24 groups and 30 group members were interviewed. The figures on CAC's transaction costs associated with group lending were also collected. Data on the transaction costs of individual lending were obtained from 12 CamCCUL credit unions. In addition, 60 individual cooperative members were interviewed. The composition and size of the sample were clearly influenced by access, time, and funding constraints but, nevertheless, the sample yields statistically significant results. It should also be pointed out that Cameroon is one of the few countries in Sub-Saharan Africa that offers a well-established rural finance organization with individual clients for research purposes. Group lending approaches are far more common but not necessarily more successful. Table 10.1 summarizes the composition of the study sample for the groups, group members, and individuals.

---

1. The exchange rate at the time of the survey was, on average, US$1 = 555 CFA francs.
2. We gratefully acknowledge the financial support of this field research by the German Academic Exchange Service (DAAD).
3. CAC, an agricultural development bank designed to operate along commercial lines, was liquidated in 1997. Government intervention and loan repayment arrears degraded its solvency and liquidity.

FIGURE 10.1 Transaction cost components in group and individual lending in Cameroon

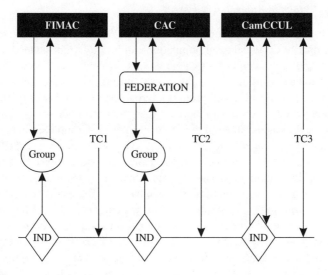

NOTES: Arrows pointing up indicate borrowers' transaction costs and arrows pointing down indicate lenders' transaction costs. FIMAC = Fonds d'Investissement des Micro-réalisations Agricoles et Communautaires; CAC = Crédit Agricole du Cameroun; CamCCUL = Cameroonian Cooperative Credit Union League; IND = individual.

TABLE 10.1 Sample composition and size

| | Group Credit | | Individual Credit | |
	FIMAC	CAC	CamCCUL	Total
Number of credit groups	40	24	. . .	64
Number of individuals affiliated with a credit group	30	30	. . .	60
Number of individuals not affiliated with a credit group	. . .	. . .	60	60

SOURCE: Belle-Sossoh (1997).

Transaction Costs of RFIs in Group and Individual Lending Approaches

The Social Linkage Approach of FIMAC

FIMAC is a food security program supported by the World Bank and targeted to economically disadvantaged populations and regions. In September 1990, FIMAC began operating in four Cameroonian provinces. By December 1991 it had established itself in all 10 Cameroonian provinces. FIMAC provides a revolving fund that finances agricultural microenterprises and community projects implemented by groups to increase local food production. The loans are given to the groups in kind and at 0 percent interest. Group members can use those funds either collectively in a joint microenterprise or individually. Because of the 0 percent interest charged on loans, FIMAC's approach is referred to as social linkage lending. The program channels loans to its credit groups with the support of local counterpart organizations. The counterpart organizations act as training units (*structure d'encadrement*) and are charged with building and consolidating the cohesion of groups before they become eligible for FIMAC loans. FIMAC provides financial assistance to the counterpart organizations and extends technical and financial assistance to eligible credit groups. The project recovers the credit granted to groups with yet another array of local counterparts, called collection structures (*structures de recouvrements*). These are autochthonous organizations or institutions that exert moral pressure on the community and the credit group members when loans become due.

All the costs incurred by the project were documented for the period of one year (July 1993–June 1994). The loan volume extended to the credit groups plus the revolving fund recovered was considered to be the operational volume for this period. FIMAC's transaction costs are summarized in Table 10.2.

The figures in Table 10.2 show that FIMAC's unit transaction costs, three years after its foundation, were at 50 percent. Christen et al. (1995) state that microfinance programs intending to become financially independent require 5–10 years to become self-sufficient in operational costs. Operational self-sufficiency, however, cannot be foreseen for FIMAC's social linkage program in the near future. The high unit transaction costs can be partly explained by the high expenditure on building and training groups, which represents about 20 percent of total program expenditure. They can also be explained by the relatively small volume of activity. Although FIMAC may be criticized for its high transaction costs, it achieves a recovery rate of 86 percent. This repayment rate is the result of tight screening of the groups and peer pressure from the counterparts. Nevertheless, a loan recovery rate of 86 percent is insufficient to become financially self-sufficient; the experiences of microfinance practitioners show that the minimum loan recovery rate needed is 95 percent (Christen et al. 1995).

The double-log cost function was used to analyze scale economies of FIMAC's transaction costs. On the one hand, the volume of activity was taken to

TABLE 10.2 Transaction costs per credit unit of FIMAC's social linkage approach, July 1993–June 1994

	Unit Transaction Costs	
Based on	Phase I (Surveyed Phase)	Phase II (Hypothetical Future Phase)
Operational volume (percent)	50	37
One credit group (CFA francs)	360,000	262,423

SOURCE: Belle-Sossoh (1997).

NOTES: Phase I comprises the building and training of groups. The unit transaction costs were calculated by adding all costs incurred by the program, including the expenses of building and training groups, divided by the total value of loans extended and recovered from the groups. To obtain the transaction costs per group, total costs were divided by the total number of groups. Phase II was not actually observed but describes a scenario after all capacity building has been done. It excludes the costs associated with building and training groups from the total costs of the project. It can be considered a sensitivity analysis to allow for a better comparison of the results with the financial organizations in the sample that have a longer operational history.

be the total value of loans extended plus funds recovered, and, on the other hand, it was taken to be the total number of credit groups benefiting from FIMAC's social linkage program. The double-log specification was

$$LOG(TC) = LOG(a) + aLOG(Q), \qquad (10.1)$$

where TC is transaction costs and Q is volume of activity.

The results for the 10 FIMAC provincial branches are shown in Table 10.3. The scale parameter of 0.42 indicates that, when the total value of FIMAC's activities increases by 10.0 percent, the transaction costs increase by just 4.2 percent.

TABLE 10.3 Estimated parameters of the double-log cost function for FIMAC

Dependent Variable	Constant (log a)	Coefficient of Volume of Activity (α)	$\bar{R}^2$	Scale Parameter	N
FIMAC's transaction costs[a]	4.117 (3.130)	0.425 (2.539)	.377	0.42[b]	10
Transaction costs per group[c]	6.065 (25.918)	0.692 (5.970)	.793	0.70[d]	10

SOURCE: Belle-Sossoh (1997).

NOTES: Figures in parentheses are *t*-values.

[a] The volume of activity is considered to be the total value in CFA francs of loans disbursed and recovered.

[b] Significant at 97 percent.

[c] The volume of activity is considered to be the total number of credit groups.

[d] Significant at 95 percent.

TABLE 10.4 Transaction costs of FIMAC groups and group members

	Cash Expenses		Opportunity Cost of Time		Total	
	CFA Francs	Percent	CFA Francs	Percent	CFA Francs	Percent
Group	55,605	69	25,526	31	81,135	100
Group member (average)	16,615	83	3,182	17	19,797	100
Leader	25,146	85	4,371	15	29,516	100
Nonleader	8,085	80	1,994	20	10,079	100

SOURCE: Belle-Sossoh (1997).

Transaction costs per group will increase by 7.0 percent if the number of groups borrowing from FIMAC increases by 10.0 percent. These results suggest that FIMAC experiences substantial economies of scale in group lending. The scale parameters of FIMAC's group operations indicate that the program could improve its transaction costs by increasing its activities and reaching more groups with its present organizational structure. No judgment can be made here regarding possible financial market distortions owing to the program's policy of a 0 percent interest rate.

To establish the transaction costs of acquiring a FIMAC loan, 40 FIMAC groups and 30 of their members were interviewed. Group members were classified as leaders and participants. The former designation comprises members of the executive committee. The transaction costs of groups and their members are shown in Table 10.4.

Table 10.4 indicates that FIMAC groups spend a substantial amount up front (81,131 CFA francs, or US$312) to obtain a loan. Almost 70 percent of this expenditure is in cash, whereas the opportunity cost of time comes to 31 percent. Group leaders spend about three times more up front per loan than ordinary members, who invest 10,079 CFA francs to acquire a loan. The credit market entry fees are substantial, ranging from about 20 percent to 55 percent of an average loan. The findings here also reflect higher initiation costs for group leaders, who are in charge of the loan contract negotiations. It should also be noted that the group leader's average loan is higher than that of the ordinary member. Table 10.5 shows group members' cash spending by item. It illustrates that FIMAC's group members face particularly high expenses for ceremonies in honor of credit officers delivering credit (76 percent of total expenses).

Table 10.6 gives the transaction costs per credit unit for the FIMAC groups and their members. The members of FIMAC groups face extremely high transaction costs of 37 percent per loan unit acquired. These high transaction costs at the client level cannot be explained by the relatively recent foundation of FIMAC. Rather they indicate that FIMAC is inefficient. The unsatisfactory

TABLE 10.5 FIMAC group members' cash expenses, by expense item

	Nonleader		Leader		Average	
Item	CFA Francs	Percent	CFA Francs	Percent	CFA Francs	Percent
Paperwork	221	2.7	800	3.2	510	3.0
Transport	818	10.0	3,239	12.9	2,028	12.0
Food and lodging	346	4.3	2,607	10.4	1,476	9.0
Reception[a]	6,700	83.0	18,500	73.5	12,600	76.0
Total	8,085	100.0	25,146	100.0	16,614	100.0

SOURCE: Belle-Sossoh (1997).

[a] "Reception costs" are all the expenses incurred by group members for the ceremony organized for the credit officers when they deliver the credit to the group.

performance of FIMAC gave rise to the World Bank's initiative of restructuring FIMAC shortly after the surveys in 1994–95. Although FIMAC's loan beneficiaries pay no explicit interest, their implicit cost burden is comparable to the average interest in the informal financial sector of 60 percent per year (Schrieder 1996a).

The Commercial Linkage Approach of CAC

After the dissolution of the Fonds National de Développement Rural (FONADER) in the late 1980s, a new agricultural bank was formed in 1987, the Crédit Agricole du Cameroun (CAC). Its objective was to collect savings and provide loans to the rural sector as a nonsubsidized private entity with limited liability. For the initial years of operation, CAC concentrated on building up its commercial banking activities. Having established itself as a credible commercial bank in the Cameroonian financial sector, operating mainly in urban areas, CAC expanded its outreach into the rural sector. In 1991, CAC launched an innovative project of rural financial institution building by creating its first village bank in Esse, the Caisse Locale d'Esse. The village bank, which CAC refers to as a

TABLE 10.6 Transaction costs per credit unit, FIMAC groups and their members

	Transaction Costs (CFA francs)	Average Loan Amount (CFA francs)	Unit Transaction Costs (percent)
Group	81,135	534,874	15
Group members	19,797	53,487	37

SOURCE: Belle-Sossoh (1997).

NOTES: See Table 10.4 for a breakdown of transaction costs. The average number of members in FIMAC groups is 10.

TABLE 10.7 Transaction costs of CAC's commercial linkage banking program

	Transaction Costs (CFA francs)	Volume of Activity (CFA francs)	Unit Transaction Costs (Percent)
CAC	1,026,300	20,975,000	4.9
Federation of credit groups	238,000	6,399,500	3.7

SOURCE: Belle-Sossoh (1997).

NOTES: Transaction costs include all noninterest expenses incurred by CAC and the federation in the process of giving or obtaining credit. The volume of activity of the bank is the total amount of credit granted plus the total amount of savings collected from the federation.

federation, mobilized and united already existing local groups (see also Figure 10.1). The village bank was allowed to formulate its own financial and organizational regulations. Credit was extended only to the federation of credit groups in a predetermined relation to the amount of savings deposited at the bank. The federation was then in charge of allocating the loan to its groups, which in turn distributed loans to individual members. The federation was also in charge of collecting loan principals and interest installments from groups, and groups were responsible for recovery from their members.

CAC granted a loan to the federation for the first time in May 1992. The federation received a total of 6.4 million CFA francs between 1992 and 1994 and distributed it among 24 of its affiliated groups. CAC extended another loan of 9 million CFA francs to the federation to help finance its commercial activities. A summary of the loan figures and transaction costs supported by the CAC and the federation is given in Table 10.7; the data used for the analysis cover the period 1992 to 1994.

Table 10.7 shows that the federation of groups lowers CAC's unit transaction costs to 4.9 percent. CAC is able to shift some of the transaction costs that would normally occur at its level to the federation. Compared with the unit transaction costs faced by FIMAC (50 percent), CAC appears to have organized its group lending activity more efficiently. The transaction costs incurred by the federation are 3.7 percent of the total amount of the loans received from the bank.

In order to determine the transaction costs incurred by groups and their members affiliated with the federation and CAC, 24 groups and 30 of their members were interviewed in 1994. Table 10.8 gives an overview of the transaction costs at the level of the groups and their members. The groups' transaction costs amounted to 7,943 CFA francs and group members spent 4,582 CFA francs (3.5 days of work) per average loan of 118,000 CFA francs. (CamCCUL's individual borrowers spend one-quarter of this amount.) On average, CAC members spent 71 percent of their transaction costs in cash and 29 percent

TABLE 10.8 Transaction costs of CAC groups and their members

	Cash Expenses		Opportunity Cost of Time		Total	
	CFA Francs	Percent	CFA Francs	Percent	CFA Francs	Percent
Group	5,621	70.76	2,322	29.23	7,943	100
Group member (average)	3,263	71.21	1,319	28.78	4,582	100
Leader	4,655	71.45	1,860	28.54	6,515	100
Nonleader	1,872	70.64	778	29.35	2,650	100

SOURCE: Belle-Sossoh (1997).

in the opportunity cost of the time spent to secure the loan. Group leaders spent more than twice the amount that nonleaders did. These leaders are usually in charge of all negotiations with the federation on behalf of the whole group.

Table 10.9 describes group members' different expenses incurred in acquiring a loan from CAC through the federation. It shows that food and lodging are the major cash expenditures (40 percent).

The unit transaction costs at each level of CAC's commercially oriented linkage banking approach are described in Table 10.10. At the bank level these costs are almost 5 percent (Table 10.10). The federation spends nearly 4 percent, the groups spend 3 percent, and the group members spend 4 percent of the credit amount received at the respective levels of intermediation. These results indicate that the bank transfers some of the transaction costs to the federation and its group borrowers (6.7 percent).

Despite the existence of the federation of credit groups, which was intended to exert pressure on each group, the recovery rate of loans was only 22 percent. Nonrecovery includes interest and principal overdue for more than one day. To some extent, this low recovery rate is the result of the federation's

TABLE 10.9 CAC group members' cash expenses, by expense item

	Nonleader		Leader		Average	
Item	CFA Francs	Percent	CFA Francs	Percent	CFA Francs	Percent
Paperwork	97	5	1,442	31	818	25
Transport	825	44	1,463	31	1,145	35
Food and lodging	950	51	1,750	38	1,350	40
Total	1,872	100	4,655	100	3,313	100

SOURCE: Belle-Sossoh (1997).

TABLE 10.10 Unit transaction costs at different levels of CAC's linkage approach

	Transaction Costs (CFA francs)	Volume of Activity (CFA francs)	Average Loan Amount (CFA francs)	Unit Transaction Costs (percent)
CAC	1,026,300	20,975,000	. . .	4.9
Federation	238,000	6,399,500	. . .	3.7
Group (average number of members)	7,943	. . .	266,545	3.0
Group member (average)	4,583	. . .	117,968	4.0
Leader	6,515	. . .	131,000	5.0
Nonleader	2,650	. . .	93,937	3.0

SOURCE: Belle-Sossoh (1997).

ineffectiveness in selecting and monitoring group members. Low recovery runs counter to the theoretical assumptions that information asymmetries are smaller and the social pressure to honor repayment obligations is higher when local organizations are included in the financial intermediation process. The federation's failure to recover the debt successfully may be due to moral hazard. The federation was particularly exposed to moral hazard behavior owing to its presumption that its own financial intermediation role between the CAC and its group members would not be a long-term relationship.

The Individual-Based Lending of CamCCUL

The Cameroonian Cooperative Credit Union League (CamCCUL) comprises 268 credit unions and discussion groups in Cameroon. The principal activity of credit unions is to collect members' savings and reallocate them to interest-bearing investments. Each credit union is autonomous in the mobilization of savings and the allocation of loans, but all of them follow the board guidelines established by CamCCUL. The credit unions contribute 25 percent of their shares and savings to CamCCUL's central liquidity fund, which is used to refinance its credit unions. CamCCUL is in charge of managing the central liquidity fund and provides technical assistance to its member credit unions. CamCCUL (1994) reports a membership of 84,900 persons, total savings of 11 billion CFA francs (equivalent to about US$22 million), and a loan portfolio of 5.9 billion CFA francs (see Figure 10.2). In the second half of the 1970s, the number of credit unions was consolidated. From the early 1980s to 1994, their number increased by 24 percent (from 204 to 268) while the membership increased even more, by 51 percent (from 41,197 to 84,900). Whereas lending activities expanded at a relatively moderate rate because of a more conservative lending

FIGURE 10.2 CamCCUL savings, credit, and reserves, 1969–94

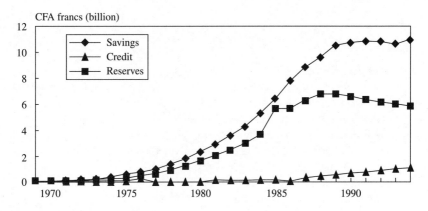

SOURCE: Belle-Sossoh (1997).

policy, and even declined toward 1994, savings and reserves rose more consistently as a result of the growth in membership.

In order to gain more insight into credit unions' transaction costs, 12 representative credit unions were selected in four provinces of Cameroon (Northwest, West, Littoral, and South). Data on their operational costs were collected for the years 1990 to 1994. The data were supplemented by semistructured interviews with managers and bookkeepers of the credit unions. Table 10.11 shows the evolution of unit transaction costs of the surveyed unions. The data indicate that unit transaction costs of the credit unions varied between 0.85 and 2.45 percent, with an average of 1.49 percent.

To analyze the cost–output relationships and to quantify scale economies in both credit and savings activities of the credit unions, the Cobb–Douglas

TABLE 10.11 Unit transaction costs of CamCCUL's credit unions

Year	Unit Transaction Costs (percent)
1990	0.85
1991	1.11
1992	1.38
1993	2.45
1994	1.66
Average	1.49

SOURCE: Belle-Sossoh (1997).

specification was used (Desai and Mellor 1993). The implicit TC function can be written as

$$TC = f(Q_1, Q_2, P_1, P_2),\qquad(10.2)$$

where

TC = transaction costs,

Q_1 = volume of loans: the total value of loans of the 12 sampled credit unions over the five-year period 1990–1994,

Q_2 = volume of savings: the total value of savings collected from the 12 sampled credit unions over the five-year period 1990–1994,

P_1 = price of labor: the total value of wages divided by the total number of employees in the 12 credit unions evaluated, and

P_2 = price of capital services: the ratio of depreciation plus rents paid over the total loan and savings portfolio.

Cost minimization for a Cobb–Douglas production function, subject to production constraints, yields a Cobb–Douglas cost function that can be written as

$$\begin{aligned}LOG(TC) = \alpha_0 + \alpha_1 LOG(Q_1) + \alpha_2 LOG(Q_2)\\ + \beta_1 LOG(P_1) + \beta_2 LOG(P_2) + \varepsilon.\end{aligned}\qquad(10.3)$$

Overall economies of scale (OES) are defined as the change in cost when total output increases (by a common factor). In the Cobb–Douglas cost function above, overall economies of scale are measured as

$$OES = \frac{\partial LOG(TC)}{\partial LOG(Q_1)} + \frac{\partial LOG(TC)}{\partial LOG(Q_2)}.\qquad(10.4)$$

Partial economies of scale for loans (ESQ_1) and savings (ESQ_2) can be calculated as

$$ESQ_1 = \frac{\partial LOG(TC)}{\partial LOG(Q_1)} = \alpha_1,\qquad(10.5)$$

$$ESQ_2 = \frac{\partial LOG(TC)}{\partial LOG(Q_2)} = \alpha_2.\qquad(10.6)$$

Results of the Cobb–Douglas specification are presented in Table 10.12. The overall economies of scale of CamCCUL's credit unions are

$$\alpha_1 + \alpha_2 = -0.0028 + 0.7528 = 0.75.\qquad(10.7)$$

This suggests that the costs of CamCCUL's credit unions increase by 7.5 percent when their volume of credit and savings increases by 10.0 percent. However, we can disassociate the effect of credit and savings in CamCCUL's economies of scale.

TABLE 10.12 Transaction cost parameters of CamCCUL's credit unions: Cobb–Douglas cost function

Parameter	Estimate	t-Value
α_0 (constant)	−0.4770	−1.442
α_1 (volume of credit: Q_1)	−0.0028	−0.105
α_2 (volume of savings: Q_2)	0.7528	8.480**
β_1 (price of labor: P_1)	0.0780	0.976
β_2 (price of capital: P_2)	−0.0540	−0.599
R^2	.961	
Adjusted R^2	.923	
F-value	148**	

SOURCE: Belle-Sossoh (1997).

NOTES: ** significant at .001 or more; $N = 54$ yearly balances (6 are missing).

- The economies of scale in connection with credit are

$$\alpha_1 = -0.0028.$$

- The economies of scale in connection with savings are

$$\alpha_2 = 0.7528.$$

These results seem to suggest that the expansion of the savings portfolio has a significantly bigger impact on cost increase (though the economies of scale are smaller than 1) than the allocation of credit has. One reason is the high cost associated with the mobilization of additional savers for an established credit union. Expanding the geographical coverage through the foundation of new credit unions and thereby mobilizing more savers is also costly. Once the credit unions are in operation, the cost of expanding the loan portfolio, given the existence of unsatisfied demand, is relatively low because of their largely honorary workforce (this also explains the negative parameter of α_1). Nevertheless, cooperative credit extension is directly linked to the prior savings mobilization because cooperative structures rely only rarely on domestic refinancing lines other than the CamCCUL's central liquidity fund. As long as the potential crediting capacity is not exhausted, credit unions can grant additional loans at very low cost.

The figures in Table 10.12 also indicate the effect of labor costs ($\beta_1 = 0.0780$) and capital costs ($\beta_2 = -0.0540$). The increase in labor costs has little impact on the increase in transaction costs. If the volume of activity of the credit unions increases by 10.0 percent, their wage bill will rise by only 0.78 percent. This reflects the fact that CamCCUL's credit unions depend to a large extent on honorary staff. Employees are recruited locally, trained on the job, and remunerated

TABLE 10.13 Costs and viability of CamCCUL's credit unions, 1990–94 (percent)

| | Year | | | | | |
	1990	1991	1992	1993	1994	Mean
Unit transaction costs	0.85	1.11	1.38	2.45	1.66	1.49
Unit financial costs[a]	5.50	5.00	6.00	7.70	6.60	6.16
Unit revenue[b]	12.00	12.00	12.00	18.00	18.00	14.40
Unit gross margin[c]	6.50	7.00	6.00	10.30	11.40	8.24
Unit net margin[d]	5.65	5.89	4.62	7.85	9.74	

SOURCE: Belle-Sossoh (1997).

[a] Unit financial costs are the interest paid on deposits.

[b] Unit revenue is the interest received on loans.

[c] Gross margin is the difference between unit revenue and unit financial costs.

[d] Net margin is the difference between gross margin and unit transaction costs.

according to local wage rates. It also indicates that, in recent years, CamCCUL has reacted to its rising transaction portfolio not by increasing the number of employees but rather by raising the productivity of the current staff and relying more on honorary personnel.

The coefficient related to capital suggests that, when the volume of activity increases by 10.0 percent, the expenses for capital investments decrease by 0.54 percent. This result can be explained by the fact that most of the credit unions are operating at a very low level of physical capital investment and maintain this basic capital structure over the years. Table 10.13 summarizes the cost and revenue structure of CamCCUL's credit unions.

Transaction Costs of CamCCUL's Individual Borrowers

In 1995, questionnaire guided interviews were conducted with 60 individual members of different rural CamCCUL credit unions in order to obtain data on transaction costs related to the acquisition of loans by individual borrowers. Individual members of CamCCUL's credit unions spend, on average, 1,400 CFA francs (equivalent to US$3 or one day's labor rate of 1,500 CFA francs) on the acquisition of a loan. The average time spent on formalities related to a loan application is three hours, valued at an opportunity cost of 350 CFA francs.

Table 10.14 recapitulates the costs at different levels of CamCCUL's direct individual lending and borrowing transactions. It shows that the transaction costs are extremely low for both the lender and the borrowers, indicating efficient operations.

TABLE 10.14 Lender and borrower transaction costs of CamCCUL's individualized microfinance approach (percent)

	Credit Union	Member
Unit transaction costs	1.5	3.4
Unit financial costs	6.2	18.0
Total costs per credit unit	7.7	21.4

SOURCE: Belle-Sossoh (1997).

Comparison of Transaction Costs between Group-Oriented and Individual-Oriented Microfinance

In this section, we compare the transaction costs of FIMAC, CAC, and Cam-CCUL at the level of the formal organization, the group intermediary, and the individual client.

Comparison at the Level of the Organization

Table 10.15 presents a comparison of the costs of group and individual lending. The total costs involved in group lending are much higher than in the case of individual lending. Nevertheless, the costs of the two group-based lending schemes also vary significantly although they address the same target group, namely the rural poor.

The transaction costs of FIMAC's social linkage approach are significantly higher (at 50.0 percent) than those of CAC's commercial linkage approach (4.9 percent). But the risk costs in the commercial linkage approach were apparently much higher than those of the social linkage approach. This result reflects the improving effect on recovery of the intensive training and close monitoring of groups in the social linkage approach. In the commercial linkage

TABLE 10.15 Comparison of the costs of group and individual lending: FIMAC, CAC, and CamCCUL (percent)

	Group Lending		Individual Lending
Costs	FIMAC's Social Linkage Approach	CAC's Commercial Linkage Approach	CamCCUL
Transaction costs	50.0	4.9	1.5
Risk costs[a]	14.0	78.0	14.0
Total costs	64.0	82.9	15.5

SOURCE: Belle-Sossoh (1997).

[a] Risk costs = 1 minus recovery rate of the institution.

approach of CAC, part of the credit transaction, and thus transaction costs, is shifted from the bank to the groups and their members. By transferring some of the bank's responsibility to the federation of the credit groups, the transaction costs at the bank level are reduced. However, in the case of CAC, the risk costs are increased, which is demonstrated by the low loan recovery rate. In this analysis, group lending approaches have been shown to have higher transaction costs than lending to individuals. Nevertheless, the group lending approach of CAC came very close to the level of transaction costs of individual lending. FIMAC's group lending approach, though inefficient in transaction costs, produced a recovery result comparable to that of CamCCUL.

However, neither group lending approach, whether socially or commercially oriented, could compete with the well-established individual lending activities of CamCCUL. This result is of interest for two reasons. First, it shows that group-oriented microfinance lending is not the panacea for solving all access problems to financial services for the poor in developing countries. There is scope for microfinance organizations to service individuals effectively and efficiently, as the case of CamCCUL demonstrates. Second, group-based microfinance lending is not a trivial undertaking, either for a donor with almost unlimited funds or for a commercial bank with professional banking expertise. The sociocultural and moral hazard aspects of group lending are important for the long-term functioning of rural finance markets. They may well hamper group lending transactions if not properly taken into account, as in the case of CAC. FIMAC implements group lending as if the long-term financing of the extremely high transaction costs were not a matter of concern. It also appears to pursue socioeconomic objectives in addition to financial market development. However, it is interesting to note that in the end the costs of borrowing for the ultimate client are similar to the interest rates in the informal financial sector, although FIMAC charges 0 percent interest. Both group lending schemes could operate more efficiently, but fail to do so for reasons of cost-intensive institution building. Institution economics has shown ways of reducing costs in institution formation.

Comparison at the Borrower Level

A total of 120 borrowers were interviewed in 1994 and 1995 to obtain data on their transaction costs. Half of the sample were members of groups affiliated either with FIMAC or with CAC and the other half were individuals (IND) who borrowed directly from CamCCUL. FIMAC and CAC group members were classified into two categories, group leaders (LEAD) and nonleaders (N-LEAD).

Table 10.16 gives the different transaction costs of each borrower category. The borrowers of FIMAC's social linkage approach have higher transaction costs than borrowers of the CAC's commercial linkage approach. Overall, individual borrowers have lower transaction costs than do the group leaders in both linkage approaches and the group members in the social linkage approach.

TABLE 10.16 Ultimate borrowers' transaction costs in group and individual lending (percent)

	Transaction Costs
Group lending	
FIMAC's social linkage approach	
LEAD$_1$	55.0
N-LEAD$_1$	19.0
CAC's commercial linkage approach	
LEAD$_2$	5.0
N-LEAD$_2$	3.0
Individual lending	
CamCCUL's individual approach (IND)	3.4

SOURCE: Belle-Sossoh (1997).

NOTES: LEAD$_1$ = FIMAC's group leaders; LEAD$_2$ = CAC's group leaders; N-LEAD$_1$ = FIMAC's group members; N-LEAD$_2$ = CAC's group members; IND = CamCCUL's individual borrowers.

Figure 10.3 summarizes graphically the transaction costs for FIMAC, CAC, and CamCCUL and their clients.

Looking at the different categories of average transaction costs, an analysis of variance (ANOVA) was applied to test whether the observed differences are random or whether there are significant differences between the five categories of borrowers. The hypothesis that the different categories of borrowers experience equal average transaction costs is formulated in the null hypothesis:

$$H_0 : \mu_{LEAD1} = \mu_{LEAD2} = \mu_{N\text{-}LEAD} = \mu_{N\text{-}LEAD2} = \mu_{IND}, \qquad (10.8)$$

where μ_i represents the mean transaction costs of the different categories of borrowers. The results of the analysis of variance are given in Table 10.17. The ANOVA shows that the average transaction costs of different borrowers are not equal. The probability that the null hypothesis is true is thus zero. Therefore, the null hypothesis of all means being equal ($H_0 = 0$) can be rejected.

The results in Table 10.17 indicate only that variations exist among borrower groups regarding their transaction costs; they do not disclose which category is significantly different from the other. A multiple comparison procedure was used to determine which borrower's average transaction costs are different. Multiple comparison procedures protect against the fallacy of calling too many differences significant. The Scheffé test was conducted for the comparison of means in pairs, because it is "conservative and requires larger differences between means for significance than other methods" (Marija 1983: 112). The results of the Scheffé multiple comparison procedure are contained in Table 10.18.

FIGURE 10.3 Overview of the different transaction costs analyzed

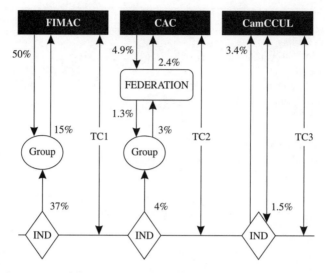

SOURCE: Belle-Sossoh (1997).
NOTES: Arrows pointing up indicate borrowers' transaction costs and arrows pointing down indicate lenders' transactions costs. FIMAC = Fonds d'Investissement des Micro-réalisations Agricoles et Communautaires; CAC = Crédit Agricole du Cameroun; CamCCUL = Cameroonian Cooperative Credit Union League; IND = individual.

In Table 10.18, the means are ordered from the smallest to the largest. Pairs of means that are significantly different at the 5 percent level are indicated with an asterisk. The asterisks in the IND column indicate that individual borrowers' transaction costs are significantly different from CAC's group leaders' transaction costs, from FIMAC's group members' transaction costs, as well as from FIMAC's group leaders' transaction costs.

TABLE 10.17 Analysis of variance by borrowers' categories

Source	Degrees of Freedom	Sum of Squares	Mean Squares	F Ratio	F Prob
Between categories	4	9,233,097,066	2,308,274,266	94	.000
Within categories	114	2,778,028,021	24,368,666.85	. . .	. . .
Total	118	. . .	. . .	. . .	. . .

SOURCE: Belle-Sossoh (1997).

TABLE 10.18 Results of the Scheffé multiple comparison procedure

Credit Approach	Mean (CFA francs)	Category	IND	N-LEAD$_2$	LEAD$_2$	N-LEAD$_1$	LEAD$_1$
CamCCUL lending	1,663	IND					
CAC							
Group lending	2,649	N-LEAD$_2$					
Individual lending	6,514	LEAD$_2$	*				
FIMAC							
Group lending	10,079	N-LEAD$_1$	*	*			
Individual lending	29,516	LEAD$_1$	*	*	*	*	

SOURCE: Belle-Sossoh (1997).

NOTES: * denotes that pairs of means are significantly different at the 5 percent level. LEAD$_1$ = FIMAC's group leaders; LEAD$_2$ = CAC's group leaders; N-LEAD$_1$ = FIMAC's group members; N-LEAD$_2$ = CAC's group members; IND = CamCCUL individual's borrowers.

Conclusion and Recommendation

In developing economies, group lending is often recommended as a way to reduce lenders' and borrowers' transaction costs. This study investigated the transaction costs of two organizations (FIMAC and CAC) that apply different approaches to group lending in Cameroon. It then compared the transaction costs of these two group lending approaches with the transaction costs of Cam-CCUL, which caters primarily for individual clients.

The FIMAC approach to group lending can be characterized as a social network approach (Schmidt and Zeitinger 1994). The microfinance technology of the Grameen Bank in Bangladesh is the most prominent example of this approach. Groups are used as an entity in order to reach poor segments of the population with the aim of supplying financial and technical agricultural training together with loans. Furthermore, the group approach of the formal organization creates the feeling that member borrowers belong to a community with common goals and interests. Thus, they experience a moral obligation to honor their financial commitments and are less likely to become delinquent.

Results indicate that the transaction costs per unit of credit lent and recovered by FIMAC are 50 percent. The high level of unit transaction costs is caused by the high costs of forming and training groups and of extending financial and technical services to group members. However, FIMAC has a relatively good loan recovery rate of 86 percent. This is due to close group monitoring and peer pressure at the group and community levels on member borrowers to honor their debts. FIMAC experiences scale economies in lending to groups with a scale parameter of 0.7.

The CAC approach to group lending is more commercially oriented. Here, the federation of groups acts as a financial intermediary or village bank. But it is the individual borrowers who remain liable to the bank for their debts; there is no joint group liability. The federation is given responsibility for carrying out key functions normally performed by the bank, in particular the selection of borrowers and the recovery of the loans. The CAC has low transaction costs of just under 5 percent per unit of credit extended and savings collected, but it experiences a poor loan recovery rate of only 22 percent.

CamCCUL, which lends directly to individuals, has unit transaction costs of 1.5 percent, a loan recovery rate of 86 percent, and an overall scale parameter of 0.8. According to these results, the microfinance organization applying direct lending to individuals performs better than those using groups to extend credit or collect savings.

This result should not be misinterpreted. The overall performance of group lending schemes can be improved by reducing transaction costs (like CAC) or by reducing risk costs through a better loan recovery rate (like FIMAC). The analysis points to the fact that it is not only specialized agricultural development banks that are prone to difficulties arising from information asymmetries and moral hazard, as pointed out by institution economics; these problems can occur in group lending too.

References

Adams, D. W. 1979. *Lending to rural poor through informal groups: A promising financial market innovation.* ESP No. 587. Columbus, Ohio, U.S.A.: Ohio State University, Department of Agricultural Economics and Rural Sociology.

Adams, D. W, and D. A. Fitchett, eds. 1992. *Informal finance in low-income countries.* Boulder, Colo., U.S.A.: Westview Press.

African Studies Center. 1978. Savings and credit institutions in rural West Africa. In *Rural Africana*, ed. M. W. DeLancey. East Lansing, Mich., U.S.A.: Michigan State University.

Belle-Sossoh, D. 1997. *Analyse comparative des coûts de transaction des crédits de groupes et des crédits individuels des marchés financiers ruraux au Cameroun.* Ph.D. thesis, University of Hohenheim. Stuttgart: Gabler Verlag.

CamCCUL (Cameroonian Cooperative Credit Union League). 1994. *CamCCUL Annual Report.* Bamenda, Cameroon.

Christen, P. R., E. Rhyne, E. C. Vogel, and C. McKean. 1995. *Maximizing the outreach of microenterprise finance: An analysis of successful microfinance programs.* Program and Operations Assessment Report No. 10. Washington, D.C.: U.S. Agency for International Development.

Cuevas, C. 1984. *Cost of financial intermediation under regulation: Commercial banks and development banks.* Columbus, Ohio, U.S.A.: Ohio State University.

Desai, B. M., 1980. *Group lending experience in reaching small farmers.* Columbus, Ohio, U.S.A.: Ohio State University.

Desai, B. M., and J. W. Mellor. 1993. *Institutional finance for agricultural development. An analytical survey of critical issues.* Washington, D.C.: International Food Policy Research Institute.

Heidhues, F. 1990. Institution, economic policies and participatory development. Paper presented at a seminar sponsored by the German Foundation for International Development (DSE), April 1990, Feldafing, Germany.

————. 1995. Rural financial markets—An important tool to fight poverty. *Quarterly Journal of International Agriculture* 34 (2).

Krahnen, J. P., and R. H. Schmidt. 1994. *Development finance as institution building. A new approach to poverty-oriented banking.* Boulder, Colo., U.S.A.: Westview Press.

Marija, N. 1983. *Introductory statistics guide.* Chicago, Ill.: SPSS Inc.

Schmidt, R. H., and C. P. Zeitinger. 1994. *Critical issues in small and microbusiness finance.* Frankfurt/Main: Interdisziplinäre Projekt Consult GmbH (IPC).

Schrieder, G. 1996a. Financial innovations combat food insecurity: The case of Cameroon. Paper presented at the International Symposium on Food Security and Innovations: Successes and Lessons Learned, March 11–13, University of Hohenheim and Eiselen Stiftung Ulm, Stuttgart, Germany.

————. 1996b. *The role of rural finance for food security of the poor in Cameroon.* Frankfurt, Germany: Peter Lang Verlag.

Zeller, M., G. Schrieder, J. von Braun, and F. Heidhues. 1997. *Rural finance for food security for the poor: Implications for research and policy.* Food Policy Review No. 4. Washington, D.C.: International Food Policy Research Institute.

PART III

Measuring the Impact
of Microfinance

11 Impact of Microfinance on Food Security and Poverty Alleviation: A Review and Synthesis of Empirical Evidence

MANOHAR SHARMA AND GERTRUD BUCHENRIEDER

Until the early 1980s, only a handful of microfinance intermediaries existed; today these institutions number more than 7,000 worldwide, reaching approximately 16 million poor people. This spectacular growth by the microfinance industry has been fueled not by anonymous market forces, but by deliberate actions of national governments, nongovernmental organizations (NGOs), and donors who view microfinance as an effective tool for alleviating poverty. This view, in turn, is based on the assumption that poor households have worthy projects that could potentially raise their living standards but that do not come to fruition because of—among other things—severe financial constraints.

Since much of the impetus behind the large and increasing support for microfinance hinges on this assumption, it is worth examining this assumption. The objective of this chapter is to review some of the emerging evidence of the impact of credit institutions—formal and informal—on their clients, with a specific focus on poverty alleviation. The chapter is divided into five parts. In the next section we address the general scope of these impact studies. We do this mainly because a purely descriptive review without some kind of perspective or background frequently creates a misunderstanding about why we care to measure what we measure or how we should go about making policy-related conclusions based on the findings. We then review what are known as "investment-led" and "insurance-led" benefit impact studies, respectively. The former compare household- or individual-level outcomes for those that have access to credit and those that do not. The latter studies look at the benefits of credit when it serves as an insurance substitute. In the fourth section we examine possible relationships between institutional performance or format and program impact. We draw policy-related conclusions in the final section.

The Policy Perspective of Impact Studies

The Market-Based Benchmark

When individuals or households decide, without any outside coercion, to borrow from a lender or participate in a credit program, potential benefits are in some sense axiomatic. In the absence of coercion, borrowing would simply not make sense if there were not the prospect of potential benefit to the borrower. Of course, this does not mean that all potential benefits are actually realized. Financed projects may fail, and the household may suffer an actual loss. Further, the potential benefits a loan applicant has in mind when joining a credit program may not necessarily match the lender's definition of benefits, which in the development context are usually couched in objectives related to poverty alleviation—usually an increase in productivity or income.

Once funds enter the household, pinpointing exactly which part of the household system they trickle down to is difficult because financial resources are fungible. Even when lending institutions impose strict conditions, credit may be used for a wide variety of purposes—such as to increase household members' leisure, repay more expensive loans from other sources, finance wedding expenses, increase the consumption of durable goods, or reallocate labor within a household. Understanding that these are indeed real benefits that accrue to the household is important.

The market-based benchmark for measuring benefits is then quite clear: a reasonable valuation of the benefits derived from credit services, as in the case of any other good or service, is expressed by willingness to pay. The monetary value of marginal benefits must be at least as high as the price paid for the service. In this sense, the general health, profitability, and dynamism of a microfinance institution are important indicators of its significant impact because they attest to the success of clients' projects: the returns accruing to the household from whatever is financed by loans are high enough to pay for services received in full.

The Public Policy Realm

What then is the case for measuring impact for policy purposes? The reasons for doing so lie in the implicit assumption that the impacts of credit programs are imperfectly measured by willingness to pay because important social benefits are not included in the measurement.[1] In the poverty alleviation policy framework—especially when the issue is one of allocating scarce *public* resources to competing ends—policymakers, NGOs, and donors ask how credit programs affect broader social goals, such as adoption of technology, income generation, attainment of food security, nutritional adequacy, and educational attainment. Sometimes even broader goals are considered, such as women's empowerment or the quality of the environment. If social benefits are indeed significant, then the provision of services based on private willingness to pay will be less than optimal.

---

1. It is also complicated by the fact that loan markets are usually characterized by nonprice rationing.

Although it is pointless to argue that financial constraints do not matter in poverty alleviation, it would be equally wrong to ascribe the "only credit matters" mentality to the advocates of microfinance. Actually, the more common assumption is that credit needs to be delivered along with other services to alleviate poverty within a reasonable time frame. Hence, the relevant question in the poverty alleviation debate is not so much whether financial constraints matter or not, but the relative weight to be attached to credit programs vis-à-vis alternative poverty alleviation programs, such as those relating to investments in infrastructure, health, education, agricultural extension, and various kinds of services related to a social safety net. What policymakers essentially need to know is the answer to the following question: Is shifting resources away from other poverty programs to credit-based programs good social policy?

By assessing the benefits of credit programs, we address this question—although only partially because measuring benefits alone does not provide us with complete information. An equally important question is whether credit programs are cost effective in delivering these services compared with other programs. Only by comparing the cost–benefit ratios of alternative programs can we soundly judge the role and size of the credit programs in the national policy portfolio. And only after we judge these programs can we begin to address complex issues regarding subsidization and other means of supporting microfinance institutions. The business of testing for and quantifying the benefits of credit institutions should therefore be viewed as a first, albeit important, step in overall program evaluation.

The Nature of Benefit Impact Studies

On the basis of theory alone we can conclude that savings and credit facilities help individuals or households build up or acquire funds for all kinds of investments. However, an important question at the practical level is whether poor households have, on their own, simultaneous access to other inputs required to start or expand an enterprise (farm or nonfarm). Credit will generally have high returns if complementary inputs are available, such as irrigated farms, secure tenancy rights, educational attainment, efficiently functioning markets, and a reasonable degree of social and infrastructure development. However, in the absence of seeds or irrigation water for the farmer, market access for the rural producer, or elementary bookkeeping skills for the would-be entrepreneur, the returns to financial services may be low or even nonexistent. The investment-led benefit impact studies (see, for example, Sebstad et al. 1995) essentially test whether this is the case and, for this reason, provide valuable information.

Another useful role for savings and credit in poverty alleviation gained recognition in the 1980s: the role of insurance substitutes. To summarize, when the poor face catastrophic risks—risks arising out of erratic rains, human illness, crop pests, diseases, and other problems—and when formal insurance markets are nonexistent, credit transactions allow the poor to borrow during bad times and repay when times are better. Note that, unlike in the case of investment-related benefits, ownership or access to other investment inputs are not prerequisites for the insurance benefits to materialize. Even so, it is hypothesized that the insurance effect does have an important bearing on resource management. By making it possible for poor households to uphold precious consumption even during income shortfalls, it emboldens them to manage their investment portfolio in a more efficient manner (see Morduch 1995, for example). Given adequate protection against the unexpected, poor households would no longer need to restrict themselves to low-risk—but also less profitable—portfolio choices. This type of thinking gave rise to a wave of empirical work testing the role that credit institutions played in maintaining adequate consumption in the face of volatile income and in assisting risk management in production. We review these in the section on insurance-led benefit impact studies.

Investment-Led Benefit Impact Studies

The Format of the Studies

The essential format of investment-led benefit impact studies consists of comparing the household- or individual-level outcomes of those who have access to credit with those who do not, controlling for various other factors that simultaneously affect household welfare, namely, levels of prior-owned human and physical capital. "Controlling for other factors" has been the key issue in these studies: to what extent can observed levels of household outcomes be attributed to credit and not something else? This attribution problem remains the most challenging part of these studies, and a great deal of effort has been made to address it.

Another problem is related to time. Investments yield a flow of returns over time, and the time lag in the accrual of benefits can be long—especially for certain types of investments such as investments in human capital. The benefits that are captured by a snapshot at a particular time—as in the one-shot household surveys upon which most impact studies have been based—clearly do not provide full information. Investment lags take different shapes, and it is not hard to find cases where some of the impact indicators (for example, income and consumption) remain unchanged for a time or even take a dip before showing any signs of increase. This is especially true when investments have been cofinanced by the household's own resources. Of course, the opposite may also be the case: projects that experience positive returns in an emerging market may eventually fail as markets play out more fully. Ideally, we should be determining the present value of future net benefits, using a reasonably long-term horizon. However, we are almost always dictated to by the time horizon set.

Leaving aside the issues of the timing of benefits, which most studies do not address, we now return to the problem of attribution. In real life, it is not possible to observe a household simultaneously with and without program participation. In the usual research setup, therefore, the welfare levels of participant households are compared with those of nonparticipant households. However, no two households are identical, which creates a problem. Although econometric methods enable us to examine the effect of a change in one factor while keeping everything else the same, they can do so only to the extent that all household characteristics are readily observable and quantifiable. What is not observable or quantifiable also cannot be controlled. This is the heart of the problem in at least the econometric impact studies (Zeller et al. 1996). Factors such as entrepreneurship, social skills, management abilities, and other abilities—whether learned or innate—make some households more productive than others but cannot be fully observed or adequately measured. These same factors also affect a household's participation or acceptance in credit programs, and attribution becomes a problem.

The extent to which observed differences in welfare outcomes between participant and nonparticipant households are due to credit access or to unobservable factors is therefore an issue that has to be resolved. In many case, benefits attributed to credit will be overestimated if the nonobservable attributes are not accounted for. As reported in Morduch (1998), selection bias can lead to overestimation of benefits by as much as 100 percent. It could also lead to underestimation of benefits in cases where programs take special care to select clients who have some inherent but unmeasurable weaknesses.

Further, if programs tend to be placed in locations that have better infrastructure, not accounting for this fact will lead to the overstating of benefits, and the opposite if they are placed in communities that are worse off. Khandker, Khalily, and Khan (1995), for example, reported that commercial banks in Bangladesh favor well-endowed areas; and Binswanger, Khandker, and Rosenzweig (1989) concluded that commercial banks in India are more likely to locate branches where the road infrastructure and marketing system are relatively advanced. Is this true of microfinance programs too? Sharma and Zeller (1999) examined the way in which three NGOs in Bangladesh place their services geographically. The results indicated that, although placement of branches of NGO institutions is tied to poverty, NGO services are geared more toward poor pockets of relatively well-developed areas rather than toward servicing the poor in remoter, less developed regions.

The challenge in measuring impact lies in finding observable and measurable factors that affect a household's access to credit but not the welfare outcome under study. This is the classic "identification" problem in econometrics. Pitt and Khandker (1996) use eligibility conditions externally imposed on the household by lending institutions—in their case, a landownership cutoff factor defining the target group of credit programs. The simplest case would be one in which a binary indicator variable indicating program eligibility is used as a measure of credit access. However, Pitt and Khandker (1996, 1998) combine this variable with various other household characteristics that are likely to affect credit demand. In addition, they use household samples from "nonprogram" villages to control for "nonrandom" placement of services. Morduch (1998, 1999) uses a very similar framework in that he evaluates program impact on the basis of differences in outcomes between eligible and noneligible households in program and nonprogram villages. The essential idea behind both approaches is that, if program impact is significant, the differences in outcomes between eligible and ineligible households should be greater in program villages than in nonprogram villages. But this kind of approach by default relies on the availability of clear-cut eligibility conditions enforced by lenders (and therefore exogenous to the household). Not all programs use clear-cut criteria. Hence, other "experimental" methods are also used.

McNelly and Dunford (1998) actually implement an experiment in which, after an initial baseline survey, programs are implemented randomly within the surveyed communities. They then use multiperiod data to compare the difference in outcomes over time between participants, nonparticipants, and control village households. They also further substantiate quantitative results from the experiment with in-depth qualitative interviews. In another series of studies, Mosley and Hulme (1998) use a similar "difference in difference" approach, using as the control group households that have not yet borrowed but that are scheduled to begin borrowing.

Not all studies use the experimental design. Those by Schrieder and Heidhues (1993), Malik (1994), Zeller (1995), Kochar (1997), Zeller, Diagne, and Mataya (1998), and Diagne and Zeller (2001) use a two-step procedure in which participation decisions are separately modeled and estimated. Information from the estimated participation equation is then used to correct for self-selectivity bias in the impact equation. Additionally, the studies by Diagne and Zeller (2001) and Kochar (1997) collected information on lender characteristics in order to identify the impact relationship. Other studies (for example, Berger 1989 and Goetz and Sen Gupta 1996) analyze loan processes and/or loan use in detail to infer possible impact. The results of these and a few other studies are reviewed in the next subsection.

Impact on Assets, Income, and Production

We begin with the now well-known Pitt and Khandker (1996, 1998) study. Using data from 87 villages in Bangladesh in 1991–92, it estimated the marginal impact of credit on a number of welfare indicators. The study showed that household income (proxied by total household expenditure) increased by 18 taka for every 100 taka lent to a woman. Pitt and Khandker also found positive net impacts of credit programs on both human and physical assets. In the case of nonland assets, they found substantial increases when borrowing was by women, but not by men. When labor supply was considered, women's labor supply was only somewhat affected, but men tended to take more leisure. They found mixed results when measuring the impact of the credit programs on education. The education of boys increased irrespective of whether the borrower was male or female; but the education of girls increases only when women borrow from the Grameen Bank.

Morduch (1998, 1999), using the same data set as Pitt and Khandker (1996, 1998) but within the difference-in-difference framework rather than the "instrumental variable" framework used by Pitt and Khandker, found average impacts to be nonexistent.[2] Zeller et al. (2001) applied Morduch's framework to household data from five program and two control villages in Bangladesh. Their results indicate a positive impact of loans on monthly total consumption expenditures (a good proxy for income). McNelly and Dunford (1998) found in their evaluation of Freedom from Hunger's "Credit with Education" program in Ghana that, over the period of program implementation (1993–96), the increase in net nonfarm monthly income for participant women was twice as high as that for both nonparticipants and the control group.

Mosley and Hulme (1998) estimated the impact of 13 microfinance intermediaries in seven developing countries.[3] The study found that, for each of the intermediaries, the impact of lending on the recipient household's income tended to increase as the debtor's income and asset position improved. This, the study surmised, was due in part to poorer debtors' greater preference for consumption loans, their greater vulnerability to asset sales forced by income shocks, and their limited range of investment opportunities. On the basis of this, Hulme and Mosley suggest an "impact frontier" highlighting the trade-off between an ultra-poor clientele with relatively low total impact and a moderately poor clientele with higher impact (Mosley and Hulme 1998; Zaman 1998). They also point out that the impact frontier itself varies with the institutional design of the intermediary: the frontier of "well-designed" schemes is well above that of "ill-designed" schemes.

A slightly different tack was used in the impact study by Diagne and Zeller (2001) in Malawi. Here the approach was to avoid equating borrowing with credit access because households that have credit access may not necessarily choose to borrow, and those that choose to borrow may not necessarily borrow to the full extent of their credit limit. Indeed, in the past the tendency has been

---

2. Two divergent conclusions derived from the same "data set" throw light on unresolved methodological issues. More will be said on this later.

3. These are Banco Solidario (BancoSol) in Bolivia; Badan Kredit Kecamantan (BKK), Kredit Usaha Rayakat Kecil (KURK), and the village banking system of the Bank Rakyat Indonesia (BRI-UD) in Indonesia; the Grameen Bank, the Bangladesh Rural Advancement Committee (BRAC), and Thana Resource Development and Employment (TRDEP) in Bangladesh; the Primary Thrift and Credit Co-operative Society (PTCC) in Sri Lanka; the Kenya Rural Enterprise Program (K-REP) and the Kenya Industrial Estates Informal Sector Programme (KIE-ISP) in Kenya; the Regional Rural Bank (RRB) in India; and the Smallholder Agricultural Credit Administration (SACA) and the Malawi Mudzi Fund in Malawi.

to classify all nonborrowers as credit constrained, which is clearly a shortcoming. In the Malawi study, households were asked both how much they borrowed as well as the maximum they could possibly borrow from formal and informal sources.[4] The interesting result of the Malawi study is that households borrowed only one-half the amount of any increase in their program credit lines. The unused credit lines were maintained partly as precautionary balances and partly because economic returns did not justify full use of the credit line. The study found that the effects of access to four institutions[5] were too small to cause any significant difference in income and food security status between program members and nonmembers. Land scarcity and the lack of complementary inputs in the cultivation of the main crop—maize—were the chief reasons for the low return on credit access: under conditions of exceedingly drought-prone agriculture, returns to fertilizer credit were likely to be poor, if not negative. However, as Zeller, Diagne, and Mataya (1998) noted, using the same data, greater access to credit did increase the share of land allocated to high-yielding maize and tobacco and reduce that allocated to local maize.

Impact on Food Security

Several studies have attempted to measure the effect of participation in credit programs on food security and nutrition specifically. Zeller and Sharma (1998) report that, in many countries, the poor spend as much as 91 percent of their income on food. Furthermore, most loans, especially in the informal sector, are for the purpose of financing consumption-related expenditure. However, when the effect of program participation on food security and nutrition was measured, the results were mixed. Positive effects on household caloric availability were found in studies conducted in Bangladesh, China, and Madagascar (Zeller and Sharma 1998). On the other hand, studies in Malawi (Diagne and Zeller 2001) and Cameroon (Schrieder 1996) did not indicate a significant impact. Pitt and Khandker (1996) also examined the effect of program participation on seasonality in consumption and found that the largest consumption effect of credit is

---

4. Asking households their credit limits presents pitfalls. First, credit limits depend on the interest rate borrowers are willing to pay for credit, which is determined by the potential payoff of the projects they intend to finance. Also, those who have borrowed close to their credit limit or have actually hit it are likely to have a better knowledge of their credit limits than are those who have not. But credit limits in many NGO credit programs are well publicized and are set under clear-cut institutional rules, so borrowers or prospective borrowers know quite accurately the maximum they can borrow at a known, constant interest rate. Hence, extracting fairly accurate formal credit limits from households in program villages is possible. This is what the survey by the International Food Policy Research Institute (IFPRI) in Malawi did.

5. The institutions were the Malawi Rural Finance Company (MRFC), the Promotion of Micro-enterprises for Rural Women (PMERW), the Malawi Mudzi Fund (MMF), and the Malawi Union of Savings and Credit Cooperatives (MUSCCO).

in the hungry season of Aus, just before the crops are harvested. They also found that households with low consumption in the Aus season are more likely to participate in credit programs.

The effect on nutritional outcomes of children is even more unclear, perhaps because good nutrition depends on a host of other factors related to sanitation, access to safe water, access to health care, and the nutritional knowledge of caregivers. Probably because of this, a significant nutritional effect was not found in Bangladesh (Pitt and Khandker 1996), Niger (Schrieder and Pfaff 1997), or Malawi (Diagne and Zeller 2001). McNelly and Dunford (1998) found that in Ghana the nutritional status of participants' one-year-old children had significantly improved between 1993 and 1996 relative to the children of nonparticipants. However, the extent to which this difference can be attributed to improved access to credit is not clear from the results reported.

Gender-Based Impact

The general expectation that the impacts of credit programs are greater for women participants has led many microfinance institutions in Africa and Asia to limit their target group to women. The Pitt and Khandker results discussed earlier implied a strong gender-differentiated impact and hence support such a stance. Since gender is used so pervasively in targeting in both Asia and Africa, we take up this issue in more detail below.

Any observed changes in gender-based differences in impact, by corollary, carry two implications. The first implication is that providing credit to women gives them additional power in household decisionmaking. Without this empowering effect, it would not matter who signed up for the loan, given the fungibility of capital. The second implication is that women's preferences are not the same as men's. Otherwise, there would be no observed difference in impact even if an empowerment effect were present.

Gender-based differences in impact are echoed in a number of other studies. Hashemi, Schuler, and Riley (1996) report that the Grameen Bank and BRAC in Bangladesh had a positive effect on eight different dimensions of women's empowerment, including in contraceptive usage. Osmani (1998) also observed improvement in the bargaining position of women in Bangladesh because of their access to credit. Schrieder (1996) presents evidence from Cameroon that giving credit to women results in resources and profits being plowed back into the development of the immediate household. This leads to better protection of the health and safety of household members—particularly the more vulnerable household members such as women and children (Pallen 1997). Indeed, studies in areas outside the field of microfinance have tended to find women's control of resources important in achieving positive welfare outcomes for children and their families in food, nutrition, education, and health (Quisumbing et al. 1995).

However, positive gender effects cannot always be taken for granted. Osmani (1998), for example, points out that, because of women's generally low absorptive capacity (for example, their limited ability to use larger amounts of credit in the prevailing cultural conditions and in the absence of economic opportunities), many women are likely to lean on their husbands to make better use of the loans. Goetz and Sen Gupta (1996) provide some evidence of this: even though 94 percent of Grameen Bank's borrowers are female, only 37 percent of them are able to exercise control over loan use. Khandker's (1998) findings are similar: only 3 percent of the borrower women out of the 150 he surveyed used money on their own; the others simply gave it to their husbands or other male relatives. However, as Goetz and Sen Gupta note, the mere fact that resources now flow through women may accord some power to them. Interestingly, as Morduch (1999) points out, it may be the very lack of women's empowerment that makes it easier for program managers to enforce loan conditions and therefore make them preferable borrowers.

Gender effects are also likely to depend on the prevailing socioeconomic and cultural environment. All the studies discussed above refer to the particular socioeconomic context of Bangladesh. Results may be different in other cultural contexts, as the study by Schrieder and Pfaff (1997) in Niger shows. In Niger, traditionally the male household head is responsible for taking care of the family's health and food needs. Schrieder and Pfaff found that women do not invest the profits from debt-financed investments in their own or their children's health but rather save the profits in kind to buy consumption goods for their daughters' dowries. Of course, if this results in daughters marrying into a richer household, the mother appears to be acting in the best interest of her daughters, at least in the long run.

Table 11.1 summarizes the results of the studies on investment-led benefit impact.

Insurance-Led Benefit Impact Studies

Many poor households in Asia and Africa live very close to bare subsistence, and downturns in income or shocks in the form of illness of family members can have grave consequences. For the poorest, a large income shock (or a series of smaller shocks) can, in the absence of some form of insurance, lead to serious reductions in food intake (which may, in turn, lead to more permanent disability, especially of children) or even lasting impoverishment if these people sell off key assets to uphold essential consumption.

The insurance-related studies have been of two types. The first type focuses on how access to financial institutions assists households in upholding consumption in the face of income or expenditure shocks. The second type investigates whether households lacking access to credit engage in economic activities that are safer but yield lower returns. We review both types below.

TABLE 11.1 Microfinance and its impact on welfare: Empirical evidence

	Capital				
Authors[a]	Human[b]	Physical[c]	Social[d]	Income	Environment
Berger (1989)			±	±	
Diagne and Zeller (2001)	±[e]			±[f]	
Hashemi, Schuler, and Riley (1996)			?[g]		
Khandker (1998)			±		
Lund and Fafchamps (1997)			+[h]		
McNelly and Dunford (1998)	±[i]			+	
Morduch (1998)			−[j]		
Mosley and Hulme (1998)				+[k]	
Osmani (1998)			±		
Pallen (1997)					+
Pitt and Khandker (1996, 1998)			+[l]		
Schrieder (1996)	±			+	
Schrieder and Heidhues (1993)		±[m]		+	
Schrieder and Pfaff (1997)	±	+	±		
Zaman (1998)			±		
Zeller (1995)	+	+		+	
Zeller, Diagne, and Mataya (1998)		±[n]		+	
Zeller et al. (2000)					+

NOTES: + indicates a positive welfare effect, ± indicates an equivocal result, and − indicates a negative result.

[a] Authors are listed alphabetically.

[b] Investments in human capital in the short run can be the securing of food consumption standards; in the long run, investment in education can be referred to as "human capital investment."

[c] Physical capital includes productive (including animal stock) and consumption goods.

[d] Social capital comprises the development of the community, its local organizations, risk-sharing capacity, and female empowerment.

[e] Positive, but not a statistically significant effect on per capita daily food expenditures or daily calorie and protein intakes.

[f] The authors look only at formal credit schemes and conclude that the marginally beneficial effect on income is due to the reduction in borrowing from informal sources; the result is not statistically significant.

[g] Evidence is unclear.

[h] Informal consumption loans resemble insurance payments in rural villages of the Philippines.

[i] The effect found was positive on children's nutrition but not on maternal nutrition.

[j] Average impact on weekly consumption expenditure is largely negative and seldom statistically significantly different from zero.

[k] Income improves at a decreasing margin.

[l] This represents moderate-sized impacts on household consumption expenditures.

[m] This represents a clear increase in consumption but not in production goods.

[n] Smallholders' participation in agricultural credit schemes had an increasing effect on the adoption of high-yielding seeds; participation in nonagricultural credit schemes had an increasing effect on the use of local varieties, but these schemes primarily targeted nonagricultural enterprises.

Consumption-Smoothing Effects

A number of studies—Paxson (1992) in Thailand, Morduch (1990) in India, Lund and Fafchamps (1997) in the Philippines, and Alderman (1994) in Pakistan—have suggested that, although households generally use savings, credit, transfers, and increased wage employment to cope with income volatility, protection of consumption is by no means complete. Much, it appears, depends on the severity of the shocks.

A study in Nepal by Sharma (1998) examined households' caloric availability when crop incomes fluctuated over agricultural seasons and also as a result of changes in crop yields owing to rainfall. The study found that poorer households that are unable to uphold food expenditures entirely through borrowing or dissaving were nonetheless able to protect caloric availability by switching from a relatively more expensive cereal (rice) to a cheaper one (maize). The study also indicated that, because loans for managing losses are usually small and need to be obtained quickly, formal banks cannot be used for such purposes. For these reasons, credit from formal and informal sources is not always substitutable, even though there is some substitutability between informal sources of credit (for example, between loans from friends and relatives and credit from village moneylenders).

The income shocks in the Nepal study were not that large; hence the finding that even poor households are fairly successful in absorbing them. When the shocks are larger, this is not always the case, as the work by Foster (1995) in Bangladesh indicates. Foster shows that when households confront severe events, such as the Bangladesh floods in 1988, the nutrition status of children of poorer households does suffer as a result of the households' insufficient access to credit. Similarly, in a study in Peru, Jacoby (1994) found that, during adverse circumstances, credit-constrained parents tend to withdraw children from school and put them into income-earning jobs, essentially substituting present consumption for future consumption.

The ability of poor households to cushion income shocks appears also to break down when smaller but repeated shocks occur. Using data collected by IFPRI in Pakistan, Alderman (1994) found that, if a household has a negative income shock following a positive shock, it does not reduce its consumption but increases debt. However, if a household has two or more negative shocks in a row, it does reduce its consumption. Also, when this happens, the household does not increase its debt but rather sells off physical assets, suggesting that credit may be harder to obtain if the household had to rely on it in the previous year. Similarly, Webb and Reardon (1992) found in another study that, in Africa, drought has relatively little impact on households, unless the drought occurs in a sequence of bad years.

Income Stabilization Effects

As Morduch (1995) suggests, we generally cannot just look at the abilities of poor households to smooth the flow of consumption and make conclusions about their ability to insure against investment losses. This is because, in anticipation of credit constraints, households may choose safer production techniques and limit exposure only to income shocks that they can handle. The implication is that, if households did not take steps to smooth their incomes in the first place, they would be much less protected. Further, income smoothing comes at substantial costs. This is the subject matter of the second type of insurance-related studies.

Bliss and Stern (1982), in their study on India, suggest that poorer farmers use less fertilizer in order to reduce investment losses in bad times, but in the process they forgo expected profits. The attempt to smooth income may also give rise to patron–client relationships in which wage laborers agree to provide a detailed set of labor services to an employer household in return for a guaranteed annual wage (Bardhan 1984; Sharma 1993).

Financial Performance and Welfare Impact

Does any relationship exist among program welfare impact, poverty outreach, and financial sustainability? As indicated earlier, a fuller policy-related assessment requires information on the costs as well as on the benefits generated by the program. Important determinants of the cost of financial performance are loan repayment rates, the level of interest rates, and the level of operating costs. At issue are two measures of sustainability. The first is operational sustainability, which measures the extent to which the revenues generated cover operating costs, but not necessarily the full capital costs. The second is financial sustainability, which relates to the extent to which a financial institution can operate free of any type of subsidy.

Few studies have addressed both welfare impact and the cost of service provision. One exception is the study by Mosley and Hulme (1998), who ranked institutions by indicators of financial sustainability and showed a positive and high correlation between financial performance and impact generation, implying that a trade-off between impact and financial performance is not necessary. However, as Morduch (1998) points out, the study suffers from quite serious methodological shortcomings related to inconsistencies in sample sizes and in the quality of control groups, making the results less than fully reliable. Further, the poverty levels of clients of different institutions are themselves quite different (both between and within countries), and it is quite risky and difficult to make straightforward comparisons.

If reliable evidence on cost–benefit ratios is hard to come by, can we still ask if some particular institutional formats outperform others in terms of impact? Even here, answers are not so clear-cut. Institutions differ not only by their type of lending technology, but also in terms of the type of noncredit services that are bundled with credit and the type of target group served (Table 11.2). For these reasons, inferences from data presented cannot be readily made and definitive conclusions have to await further analysis.

TABLE 11.2 Organizational diversity in microfinance and areas of impacts

	Service Package		Target Group		Liability		Loan Repayment	Positive Impact Reported on	Sources on Impact
	Minimalist	Finance-Plus	Women	Men	Group-Based	Individual			
Africa									
Ghana Freedom from Hunger		x	100%		x	x	84–100%	Income, nutrition, empowerment	McNelly and Dunford (1998)
Kenya-REP Juhudi	...	...	60%	x	x		97.7%	Income	Mosley and Hulme (1998)
Malawi Mudzi Fund	x		100%		x		56.6%	Income	Mosley and Hulme (1998)
Marocco Je Recycle		x		x		x	...	Environment	Srinivas and Pallen (1998)
Niger PMR-RFA	x		47%	x		x	77%	Income, assets	Schrieder and Pfaff (1997)
Asia									
Indonesia BRI-UD	x		24%	x		x	92.5%	Income	Mosley and Hulme (1998)
Indonesia BKK	x		x	x		x	95%	Income	Mosley and Hulme (1998)
Indonesia KURK	x		...	...		x	86.3%	Income	Mosley and Hulme (1998)

Institution							Sources
Bangladesh Grameen Bank	x	94%	x	x	98%	Income, consumption, empowerment	Mosley and Hulme (1998); Khandker (1998); Osmani (1998); Pitt and Khandker (1996, 1998)
Bangladesh BRAC	x	80%	x	x	98%	Income, empowerment	Mosley and Hulme (1998); Khandker (1998); Zaman (1998)
Bangladesh TRDEP	...	...	...	...	100%	Income	Mosley and Hulme (1998)
Sri Lanka PTCC	...	...	...	...	96%	Income	Mosley and Hulme (1998)
Sri Lanka SEWA	x	x	x	x	...	Assets, empowerment	Mosley and Hulme (1998); Berger (1989)
India RRB	...	...	...	...	58%	Income	Mosley and Hulme (1998)
Latin America							
Bolivia BacoSol	x	71%	x	x	100%	Income	Mosley and Hulme (1998)
El Salvador FINCA	x	x	x	x	98%	Consumption	Mosley and Hulme (1998)

OTHER SOURCES: Christen et al. (1995); Jahangir and Zeller (1995).

Conclusions

Overall, the investment-led benefit impact studies present mixed results on the impact of credit on various household outcomes. Apart from methodological differences, country-specific and program-specific conditions drive the results of these studies. One important factor is the extent to which households have access to other complementary production inputs that affect the returns to credit. Several studies reiterate that credit is likely to carry good returns to poor households only if other complementary inputs are adequately available. For example, unless conditions of modern agriculture, such as advancements in irrigation and market infrastructure, are fulfilled, providing credit service in the hope that it will trigger income generation based on increased use of chemical fertilizer is indeed wasteful. In such cases, credit constitutes a one-shot transfer to households, leading either to poor repayment rates in lending, or even to a reduced level of consumption in the longer term if cheap credit increases current consumption at the expense of future consumption.

We also found that investment-led benefit impact studies are still somewhat clouded by methodological issues and that further efforts are required to improve the methodology of impact evaluation. The sharply differing estimates, especially when two similar methods are used on the same data (Pitt and Khandker 1996; Morduch 1998, 1999), are rather disturbing. Several observations are worth noting regarding methodology:

- Most of the credit programs studied are actually hybrid programs that bundle credit with services such as health, education, and enterprise management, and the impact observed must also be attributed to this bundling of services. Disentangling credit from noncredit impact is a challenging task. Morduch (1998, 1999), for example, refers to a study that suggests that noncredit services alone may explain about half the observed impact. Further, accounting for the full range of benefits produced by programs is obviously difficult. Many microfinance programs also induce empowerment at the community level by enabling collective action as well as by setting the foundation for sustainable community-based organizations (Pallen 1997; Srinivas and Pallen 1998). Pallen (1997), Srinivas and Pallen (1998), and Zeller et al. (2000) also report significant and positive impacts of credit programs on the environment. A more complete evaluation needs to account for these types of benefits.
- All studies estimate net impacts relative to the control communities. If these controlled communities are served by other social programs, then the difference between control and program villages will remain small. A recent study from the Bangladesh Institute of Development Studies reports that finding a village in Bangladesh that is not served either by some NGO or by some kind of a microcredit program is difficult. However, in some sense, this is what we want if we want to compare the net benefits of credit programs relative to other services.

- The impact studies, especially those that rely on a quasi-experimental research setup, fail to reveal the exact processes by which poverty indicators are affected. They are instead left in a black box, which has created a certain amount of disconnection between researchers and practitioners. To improve the impact of microfinance, more explicit discussion and more qualitative and participatory assessment of the actual mechanism of impact is needed.
- Impacts in Bangladesh as well as in other countries have been evaluated only for the most successful programs. Generalization of this result to other programs can be dangerous.

Compared with the investment-led benefit impact studies, the insurance benefit studies show better evidence of consistent positive impact. This may be because insurance benefits, unlike investment benefits, are conditioned less on access to or ownership of other complementary inputs. Further, compared with the investment-led benefit impact studies, insurance-led benefit impact studies take a fuller account of access to informal sources of credit. This latter consideration has an important implication: policy discussion needs to address the extent to which additional public intervention may simply displace existing mechanisms and produce limited net gains. How limited the net gains will be in actual practice is not yet known. Clever insurance schemes do hold much promise in terms of reducing poverty and improving the lives of the poorest, and may even lead to actual savings in other compensation programs (such as food subsidies) that are already in place even in the poorest countries. However, insurance schemes are also the ones most plagued by informational and enforcement problems. Hence, in the short to medium term, continued reliance will likely have to be placed on credit and saving to provide insurance-like services to the poor.

The challenge ultimately is to reduce the cost of providing financial services to the poor. Whatever the current size of impact, further increases in benefits per dollar of investment critically depend on cost-saving innovations. Public support is critical, especially since private market-based initiatives are hardly forthcoming. Our review shows that returns on such efforts will be substantial, but strongly conditioned on access to other complementary inputs. Our review also indicates that impact studies themselves have to be improved to make more accurate assessments of benefits. This is an important task, because it is only through cycles of innovation, experimentation, and evaluation that we can hope eventually to establish lasting institutions that alleviate the financial constraints faced by the poor.

References

Alderman, H. 1994. Savings and economic shocks in rural Pakistan. Photocopy. Policy Research Department, World Bank, Washington, D.C.

Bardhan, P. K. 1984. *Land, labor, and rural poverty: Essays in development economics*. Oxford: Oxford University Press.

Berger, M. 1989. Giving women credit: The strengths and limitations of credit as a tool for alleviating poverty. *World Development* 17 (7): 1017–1032.

Binswanger, H., S. R. Khandker, and M. Rosenzweig. 1989. *How infrastructure and financial institutions affect agricultural output and investment in India*. Working Paper No. 163. Washington, D.C.: World Bank.

Bliss, C., and N. Stern. 1982. *Palanpur: The economy of an Indian village*. Oxford: Oxford University Press.

Christen, R. P., E. Rhyne, R. C. Vogel, and C. McKean. 1995. *Maximizing the outreach of microenterprise finance: An analysis of successful microfinance programs*. USAID Program and Operations Assessment Report No. 10. Washington, D.C.: IMCC and United States Agency for International Development (USAID).

Diagne, A., and M. Zeller. 2001. *Access to credit and its impact on welfare in Malawi*. Research Report No. 116. Washington, D.C.: International Food Policy Research Institute.

Foster, A. 1995. Prices, credit markets, and child growth in low-income areas. *Economic Journal* 105 (430): 551–570.

Goetz, A. M., and R. Sen Gupta. 1996. Who takes credit? Gender, power, and control over loan use in rural credit programs in Bangladesh. *World Development* 24 (1): 45–64.

Hashemi, S., S. Schuler, and A. Riley. 1996. Rural credit programs and women's empowerment in Bangladesh. *World Development* 24 (4): 635–654.

Jacoby, H. 1994. Borrowing constraints and progress through school: Evidence from Peru. *Review of Economics and Statistics* 76 (1): 151–160.

Jahangir, A. S. M., and M. Zeller. 1995. Overview paper on rural finance programs for the poor in Bangladesh. A review of five major programs. International Food Policy Research Institute, Washington, D.C.

Khandker, M. 1998. Socio-economic and psychological dynamics of empowerment of Grameen Bank and BRAC borrowers. In *Workshop proceedings "Recent research on micro-finance: Implications for policy,"* ed. I. Matin, S. Sinha, with P. Alexander. Brighton, Sussex, U.K.: University of Sussex, Poverty Research Unit at Sussex.

Khandker, S., B. Khalily, and Z. Khan. 1995. *Grameen Bank: Performance and sustainability*. Discussion Paper No. 306. Washington, D.C.: World Bank.

Kochar, A. 1997. Does lack of access to formal credit constrain agricultural production? Evidence from the land tenancy market in rural India. *American Journal of Agricultural Economics* 79: 754–763.

Lund, S. M., and M. Fafchamps. 1997. *Informal credit, insurance networks, and risk-sharing: Empirical evidence from the Philippines*. Stanford, Calif., U.S.A.: Stanford University.

McNelly, B., and C. Dunford. 1998. *Impact of credit with education on mothers' and their young children's nutrition: Lower Pra Rural Bank Credit with Education Program in Ghana*. Davis, Calif., U.S.A.: Freedom from Hunger.

Malik, S. 1994. Credit use, poverty, and the role of institutional rural credit. Mimeo. International Food Policy Research Institute, Washington, D.C.

Morduch, J. 1990. Risk, production and savings: Theory and evidence from Indian households. Photocopy. Harvard University, Cambridge, Mass., U.S.A.

————. 1995. Income smoothing and consumption smoothing. *Journal of Economic Perspectives* 9 (3): 103–114.

————. 1998. Does microfinance really help the poor? Unobserved heterogeneity and average impacts of credit in Bangladesh. Harvard University, Department of Economics, and Harvard Institute for International Development, Cambridge, Mass., U.S.A.

————. 1999. The microfinance promise. *Journal of Economic Literature* 37 (4): 1569–1614.

Mosley, P., and D. Hulme. 1998. Micro-enterprise finance: Is there a trade-off between growth and poverty alleviation. In *Workshop proceedings "Recent research on micro-finance: Implications for policy,"* ed. I. Matin, S. Sinha, with P. Alexander. Brighton, Sussex, U.K.: University of Sussex, Poverty Research Unit at Sussex.

Osmani, L. N. K. 1998. Credit and relative well-being of women: The experience of the Grameen Bank, Bangladesh. In *Workshop proceedings "Recent research on micro-finance: Implications for policy,"* ed. I. Matin, S. Sinha, with P. Alexander. Brighton, Sussex, U.K.: University of Sussex, Poverty Research Unit at Sussex.

Pallen, D. 1997. Environmental source book for micro-finance institutions. Canadian International Development Agency (CIDA), Asia Branch. Available at <http://www.soc.titech.ac.jp/icm/environ/environ.html>.

Paxson, C. 1992. Using weather variability to estimate the response of savings to transitory income in Thailand. *American Economic Review* 81 (1): 15–33.

Pitt, M. M., and S. R. Khandker. 1996. *Household and intrahousehold impact of the Grameen Bank and similar targeted credit programs in Bangladesh.* World Bank Discussion Papers No. 320. Washington, D.C.: World Bank.

————. 1998. The impact of group-based credit programs on poor households in Bangladesh: Does the gender of participants matter? *Journal of Political Economy* 106 (5): 958–996.

Quisumbing, A. R., L. R. Brown, H. Sims Feldstein, L. Haddad, and C. Peña. 1995. *Women: The key to food security.* Food Policy Report. Washington, D.C.: International Food Policy Research Institute.

Schrieder, G. 1996. *The role of rural finance for food security of the poor in Cameroon.* Frankfurt, Germany: Lang Verlag.

Schrieder, G., and F. Heidhues. 1993. Credit for the rural poor: Cameroon country case. Part 3 of the Final Report to the GTZ. International Food Policy Research Institute, Washington, D.C.

Schrieder, G., and K. Pfaff. 1997. *Mise en place d'un réseau de caisses d'épargne villageoises au Niger.* Working Paper No. 28. Stuttgart, Germany: University of Hohenheim.

Sebstad, J., C. Neill, C. Barnes, and G. Chen. 1995. *Assessing the impacts of micro-enterprise interventions: A framework for analysis.* Washington, D.C.: USAID/ Global Bureau/Office of Microenterprise Development.

Sharma, M. 1993. Institutions of insurance in rural Nepal: The case of contractual arrangements in credit, land and labor. In *Indigenous management of natural resources in Nepal,* ed. D. Tamang, G. J. Gill, and G. B. Thapa. Kathmandu, Nepal: His Majesty's Government, Ministry of Agriculture/Winrock International.

————. 1998. Rural credit-based institutions and subsistence consumption: An empirical study based on household data from Nepal. Ph.D. dissertation. Cornell University, Department of Agricultural Economics, Ithaca, N.Y., U.S.A.

Sharma, M., and M. Zeller. 1999. Placement and outreach of group-based credit organizations: The cases of ASA, BRAC, and PROSHIKA in Bangladesh. *World Development* 27 (12): 2123–2136.

Srinivas, H., and D. Pallen. 1998. The environmental colors of microfinance. Available at <http://www.soc.titech.ac.jp/icm/environ/environ.html>.

Webb, P., and T. Reardon. 1992. Drought impact and household response in East and West Africa. *Quarterly Journal of International Agriculture* 31 (3): 230–246.

Zaman, H. 1998. BRAC's impact on poverty and empowerment: A summary of findings from Matlab. In *Workshop proceedings "Recent research on micro-finance: Implications for policy,"* ed. I. Matin, S. Sinha, with P. Alexander. Brighton, Sussex, U.K.: University of Sussex, Poverty Research Unit at Sussex.

Zeller, M. 1995. The demand for financial services by rural households: Conceptual framework and empirical findings. *Quarterly Journal of International Agriculture* 34 (2): 149–170.

Zeller, M., and M. Sharma. 1998. *Rural finance and poverty alleviation.* Washington, D.C.: International Food Policy Research Institute.

Zeller, M., A. Diagne, and C. Mataya. 1998. Market access by smallholder farmers in Malawi: Implications for technology adoption, agricultural productivity, and crop income. *Agricultural Economics* 19: 219–229.

Zeller, M., M. Sharma, A. Ahmed, and S. Rashid. 2001. *Group-based financial institutions for the rural poor in Bangladesh: An institutional- and household-level analysis.* Research Report No. 120. Washington, D.C.: International Food Policy Research Institute.

Zeller, M., A. Ahmed, S. Babu, S. Broca, A. Diagne, and M. Sharma. 1996. Rural financial policies for food security of the poor: Methodologies for a multicountry research project. Food Consumption and Nutrition Division Discussion Paper No. 11. International Food Policy Research Institute, Washington, D.C.

Zeller, M., C. Lapenu, B. Minten, E. Ralison, D. Randrianaivo, and C. Randrianarisoa. 2000. Pathways of rural development in Madagascar: An empirical investigation of the critical triangle of environmental sustainability, economic growth, and poverty alleviation. Food Consumption and Nutrition Division Discussion Paper No. 82. International Food Policy Research Institute, Washington, D.C., March.

12 Impact of Access to Credit on Maize and Tobacco Productivity in Malawi

ALIOU DIAGNE

The continuing inadequate access of African farmers to credit is believed to have significant negative consequences for various aggregate and household-level outcomes, including technology adoption, agricultural productivity, food security, nutrition, health, and overall household welfare. It has long been recognized that without well-functioning financial markets there is little prospect for increasing the agricultural productivity and living standards of the African rural population in any significant and sustainable way. During the past 40 years, African governments and donors have set up credit programs aimed at improving rural household access to credit. However, the vast majority of these credit programs, especially the agricultural development banks, which provided credit at subsidized interest rates, have failed to achieve their objective of serving the rural poor as sustainable credit institutions (Adams, Graham, and Von Pischke 1984; Adams and Vogel 1985; Braverman and Guasch 1986).

In response to these failures and recognizing that traditional commercial banks typically have no interest in lending to poor rural households because the poor lack viable collateral and because the transaction costs associated with small loans are high, innovative credit delivery systems are being promoted as a more efficient way of improving rural households' access to formal credit with no or minimal government involvement. Most of these lending programs are group based. They use joint liability and peer pressure as collateral substitutes and community-based credit delivery systems to reduce transaction costs. The Grameen Bank in Bangladesh is a well-known example of these innovative credit programs. The Grameen Bank has a proven record in reaching the poorest and simultaneously achieving very high repayment rates.

Like many developing countries, Malawi has recently seen the emergence of several innovative microcredit programs targeted to the rural population. The Smallholder Agricultural Credit Administration in Malawi (SACA) used to be the prime example in Africa of a successful government-supported credit program because its repayment rates averaged over 97 percent from 1968 to 1991. But SACA collapsed in 1991 when the repayment rate plummeted to less than

25 percent owing to a combination of severe drought and political liberalization.[1] Although SACA was replaced by the newly created Malawi Rural Finance Company (MRFC) and microcredit programs run by nongovernmental organizations (NGO) have become increasingly important in Malawi, most smallholders continue to be left out of the main extension and credit systems. For example, a census of 4,800 households in 45 villages with credit programs conducted at the beginning of a survey by the International Food Policy Research Institute (IFPRI) and the Rural Development Department (RDD) at Bunda College of Agriculture found that only 14 percent of the smallholder farmers had access to formal credit. Furthermore, this figure significantly overstates the incidence of smallholders with access to credit because the vast majority of villages in Malawi do not host any credit program.

Poor households in Malawi generally have landholdings of less than 1 hectare. They are unable to grow enough food to feed themselves, even though they concentrate almost exclusively on maize production. To break the poverty cycle, these food-insecure households, often with severely malnourished children, need some form of assistance to obtain adequate modern agricultural inputs to raise their land and labor productivity (Malawi 1994). It has been argued, however, that most of these farmers are too poor and cash strapped to benefit from any kind of access to credit, and that, even if they had adequate supplies of the right inputs, their land constraints are so severe that any increase in productivity would still fall short of guaranteeing their food security (Malawi 1995). For these households, credit for nonfarm income-generating activities has been suggested as a policy alternative for addressing their food insecurity and malnutrition problems.

The objectives of this chapter are to analyze the socioeconomic determinants of household productivity and technical efficiency in growing maize and tobacco in Malawi and to assess the impact of access to credit on them. The rest of the chapter is organized into three sections. First, I present the methodology used to measure the impact of access to credit on productivity. I then describe the data and present the empirical results. I conclude with some remarks on the policy implications of the analysis.

Methodology for Measuring the Impact of Access to Credit on Productivity

A stochastic frontier production function framework is used to assess the impact of access to formal credit on maize and tobacco productivity (see, for

---

1. A study on the causes of the collapse of SACA revealed that the exceptionally high repayment rates, achieved under the one-party system, were to a large extent the result of the draconian and coercive loan recovery methods employed by the "campaigners" from the youth organization of the then ruling Malawi Congress Party (Msukwa et al. 1994).

examples, Aigner, Lovell, and Schmidt 1977; Schmidt 1985; and Battese 1992). Within this framework, the frontier production function is the maximum output a farmer could obtain from given fixed quantities of basic inputs (land, seed, fertilizer, and water). This maximum output is the potential that can be achieved from a given technology embodied in seed and fertilizer. It depends on soil characteristics and other physical constraints that are specific to each farm. Once these physical constraints are controlled for, any deviation from the potential is attributed to the farmer's technical inefficiency in production. Formally, the stochastic frontier production model is defined, for a given product, as

$$y = f(x)e^{u + v}, \qquad (12.1)$$

where y is the farmer's observed or realized output; f is the production function frontier, which describes the technological parameters of the production process; x is a vector of given levels of basic inputs with observable and unobservable intrinsic physical characteristics; $f(x)$ is the potential or maximum possible output that *any* farmer can achieve using x and the production technology embodied in f; u is a negative random variable that measures the systematic deviation of the farmer's realized output from the potential; and v is a statistical error term. Thus, the nonnegative ratio $e^u = f(x)e^v/y$ measures the level of technical efficiency of a farmer. The same ratio measures the deviation from the potential marginal productivity independently of the level of input use. Farmers are technically efficient when the ratio reaches its maximum value, which is 1 (corresponding to the value zero for the deviation u). Otherwise they are technically inefficient and therefore can potentially achieve higher output for the same level of inputs (or, equivalently, higher marginal productivity at all levels of input use). The random variable u is usually assumed to follow a truncated normal distribution, and the individual farm-level technical efficiency index is estimated by the conditional expectation $E(e^u|\xi)$; where $\xi \equiv u + v$.[2]

The technical inefficiency of a farmer is explained by sociodemographic factors that include management practices and access to extension services, credit, infrastructure, age, education, and other household demographics (see, for example, Kalirajan 1981; Pitt and Lee 1981; and Battese 1992). Following Kumbhakar, Ghosh, and McGuckin (1991), Huang and Liu (1994), and Battese and Coelli (1995), the dependence of the technical inefficiency of a farmer on sociodemographic factors is formulated as

$$u = z\beta + \varepsilon, \qquad (12.2)$$

where z is the vector of sociodemographic variables, β is a vector of parameters to be estimated, and ε is a normally distributed random variable with zero

---

2. See, for example, Battese and Coelli (1988) or Kalirajan (1991) for the exact expressions of the conditional expectation.

mean and truncation point defined by $\varepsilon \leq -z\beta$. The vector of parameters, β, is estimated jointly with the technological parameters of the production function f using a maximum likelihood estimation (MLE) procedure (see, for example, Battese and Coelli 1995, or Battese, Malik, and Gill 1996).

Access to credit affects farmers through at least two channels. First, credit increases the ability of poor farmers with little or no savings to acquire needed agricultural inputs. Credit also allows nonpoor farmers to acquire farm equipment that is too expensive to finance out of their own resources. For example, a study by Diagne, Zeller, and Mataya (1996) found that the 1995 average input expenditures of smallholders without access to credit in Malawi was US$3, compared with US$20 for those with access to credit. The study also found that fewer than 25 percent of the agricultural inputs acquired by smallholder farmers in Malawi are financed through credit. More than two-thirds of their input acquisitions were financed through their own meager resources (the 1995 average per capita annual income was US$51).

Second, access to credit helps rural households by increasing their risk-bearing ability and altering their risk-coping strategies. Just the knowledge that credit will be available in case of crop failure can induce farmers to adopt new and more risky technologies. The evidence from Malawi suggests that, without access to credit, the ability of smallholder farmers to recover from a crop fail-ure is extremely limited, as shown by the significant drop in their input expen-ditures (a 50 percent drop, compared with an 18 percent increase for those with access to credit). Similarly, the option to borrow, even if not exercised, helps avoid risk-reducing but inefficient income diversification strategies and pre-cautionary savings (Deaton 1989; Eswaran and Kotwal 1990).

To satisfactorily assess the impact of access to credit on a farmer's level of technical efficiency, a distinction is made between *access to credit* (formal or informal) and *participation* in formal credit programs or in the informal credit market. A household has access to a particular source of credit if it is able to borrow from that source, although it may choose not to borrow. The extent of access to credit from a given source is measured by the maximum amount a household can borrow from that source (its credit limit). A household is par-ticipating if it is borrowing from a source of credit. The impact of access to credit on any household outcome variables is then measured by the marginal effect of the credit limit variable on that outcome variable. For more details on the methodology, see Diagne (1998 and 1999) and Diagne and Zeller (2001).

The distinction between access and participation is important because the impact of access to credit on the farmer's technical efficiency is through the sec-ond channel and is different from the effect it has on output by allowing the smallholder to use more fertilizer or seed through borrowing, which is the first channel (see Zeller, Diagne, and Mataya 1998 for an analysis of the impact of participation on technology adoption in Malawi). Indeed, by definition, techni-cal inefficiency is measured for a given level of basic input use, and a household may benefit from mere access to credit even if it does not borrow. Access to credit enhances farmers' technical efficiency by enabling them to specialize in the crops in which they have a comparative advantage in human and physical capital. Furthermore, without an adequate level of access to credit on which they can rely in times of crop failure, smallholders may be forced to use risk-reducing, but inefficient, production practices such as mixed cropping, late planting, and bad timing of input applications.

Finally, because the household level of access to credit is determined by the same sociodemographic variables that affect its technical efficiency, reduced form models of the determination of the household's credit limits from formal and informal sources of credit are estimated first. This enables calculation of the overall effects of the sociodemographic variables on the household level of technical efficiency in growing maize and tobacco.

Description of the Sample and Data and of the Results

The Sample and Data

The data used in the analysis come from a year-long, three-round survey (February 1995–December 1995) of 404 households in 45 villages in five districts of Malawi where the four microcredit programs studied were operating. The four microcredit programs are the Malawi Rural Finance Company (MRFC), a state-owned nationwide agricultural credit program; the Promotion of Micro-Enterprises for Rural Women (PMERW), a microcredit program for nonfarm income generation activities supported by the German Agency for Technical Cooperation (GTZ); the Malawi Mudzi Fund (MMF), a program funded by the International Fund for Agricultural Development (IFAD) and modeled on the Grameen Bank and now incorporated into MRFC; and the Malawi Union of Savings and Credit Cooperatives (MUSCCO), a union of locally based savings and credit unions. All the programs are based on group lending except MUSCCO. A choice-based stratified random sampling procedure was used to select the households surveyed. About half of the sample was selected from participants of the four credit programs. The other half of the sample was equally divided between past participants (mostly from a failed government credit program) and households that had never participated in any formal credit program. See Diagne, Zeller, and Mataya (1996) for details on the survey and data collection methodology and Diagne (1998 and 1999) and Diagne and Zeller (2001) for the statistical corrections required because of the choice-based sampling.

The information collected in the survey includes household demographics, land tenure, agricultural production, livestock ownership, asset ownership and transactions, food and nonfood consumption, credit, savings and gift transactions, wage, self-employment income and time allocation, and anthropometric status of preschoolers and their mothers. The agricultural data cover the 1993/94 and 1994/95 seasons. The questionnaire on credit and savings was administered to all adult household members (over 17 years old) in the sample. In each round, respondents were asked what was the maximum amount they *could* borrow during the recall period from both informal and formal sources of credit. If the respondent was involved in a loan transaction as a borrower, the question was asked for each loan transaction (for both granted and rejected loan demands). In this case, the credit limit refers to the time of borrowing and to the lender involved in that particular loan transaction. If the respondent did not ask for any loan, the question was asked separately for formal and informal sources of credit with no reference to particular formal or informal lenders. Respondents who were granted loans were also asked the same general question (that is, with no reference to particular formal or informal lenders) in a way that elicited the credit limit they would face if they wanted more loans not just from the same lender, but from the same sector of the credit market (formal or informal) in which they had already borrowed. Consequently, for both formal and informal credit, the maximum formal and informal credit limits of each adult household member were obtained in each round, even if the respondent was not involved in any loan transaction.

Demographic Characteristics and Asset Ownership of Sample Households

Table 12.1 shows that 28 percent of the households in the sample are headed by females. This figure is close to the widely cited figure of 30 percent for Malawi as a whole. The table also shows that the average household size in the survey areas is five persons per household, which is the same for both male- and female-headed households. The average age of household heads in the sample is 42, with female heads of household being, on average, 4 years older than male ones. Overall, 68 percent of household heads attended primary school, but only 17 percent have a Primary School Leaving Certificate; female household heads tend to have a lower primary school attendance rate than male ones (63 versus 71 percent). Farming is the primary occupation of two-thirds of household heads, both male and female. Other self-employment activities and wage labor are second and third, respectively, as primary occupations of household heads (18 and 8 percent, respectively).

Table 12.1 also shows that the average total value of all household assets is 6,681 Malawian kwacha (MK) or approximately US$450.[3] The average value of land is MK 3,306 and of livestock MK 1,571. In total, productive assets, including those for off-farm income generation activities, make up 57 percent of the value of household assets. On-farm assets (cultivable land, farm equipment, and oxen) constitute 44 percent of the total value of household assets and livestock 11 percent. There are noticeable differences between male- and female-

---

3. The exchange rate was US$1 for 15 kwacha (MK) at the time of the survey.

TABLE 12.1 Demographic characteristics of households

	Male	Female	All
	Gender of Household Head		
Sample size (number)	291	111	402
Sample size (percent)	82	28	100
Household size	5	5	5
Adult equivalent population	3.6	3.6	3.6
Dependency ratio	.4	.5	.4
Mean age of head	40	44	42
Head attended primary school (percent)	71	63	68
Head has Primary School Leaving Certificate (percent)	21	10	17
Primary occupation of heads (percent)			
Farming	62	74	66
Household work	0	7	3
Wage laborer	11	2	8
Other self-employment	18	17	18
Student	1	0	0
Unemployed	3	0	2
Other	5	0	3
Average value of all assets (MK)	7,551	4,841	6,681
Land (MK)	3,866	2,148	3,306
Livestock (total MK)	1,440	1,848	1,571
Productive assets[a] (MK)	4,537	3,343	4,154
Nonproductive assets[b] (MK)	3,014	1,498	2,528
Share of total household assets held in the form of			
Productive assets	57	58	57
On-farm assets	43	46	44
Livestock	11	12	11
Land	56	59	57
Average hectares of land	1.8	1.4	1.7
Household with			
Less than 0.5 hectare	4	9	6
0.5 to 1.0 hectare	17	21	18
1.0 to 1.5 hectares	24	35	28
1.5 to 3.0 hectares	42	30	38
Over 3.0 hectares	12	5	10

SOURCE: Rural finance survey, conducted by the International Food Policy Research Institute (IFPRI) and the Rural Development Department (RDD) at Bunda College of Agriculture, Malawi, 1995.

NOTE: The exchange rate was US$1 = MK 15 in 1995.

[a] Noncultivable land, the buildings, furniture, and utensils in the house.

[b] On-farm assets (cultivable land, farm equipment, and oxen) and livestock.

headed households. In particular, the total value of all assets is significantly higher for male-headed households (about MK 7,600) compared with female-headed households (about MK 4,800), who also own less land (1.4 versus 1.8 hectares). Overall, land is scarce; more than half of all households in the survey areas have landholdings of less than 1.5 hectares.

The Extent of Access to Credit of Smallholder Households

Table 12.2 presents the average informal and formal credit limits and unused credit lines observed in the survey, for the whole population and separately for when a formal loan was granted, rejected, or not requested. The table shows that for the population as a whole the mean credit limit is MK 44 for formal credit and MK 46 for informal credit (about US$3). To put these figures in perspective, Malawi's 1995 per capita GNP was US$170 (MK 2,550) and the average per capita income in the sample was MK 1,190. The average formal credit limit is significantly higher for cases where formal loans were granted (MK 679, on average) than for cases where informal loans were granted (MK 35). One should also note that some rejected borrowers and respondents who did not ask for loans could nevertheless borrow from both sectors.[4]

The distribution of the credit limits and unused credit lines presented in Table 12.2 gives a better picture of the extent of access to credit in Malawi. The median formal and informal credit limits in the population as a whole are both zero. The distribution of the unused credit lines shows that borrowers more often exhaust their credit lines in the formal sector compared with the informal sector. This, taken together with the fact that informal loan sizes and credit limits are significantly lower than the corresponding formal ones, suggests that the two types of credit are not perfect substitutes. Otherwise, because almost all informal loans do not carry an interest rate, one would expect to see households reach their credit limits more frequently in the informal sector than in the formal sector.

Crop Choice, Input Use, and Yields of Smallholder Households

Table 12.3 shows the average hectares of land cultivated by the smallholder households in the sample and the shares allocated to each crop for the 1994/95 agricultural season, differentiated by program membership. On average, each household cultivated 0.7 hectares; hybrid maize had the highest share of land allocated to it (46 percent), followed closely by local maize (38 percent). The

---

4. A small number of borrowers whose loan demand was rejected could borrow a lesser but positive amount from the same lender but chose not to do so. The main reason a rejected borrower chooses to go without a loan instead of accepting a lesser amount is that the lesser amount is usually too small for the intended purpose of the loan. Often when a loan demand is rejected by one sector of the credit market (formal or informal), the potential borrower could borrow at least some amount from the other sector.

TABLE 12.2 Distribution of formal and informal credit limits and unused credit lines, October 1993–December 1995

	Formal Credit Limit and Unused Credit Line (MK)					Informal Credit Limit and Unused Credit Line (MK)				
	Mean	Median	Standard Deviation	Minimum	Maximum	Mean	Median	Standard Deviation	Minimum	Maximum
All respondents										
Credit limit	44	0	248	0	10,000	46	0	188	0	12,000
Unused	19	0	137	0	6,575	36	0	112	0	5,000
When formal loan was granted										
Credit limit	679	500	911	13	10,000	95	20	500	0	12,000
Unused	148	0	474	0	6,575	69	10	202	0	4,000
When informal loan was granted										
Credit limit	35	0	149	0	1,000	127	50	369	5	12,000
Unused	13	0	76	0	1,000	52	12	134	0	4,000
When loan demand was rejected										
Credit limit	72	0	254	0	4,000	46	0	89	0	400
Unused	53	11	215	0	4,000	34	0	69	0	300
When no loan was requested										
Credit limit	12	0	88	0	5,000	32	0	104	0	5,000
Unused	12	0	88	0	5,000	32	0	104	0	5,000

SOURCE: Rural finance survey, conducted by the International Food Policy Research Institute (IFPRI) and the Rural Development Department (RDD) at Bunda College of Agriculture, Malawi, 1995.

NOTE: The exchange rate was US$1 = MK 15 in 1995.

TABLE 12.3 Household land and fertilizer allocation among crops in the 1994/95 season, by credit program membership

| | All Households | Current Members | | | | | | | Past Members | Never Been Members |
		MRFC	Mudzi Fund	MUSCCO	PMERW1	PMERW2	Other	All		
Average hectares planted to										
Local maize	0.9	10.3	0.7	0.7	0.7	0.8	20.4	10.2	0.9	0.8
Hybrid maize	0.8	0.9	0.9	0.9	0.6	0.7	10.3	0.9	0.8	0.8
Tobacco	0.3	0.4	0.0	0.6	0.7	10.0	20.6	0.5	0.3	0.2
Other crops	0.4	0.3	...	0.4	0.4	0.4	0.7	0.4	0.3	0.4
All crops	0.7	0.9	0.8	0.8	0.6	0.7	10.4	0.9	0.7	0.7
Average shares planted to										
Local maize	38	43	9	13	12	21	37	35	51	36
Hybrid maize	46	49	91	65	71	47	54	53	30	46
Tobacco	2	3	0	13	5	25	2	4	3	1
Other crops	14	5	...	9	12	7	7	8	16	16

Percentage of households using chemical
fertilizer in

No crop	36	5	29	9	10	16	26	11	53	40
Local maize	19	54	11	2	11	22	42	40	19	12
Hybrid maize	49	72	67	91	82	76	74	71	35	45
Tobacco	8	14	0	32	9	36	2	13	12	5
Other crops	0	0	0	0	1	0	0	0	3	0
Percentage of total chemical fertilizer used on										
Local maize	26	39	11	2	8	12	41	31	31	21
Hybrid maize	65	50	89	79	76	49	53	57	54	75
Tobacco	8	11	0	20	15	39	6	12	12	4
Other crops	0	0	...	...	0	...	...	0	2	...

SOURCE: Rural finance survey, conducted by the International Food Policy Research Institute (IFPRI) and the Rural Development Department (RDD) at Bunda College of Agriculture, Malawi, 1995.

NOTES: MRFC = Malawi Rural Finance Company; MUSCCO = Malawi Union of Savings and Credit Cooperatives; PMERW1 = PMERW revolving fund for rural women; PMERW2 = PMERW credit program for experienced business women.

share allocated to tobacco was very small (2 percent). Credit program members allocated 53 percent of their land to hybrid maize and 35 percent to local maize compared with 30 and 51 percent, respectively, for past participants (mostly from the SACA program) and 46 and 36 percent, respectively, for households that had never participated in any credit program. In Table 12.3, current household membership is differentiated by program type. Two subprograms are distinguished within PMERW. PMERW1 is a revolving fund providing two-year loans to women's clubs, each consisting of 10–15 poor, entrepreneurial women who have completed training courses with a Community Development Assistant. PMERW2 provides loans to highly skilled business women, most with prior successful credit repayments histories (see Diagne and Zeller 2001 for further details). Among program members, Mudzi Fund and PMERW1 households have relatively high shares of their cultivated land planted with hybrid maize (91 and 71 percent, respectively) while PMERW2 households have significantly higher shares of land allocated to tobacco (25 percent compared with an average of 4 percent for all program members).

Table 12.3 also shows that only 11 percent of program households did not apply chemical fertilizer in 1995. In comparison, 53 percent of past members and 40 percent of households that had never belonged to a credit program did not use chemical fertilizers, indicating that program participation and fertilizer use are highly correlated. Table 12.3 reveals an interesting pattern regarding the allocation of chemical fertilizer among the different crops: chemical fertilizer, when applied, is most frequently used for hybrid maize, followed by local maize, and then tobacco. Other crops seldom receive chemical fertilizer. For example, 50 percent of the chemical fertilizer acquired in 1994/95 by MRFC members was used on hybrid maize, compared with 11 percent used on tobacco and 39 percent used on local maize. Even smallholder tobacco farmers applied chemical fertilizer on tobacco and hybrid maize in about equal amounts. Moreover, MRFC members supposedly receive more in-kind loans for tobacco than for hybrid maize (Diagne and Zeller 2001). This indicates that MRFC members are diverting a large portion of their tobacco loan packages toward their food crops.

Table 12.4 presents yields, input expenditures per hectare, and gross margins for local maize, hybrid maize, and tobacco for the 1995 production year, differentiated by program membership. Several general patterns can be identified when the results are differentiated by program membership. First, the average maize yield of current program members is much lower than that for past members. However, program members perform better than households that have never had access to credit. Current program members also have an average gross margin per hectare for hybrid maize that is 51 percent lower than that for past members of credit programs. This is somewhat surprising in view of their higher input intensity. However, current members have higher yields and gross margins per hectare of tobacco than past members. Households that have never had access to formal credit have the lowest aggregate gross margins per hectare for all crops (MK 1,240 compared with MK 1,482 for current members and MK 1,773 for past members). Hence, although current members appear to be inefficient at growing hybrid maize, they are much better tobacco farmers than either past members or households that have never been members. Still, the results raise the question of whether the extension advice and credit packages recommended are suboptimal, especially those of MRFC, the Mudzi Fund, and MUSCCO. Perhaps they encourage too much use of fertilizer and seed with a view to enhancing yield instead of profitability.

Results of the Econometric Analysis

A translog functional form was specified for the production function *f*. The results of the estimation of the production function frontier, marginal productivity, and technical efficiencies for hybrid maize, local maize, and tobacco are reported in Tables 12.6 and 12.7 (the definition and summary statistics of the variables used in the econometric analysis are presented in Table 12.5). As noted above, the technical efficiency estimates measure deviations from both potential output and marginal productivity.[5]

The socioeconomic determinants of the technical efficiency of a household in growing hybrid maize, local maize, and tobacco are presented in Table 12.6. The chi-square statistics of the log-likelihood test indicate that the management and demographic variables are jointly significant in explaining household technical inefficiency in growing hybrid maize and tobacco, but not for local maize. However, taken individually, the coefficients for most of the variables are not statistically significant. There are a few notable exceptions. More days of late planting (LPDOPHMZ) lower the technical efficiency (thus the marginal productivity) in growing hybrid and local maize. The more educated the spouse (YYEDUCS), the more technically efficient is the household in growing both types of maize. In constrast, the education of the household head (YYEDUCH) does not significantly affect technical efficiency except in lowering the efficiency for hybrid maize. Interestingly, access to extension services, as measured by the number of visits of extension agents during the previous two years (NEXTVC2Y), has no significant effect on household technical efficiency. The effect of access to formal credit (FLOANMAX), including its interaction with landholding size (FLNMXLND), is significant only for local maize. Finally, households in the south tend in general to be less technically efficient than households in the other regions.

---

5. The estimation results for the socioeconomic determinants of the formal and informal credit limit equations are not discussed in this chapter in order to keep it short and focus on assessing the impacts of access to formal credit on household technical efficiency and productivity in growing maize and tobacco. For a full discussion of these results, see Diagne and Zeller (2001), which also discusses the estimation procedure in greater detail.

TABLE 12.4 Average yield and net income per hectare for the 1995 rainfed crops, by program membership

	All Households	Current Members							Past Members	Never Been Members
		MRFC	Mudzi Fund	MUSCCO	PMERW1 (S&C)	PMERW2 (CBM)	Other	All		
Yield (kilograms per hectare)										
Local maize	833	917	424	78	11,128	1,160	972	899	1,159	699
Hybrid maize	799	714	629	1,512	517	1,127	730	799	1,198	728
Tobacco	603	798	0	780	1,037	1,397	1,044	788	532	478
Other crops	1,224	387	...	1,623	1,510	1,215	1,514	945	656	1,471
All crops	907	743	609	1,299	770	1,193	900	847	972	912
Total input expenditure per hectare (MK)[a]										
Local maize	130	304	166	108	170	279	270	280	71	103
Hybrid maize	281	341	260	543	349	524	369	367	303	234
Tobacco	612	1,050	0	659	939	1,186	693	951	592	322
Other crops	146	342	...	122	292	466	195	296	84	133
All crops	216	382	251	414	349	586	325	376	166	170
Total value of inputs per hectare (MK)[a]										
Local maize	232	333	843	114	681	752	376	367	128	225
Hybrid maize	313	353	285	551	353	550	369	380	321	278
Tobacco	619	1,050	0	659	939	1,186	693	951	592	338
Other crops	187	365	...	122	360	488	205	324	147	170
All crops	271	399	340	418	412	693	350	410	211	235

Gross margin per hectare (MK)[b]

Local maize	981	1,047	−264	991	916	1,012	1,405	975	1,559	782
Hybrid maize	622	419	177	1,322	196	817	617	542	1,061	584
Tobacco	6,283	9,772	0	8,447	11,288	22,031	23,896	8,923	4,626	4,864
Other crops	1,959	971	. . .	1,846	3,454	1,692	1,591	1,678	1,877	2,048
All crops	1,331	1,374	133	2,557	1,330	4,731	1,170	1,449	1,727	1,175

Net crop income per hectare (MK)[c]

Local maize	1,083	1,075	412	997	1,427	1,485	1,510	1,063	1,616	904
Hybrid maize	654	431	201	1,329	200	843	617	555	1,079	627
Tobacco	6,290	9,772	0	8,447	11,288	22,031	23,896	8,923	4,626	4,880
Other crops	2,000	995	. . .	1,846	3,522	1,715	1,601	1,705	1,940	2,086
All crops	1,385	1,391	222	2,562	1,392	4,837	1,195	1,482	1,773	1,240

SOURCE: Rural finance survey, conducted by the International Food Policy Research Institute (IFPRI) and the Rural Development Department (RDD) at Bunda College of Agriculture, Malawi, 1995.

NOTES: US$1= MK 15. MRFC = Malawi Rural Finance Company; MUSCCO = Malawi Union of Savings and Credit Cooperatives; S&C = Saving and Credit groups; CBM = Commercial Bank of Malawi; PMERW1 = PMERW revolving fund for rural women; PMERW2 = PMERW credit program for experienced business women.

[a] Includes the imputed values of home-produced seeds and of inputs received as gifts.

[b] The gross margin is calculated as the total value of production less the total value of all inputs used.

[c] The net cropping income is calculated using the total costs of inputs excluding the values of home-produced seeds and inputs received as gifts.

TABLE 12.5 Definition and summary statistics of variables used in the econometric analysis

Variable	Mean	Standard Deviation	Minimum	Maximum	N	Label
AGEH	45.82	13.76	20.00	86.0	1,885	Age of head
AREAPHMZ	0.89	0.63	0.00	4.90	497	Hybrid maize area planted (hectares)
AREAPLMZ	0.87	0.55	0.10	4.90	428	Local maize area planted (hectares)
AREAPTOB	0.57	0.54	0.10	2.80	121	Tobacco area planted (hectares)
CVG9495P	1.24	0.34	0.85	2.03	1,885	Coefficient of variable, 1994/95 gaps within-peak season
CVGAPYYP	0.30	0.06	0.20	0.45	1,885	Coefficient of variable, across years, days of gaps (no rain)
DISTFA	2.33	3.75	0.00	15.00	1,885	Distance to home of field assistant / community development assistant (FA/CDA)
DISTPO	6.64	7.70	0.00	26.00	1,885	Distance to post office
DISTPSCH	1.65	1.76	0.00	5.00	1,885	Distance to primary school
DISTTCEN	5.04	5.16	0.00	15.00	1,885	Distance to trading center
DPLTHMZ	17.90	11.64	0.00	54.00	490	Hybrid maize days away optimal planting
FATMHMZ	51.24	41.83	7.00	120.00	493	Hybrid maize week of fertilizer application from planting
FLOANMAX	70.50	172.91	0.00	2,600	1,603	Maximum formal credit limit
ILOANMAX	25.14	49.39	0.00	743	1,511	Maximum informal credit limit
LANDAREH	1.96	1.41	0.10	13	1,885	Total hectares of household land

Variable	Mean	Std. Dev.	Min	Max	N	Description
LDAOWNS	0.43	0.47	0.00	1.00	1,885	Share of acres of household land owned by spouse
LPDOPHMZ	15.97	12.52	0.0000	54.0000	497	Log of hybrid maize days away optimal planting
LPLTHMZ	0.77	0.42	0.00	1.00	497	1 = late planting of hybrid maize
MALEHEAD	0.72	0.45	0.00	1	1,885	1 = male-headed household
MALELEND	0.09	0.29	0.00	1	1,885	1 = lender is a male
NEXTVC2Y	9.87	18.45	0.00	100	754	Cumulative number of extension visits in the past two years
PLTMHMZ	41.44	25.40	45.00	84	490	Hybrid maize planting time from first rain
POPADL15	2.56	1.26	0.00	8	1,885	Adults household members between 15 and 64
QSEEDLMZ	12.57	14.74	0.00	100.0	754	Local maize quantity of seed (kilograms)
QFERTLMZ	25.16	61.89	0.00	500.0	754	Local maize quantity of fertilizer (kilograms)
QSEEDHMZ	12.93	19.11	0.00	300.0	754	Hybrid maize quantity of seed (kilograms)
QFERTHMZ	74.68	133.18	0.00	1260.0	754	Hybrid maize quantity of fertilizer (kilograms)
QSEEDTOB	0.00	0.04	0.00	1.0	754	Tobacco quantity of seed (kilograms)
QFERTTOB	23.44	90.90	0.00	1000.0	754	Tobacco quantity of fertilizer (kilograms)
SOUTH	0.24	0.43	0.00	1	1,885	1 = Southern region
TRAIN	591.32	171.21	261.10	1121.80	754	Cumulative rainfall for the season
WSL12MHH	1.01	1.92	0.00	17.33	1,885	Average weeks of sickness in last 12 months in household
YYEDUCH	4.20	3.32	0.00	12.00	1,885	Years of schooling of head
YYEDUCS	3.14	3.05	0.00	10.00	1,885	Years of schooling of spouse

TABLE 12.6 MLE parameter estimates of the translog production frontier functions and marginal effects on technical efficiency for hybrid maize, local maize, and tobacco

Input Variables	Estimated Coefficient			Management and Demographic Variables	Estimated Coefficient			Total Marginal Effects on the Technical Efficiency in the Production of		
	Hybrid Maize	Local Maize	Tobacco		Hybrid Maize	Local Maize	Tobacco	Hybrid Maize	Local Maize	Tobacco
CONSTANT	393.10	−229.00	2,479.70	CONSTANT	−3.84	−3.26	−1.69	−0.0683	−0.0468	−0.0781
s.e.[a]	56.62	38.63	492.32	s.e.	41.70	0.61	0.62			
AREA	1.68	−9.44	2.99	DPLTHMZ	0.00	0.01	0.00	−0.0002	−0.0000	−0.0002
s.e.	1.63	2.47	5.80	s.e.	0.00	0.00	0.00			
SEED	−9.49	14.41	6.41	LPLTHMZ	0.17	0.20	0.29	−0.0017	−0.0016	−0.0080
s.e.	2.01	2.46	2.87	s.e.	0.17	0.13	0.31			
FERT	1.06	−2.81	4.09	LPDOPHMZ	−0.02	−0.01	−0.01	−0.0004	−0.0002	−0.0009
s.e.	0.60	0.76	5.43	s.e.	0.01	0.00	0.01			
RAINFALL	−96.31	62.75	−697.10	FATMHMZ	−0.00	−0.00	0.00	−0.0000	−0.0000	0.0003
s.e.	8.84	10.19	136.70	s.e.	0.00	0.00	0.00			
DGAPRAIN	−97.41	27.04	−392.10	LANDAREH	−0.03	0.06	0.12	0.0003	0.0006	0.0049
s.e.	10.24	8.80	83.81	s.e.	0.05	0.04	0.09			
AREAAREA	0.02	−0.05	−0.06	LDAOWNS	0.13	−0.20	0.39	0.0023	−0.0028	0.0181
s.e.	0.06	0.07	0.10	s.e.	0.11	0.09	0.22			
AREASEED	−0.13	−0.05	−0.04	AGEH	−0.00	0.00	−0.00	−0.0000	0.0001	−0.0000
s.e.	0.12	0.10	0.07	s.e.	0.00	0.00	0.00			
AREAFERT	0.04	−0.01	−0.29	MALEHEAD	0.23	−0.08	0.12	−0.0039	−0.0009	−0.0108
s.e.	0.03	0.03	0.11	s.e.	0.11	0.09	0.27			
AREARAIN	0.11	1.67	0.04	YYEDUCH	−0.05	0.00	0.04	−0.0010	0.0000	0.0018
s.e.	0.21	0.35	0.87	s.e.	0.01	0.01	0.04			
AREADGAP	−1.26	−0.28	−1.94	YYEDUCS	0.08	0.05	0.02	0.0014	0.0007	0.0013
s.e.	0.26	0.40	0.65	s.e.	0.01	0.01	0.04			
SEEDSEED	0.22	0.00	0.06	POPADLI5	−0.00	−0.00	0.19	−0.0000	0.0005	0.0092
s.e.	0.05	0.03	0.03	s.e.	0.03	0.03	0.06			

Table — stochastic frontier / Tobit estimation results

Panel A

Variable	(1)	(2)	(3)
SEEDFERT	−0.13	−0.03	0.06
s.e.	0.03	0.03	0.05
AREADGAP	−1.26	−0.28	−1.94
s.e.	0.26	0.40	0.65
SEEDSEED	0.22	0.00	0.06
s.e.	0.05	0.03	0.03
SEEDFERT	−0.13	−0.03	0.06
s.e.	0.03	0.03	0.05
SEEDRAIN	1.02	−2.29	−0.95
s.e.	0.25	0.36	0.41
SEEDDGAP	1.81	0.32	−0.05
s.e.	0.35	0.34	0.43
FERTFERT	0.05	0.10	0.06
s.e.	0.02	0.02	0.03
FERTRAIN	−0.11	0.37	−0.57
s.e.	0.07	0.11	0.77
FERTDGAP	−0.12	0.09	−0.28
s.e.	0.10	0.07	0.44
RAINRAIN	6.02	−3.95	48.50
s.e.	0.55	0.67	9.42
RAINDGAP	12.97	−4.47	61.54
s.e.	1.37	1.15	12.46
DGAPDGAP	3.41	−0.00	−0.67
s.e.	0.74	0.72	3.33
σ	1.57	0.79	0.47
s.e.	0.00	0.00	0.00
γ	0.89	0.88	0.79
s.e.	0.05	0.04	0.20

Panel B

Variable	(1)	(2)	(3)	(4)	(5)	(6)
WSLI2MHH	−0.08	0.00	−0.05	−0.0015	0.0001	−0.0026
s.e.	0.02	0.02	0.04			
YYEDUCS	0.08	0.05	0.02	0.0014	0.0007	0.0013
s.e.	0.01	0.01	0.04			
POPADLI5	−0.00	0.03	0.19	−0.0000	0.0005	0.0092
s.e.	0.03	0.03	0.06			
WSLI2MHH	−0.08	0.00	−0.05	−0.0015	0.0001	−0.0026
s.e.	0.02	0.02	0.04			
NEXTVC2Y	−0.00	0.00	0.00	−0.0000	0.0000	0.0000
s.e.	0.00	0.00	0.00			
DISTPO	0.01	−0.00	−0.02	0.0002	−0.0000	−0.0010
s.e.	0.01	0.00	0.07			
DISTTCEN	−0.02	−0.01	−0.08	−0.0005	−0.0001	−0.0037
s.e.	0.01	0.00	0.07			
SOUTH	−1.55	−1.73	⋯	0.0116	0.0103	⋯
s.e.	0.23	0.21	⋯			
FLOANMAX	−0.00	0.00	−0.00	−0.0000	−0.0000	0.0000
s.e.	0.00	0.00	0.00			
ILOANMAX	−0.00	−0.00	0.00	0.0000	−0.0000	−0.0004
s.e.	0.00	0.00	0.00			
FLNMXLND[b]	−0.00	−0.00	0.00	−0.0000	−0.0000	0.0000
s.e.	0.00	0.00	0.00			
ILNMXLND[c]	0.00	0.00	−0.00	0.0000	0.0000	−0.0000
s.e.	0.00	0.00	0.00			
σ_u	0.83	0.58	0.42			
log-likelihood	−1.367	−1,006	−165			−126
$2(L^* - L)$					496	−126
$\chi_{(22)}$						

[a] Standard errors.

[b] FLNMXLND = interaction terms for the formal credit limit (FLOANMAX) and Land (LANDAREH) variables.

[c] ILNMXLND = interaction terms for the informal credit limit (ILOANMAX) and Land (LANDAREH) variables.

The direct and indirect marginal effects of the management and demographic variables on household technical efficiency, evaluated at the current level of technical efficiencies, are reported in Table 12.6. They are all negligible in magnitude except for the share of household land owned by the spouse (LDAOWNS). This is consistent with the fact that, by and large, households are operating close to their potential (given the currently used technology embodied in the seed and fertilizer and the prevailing climatic conditions). Indeed, except for a few outliers, all households in all three regions of Malawi are operating at more than 80 percent of their potential, as shown by the distributions of household technical efficiencies in maize and tobacco in Table 12.7. The table shows the means of technical indices, which range from 87 percent to 91 percent. A notable exception is tobacco in the Northern region, where a significant number of households are operating below 80 percent of their potential, with a mean index of 79 percent. This means that there is scope for a significant increase in tobacco productivity in the Northern region. The results also show that the distributions of household technical efficiencies are not affected by the level of access to credit. An exception to this may be for tobacco, grown only in the Central and Northern regions, for which access to credit seems to induce a slight improvement in household technical efficiency.

Finally, the marginal productivity estimates for the basic inputs (land, seed, and fertilizer) were calculated from the production frontier isolated from the influence of the management and demographic variables. Their distributions are shown in Table 12.7. For all crops, only land has a positive marginal productivity. The marginal productivities of fertilizer and seed are either zero or negative. This means that, holding rainfall at the 1993/94 and 1994/95 levels (drought years), seed and fertilizer were used at or beyond their optimal levels. Hence, rainfall and land were the constraining factors for achieving higher outputs in 1993/94 and 1994/95. Therefore, the econometric analysis confirms the tentative conclusion reached from the descriptive analysis, which suggested that smallholder farmers were using too much fertilizer.

The finding that smallholder farmers are applying fertilizer beyond optimal levels is consistent with Diagne and Zeller (2001), who found that the in-kind loan package given to smallholder farmers had a negative impact on household net crop income. The finding is also supported by a number of studies conducted during the 1990s (HIID 1994; Msukwa et al. 1994; Simler 1994; Benson 1997; Smale and Phiri 1998). Byerlee (1992, cited in Simler 1994) had already observed that, although the official recommended fertilizer application level will produce the highest yields, lower levels of fertilizer use are generally more profitable for farmers. Similarly, the HIID study (1994) concluded that the single nationwide recommendation for fertilizer application for maize means that in many regions, farmers are asked to apply too much fertilizer, especially phosphate, and that region- and soil-specific recommendations are urgently required (HIID 1994). These conclusions were confirmed in a more recent study by Benson (1997), using on-farm trials data from more than 1,600 sites in Malawi. Benson concluded that the recommended levels of fertilizer use per hectare of maize were suboptimal even in years with above-average rainfall. In fact, according to Benson (1997:14), "under current prices the use of fertilizer on hybrid maize in Malawi cannot be recommended for virtually all of the country." A new fertilizer recommendation that calls for a much smaller fertilizer package for different soils and regions was adopted following the Benson study.

Conclusions

Under the climatic conditions that prevailed in 1993/94 and 1994/95, smallholder farmers in Malawi were operating close to their potential, given the characteristics of their soil and the technology embodied in the seed and fertilizer used. Therefore, more emphasis on extension to promote better use of the current technology (embodied in the seed and fertilizer) will not bring a significant increase in productivity and output in Malawi if the 1993–95 climatic conditions continue to prevail. Under these climatic conditions, the prospects for significantly increasing agricultural productivity can come only through the alleviation of the severe land constraints facing smallholders and the development and diffusion of new seed varieties and soil fertility technologies better adapted to those climatic conditions. A notable exception is with respect to tobacco in the Northern region, where there is scope for a significant increase in tobacco productivity. Furthermore, household technical efficiency in growing the various crops is not affected by the level of access to credit. An exception to this is again tobacco, grown only in the Central and Northern regions, for which access to credit induces a slight improvement in household technical efficiency.

Therefore, policy reforms should emphasize a more equitable land distribution to ease the land constraints facing smallholder farmers and to encourage efficient and sustainable use of the existing cultivable land. However, the scope for alleviating the land constraints of smallholders through land reform in the estate sector is likely to be limited. Indeed, more than 80 percent of the cultivable land in Malawi is already being farmed under the customary tenure system by smallholder households with an average landholding of 1.1 hectares. Furthermore, 55 percent of these farms are less than 1.0 hectare each and 95 percent are less than 3.0 hectares (World Bank 1987). Therefore, policy reforms should put more emphasis on promoting better terms of trade for agricultural products to give smallholder farmers the incentive to invest in soil fertility technologies and to use new seed varieties that are better adapted to the existing climatic conditions. Given that farmers have been applying too much fertilizer under the previous fertilizer recommendation, more effort should be put on extension to promote the new fertilizer package, which recommends lower amounts for different soils and regions. However, one should expect farmers to

TABLE 12.7 Estimated technical efficiency and marginal productivity in growing hybrid maize, local maize, and tobacco at different levels of access to credit

	Hybrid Maize			Local Maize			Tobacco		
	Central	South	North	Central	South	North	Central	South	North
Technical efficiency									
At household predicted current credit limits									
Mean	.87	.89	.87	.90	.87	.89	.89	…	.79
Median	.87	.90	.87	.91	.94	.89	.93	…	.83
Standard deviation	.02	.05	.03	.03	.13	.02	.08	…	.11
Minimum	.79	.43	.56	.45	.57	.80	.29	…	.53
Maximum	.91	.93	.91	.98	.95	.94	.94	…	.94
At zero credit limit for all households									
Mean	.87	.89	.87	.90	.91	.89	.89	…	.78
Median	.87	.90	.87	.91	.94	.89	.92	…	.83
Standard deviation	.02	.05	.03	.03	.05	.02	.10	…	.11
Minimum	.79	.45	.55	.45	.78	.84	.10	…	.48
Maximum	.91	.93	.90	.98	.95	.95	.94	…	.94

Marginal productivity[a]

Land									
Mean	695	13	1,264	388	173	777	23	...	550
Median	589	2	1,128	332	157	766	28	...	350
Standard deviation	447	158	818	304	328	457	274	...	846
Minimum	32	-732	5	1	-762	128	-687	...	-1,239
Maximum	3,040	737	7,615	2,651	639	2,762	3,160	...	3,151
Seed									
Mean	0.002	0.015	-0.029	0.004	0.006	0.007	-6.500	...	-8.700
Median	0.008	0.011	-0.006	0.004	0.008	0.002	-0.200	...	-0.200
Standard deviation	0.037	0.030	0.060	0.019	0.011	0.170	30.000	...	33.000
Minimum	-0.570	-0.014	-0.340	-0.190	-0.008	-0.020	-326.000	...	-234.000
Maximum	0.141	0.330	0.028	0.050	0.053	5.000	20.000	...	58.000
Fertilizer									
Mean	-34	-30	-60	-145	-34	-243	1	...	3
Median	1	0	-13	-97	0	-184	1	...	2
Standard deviation	86	67	92	160	52	223	12	...	5
Minimum	-630	-449	-396	-722	-231	-1,960	-261	...	-65
Maximum	37	66	33	12	7	11	6	...	14

[a] Kilograms of output per additional unit of input, holding the quantities of the other inputs constant at observed levels.

be less receptive of fertilizer-intensive technologies unless current market conditions change in favor of farmers. Indeed, gross margin calculations using on-farm trial data have shown that, even in relatively favorable climatic conditions for growing maize, the major crop grown on over 75 percent of the cultivable land in Malawi is barely profitable because the price of maize is very low compared with that of fertilizer (Msukwa et al. 1994; Benson 1997). The results of these earlier studies are reinforced by the findings here.

References

Adams, D. W., and R. C. Vogel. 1985. Rural financial markets in low-income countries: Recent controversies and lessons. *World Development* 14 (4): 477–487.

Adams, D. W., D. H. Graham, and J. D. Von Pischke, eds. 1984. *Undermining rural development with cheap credit.* Boulder, Colo., U.S.A.: Westview Press.

Aigner, D. J., C. A. K. Lovell, and P. Schmidt. 1977. Formulation and estimation of stochastic frontier production function models. *Journal of Econometrics* 6: 21–37.

Battese, G. E. 1992. Frontier production functions and technical efficiency: A survey of empirical applications in agricultural economics. *Agricultural Economics* 7: 185–208.

Battese, G. E., and T. Coelli. 1988. Prediction of firm-level technical efficiencies with a generalized frontier production function and panel data. *Journal of Econometrics* 38: 387–399.

————. 1995. A model for technical inefficiencies effects for a stochastic frontier production function for panel data. *Empirical Economics* 20: 325–332.

Battese, G., S. Malik, and M. Gill. 1996. An investigation of technical inefficiencies of production of wheat farmers in four districts of Pakistan. *Journal of Agricultural Economics* 47 (1): 37–49.

Benson, T. 1997. The 1995/96 Fertilizer Verification Trial-Malawi: Economic analysis of results for policy discussion. Report by Action Group I, Maize Productivity Task Force, Ministry of Agriculture and Livestock Development, Government of Malawi.

Braverman, A., and J. L. Guasch. 1986. Rural credit markets and institutions in developing countries: Lessons for policy analysis from practice and modern theory. *World Development* 14 (10/11): 1253–1267.

Deaton, A. 1989. Saving in developing countries: Theory and review. *World Bank Economic Review* 4.

Diagne, A. 1998. Impacts of access to credit on income and food security in Malawi. Food Consumption and Nutrition Division Discussion Paper No. 46. International Food Policy Research Institute, Washington, D.C.

————. 1999. The determinants of household access to and participation in formal and informal credit markets in Malawi. Food Consumption and Nutrition Division Discussion Paper No. 67. International Food Policy Research Institute, Washington, D.C.

Diagne, A., and M. Zeller. 2001. *Access to credit and its impact on welfare in Malawi.* Research Report No. 116. Washington, D.C.: International Food Policy Research Institute.

Diagne, A., M. Zeller, and C. Mataya. 1996. Rural financial markets and household food security: Impacts of access to credit on the socioeconomic situation of rural households in Malawi. Final report submitted to the Ministry for Women, Children Affairs, Community Development and Social Welfare, and to the German Agency for Technical Cooperation in Malawi. Bunda College of Agriculture, University of Malawi, and International Food Policy Research Institute, Washington, D.C.

Eswaran, M., and A. Kotwal. 1990. Implications of credit constraints for risk behavior in less developed economies. *Oxford Economic Papers*, N.-S. 42 (2): 473–482.

HIID (Harvard Institute for International Development). 1994. Fertilizer policy study: Market structure, prices, and fertilizer use by smallholder maize farmers. Report prepared for the Ministry of Economic Planning and Development, Government of Malawi. Lilongwe, Malawi.

Huang, C. L., and J.-T. Liu. 1994. Estimation of a non-neutral stochastic frontier production function. *Journal of Productivity Analysis* 5: 171–180.

Kalirajan, K. 1981. An econometric analysis of yield variability in paddy production. *Canadian Journal of Agricultural Economics* 29: 283–294.

———. 1991. The importance of efficient use in the adoption of technology: A micro panel data analysis. *Journal of Productivity Analysis* 2: 113–126.

Kumbhakar S., S. Ghosh, and J. McGuckin. 1991. A generalized production frontier approach for estimating determinants of inefficiency in U.S. dairy farms. *Journal of Business and Economic Statistics* 9 (3): 279–286.

Malawi. 1994. Implementation of the poverty alleviation program. Government of Malawi.

———. 1995. The agricultural and livestock development strategy and action plan. Ministry of Agriculture and Livestock Development (MoALD), Government of Malawi, Lilongwe, Malawi.

Msukwa, L., W. Chilowa, H. Bagazonzya, A. Mawaya, F. Nankhuni, and T. Bisika. 1994. *Smallholder credit repayment study*. Lilongwe, Malawi: Center for Social Research, University of Malawi.

Pitt, M. M., and L. F. Lee. 1981. Measurement and source of technical inefficiency in the Indonesian weaving industry. *Journal of Development Economics* 9: 43–64.

Schmidt, P. 1985. Frontier production functions. *Econometric Reviews* 4: 289–328.

Simler, K. 1994. *Agricultural market liberalization and technological innovation in Malawi: Modeling responses and outcomes in the smallholder subsector*. Working Paper No. 12 for the Agricultural Sector Memorandum. Washington, D.C.: World Bank.

Smale, M., and A. Phiri. 1998. Institutional change and discontinuities in farmers' use of hybrid maize in Malawi: Findings from the 1996–97 CIMMYT/MOALD. CIMMYT Economics Working Paper 98-01. Mexico City: Centro Internacional de Mejoramiento de Maíz y Trigo (CIMMYT).

World Bank. 1987. *Malawi: Smallholder agricultural credit project*. Staff Appraisal Report. Washington, D.C.: World Bank, February.

Zeller, M., A. Diagne, and C. Mataya. 1998. Market access by smallholder farmers in Malawi: Implications for technology adoption, agricultural productivity and crop income. *Agricultural Economics* 19 (2): 219–229.

13 Explaining Poverty: An Empirical Analysis of the Effects of Ill Health and Uncertainty on the Savings of Rural Pakistani Households

ANJINI KOCHAR

This chapter examines the effects of adult male illness on the savings decisions of rural Pakistani households. In particular, it analyzes the way illness affects the composition of asset portfolios. The chapter contrasts the effects of illness with those of income uncertainty and anticipated changes in income stemming from sources other than the illness of adult males. The focus on the effects of ill health distinguishes this work from previous research on household savings in developing economies, which largely concentrated on analyzing the effects of crop income uncertainty, particularly that attributable to variable weather conditions.

An influential strand of research in development economics argues that anticipated and unanticipated income volatility contribute significantly to the chronic poverty of rural households. The link between the income process and poverty is attributed to the effects of income volatility on household savings decisions, particularly the composition of asset portfolios. The literature argues that the lack of insurance markets in such economies, in conjunction with imperfectly functioning credit markets, forces households to accumulate assets primarily to smooth consumption. Such behavior may yield portfolios that favor relatively low-yielding "liquid" assets over high-yielding illiquid assets such as the physical capital required to increase crop incomes. If so, households will experience lower lifetime wealth and, hence, higher poverty.

Whereas a number of studies have shown that households in developing economies are forward looking in that savings decisions reflect expectations of future income, far less research has examined the effects of such expectations on asset portfolios. Even fewer studies have analyzed the effects of idiosyncratic or household-specific measures of income uncertainty on household savings decisions. This study does so by developing household-specific measures of the forecast error variance in incomes, recognizing that the considerable variability in the sources of income in rural areas of developing economies implies that the forecast error variance in income must vary with the household's choice of occupations.

The main results of this study show that anticipated changes in ill health do affect household savings and portfolio choices, but that this effect varies across households according to the number and age composition of their male members. Moreover, income uncertainty adversely affects portfolio choices only in households that have experienced the illness of adult males. These results suggest that a link exists between adult male illness and the poverty of rural households. This hypothesis is tested by considering the effects of adult illness on household lifetime wealth, as reflected in estimates of the marginal utility of wealth recovered from consumption regressions. These regressions support the hypothesis that adult male illness is a significant determinant of poverty.

The next section reviews the existing literature on the effects of income volatility on household savings. The section after that describes the IFPRI data set used for the empirical analysis in this study and discusses the economic characteristics of the sample households that are relevant for an analysis of savings. The third section presents the methodology used to estimate the forecast error variance in individual incomes. The theoretical framework underlying the savings regressions and the estimating equations are detailed and results are presented. Subsequently the method for estimating the effects of shocks such as illness on poverty and the results of such an exercise are reported. The final section offers conclusions.

Empirical Evidence on the Effect of Income Volatility on Household Savings

The level at and forms in which households save are of particular importance in developing economies, given that large numbers of households derive their income from self-employment by combining their accumulated human and physical capital. This link between savings and income underlies the belief that the poverty of households in developing economies, reflected in low levels of lifetime income, can best be understood by analyzing the factors that affect savings decisions. The level of household investment in "productive" assets that contribute directly to farm income or income earned from other household enterprises is particularly important.

It is commonly argued that "high-frequency" consumption smoothing against the volatility of income in the short run is a primary motive for savings in developing economies. This motive reflects both anticipated changes, such as the seasonal fluctuations in income that occur within a year, as well as season-to-season and year-to-year uncertainty in incomes (Deaton 1989). This motive for savings, in conjunction with absent or imperfectly functioning insurance and credit markets, is said to explain low levels of investment in productive assets. Since high-frequency consumption smoothing necessitates stocks of relatively liquid assets, households may choose to accumulate such assets at the cost of investment in illiquid capital. The latter form of capital contributes directly to farm and other household income, particularly when households lack access to credit markets (Eswaran and Kotwal 1989; Rosenzweig and Wolpin 1993; Morduch 1994).

A significant body of empirical research has established that households in developing economies *do* save in response to anticipated changes in income (Deaton 1992a; Paxson 1992). Little evidence is available, however, on the effect of such income changes on asset portfolios. Moreover, scant evidence exists on the importance of precautionary savings against uncertainty in individual incomes in developing economies, or on the effect of such savings on asset portfolios.[1] Although research has shown that households reduce savings in periods of low income and in response to idiosyncratic shocks (Rosenzweig and Wolpin 1993; Udry 1995), such ex post responses do not necessarily imply that income uncertainty affects the level and form of savings ex ante.

Whereas studies of precautionary savings in economies such as that of the United States recognize the many sources of uncertainty households face (Hubbard, Skinner, and Zeldes 1994), development literature has almost exclusively concentrated on the effects of crop income uncertainty, particularly that caused by variable weather conditions. This focus reflects the belief that incomes in the rural economy depend critically on conditions in the agricultural sector and hence on the vagaries of weather. Even so, rural households face a number of other equally important sources of risk. A particularly important one is the risk of illness among working members of the household. The complete lack of medical insurance in the rural areas of many developing economies can make even a few days of illness result in a significant loss in income.

The effects of illness on savings can be very different from those of volatility in income caused by weather. One reason is the difference in their effects on the income process. Episodes of illness are more likely to be persistent or positively correlated over time than are variations in crop income caused by factors other than illness. As noted by Deaton (1992b), the income process has implications for the level of savings required to protect consumption from income fluctuations. Whereas positively autocorrelated income shocks create a strong incentive for asset accumulation, households may be able to maintain consumption levels in the event of independently and identically distributed or negatively correlated shocks with a relatively low stock of assets, because "bad" years will generally be followed by good ones.

---

1. Research by Rosenzweig and Binswanger (1993) has, however, shown that *aggregate* income uncertainty, as measured by the moments of the village-level rainfall distribution, causes Indian farm households to hold less risky portfolios, and that they trade off expected returns in doing so.

The fact that capital is used directly in the production of income from both farm and nonfarm sources provides another reason to expect the effects of illness on savings to differ from those of other income shocks. The productive nature of capital implies that income shocks will directly affect the return to capital and, hence, investment decisions through the production function. If different income shocks affect the return to capital in different ways, they will in turn have different effects on savings decisions. The considerable choice of crops and techniques of production available to farm households yields a relatively high elasticity of farm capital with respect to factors such as weather variations. Anticipated variations in rainfall, as well as crop income shocks caused by weather-related factors, are known to affect crop choices and levels of investment in farm machinery significantly (Walker and Ryan 1990). It may be harder, however, to minimize the income consequences of illness through such adjustments in farm capital.

From a policy point of view, it is more important to identify the particular factors that explain investment decisions than to show that the level and forms of savings are a response to the volatility in short-run incomes. The belief that low levels of investment in productive assets are primarily attributable to crop income uncertainty has led many researchers to suggest the need for interventions in credit markets, given the costliness of instituting effective crop insurance programs. If, however, the ill health of individuals plays a greater role in explaining low levels of productive investment, a more effective means of raising investment would be through interventions to improve health and sanitary conditions in rural areas.

The Data, the Survey Area, and the Economic Characteristics of the Sample Households

Data

The data used in this study are the International Food Policy Research Institute's (IFPRI's) panel data set of rural households in Pakistan. The survey provides information on 975 households distributed among 46 villages during a three-year period, 1986/87 to 1988/89. Households were interviewed at six different times during the first year of the survey, and three times, at approximately four-month intervals, in the second two years. In the first "round" of the survey, that is at the initial interview date in the first year of the survey, retrospective data for the 1985/86 year were also collected. In addition to the usual demographic information, the survey provides detailed income and consumption data, as well as data on the stock of assets and transactions in the major assets. Income and demographic details and details on asset transactions are based on recall since the previous interview date. The consumption data are generally based on the amounts consumed in the week prior to the interview.

Household Structures and Their Importance for Income and Savings

One distinguishing feature of the rural Pakistan economy is the considerable diversity in household structures, that is, in the size and age composition of its members. The two predominant household structures are intergenerational households, in which two or more adult generations reside with the dependent children of the younger generation, and nuclear households, comprising just one adult male of the younger generation. In the sample data, intergenerational households, defined here as households comprising adult males aged 20–45 as well as adult males aged 45 and above, represent 49 percent of all households, while nuclear households with just one male between the ages of 20 and 45 represent 23 percent of all households. Intergenerational households, with an average of 11 members, are much larger than nuclear households, which average 7 members. This difference in family size reflects not just more adults of the older generation, but also more younger men (an average of 2.0 in intergenerational households), as well as more children (5.2 in intergenerational households versus 4.5 in nuclear households).

Previous empirical research on household savings has accorded a perfunctory role to household demographics. That research includes measures of the household's demographic composition among the regressors on the grounds that such variables reflect the heterogeneity in preferences for consumption across households. The savings equation, however, is assumed to be the same for all households, even though there are several good reasons to allow its determinants to vary across household structures. One reason is that preferences for consumption are likely to vary across households distinguished by the number and age composition of their adult members. Such demographic differences are also likely to result in differences in sources of income and income profiles. Indeed, the survey data (Table 13.1) reveal that whereas as many as 19 percent of intergenerational households report that their main source of income comes from "other" sources (notably pensions, rental income, and remittances), only 6 percent of nuclear households report this as their major source of income.

The effect of anticipated changes in income and consumption on savings also depends on households' access to credit and insurance markets. In order to allow for differences in the availability of credit and insurance, the empirical literature has generally separated households by income levels (Alderman 1996) or landownership (Morduch 1990), on the assumption that a household's access to sources of credit and insurance depends on these variables. However, this treatment ignores the theoretical literature and argues that the most effective source of credit and insurance, particularly in economies characterized by imperfectly functioning markets for these inputs, is the family unit itself (Ben-Porath 1980; Kotlikoff and Spivak 1981). This theoretical literature is supported by empirical research on the insurance and credit functions of income transfers across geographically dispersed household units (Rosenzweig 1988). Studies

TABLE 13.1 Sources of income for the sample households

	Total Households	Inter-generational	Nuclear	With Land	Landless
Number of	2,482	1,224	562	1,535	947
households	(100.00)	(100.00)	(100.00)	(100.00)	(100.00)
Number reporting					
Crop income	1,553	779	351	1,075	478
	(62.6)	(63.64)	(62.46)	(70.03)	(50.48)
Wage income	1,957	965	462	1,095	862
	(78.8)	(78.84)	(82.21)	(71.34)	(91.02)
Dairy income	595	283	148	403	192
	(24.0)	(23.12)	(26.33)	(26.25)	(20.27)
Craft income	380	207	79	201	179
	(15.3)	(16.91)	(14.06)	(13.09)	(18.90)
Multiple sources	1,601	807	383	981	620
of income	(64.5)	(65.9)	(68.20)	(63.91)	(65.47)
Number for whom					
main source					
of income is					
Crop income	940	455	226	642	298
	(37.9)	(37.17)	(40.21)	(41.82)	(31.47)
Wage income	1255	633	264	700	555
	(50.6)	(51.72)	(46.98)	(45.60)	(58.61)
Dairy income	123	57	30	95	28
	(5.0)	(4.66)	(5.34)	(6.19)	(2.96)
Craft income	363	187	69	227	136
	(14.6)	(15.28)	(12.28)	(14.79)	(14.36)
Mean income by					
source					
Total	31,536	37,433	21,175	37,851	21,301
	(100.00)	(100.00)	(100.00)	(100.00)	(100.00)
Crop income	8,103	9,262	5,908	9,810	5,337
	(25.70)	(24.74)	(27.90)	(25.92)	(25.06)
Wage income	9,661	11,388	7,091	9,247	10,333
	(30.64)	(30.42)	(33.49)	(24.43)	(48.51)
Dairy income	79	124	17	136	−12.72
	(0.25)	(0.33)	(0.08)	(0.10)	(...)
Craft income	9,207	9,661	8,038	10,757	6,693
	(29.20)	(25.81)	(37.96)	(28.42)	(31.42)
Nonfarm wage	9,449	11,181	6,873	9,124	9,978
income	(29.96)	(29.87)	(32.46)	(24.11)	(4.59)

NOTE: Figures in parentheses are percentages.

by Rosenzweig and Stark (1989) and Cox and Jimenez (1992) find that the net flow and direction of remittances depend on the age, gender, and marital status of its members and, by implication, on household type. As mentioned earlier, the data used here support such research, with intergenerational households reporting a greater dependence on remittances and pensions. There is also evidence (Kochar 1999) that households are able to substitute for the lack of crop insurance through increases in male members' off-farm hours of work. As a result, a household's vulnerability to crop income shocks depends on its demographic composition.

Differences in preferences, income processes, and the availability of credit and insurance across household types suggest that the determinants of savings must vary across intergenerational and nuclear households. The empirical work in this study accordingly distinguishes between these two groups of households and estimates separate regressions for each of these subsamples. This separation of the sample raises questions about the endogeneity of household structure and the possibility that the division of households into intergenerational and nuclear households is determined by economic considerations that also determine household savings. Unfortunately, an empirical analysis of the factors determining household structure is beyond the scope of this research because of the small number of household partitions observed in the relatively short time series of the data. The empirical analysis thus does not account for any potential selection bias.

Though one would like to test for the importance of sample selection bias, there are reasons to believe that any bias that exists is likely to be small. A sociological literature on demographic life cycles (Cain 1978; Caldwell, Reddy, and Caldwell 1988) attests to the fact that individuals in the South Asian economies do not choose between living in intergenerational and nuclear households on the basis of economic factors. Rather, social customs dictate that individuals move from one structure to another over the course of their life cycles. Most children grow up in intergenerational households. Nuclear households, generally those of the eldest son in the household, then separate out from the parent unit as younger sons get married and family size increases. These nuclear units in turn mature into intergenerational units. Thus, any given individual divides his or her lifetime between these two broad structures, moving from an intergenerational household to a nuclear household, and then spending elderly years in an intergenerational unit again.[2]

---

2. Such patterns are borne out in household data. Thus, an analysis of the data in the World Bank's Living Standards Measurement Survey (LSMS) for Pakistan (Kochar 1996) reveals that the overwhelming majority of adult males between the ages of 15 and 30 reside in intergenerational households. Nuclear households become more common among men in the 30–50 age group, with more men in the 35–45 age group living in such households than in intergenerational households. Elderly men, however, almost exclusively reside in intergenerational households: more than 80 percent of the men aged 55 and older reside in such households.

The Prevalence of Ill Health in the Rural Pakistan Economy

The poverty of rural households in the South Asian economies is readily apparent to any casual visitor, but so, too, is the ill health of rural residents. Data from the 1982–83 Pakistan National Health Survey, reported in Feachem et al. (1992), reveal that, by relatively stringent criteria,[3] 14 percent of men and 17 percent of women in a sample of 11,000 rural and urban households reported being ill in the month prior to the survey. More than 50 percent of these illnesses were due to acute respiratory infections and fevers or malaria. High levels of ill health reflect deplorable health and sanitary conditions in the rural economy. In rural Pakistan only 50 percent of the population have access to safe water, and only 35 percent have ready access to health services. Further, only 17 percent have access to sanitary means of waste disposal, including outdoor toilets and composting (UNDP 1995).

The IFPRI data also reveal relatively high levels of adult morbidity: 35 percent of sample households reported illness resulting in lost days of work among adult female members and 50 percent reported illness among adult male members in the period since the previous interview date, an interval of approximately four months. The greater incidence of male illness in this sample contradicts the usual finding of a greater incidence of reported illness among females (Feachem et al. 1992; Strauss et al. 1993), and probably reflects an underestimate of female illness owing to the collection of data for only members of the household who usually work.

A limitation of the survey data is the lack of any information on the severity or type of illness. Some indication of the severity of adult illness is contained in evidence of its persistence. Simple correlation coefficients of days of illness reported by individual adult males in the last year of the survey are correlated with years of illness both in the previous year (correlation coefficient = .25, $N = 1,404$) and in the first year of the survey (correlation coefficient = .15, $N = 1,279$).

Survey Data on Household Wealth and Savings

Whereas data on asset transactions are available in each round of the survey, data on the stock of household assets were collected at only two points in time. Moreover, no information is available on the value of stocks of cash, foodgrains, and other agricultural crops. Data are available, however, on the value of consumer durables, jewelry, livestock, and "productive assets," which are defined as stocks of tools, machinery (including tubewells and tractors and sheds for these investments), and buildings used in both agricultural and

---

3. Individuals were considered to be ill if they reported one or more of the following: inability to conduct their daily routine for at least 24 hours; inability to eat normal food for at least 24 hours; or illness requiring bed rest for at least 24 hours.

TABLE 13.2 Household wealth by asset type

	Nonland Wealth[a]	Productive Assets[b]	Durables	Jewelry	Livestock
Mean value (Rs)					
Full sample	36,646	16,390	7,175	7,685	5,397
	(100.00)	(44.72)	(19.58)	(20.97)	(14.73)
Intergenerational households	44,439	20,336	7,894	9,836	6,374
	(100.00)	(45.76)	(17.76)	(22.13)	(14.34)
Nuclear households	22,669	8,265	5,450	4,417	4,538
	(100.00)	(36.46)	(24.04)	(19.48)	(20.02)
Households with land	50,639	23,353	10,600	10,457	6,229
	(100.00)	(46.12)	(20.93)	(20.65)	(12.30)
Landless households	13,996	5,118	1,631	3,197	4,050
	(100.00)	(36.57)	(11.65)	(22.84)	(28.94)
Number reporting ownership					
Full sample	2,376	2,213	2,128	1,424	1,757
($N = 2,480$)	(95.81)	(89.23)	(85.81)	(57.42)	(70.85)
Intergenerational households	1,192	1,117	1,127	759	920
($N = 1,223$)	(97.46)	(91.33)	(92.15)	(62.06)	(75.22)
Nuclear households	535	494	436	307	374
($N = 561$)	(95.37)	(88.06)	(77.72)	(54.72)	(66.67)
Households with land	1,467	1,409	1,361	1,005	1,161
($N = 1,533$)	(95.69)	(91.91)	(88.78)	(65.56)	(75.73)
Landless households	909	804	767	419	596
($N = 947$)	(95.99)	(84.90)	(80.99)	(44.24)	(62.94)

NOTES: Figures in parentheses are percentages. Household data totals given here differ slightly from those in Table 13.1 because of missing savings data for some households.

[a] Nonland wealth refers to the sum of wealth in the four categories enumerated.

[b] Productive wealth is the sum of the value of all tools and machinery used in farm and nonfarm enterprises, buildings used to house such machinery and other buildings used for these enterprises, and inventories maintained for nonfarm enterprises.

nonagricultural enterprises, as well as on the value of inventories of goods and inputs used in nonagricultural enterprises. The value of these assets is presented in Table 13.2.

The data reveal significant wealth differences between intergenerational and nuclear households and between landed and landless households. Productive assets are important, however, for all groups of households. Thus, 89 percent of households report ownership of productive assets, which account for 45 percent of the total nonland wealth of the average household. Productive assets are also important for landless households. As many as 85 percent of such households report owning productive assets, which account for 37 percent of nonland wealth. The importance of productive assets in this and other Asian economies attests to their critical role in determining the income of rural households and lends support to the hypothesis that asset accumulation and savings decisions are intimately related to household income decisions.

Since data on the value of assets such as cash holdings and stocks of agricultural products are not available, the data on assets do not significantly inform analyses of the motives for savings and, in particular, the role of short-run income volatility in explaining savings. But because data on income and consumption are available, the level of household savings can be measured directly as the difference between income and consumption over the course of the year.[4] The IFPRI data also contain information on transactions in broad categories of assets in each round of the survey. Information on loans made and borrowings from the "informal" credit sector, which comprises other households in the village and professional moneylenders, makes up this part of the data set. Table 13.3 presents descriptive statistics on household savings as well as informal borrowings.

Although much of the theoretical and empirical literature on household consumption and savings routinely assumes that a significant percentage of households lack access to credit markets and hence are constrained to save nonnegative amounts in each period, the data in Table 13.3 reveal that this assumption is invalid for the Pakistani economy. For the pooled sample, 56 percent of households report nonpositive savings, while 44 percent report positive savings. The number of households with negative savings is high even among landless households (55 percent). Thus, whereas the mean level of savings for the sample as a whole is positive at Rs 7,436, savings for the median household are negative at Rs −1,707.

Low and negative savings are commonly revealed in data from developing countries and are frequently attributed to the underreporting of income by self-employed households. The IFPRI data, however, reveal that households *do* have the potential to dis-save, in that they appear to have widespread access to informal credit. Table 13.3 reveals that almost all households (91 percent) report borrowing from the informal sector and that the percentage of borrower households is highest among landless households (95 percent). The average amount borrowed by landless households, Rs 5,324, is far less than that borrowed by landowning households, Rs 8,482. Similarly, nuclear households report smaller loans on average (Rs 4,831) than do intergenerational households (Rs 8,180).

This widespread access to informal credit undermines the premise of "buffer stock" models of savings, wherein households are required to maintain stocks of real assets to smooth consumption because of a lack of access to credit.

---

4. For the purposes of this exercise, consumption includes expenditures on food, nonfood items (clothing, hygiene, tobacco, medical expenditures, travel, entertainment), education, and ceremonies.

TABLE 13.3 Descriptive statistics on household savings

	Total Households	Inter-generational	Nuclear	With Land	Landless
Number of households	2,480	1,223	561	1,533	947
	(100.00)	(100.00)	(100.00)	(100.00)	(100.00)
Mean savings (Rs)	7,436.29	8,159.42	3,921.55	10,307.57	2,788.27
Households with savings > 0	1,089	566	233	691	426
	(43.90)	(46.28)	(41.53)	(45.08)	(44.98)
Households with no savings	1,391	657	328	842	521
	(56.10)	(53.72)	(58.47)	(54.92)	(55.02)
Percentage of households with savings > 0 in year 1 who also have savings > 0 in year 2	63.36	63.32	62.56	65.80	59.68
Percentage of households with savings > 0 in years 2 and 3	67.53	62.26	62.23	66.82	68.75
Number of households borrowing from informal sector	2,257 (91.01)	1,113 (91.01)	516 (91.98)	1,356 (88.45)	901 (95.14)
Mean informal borrowings (Rs)	7,277	8,180	4,831	8,482	5,324

NOTES: Figures in parentheses are percentages. Household data totals given here differ slightly from those in Table 13.1 because of missing savings data for some households.

Buffer stock models also assume that households have little motivation to accumulate assets over the years, and that savings will fluctuate from positive to negative amounts within the year. The data, however, do reveal some tendency for long-term capital accumulation, in that a significant percentage of households maintain positive levels of savings across the survey years. Thus, of the households that reported positive savings in the first year of the survey, as many as 63 percent reported positive savings in the second year as well. Similarly, 68 percent of the households who were saving positive amounts in the second survey year were also saving positive amounts in the third year.

Estimating the Uncertainty in Individual Incomes

Income Regressions

As discussed in the previous section, sample households earn income from several different sources, most notably from the nonfarm wage labor market and crop production. Each of these types of income is likely to be characterized by a different income process, so that the determinants of household income will vary across households according to income source. If households specialize by occupation, earning income primarily from one source, differences in the income process across households could be handled by dividing the sample by occupational status. However, the importance of any given source of income varies tremendously across households. Thus, even if attention is restricted to households whose major source of income is wages, the ratio of wage income to total household income will vary from 0.01 at the 25th percentile to 0.84 at the 75th percentile, and is 0.35 for the median household.

Rather than attempt to group households by occupational status, a more appealing alternative is to allow the parameters of the income process to vary with variables that affect occupational choice. The most important determinants of this choice are likely to be landownership and household structure. Whether these variables imply differences in the income process across households is tested by standard Chow tests. Thus, a "basic" income regression is estimated and whether its coefficients differ across intergenerational and nuclear house-holds and across landowning and landless households is tested. The "basic income" regression is to predict household expectations of income in period t on the basis of period $(t-1)$ information, so as to estimate the forecast error variance in income. The regressors in this equation are the number of males and females in the age groups 20–45 and 45 and above; the average age and age squared of members of each of these four demographic groups; the number of literate members in these four groups; the number of boys and, separately, the number of girls in the age groups 0–5, 5–10, 10–15, and 15–20; the amount of land owned by the household,[5] and a full set of district/year dummy variables. The regressors also include household savings in period $(t-1)$ and days of illness by adult males of both generations in period $(t-1)$. If households *do* save in anticipation of future income earnings, then, as noted by Campbell (1987), including lagged savings in income regressions provides a means of incorporating the household's "superior information" regarding its income prospects. Similarly, persistence in illness implies that lagged illness provides information on household expectations of income in the following years.

Interactions of this full set of regressors with the dummy variable for intergenerational households reveal that the constant and slope coefficient for intergenerational households are jointly significantly different from those for nuclear households ($F(34,2062) = 1.70$, p value $= .0099$). Whereas the amount of land owned by the household is a significant determinant of income, dividing households according to whether they own land or not yields no

---

5. The assumption made here follows the empirical literature as it relates to South Asian economies: landownership is exogenous, given the scarcity of land transactions in these economies. Land transactions appear to be primarily in the way of bequests or gifts, and regressions of such transactions, reported later in this chapter, have little explanatory power.

significant difference in income regressions (the F statistic to test the difference between these two groups, $F(38,2058)$, is 1.11, p value = $.2982$). As a first step in characterizing the income process for sample households, households are divided into intergenerational and young households, and separate income regressions are run for these two subsamples.

In order to capture the variability in occupational choice within each of these two subsamples, a flexible income regression is estimated in which all the determinants of the "basic income" regression described above, including the set of district/year dummy variables, are interacted with a set of "interaction variables" that may determine occupational choice. The latter variables are the number of adult members in four gender–age demographic groups, the average age of males in the two age groups, and the amount of land owned by the household. The corresponding interaction variables for nuclear households are ownership of land, the average age of the sole male member, and the number of females in the household.

The final income regressions used to estimate the forecast error variance in income are household fixed-effects, least squares regressions, which, in addition to the set of household fixed effects, include all the determinants of the basic income regression and interactions of all these variables with the relevant set of "interaction variables." For both subsamples, the regressions explain much of the variation in income; for the sample of intergenerational households, the relevant R^2 statistic is $.88$, whereas it is $.89$ for young households. In the interests of brevity the regression results are not reported.

Residual Regressions

While there has been little research that identifies the moments of the income process in developing economies, several such estimates are available for developed economies. The uncertainty in incomes in these economies is typically measured as the variance in the residual error term in regressions of income on a set of regressors explaining household income. As emphasized in this research, the variability in income depends on the nature of the income process. Thus, persistence in income, as might exist if the error structure were characterized by an autoregressive process, implies a higher level of income uncertainty than is obtained if there was no autocorrelation in the error terms. Although it is possible to test for the nature of the income process (MaCurdy 1982), the ability to allow for high-order income processes is frequently limited by the duration of the available panel data. Much of the research in this area typically assumes that the income process follows an AR1 (auto-regressive 1) structure.

Studies that estimate the forecast error variance in income generally restrict their sample of households to a fairly homogeneous group, by conditioning either on demographic variables such as age, race, and marital status (MaCurdy 1982) or on years of education (Hubbard, Skinner, and Zeldes 1994).

The wide variation in sources of income observed in the IFPRI data, even within homogeneous demographic groups such as intergenerational or young households, suggests that the forecast error variance will vary across members of such groups with their occupational choices. Such variability implies that the error terms in the income regressions are likely to be heteroskedastic.[6]

To incorporate heteroskedasticity in error terms, the degree of persistence in incomes is allowed to vary with the interaction variables determining income choice. The persistence in income is also likely to be determined by the number of days of illness of adult males. A residual regression of the form can thus be estimated,

$$e(t) = \rho(\alpha_o + \alpha_1 X(t) + \alpha_2 i(t-1))e(t-1) + \upsilon(t), \qquad (13.1)$$

where $X(t)$ is the set of variables determining occupational choices and $i(t-1)$ is the days of illness of young and old adult males in period $(t-1)$. $\upsilon(t)$ is assumed to be white noise. The results of these residual regressions are reported in Table 13.4. This table reports results from two sets of regressions, which differ in that regression 2 imposes some of the exclusion restrictions suggested by regression 1. Regression 2 is used to estimate the forecast error variance. For both subsamples we can reject the null hypothesis of homoscedastic variances.

The residual regressions estimate a negative value for $\rho(t)$, the correlation between $e(t-1)$ and $e(t)$, for both intergenerational and nuclear households.[7] This negative correlation is at odds with the positive correlation that characterizes income in, for example, the United States. One reason for negative correlation is, of course, the agrarian nature of the economy, where agricultural output follows cyclical patterns. As noted earlier, negatively correlated residuals imply that households need hold only small stocks of assets in order to smooth consumption, because years of low income will generally be followed by years of high income.

The illness of older males and of males in young households adds to the persistence of income and, as one would expect, reduces the negative correlation of income. Unlike other factors that result in a negative value of ρ, adult male illness provides a motive to accumulate assets across years, because it implies low income not just in the current year but also in future years.

---

6. Unlike in pure time series, such patterns of heteroskedasticity can be accommodated in panel data sets, since the asymptotic results in this case obtain as N, the size of the cross section, tends to ∞.

7. Stationarity in incomes requires the absolute value of ρ to be less than one. This condition is met for all but 1 percent of the intergenerational households and 2 percent of nuclear households. Those households for whom $|\rho| > 1$ are excluded from the savings regressions are reported later in this chapter.

TABLE 13.4 Residual regressions

Variable	Regression 1	Regression 2
Intergenerational households		
Lagged residual	.4581* (.2737)	.4573* (.2732)
Interactions with		
Days ill, young males	.0003 (.0008)	.0003 (.0008)
Days ill, old males	.0021** (.0011)	.0021** (.0010)
Land	.0001 (.0013)	.0001 (.0012)
Number young males	.0750 (.0221)	.0754** (.0209)
Number old males	.0925 (.0825)	.0946 (.0796)
Number young females	.0014 (.0276)	. . . . . .
Number old females	.0057 (.0565)	. . . . . .
Average age young males	.0105* (.0064)	.0105* (.0062)
Average age old males	.0073** (.0036)	.0073** (.0036)
Mean value of correlation coefficient	.55.55	
F test for significance of interacted terms	$F(9,772) = 3.38$	$F(7,776) = 4.36$
Nuclear households		
Lagged residual	.8492** (.3925)	.9104** (.1825)
Interactions with		
Days ill, males	.0047** (.0021)	.0047** (.0021)
Land	.0040 (.0087)	.0047 (.0086)
Number of females ages 20–45	.2727* (.1627)	.2593* (.1583)
Number of females ages 45+	.0725 (.1483)	. . . . . .
Average age, males	.0018 (.0088)	. . . . . .
Mean value of correlation coefficient	.58	.58
F test for significance of interacted terms	$F(5,309) = 1.56$	$F(3,311) = 2.52$

NOTE: Standard errors are shown in parentheses.
** significant at 5 percent level; * significant at 10 percent level.

The Savings Equation

Theoretical Framework

The savings equation used next follows from standard models of intertemporal choice, in which savings reflect household expectations of future income or consumption requirements. For example, assuming negative exponential utility and under a set of normality assumptions, it is possible to derive a savings equation, following Campbell (1987), of the following form:

$$
s(t) = -\sum_{k=1}^{\infty} E_t \frac{\Delta Y(t+k)}{(1+r)^k} + \sum_{k=1}^{\infty} E_t \frac{\Delta \theta(t+k)}{(1+r)^k}
$$
$$
+ \frac{\gamma}{2(1+r)} \sum_{k=0}^{\infty} \frac{\Omega_t(t+k)}{(1+r)^k} + \frac{\ln(r-\delta)}{r}.
$$

(13.2)

In this equation, Y is household income, θ represents a set of variables that condition preferences, δ is the household's discount rate, r is the interest rate, Ω is the forecast error variance, and γ is a preference parameter representing the household's degree of "prudence." Equation (13.2) makes explicit the forward-looking nature of savings, in that savings reflect the change in income and preferences anticipated by the household in all future planning periods. To the extent that households are prudent (parameter γ), savings also reflect the variability in consumption. Thus, households facing greater variability in uninsured income will save more.

Rather than attempt to model the household's expectation of future income changes, the change in savings is analyzed: $\Delta s(t + 1) = s(t + 1) - s(t)$. From equation (13.2),

$$\Delta s(t+1) = \frac{1}{(1+r)}\left\{E_t\Delta y(t+1) - E_t\Delta\theta(t+1) - \frac{\gamma}{2}\Omega(t) - \eta^*(t+1)\right\}, \quad (13.3)$$

where $\eta^*(t + 1) = \eta(t + 1) + E_t\eta(t + 1)$, and $\eta(t + 1)$ is a vector of income and preference shocks in period $(t + 1)$. Thus, $\eta^*(t + 1)$ is the forecast error in period $(t + 1)$ shocks, which are assumed to be orthogonal to the other determinants of $\Delta s(t + 1)$.

Equation (13.3) makes clear that, unlike the case for the level of savings, the change in savings from period t to period $(t + 1)$ is positively correlated with the anticipated increase in income. Households expecting higher income in period $(t + 1)$ will save less in the current period, resulting in higher growth in savings. Similarly, greater uncertainty reduces savings growth, because it causes higher savings in period t.

The Estimating Equation

Equation (13.3) provides the basis for the equation applied to the data. The regressors include both anticipated changes in income and anticipated changes in the days of work lost owing to illness ($E_t\Delta i(t + 1)$). Ill health affects both preferences and income, and hence its effect on household savings is likely to differ from that of a change in income owing to other factors. The terms $E_t\Delta y(t + 1)$ and $E_t\Delta i(t + 1)$ are replaced, as is conventional in this literature, by the actual change $(y(t + 1) - y(t))$ and $(i(t + 1) - i(t))$. The resulting equation is estimated using variables that determine the household's expectations of income and illness as instruments. The coefficients on $\Delta y(t + 1)$ and $\Delta i(t + 1)$ thus reflect the household's response to anticipated changes. The set of instruments is described more fully below.

Equation (13.3) also relates the change in savings to the period t variability in consumption in period t. In the absence of insurance, this variability is determined by the variability of (uninsured) income, and the forecast error variability in income is accordingly included among the set of regressors from the previous section. The coefficient on the forecast error variance reflects the degree of "prudence" or the preference parameter that, for the utility function specified in equation (13.2), reflects the coefficient of relative risk aversion for the household. Since illness can also affect preferences for consumption, I also include an interaction of days of adult male illness with the variance in income among the set of regressors.

The panel nature of the data set makes it important to include the "aggregate shock" in income among the set of regressors because the assumption that aggregate shocks are uncorrelated with the household's prior information, and hence with the set of regressors, is unlikely to hold when data are available for only a few years. In order to incorporate aggregate shocks, the regressors include a full set of district/year dummy variables. Because the effects of aggregate shocks are likely to differ across households with their occupational choices, the analysis includes interactions of these dummy variables with the variables that determine occupational choice (the number of old and young males and females, the average age of males in both age groups, and the household's ownership of land for intergenerational households; the number of males and females, the average age of males, and the amount of landownership for young households).

The estimating equation for household j in district k is thus

$$\Delta s_{jk}(t+1) = \alpha_0 + \alpha_1 \Delta y_{jk}(t+1) - \alpha_2 \sum_m \Delta i_{jkm}(t+1) - \alpha_3 \sum_i \Delta \theta_{jkl}(t+1)$$
$$- \alpha_4 \Omega_{jk}(t) + \alpha_5 \mu_k(t+1) + \alpha_6 x_{jk} \mu_k(t+1) - \eta^*_{jk}(t+1). \tag{13.4}$$

As previously noted, $y(t+1)$ and $i(t+1)$ represent income and days of illness of adult male members respectively, with $m = 1,2$ indexing the two adult male generations in the case of intergenerational households ($m = 1$ for young households). θ_l, $l = 1$ to L, are variables reflecting preference shifts. These include changes in the number of adult members of the four gender–age adult demographic groups (three for young households) and the number of children in eight gender–age groups. $\mu_k(t+1)$ represents the effect of all variables, including aggregate shocks that affect all households in a given district k at time $(t+1)$. $x_{jk}(t+1)$ is the set of variables determining occupational choices.

Since asset-specific data on transactions are available, equation (13.4) is applied to both total savings and savings in specific assets (total savings measured as the difference between household income and consumption). Such savings include the rare transactions in land. Because land transactions occur infrequently, and primarily reflect bequests and gifts, the value of such transactions is removed so that the resultant measure of savings reflects savings in nonland assets. The individual assets for which transactions data are available are used in farm or nonfarm enterprises. These assets are aggregated to form a category of "productive assets" that include livestock and consumer durables. Data are also available for all financial transactions, including loans made and received by the household, separately for the formal and informal sectors. The "residual" category for which data are not available is savings in cash and stocks of foodgrains and other agricultural products. A crude measure of such savings is the difference between total nonland savings (as defined above) and savings in all the enumerated assets. Because this is a residual measure, changes in such savings obviously reflect changes in total savings and in other assets.

Measurement Error and the Choice of Instruments

SYSTEMATIC MEASUREMENT ERROR.   Research on the determinants of adult health status in both developed and developing economies typically have found considerable measurement error in the number of days of illness reported by survey respondents (Strauss et al. 1993). Wealthier and more educated adults are more likely to report days of illness than are poorer, less educated adults. Such measurement error in reported days of illness, but also in incomes, which is systematically correlated with unobserved individual or household traits, will yield biased estimates of the determinants of savings. The bias introduced by systematic measurement error, which is correlated with time-invariant household characteristics, can be eliminated by running the savings regression in first differences, as is done in this research.

RANDOM MEASUREMENT ERROR.   Income and illness measures, however, also contain random measurement error, and first differencing increases the bias introduced by such error. The presence of random measurement error in the first differenced regression also implies that the time t variables conventionally used to identify the effect of changes in income and health between periods $t + 1$ and t are invalid instruments. Instead, lagged income and illness in period $(t - 1)$ are used as instruments here, along with interactions of these lagged variables with demographic variables. The latter include the number of females in each of two adult age groups (20–45 and 45+) and, for intergenerational households, the number of males in these age groups. Since these demographic variables explain occupational choices, the extent of correlation between current and lagged values of income and illness will, in all probability, vary by these same demographic variables.

The number of days of illness is also likely to be correlated with variables reflecting the household's health environment. The set of instruments thus also includes interactions of lagged days of illness with a set of indicator variables that record whether there is a toilet in the household, whether the household's source of water is a private tap or pump, and whether there is a dispensary or clinic located in the village.

Because the savings equation is overidentified, the validity of the set of instruments can be verified by standard Basmann overidentification tests that determine whether the instruments have any independent power in explaining household savings. These test statistics are reported in the relevant tables.

TABLE 13.5 Savings regressions: Intergenerational households

Dependent Variable, $\Delta s(t-1)$ by Asset Type	Δ Income	Δ Ill Days			$\sigma^2 \times$ Illness	
		Young Males	Old Males	σ^2	Young Males	Old Males
Nonland savings	0.88**	−281.34*	−165.88	16.83	−0.24	−0.18
	(0.06)	(170.22)	(272.18)	(13.91)	(0.15)	(0.29)
Savings in productive	0.40	1,280.56	0.93	−95.89	1.13	0.04
assets	(0.06)	(282.95)	(389.51)	(22.35)	(0.25)	(0.41)
Savings in livestock	0.01	−32.28	−119.54**	1.31	−0.02	−0.13
	(0.01)	(29.95)	(48.58)	(2.44)	(0.03)	(0.05)
Consumer durables	−0.02	35.88	−359.90**	1.24	0.03	−0.35**
	(0.03)	(104.32)	(166.02)	(8.71)	(0.10)	(0.17)
Formal financial savings	0.004	−137.45	−4.50	6.81	−0.09	0.05
	(0.03)	(109.75)	(176.39)	(8.94)	(0.10)	(0.19)
Informal financial	0.03*	17.80	−108.16	−2.00	−0.02	−0.11
savings	(0.02)	(75.99)	(117.57)	(6.20)	(0.07)	(0.13)
Residual savings	0.30**	−165.09	−650.93*	−3.32	−0.10	−0.78*
	(0.09)	(269.70)	(416.00)	(22.10)	(0.24)	(0.45)

NOTES: Standard errors are shown in parentheses.

In addition to the regressors listed above, the set of regressors includes the change in the number of males and females in two age groups (15–45 and 45+), the change in the number of boys and girls in four age groups, a set of district/year dummy variables, and interactions of these dummies with the household's ownership of land, the age of the adult males in two age groups, and the number of women in the two age groups. The regression is run on the sample of intergenerational households.

The changes in income and ill days are treated as endogenous variables, and are instrumented by lags of income and days ill and interactions of these variables with demographic variables. The $F_{(19,672)}$ statistics from a Basmann overidentification test on the independent explanatory power of the instruments are 0.67, 1.80, 1.74, 1.13, 0.96, 0.86, and 0.98 for nonland savings, productive savings, savings in livestock, consumer durables, formal financial savings, informal financial savings, and residual savings, respectively.

** significant at 5 percent level; * significant at 10 percent level.

Results from Savings Regressions

INTERGENERATIONAL HOUSEHOLDS.   Table 13.5 presents results from instrumental variable regressions of the savings of intergenerational households run on the set of regressors described in the previous section.

The regression results support the hypothesis that rural households, even in very poor economies, do save in anticipation of future income changes, confirming similar results reported by other researchers (Deaton 1992a; Paxson 1992). Since the regressions are run on annual data, the results imply that households save not just in anticipation of seasonal changes in income within a year, but also across years. Although the increase in savings attributable to anticipated shortfalls in income implies an increase in liquid assets ("residual savings"), households also significantly increase their savings in productive assets and informal financial assets (the value of loans to others minus borrowings from the informal sector). Because productive assets contribute directly to income, this result suggests that anticipated changes in income may cause households to modify their income profiles through changes in the assets that directly contribute to income.

Anticipated changes in the number of workdays lost owing to illness by both young and old males also increase savings, although this effect is statistically significant only for young males. Illness also affects portfolio composition, but its effect differs strikingly from that of anticipated changes in income attributable to causes other than ill health. Thus, the expectation of a further loss of workdays owing to ill health of both young and old males causes households to reduce their investment in productive assets. Again, this effect is statistically significant only in the case of illness of young males. For such episodes of illness, the reduction in productive assets appears to be counterbalanced by an increase in liquid assets and livestock, although neither of these effects is statistically significant. The illness of older males, however, significantly increases investment in livestock and consumer durables.

As noted in the second section, it is frequently suggested that income uncertainty attributable primarily to unpredictable weather and crop incomes, in conjunction with limited access to credit markets, causes households to increase savings in liquid assets at the cost of investment in productive assets. The results in Table 13.5 reveal, in fact, that uncertainty in income by itself increases investment in productive assets. The predicted negative effect of income uncertainty on productive assets occurs only in households that report the current illness of prime age males. Thus, to the extent that income uncertainty contributes to poverty through adverse portfolio effects, it appears to be the result of the illness of young males.

This research also finds that intergenerational households do increase their savings in informal financial assets in response to anticipated income shortfalls, suggesting that informal credit is available to smooth consumption against such changes in income. Anticipated changes in adult male illness, however, do not significantly increase financial savings in either the formal or the informal sector. It may very well be the case that the inability or unwillingness of households to borrow in the event of illness causes households to reduce their investment in productive assets in order to increase stocks of more liquid assets.

Although constrained access to credit in the event of ill health provides one explanation for the regression results in Table 13.5, the fact that households are able to increase their total savings in such instances suggests that a reduction in the stock of productive assets may not be necessary to increase stocks of liquid assets. The decline in productive assets may, then, reflect adjustments to income in response to the changing expectations of the health of adult males.

In sum, the results for intergenerational households suggest that the illness of adult males significantly affects the forms in which households save. The reduction in productive assets caused by the illness of young males suggests a potential link between ill health and poverty. It is commonly believed that crop income uncertainty is linked to poverty through such portfolio effects, but the results here support this hypothesis only in the case of households that report illness of young males. There is no evidence of a negative effect of uncertainty on stocks of productive assets in the case of other households.

NUCLEAR HOUSEHOLDS. Table 13.6 reports the results from similar regressions for nuclear households. In general, anticipated changes in both income and days of illness affect the savings of nuclear households more than they do those of intergenerational households. The difference in the savings regressions for the two subsamples of households supports the hypothesis that the determinants of income and preferences and, possibly, the set of constraints households face, vary across household types. This in turn suggests that differences exist in the methods used by different types of households to protect consumption against volatility in income, and possible differences exist in the extent to which consumption correlates with income changes.

Anticipated shortfalls in income for nuclear households, as for intergenerational households, result in an increase in overall savings, and in savings in productive assets, consumer durables, net formal financial assets (deposits minus borrowings), and the residual category of liquid assets. Households, however, reduce informal financial assets. Ill health also produces effects similar to those in intergenerational households, causing reductions in productive assets, consumer durables, and formal financial assets. The reduction in such assets is counterbalanced by an increase in livestock and informal financial savings.

Supporting the hypothesis that the potentially adverse effects of income uncertainty are related to the illness of males, results show that only in households reporting such illness does income uncertainty lead to a significant reduction in productive assets. In other households, income uncertainty increases savings in productive assets. As with anticipated changes in income, this response is consistent with the hypothesis that households react to income uncertainty by attempting to modify their income profiles through their asset decisions.

Nuclear households differ from intergenerational households in the responsiveness of their financial savings to anticipated changes in income, ill health, and uncertainty. Table 13.6 shows that the anticipated illness of adult males and the uncertainty induced by such an event cause nuclear households to reduce their loans from the informal sector. Unlike their intergenerational counterparts, nuclear households appear to use informal credit to protect consumption against the ill health of their (sole) adult male. And nuclear households appear to reduce informal savings in response to anticipated shortfalls in income, perhaps to finance their increased investment in productive assets, consumer durables, and, possibly, formal financial assets.

TABLE 13.6 Savings regressions: Nuclear households

Dependent Variable, $\Delta s(t-1)$ by Asset Type	Regressors				Regression $F(45,266)$	Overidentification Test $F(5,261)$
	Δ Income	Δ Ill Days	σ^2	$\sigma^2 \times i(t-1)$		
Nonland savings	1.04** (0.06)	75.78 (192.41)	-12.52 (38.48)	0.12 (0.28)	39.73	0.24
Savings in productive assets	0.55** (0.13)	422.35** (219.89)	-81.53** (42.69)	0.61** (0.31)	1.35	0.74
Savings in livestock	-0.01 (0.02)	-112.37** (58.21)	18.96* (11.26)	-0.14* (0.08)	1.29	0.60
Consumer durables	0.11** (0.02)	160.50* (97.94)	-30.21 (19.65)	0.2 (0.14)	1.49	2.02
Formal financial savings	0.33** (0.04)	266.79* (144.16)	-43.12 (28.82)	0.35* (0.21)	2.29	1.61
Informal financial savings	-0.57** (0.08)	-429.43* (253.94)	65.74 (50.77)	-0.53 (0.37)	1.53	0.66
Residual savings	0.76** (0.10)	-149.98 (345.56)	39.49 (69.07)	-0.26 (0.50)	9.83	0.34

NOTES: Standard errors are shown in parentheses.

In addition to the regressors listed above, the set of regressors includes the change in the number of females in two age groups (15–45 and 45+), the change in the number of boys and girls in four age groups, a set of district/year dummy variables, and interactions of these dummies with the household's ownership of land, the age of the adult male, and the number of women aged 20–45 years. The regression is run on the sample of households with just one adult male aged 20–45 years.

The changes in income and ill days are treated as endogenous variables instrumented with second lag of income and days ill, and interactions of these variables with demographic variables and indicators of health environment.

** significant at 5 percent level; * significant at 10 percent level.

Does Illness Contribute to Poverty?

The results in the previous section suggest that it is adult male illness, particularly of prime age males, that has the potential to increase the poverty of rural households through its effect on the composition of asset portfolios. Although the results suggest this hypothesis, they provide no direct evidence for it. The hypothesis is tested below by analyzing the effect of the illness of prime age males on household consumption.

An extensive literature has tested the effects of both income shocks and anticipated changes in income on the period-to-period change in consumption (Deaton 1992b; Townsend 1994). Much of this literature concludes that households in developing economies are well insured against both income shocks and anticipated fluctuations in income. The literature, however, provides no evidence on the effects of income shocks on poverty. Although such shocks may reduce lifetime wealth and lower consumption in every period, regressions of the change in consumption or, equivalently, a household fixed-effects regression of the level of consumption show a "net out" effect of all fixed factors, including the household's lifetime wealth. Thus, a downward shift in the household's consumption profile is quite consistent with no observed effect of the adverse shock on the difference in consumption from period to period.

The Frisch framework, which relates consumption to a lifetime variable, the marginal utility of wealth, $\lambda(t)$, and a set of period-specific variables that determine intraperiod choices, is convenient for an analysis of the effects of illness on lifetime wealth. As detailed in MaCurdy (1985), the framework yields household consumption as a function of $\lambda(t)$ and a set of period-specific preference shifters and prices. In turn, the household's marginal utility of wealth, $\lambda(t)$, is itself an endogenous variable; the household constantly revises its expectations of wealth and the marginal utility it derives from wealth, on the basis of the additional information contained in current income and preference shocks.

Since the household's marginal utility of wealth, $\lambda(t)$, directly reflects the household's period t expectations of lifetime wealth, one can estimate the effect of illness on poverty by regressing estimates of $\lambda(t)$ on days of illness along with the other determinants of the marginal utility of wealth. $\lambda(t)$, however, varies from period to period, so that it cannot be recovered as the fixed effect from a straightforward fixed-effects regression of consumption on a set of regressors. Instead, the consumption regression needs to take into account the relationship between $\lambda(t+1)$ and $\lambda(t)$ in order to recover $\lambda(t)$ consistently. As shown by MaCurdy (1985), $\lambda(t)$ follows a random walk with drift so that, if $\varepsilon(t)$ is the forecast error in expectations, then

$$\ln\lambda(t) = \ln\left(\frac{1+\delta}{1+r}\right) - \ln(E_{t-1}\{\exp[\varepsilon(t)]\}) + \ln\lambda(t-1) + \varepsilon(t). \quad (13.5)$$

A first-order linear approximation of the period t consumption for household j in district k is then given by

$$c_{jk}(t) = \alpha_0 \ln\lambda_{jk}(t) + \alpha_1 x_{jk}(t) + \alpha_2 \mu_k(t) + \varepsilon_{jk}(t), \tag{13.6}$$

where x_{jk} represents the set of preference shifters determining current period preferences, μ represents aggregate district-wide shocks and the effects of other district-specific and time-varying variables, and ε_{jk} is the current idiosyncratic shock to consumption. Substituting in from equation (13.5) for $\lambda(1 + k)$, $k = 1,2$, the following systems of equations then applies to household j over the three years of the IFPRI panel:

$$\begin{bmatrix} c(t+2) \\ c(t+1) \\ c(t) \end{bmatrix} = [\lambda^*(t)] + \begin{bmatrix} 0' & \delta_{11}' & \delta_{21}' & 0' & \delta_{41}' & \delta_{51}' \\ 0' & \delta_{12}' & 0' & 0' & \delta_{42}' & 0' \\ \delta_{30}' & 0' & 0' & \delta_{33}' & 0' & 0' \end{bmatrix} \begin{bmatrix} x(t) \\ x(t+1) \\ x(t+2) \\ \varepsilon(t) \\ \varepsilon(t+1) \\ \varepsilon(t+2) \end{bmatrix} + \delta_6 \begin{bmatrix} \mu(t+2) \\ \mu(t+1) \\ \mu(t) \end{bmatrix}. \tag{13.7}$$

In equation (13.7), $\lambda^*(t)$ is a linear function of the marginal utility of wealth in year t and any other preference parameters that remain fixed (for the household) over time. Consumption in period $(t + k)$, $k > 0$, thus depends on $\lambda^*(t)$, current and lagged values of the variables $x(t + k)$ and the vector of forecast errors, $\varepsilon(t + k)$, and a set of district-year specific variables $\mu_k(t + k)$. As equation (13.7) makes clear, it is necessary to allow the coefficients on, for example, $x(2)$ to vary across equations, so that $x(2)$ affects consumption in period $(t + 1)$ and period $(t + 2)$ differently. Similarly, the coefficient on $\varepsilon(2)$ varies from period 2 to period 3.

Stacking observations for all households, one can then run a fixed-effects regression on household consumption to recover $\lambda(1)$.[8] The generated estimates of $\lambda(1)$, $\lambda^*(1)$, can be used to assess the effect of ill health on household wealth. Lagging equation (13.5) back to the initial period implies that $\lambda^*(1)$ is a function of the household's initial marginal utility of wealth and the household's entire history of forecast errors. This yields the following equation for household j in district k:

$$\ln\lambda^*_{jk}(1) = \lambda_0' x_{jk}(1) + \gamma_1' x_{jk}(0) + \gamma_2 i_{jk}(1) + \gamma_3 \mu_i(1) + v_{jk}. \tag{13.8}$$

---

8. This equation regresses the log of household consumption on a fixed effect, a set of demographic variables, a set of household income shocks and a set of district/year dummies. Results from this regression are available on request.

The error term in this equation, v_{jk}, includes the value of all income and preference shocks up to year 1. x_o represents variables determining the household's initial marginal utility of wealth. Since data are available on the land inherited by the head and his wife, these variables are used as components of x_o. The regression additionally includes the number of adults in the four adult gender- and age-specific demographic groups, education levels and years of education of members of these groups, the number of children in eight age- and gender-specific groups, and a set of district dummies. The estimate of the forecast error in variance in year 1 is also included among the set of regressors, in order to assess the effects of income uncertainty on lifetime wealth. This regression is run on the sample of intergenerational households, using data from year 1 only.

Days of illness experienced in the first year of the survey, $i(1)$, will be correlated with previous episodes of illness and with the error term in the regression, necessitating the use of instrumental variables to obtain consistent estimates. Lagged values of illness, however, are invalid instruments in that they will be correlated with the error term. Since the effect of previous ill health on current illness varies with age, interactions of lagged illness are used with current age and age squared as instruments.[9]

Estimates of equation (13.8) are in Table 13.7. Male ill health has a significant positive effect on the current marginal utility of wealth, implying a reduction in the household's expectations of lifetime wealth. Thus, the results support the hypothesis that the illness of prime age males contributes to the poverty of rural households. In contrast, income uncertainty appears to have no significant effect on wealth.

Conventional ordinary least squares (OLS) regressions of the change in consumption between successive years on the lagged illness of young males, or the alternative instrumental variables regression of the change in consumption on current days of illness, using lagged illness as an instrument, produce insignificant effects of anticipated illness on change in consumption.[10] Similarly, an OLS regression of the change in consumption on current days of illness in addition to lagged illness and interactions of lagged illness with age and age squared yielded no significant effect of current illness on the change in consumption (coefficient = 11.14, standard error = 49.85). Since this regression controls for the household's expectation of current illness through measures of lagged illness, the coefficient on current illness reflects the effect of the fore-

---

9. Lagged days of illness are available for year 1, because retrospective data on the previous year were collected in the initial interview. The validity of the set of instruments is confirmed through a standard Basmann overidentification test ($F(2,337) = 0.5372, p = .5849$).

10. The coefficient on lagged illness is 1.69 with a standard error of 65.55 in the OLS regression, while the coefficient on current illness in the instrumental variables regression is 88.84, with a standard error of 300.86.

TABLE 13.7 Instrumental variables regression of the effect of illness on the marginal utility of wealth in year 1

Variable	Coefficient	Standard Error
Days ill, young males[a]	0.0082**	(0.0031)
σ^2	−0.000029	(0.000033)
Number of		
Males 20–45	0.0677*	(0.0466)
Males > 45	−0.1403	(0.1285)
Females 20–45	0.0032	(0.0519)
Females > 45	−0.2821**	(0.1423)
Boys 0–5	−0.1142**	(0.0340)
Boys 5–10	−0.0793*	(0.0423)
Boys 10–15	0.0498	(0.0471)
Boys 15–20	0.0355	(0.0469)
Girls 0–5	0.1597**	(0.0379)
Girls 5–10	0.0628	(0.0441)
Girls 10–15	0.1291**	(0.0607)
Girls 15–20	−0.0138	(0.0451)
Regression $F(38,339)$	5.842**	
Overidentification test for valid instruments $F(2,333)$	0.55	

NOTES: The sample is intergenerational households, year 1. In addition to the regressors listed above, the regression includes levels and years of education of all members of the four adult demographic groups, the land inherited by the head and his wife, and a set of district dummies.

[a] Instrumental variable, instrumented by interactions of lagged illness with age and age squared.

** significant at 5 percent level; * significant at 10 percent level.

cast error in illness on consumption. According to these results, evidence that households are insured against illness shocks or can protect consumption from anticipated illness episodes is consistent with a significant effect of illness on poverty.

Conclusion

It is commonly believed that income volatility contributes to the poverty of rural households in that it causes households to reduce stocks of productive assets in order to accumulate more liquid assets. Any number of underlying factors can, however, cause incomes to fluctuate. This chapter provides evidence that the ill health of male members of the household most affects the poverty of households through adverse portfolio shifts. This result suggests that policy interventions in health infrastructure might have a substantial impact on income levels, not just on welfare as measured by improved health.

Adverse effects of income shocks on productive investments are commonly attributed to imperfectly functioning credit markets, but the findings here suggest that this may not be so. Nuclear households appear to increase savings in informal transactions in anticipation of a loss in income owing to ill health, suggesting that informal credit *is* available to finance consumption in the event of such losses. And although ill health has little effect on the financial savings of intergenerational households, the increase in their overall savings implies that the reduction in productive assets is not necessary to finance an increase in liquid assets. It appears more likely that the response of productive assets to ill health and anticipated income shortfalls reflects adjustments in occupational patterns to such potential changes, rather than the effect of credit constraints. This hypothesis, however, needs to be substantiated by empirical research that takes into account the correlation between the various asset choices made by the household.

The study also reveals important differences in the determinants of savings of nuclear and intergenerational households, particularly in response to ill health and financial savings. Whereas intergenerational households are able to increase savings in response to an anticipated reduction in workdays owing to illness, nuclear households appear unable to do so. Perhaps because of this inability, nuclear households appear more likely to use informal credit to protect consumption from episodes of illness. Given that the costs of informal credit are known to be high and to increase with loan amounts, the costs of protecting consumption from episodes of illness may be higher for nuclear households.

Finally, this research also indicates important differences in the responsiveness of the savings of intergenerational households to the illness of younger and older males. In contrast to the illness of prime age males, that of older males produces no significant increase in overall savings, perhaps because the ill health of elderly males affects household income less than the ill health of younger males. The difference in precautionary savings rates may reflect the utility loss associated with the illness of elderly males compared with that of prime age males, or it may simply reflect preferences. This, too, constitutes an area for further research.

References

Alderman, H. 1996. Saving and economic shocks in rural Pakistan. *Journal of Development Economics* 51: 343–365.

Ben-Porath, Y. 1980. The F-connection: Families, friends, and firms and the organization of exchange. *Population and Development Review* 6 (1): 1–30.

Cain, M. 1978. The household life cycle and economic mobility in rural Bangladesh. *Population and Development Review* 4 (3): 421–438.

Caldwell, J. C., P. H. Reddy, and P. Caldwell. 1988. *The causes of demographic change: Experimental research in South India.* Madison, Wis., U.S.A.: University of Wisconsin Press.

Campbell, J. Y. 1987. Does saving anticipate declining labor income? An alternative test of the permanent income hypothesis. *Econometrica* 55: 1249–1273.

Cox, D., and E. Jimenez. 1992. Social security and private transfers in developing countries: The case of Peru. *World Bank Economic Review* 6 (1): 155–169.

Deaton, A. 1989. Saving in developing countries: Theory and review. In *Proceedings of the World Bank Annual Conference on Development Economics*, pp. 61–96. Washington, D.C.: World Bank.

————. 1992a. Saving and income smoothing in Côte d'Ivoire. *Journal of African Economies* 1 (1): 1–24.

————. 1992b. *Understanding consumption*. Oxford: Clarendon Press.

Eswaran, M., and A. Kotwal. 1989. Credit as insurance in agrarian economies. *Journal of Development Economics* 31 (1): 37–53.

Feachem, R. G. A., et al. 1992. *The health of adults in the developing world.* New York: Oxford University Press.

Hubbard, R. G., J. Skinner, and S. P. Zeldes. 1994. The importance of precautionary motives in explaining individual and aggregate saving. *Carnegie-Rochester Conference Series on Public Policy* 40: 59–125.

Kochar, A. 1996. Are cross-sectional household data useful for research on savings? Inferring savings motives from cross-sectional consumption- and income-age profiles. Manuscript. Stanford University, Stanford, Calif., U.S.A.

————. 1999. Smoothing consumption by smoothing income: Hours of work responses to idiosyncratic crop income shocks in rural India. *Review of Economics and Statistics* 8 (1): 50–61.

Kotlikoff, L., and A. Spivak. 1981. The family as an incomplete annuities market. *Journal of Political Economy* 89 (4): 706–732.

MaCurdy, T. E. 1982. The use of time series processes to model the error structure of earnings in a longitudinal data analysis. *Journal of Econometrics* 18: 83–114.

————. 1985. Interpreting empirical models of labor supply in an intertemporal framework with uncertainty. In *Longitudinal analysis of labor market data,* ed. J. J. Heckman and B. Singer. New York: Cambridge University Press.

Mordoch, J. 1990. Risk, production, and savings: Theory and evidence from Indian households. Mimeo. Harvard University, Cambridge, Mass., U.S.A.

————. 1994. Poverty and vulnerability. *American Economic Review Papers and Proceedings* (May): 221–225.

Paxson, C. H. 1992. Using weather variability to estimate the response of savings to transitory income in Thailand. *American Economic Review* 82 (1): 15–33.

Rosenzweig, M. R. 1988. Risk, implicit contracts and the family in rural areas of low-income countries. *Economic Journal* 98: 1148–1170.

Rosenzweig, M. R., and H. Binswanger. 1993. Wealth, weather risk and the composition and profitability of agricultural investments. *Economic Journal* 103 (1): 56–78.

Rosenzweig, M. R., and O. Stark. 1989. Consumption smoothing, migration and marriage: Evidence from rural India. *Journal of Political Economy* 97: 905–926.

Rosenzweig, M. R., and K. I. Wolpin. 1993. Credit market constraints, consumption smoothing and the accumulation of durable production assets in low-income countries: Investments in bullocks in India. *Journal of Political Economy* 101 (2): 223–244.

Strauss, J., P. J. Gertler, O. Rahman, and K. Fox. 1993. Gender and life-cycle differentials in the patterns and determinants of adult health. *Journal of Human Resources* 28 (4): 790–837.

Townsend, R. 1994. Risk and insurance in village India. *Econometrica* 62 (3): 539–592.

Udry, C. 1995. Risk and saving in Northern Nigeria. *American Economic Review* 85 (5): 1287–1300.

UNDP (United Nations Development Programme). 1995. *Human development report.* Oxford: Oxford University Press.

Walker, T. S., and J. G. Ryan. 1990. *Village and household economies in India's semi-arid tropics.* Baltimore, Md., U.S.A.: Johns Hopkins University Press.

PART IV

Toward Economic Sustainability of
Rural Financial Systems for the
Poor: The Role of Public Action
and the Private Sector

14 The Microfinance Revolution: Implications for the Role of the State

CÉCILE LAPENU

Microfinance arouses enthusiasm among donors, practitioners, researchers, and the state. This interest is based on the success of a few well-known financial institutions in mobilizing savings and distributing large amounts of credit, with high repayment rates and good outreach on a rather sustainable basis. Microfinance has allowed millions of households usually excluded from traditional financial services to begin their own economic activities or to reinforce existing efforts and become microentrepreneurs.

Yet many difficulties remain that need to be resolved in view of the ambitious objectives attached to microfinance programs. Three main issues require clarification. First, a large number of poor households still lack access to financial services. Impact studies indicate that the poorest of the poor do not participate in microfinance programs, in part because the necessary environment is not yet in place to support their needs. Second, most of the microfinance institutions (MFIs) have not yet been able to demonstrate their capacity to reach a break-even point that would allow them to operate without subsidies. The trade-off between becoming financially sustainable and reaching the poor is frequently debated and much additional work is needed to add insight into the nature and degree to which trade-offs exist. Finally, although governments and donors have increased funding to microfinance to accelerate the development of new MFIs and to reach an increasing number of clients, much of this funding was poorly directed to unsustainable institutions and government support programs. Building efficient financial institutions requires time, skill, appropriate institutional design, and a favorable macroeconomic and regulatory environment.

These three issues raise questions about the role the state can assume in order to improve the sustainability, outreach, and impact of MFIs: (1) Are state-owned microfinance institutions necessary? (2) What level of MFI subsidization is desirable? (3) What are the state's investment options in financial institutions or complementary services? (4) How can the state create and instill confidence in a regulatory framework for microfinance?

This chapter focuses on microfinance within rural financial systems because of the widespread and severe shortage of traditional financial services in rural areas. A number of country case studies in Asia and Africa are examined to illustrate the role of the state in developing rural financial systems. The countries use different forms of government intervention to introduce and support microfinance innovations: microfinance is sometimes integrated into the public sector (the model of "integration" in India or Viet Nam); microfinance can be complementary to state-owned institutions (the model of "complementarity" in Indonesia or Burkina Faso); or microfinance can be an alternative to the rather deficient role of the government (the "alternative" model in Madagascar or West Africa). Among the three intervention types, the structure, conduct, and performance of both the MFIs and rural financial systems can be compared in order to improve understanding of the complementarities and trade-offs between public institutions and private sector activities (for-profit institutions and NGOs) that can lead to an efficient rural financial system benefiting the poor.

The chapter first presents the evolution of theoretical and empirical points of view on the role of the state in financial system development, from the interventionist period of the 1960s and 1970s to the current period of liberalization. The respective roles of the state, NGOs, and private commercial banks in facilitating innovations and outreach are reviewed to identify when the state can promote, support, develop, or impede microfinance development in rural areas. Finally, issues related to microfinance regulation and how these compare with commercial bank regulation are analyzed.

Theoretical Justification for the Role of the State

Distinction between the Public and Private Sectors

Regarding the role of the state, the World Bank defines the state and the government as follows:

> State, in its wider sense, refers to a set of institutions that possess the means of legitimate coercion, exercised over a defined territory and its population, referred to as society. The state monopolizes rule-making within its territory through the medium of an organized government. . . . Government is normally regarded as consisting of three distinct sets of powers. . . . One is the legislature, whose role is to make the law. The second is the executive . . . which is responsible for implementing the law. The third is the judiciary, which is responsible for interpreting and applying the law. (World Bank 1997:20)

The private sector can be divided into the for-profit private sector and the not-for-profit private sector, represented by the nongovernmental organizations (NGOs). In this chapter, NGOs in microfinance represent both institutes that promote grassroots MFIs (henceforth called "operators") and member-based organizations such as village banks, solidarity groups, and cooperatives implemented by operators. The role of donors as funders is included when analyzing the use of subsidies in MFI development.

Justification of the Role of the State

Neoclassical theory stipulates that individuals are rational and that the free functioning of the market should lead to an optimal allocation of resources. Yet the need for intervention and technical assistance exists even when financial repression is abolished (Krahnen and Schmidt 1994). The state has a responsibility to build a conducive environment for both financial markets and the rest of the economy (through infrastructure, liberalization of the markets, macroeconomic stability, and so forth). The role of the state in the financial system may be justified to cope with market failures and to improve equity. Table 14.1 classifies the functions of the state in this regard (World Bank 1997).

ADDRESSING MARKET FAILURES. Advances in theoretical economics over the past 20 years have provided a framework to identify constraints leading to market failures. Addressing these market failures is a first possible rationale for state intervention in the financial system (Stiglitz 1992; Besley 1994). One must recognize, though, that governments may have only limited ability to reduce or eliminate market failures.

The state's role in defining the regulatory framework and fiscal and monetary policy is widely accepted as providing a public good. As a minimal function for macroeconomic management, state intervention in the financial system mainly seeks to ensure macroeconomic stability. However, many states in developing countries have failed to ensure macroeconomic stability. Governments may actually exacerbate instability in the financial system by, for example, forgiving the loans of influential but delinquent borrowers in order to realize political gains (Besley 1994).

In assessing the role of the state, a number of questions remain for determining the course of microfinance development. In the absence of macroeconomic stability, what are the implications for developing microfinance? How should a regulatory framework be implemented for microfinance institutions? Is intervention using public funds justified, and, if so, in what circumstances?[1] Another public good in the new microfinance market is represented by institutional innovations. Because pilot projects in microfinance target clients previously excluded from the formal financial system, they may face high risk and information and start-up costs. The returns from successful innovation are

---

1. Public funds (from the state or donors) can be distributed either as subsidies to reduce the on-lending rate, or through public investment in physical or human capital as well as institutional experimentation leading to innovations and up-scaling of microfinance institutions. In this chapter, the second option is advocated rather than the first.

TABLE 14.1 Functions of the state

	Addressing Market Failures		Improving Equity
Minimal functions	Providing pure public goods (defense, law and order, property rights, macroeconomic management, public health)		Protecting the poor (antipoverty programs, disaster relief)
Intermediate functions	Addressing externalities (basic education, environmental protection)	Regulating monopoly (utility regulation, antitrust policy)	Overcoming imperfect information (insurance, financial regulation, consumer protection)	Providing social insurance (redistributive pensions, family allowances, unemployment insurance)
Activist functions	Coordinating private activity (fostering markets, cluster initiatives)		Redistribution (asset redistribution)

SOURCE: World Bank (1997).

likely to be captured by the rest of the financial system. As a public good, innovation in microfinance may benefit from donor and state investments that help design services and structures to improve MFI outreach, sustainability, and impact. Once successful, these services and structures can be broadly replicated.

Regulating monopolies and compensating for missing markets[2] are two common justifications for public support for financial institution development. However, it is not clear that monopoly power, such as that exercised by village moneylenders, is socially inefficient even though its redistributive consequences may be viewed as negative for the poor (Besley 1994). Providing credit alternatives may be a reasonable response based on distributional concerns but may have little to do with market failures. For example, to fill gaps in the types of credit provided by private entities, several East Asian governments have created development banks and used directed credit with relative success because of their flexibility and good incentive and monitoring structures (Stiglitz and Uy 1996).

Financial markets are especially subject to imperfect information owing to the characteristics of exchange: money is given up today in exchange for a promise to repay in the future. Such promises are frequently broken and the financial institutions face problems of imperfect information. MFIs in particular need to cope with risks associated with opportunistic behavior by clients (moral hazard), difficulty in the selection of borrowers (adverse selection), problems of lack of collateral, and missing insurance markets. Governments face similar problems arising from imperfect information and may have no better incentives to induce repayment within the financial market (Besley 1994). However, government intervention may increase efficiency by facilitating improved use of collateral, such as providing clear definitions of property rights,[3] and improving access to insurance markets.

Finally, based on the activist functions underscored by the World Bank (1997) and new analysis approaches developed by Stiglitz (1998), there is now greater understanding of how governments and private sectors can act together as partners. For example, governments can create rents that enhance the incentives for prudential behavior in the financial sector. In East Asia, government policies spurred growth by using and directing markets and market forces rather than replacing these, and government lending programs, employing commercial standards, complemented private lending (Stiglitz and Uy 1996).

IMPROVING EQUITY.   The need to improve equity may also justify state intervention even in the absence of market failure. Competitive financial markets can distribute capital in socially unacceptable ways so that government action

---

2. A missing market can be identified when goods or services are not provided despite a willingness to pay for them—this demand having been confirmed through surveys.

3. This type of indirect role of the state is not examined in this chapter.

may be required to protect and assist the vulnerable (World Bank 1997). Microfinance institutions developed in this new framework have aimed at reaching the excluded population or sought to undermine the monopoly power of local moneylenders.

The role of microfinance in increasing income and smoothing consumption can help provide safety nets. Two elements can justify government intervention to provide social insurance: as explained above, governments can invest in innovation, and governments have the capacity to work at the national level to cope with covariant risks. Innovative arrangements can improve equity by providing microfinance services in underserved rural areas and for the poor population. As expressed by Besley (1994), for both political and incentive reasons, credit market intervention to help the poor may make sense as an alternative to attempting interventions to redistribute assets.

Causes and Consequences of Government Intervention in the 1960s and 1970s

Development of the Public and Private Agricultural Banks

One of the main objectives of developing countries during the 1960s and 1970s was to increase agricultural production by facilitating farmers' adoption of improved technologies. Improving farmers' access to credit was seen as a key requirement, based on the following assumptions:

- The main constraint for farmers is access to capital and to new technologies; capital must be injected into the rural areas through in-kind credit packages, including fertilizers, pesticides, improved seeds, or equipment. Public institutions were developed to channel these packages to the farmers.
- Farmers often depend on usurious moneylenders for access to capital to finance their inputs; to break these links with expensive sources of funds, interest rates needed to be subsidized.
- The rural population is too poor and subject to too many shocks to save, so savings schemes were not implemented. The objective was to inject funds into the rural areas, not to act as intermediaries between savers and borrowers.

There was little concern for building an efficient rural financial market. Economic policies focused on direct government intervention, rather than on developing a conducive economic environment that could lead to sustainable financial institutions.

Based on these assumptions, most developing countries created agricultural development banks or implemented subsidized credit programs within agricultural development projects. Following independence in 1948, the government of India pioneered the practice of state-sponsored rural development banking. Acting through the Reserve Bank of India, the government provided "social banking" in competition with the private moneylenders, with affordable loans for rural producers. It created land development banks for long-term finance and cooperative banks for short-term finance, and it nationalized 20 major commercial banks in 1969 and in 1980. It implemented 25 poverty alleviation schemes, including the Integrated Rural Development Program (IRDP), initiated in 1979, which served some 20 million rural families by the mid-1990s (Hulme and Mosley 1996). In Indonesia, drawing on its oil income, the government was able to build two networks to implement its green revolution program: 3,600 "village units" of the Bank Rakyat Indonesia (BRI-UD) were directed at the channeling of subsidized loans, and more than 6,000 "village cooperatives" (Koperasi Unit Desa, KUD) provided technical support for improved technology on rice production.

In francophone West Africa, public agricultural development banks (Banque Nationale de Développement Agricole, BNDA) were established to provide financing to producer organizations for technical support of agricultural projects or development companies. The system of financing differed slightly between countries and changed over time. In general, however, financing consisted of producer loans in kind (seeds, fertilizers, pesticides, equipment), which were repaid at harvest time. Loans were subsidized through external donor funds and export taxes. Financing was designated primarily for cash crops; food crop production benefited only indirectly through the reallocation of inputs.

Failures and Achievements of the Public Agricultural Banks

Most government financing institutions quickly faced problems, the most visible being low repayment rates, which forced institutions to rely more and more on subsidies. Impact studies also revealed that the development banks generally did not reach small farmers (Adams and Vogel 1986).

Several factors can help to explain decreasing repayment rates among borrowers. Political interference and poor accountability among bank staff led to biased selection of borrowers and arbitrary loan waivers. In India, for example, nonbank staff, including local government officials charged with the allocation of IRDP loans, conducted some loan appraisals. As a consequence, the banks did not regard the IRDP as their program and tended to implement it in a mechanical manner (Hulme and Mosley 1996). Moreover, there were no rewards for bank employees for good repayment performance. When a performance appraisal did exist, it was based on the volume of loans distributed or the rate of adoption of new technologies among borrowers. In fact, there was little incentive for bank staff to motivate borrowers to repay. From the borrowers' viewpoint, the lack of flexibility associated with in-kind loans and rigidity in loan size, defined by the borrower's enterprise, decreased their interest in the financial services and their willingness to repay.

Interest rate ceilings, low repayment rates, lack of savings mobilization, and institutional mismanagement led to low or negative financial profitability for the state-owned institutions. Most of the West African agricultural development banks failed as a result of a combination of climatic shocks and political intrusion, because they had not addressed covariant risks. Two of them still finance cotton production (CNCA Burkina Faso and BNDA Mali).

Based on a review of state-owned institutions, the most important catalyst for government change appears to be financial constraints. In Indonesia, the 1983–84 drop in oil income and deteriorating repayment rates forced a major restructuring of BRI. In India, the macroeconomic and debt crisis in 1991, when inflation rose and foreign exchange reserves decreased, pushed the government to undertake a structural adjustment program that led to restructuring of its financial system. In West Africa, most government banks were dismantled or transformed as part of the structural adjustment programs of the 1990s. In Madagascar, structural reform and liberalization programs began in the 1980s; as a result, the public rural bank (BTM) created in 1975 is now privatized.

In spite of the crises and much-needed adjustments, government development banks achieved some positive impacts. Most notably, networks of financial branches were built in the rural areas. In Indonesia, more than 9,000 BRI village banks and villages cooperatives (KUD) are currently spread through rural areas, while rural India is served by 126,000 financial institutions.[4] Even where branch networks have been closed, rural financial services may be more readily reintroduced once liberalization is complete.

Moreover, policies aimed at improving agricultural production have led to the adoption of new technologies, such as increased use of animal traction in West Africa[5] and improved seeds and fertilizers for rice in India and Indonesia. Indonesia became self-sufficient in rice in 1984, having been the world's largest importer in 1970. Achieving such increases in production was many governments' primary reason for directly intervening in rural financial policy.

Current Realities of the Role of the State in the Financial System

Since the 1980s, owing to the failure of state-owned financial institutions in developing countries, governments have shifted their financial policies toward

---

4. These include 94,000 Primary Agriculture Cooperative Societies, 890 Primary Land Development Banks, 18,300 rural branches of the 20 nationalized commercial banks, and 12,800 branches of the Regional Rural Banks.

5. In Senegal, among groundnut producers, for example, there was a notable shift from manual work to mechanization as well as increased use of fertilizer and improved maize seed. This was partly the result of access to subsidized in-kind loans. Now, owing in particular to the failure of the state-financed program (1981), the equipment has not been repaired, the corn area is decreasing, and soil fertility is declining with the drop in the use of fertilizer.

greater market liberalization. These policy measures and reactions have been diverse, however, and have led to different equilibria between the roles of the state, private for-profit institutions, and NGOs. Microfinance institution development is linked to state intervention through three broad types of model: the integration, complementarity, and alternative models.

The Model of Integration

In countries such as India and Viet Nam, the state maintains a strong financial policy presence, including integration of microfinance innovations. Since the early 1950s, India has implemented programs to promote assured access to banking services for the rural poor. A major justification for bank nationalizations in 1969 was to force more extensive lending to rural areas and particularly to the rural poor (Kabeer and Murthy 1996). Currently there are approximately 126,000 public financial institutions or branches spread over India, implementing 25 poverty alleviation schemes such as the pilot project to link banks with self-help groups initiated by the National Bank for Reconstruction and Development (NABARD), the apex agricultural credit bank (Srinivasan and Rao 1996). Only a few state-owned institutions have undergone reorganizations. As the government's halting progress in reorganizing the Regional Rural Banks indicates, trade union pressure and possibly political lobbying by the landowning borrowers (who benefit most from subsidized interest and from loan and interest waivers) would need to be overcome before restructuring of the rural credit system can be attempted (Mahajan and Ramola 1996).

As Viet Nam evolves toward a market economy, state intervention continues within its rural financial system (Johnson 1996; Colliot and Ngan 1997; Creusot et al. 1997). The state-supported Viet Nam Bank for Agriculture, created in 1990, is a commercial bank using standard banking criteria to distribute loans (such as physical guarantees and risk analysis). By 1996, it had a nationwide outreach of more than 1,800 branches spread throughout the country. In 1995, the state created a nonprofit branch of the bank, the Viet Nam Bank for the Poor. Relying on subsidized credit and founded out of political concerns, its capacity to reach financial sustainability is questionable. In Viet Nam, despite approximately 60 NGO-implemented microfinance programs, the formal rural financial system is still mainly driven by the state. In fact, new microfinance programs face state-instigated financial and legal constraints, such as an interest rate ceiling, that impede their development.

The Model of Complementarity

In some countries, the state and private sector complement rather than exclude each other. Both private and public sectors can initiate microfinance innovations. One of the most interesting examples of this comes from Indonesia, where BRI's village banks were successfully restructured, spurred by a precipitous decline in loan repayments in 1983–84.

BRI is a public bank, but the principles guiding village bank transformation involved "privatizing" their internal operations (decentralized decisionmaking, a profit orientation, giving employees a stake in performance and incentives), improved staff professionalism, and increased flexibility. The government assumed the full transformation costs; it covered losses incurred under the green revolution program (Bimas), capitalized the village units, and established training programs for staff. State guarantees for savings in public banks generate incentives to save.

BRI-UD's transformation took place within the context of an overall financial sector deregulation (Mukherjee 1997), with a new regulatory framework being progressively defined since 1983. The framework offers in particular a clear and flexible status for the small banks, which are called Bank Perkreditan Rakyat (BPRs).[6] In June 1993, around 900 new BPRs were operating, 95 percent of which were private. This large network of private financial institutions adopts and develops innovations to reach rural areas, such as linkages, incentives to mobilize savings, Islamic principles of profit sharing, and interregional network building (Lapenu 1996, 1998). Before Indonesia's 1997 financial crisis,[7] the rural financial system was characterized by its strong public banking system supporting various microfinance programs, cooperatives, and the diversified competing network of BPRs. In this model of complementarity, competition and technical and financial links between the institutions strengthened the overall financial system.

The Alternative Model

In some developing countries, market and state failures in reaching the poor and rural areas are manifold, and microfinance institutions develop as an alternative.

In Madagascar, the agricultural public bank (BTM) has never really managed to reach rural households or to offer microfinance services. In response to these deficiencies, five main networks largely based on mutualist principles have developed with support from foreign associations and international donors. However, their outreach is still quite limited, reaching only an estimated 25,000 house-

---

6. Bank Perkreditan Rakyat means people's credit bank or rural bank. These banks are required to provide a minimum capital of US$25,000 (Rp 50 million 1995), compared with US$5 million (Rp 10 billion) for the commercial banks.

7. Nowhere in the Asian region has the impact of the crisis been more severe than in Indonesia. In January 1998, to protect the financial system, the central bank (Bank Indonesia) declared a guarantee on bank deposits and pumped liquidity into the banking system. But neither the guarantee nor the liquidity support were extended to the BPRs, which now face liquidity constraints. Because the BRI village units are not engaged in foreign exchange, they have been partly protected from the crisis, and savings volume increased in the village unit network. The value of loans outstanding in BRI village units and the BPRs has fallen 25 to 50 percent in constant prices since the beginning of the crisis. Most, if not all, microfinance programs have experienced lower repayment rates. For more details, see McGuire and Conroy (1998).

holds. At the national level, the structure of the rural financial system remains segmented. In some regions, virtually no formal financial services are available to rural households. As the BTM is now privatized, a large number of the 73 rural branches could be closed, which would further weaken the rural financial system.

In West Africa, the failure of most agricultural development banks led either to a dismantling of public sector institutions (in Benin, Côte d'Ivoire, Niger, and Togo) or to a return to specialized lending for cash crop production, as can be seen with cotton (in Burkina Faso and Mali). The success of microfinance, particularly in Asia, raised donor and government hopes that NGOs would be able to fill rural finance gaps and respond to the needs of the rural population. The multiplication of microfinance projects that collect savings prompted the Central Bank of West African States to define a regulatory framework, called Parmec law.[8] Although the Parmec law made important headway toward regulating informal finance, issues remain regarding the treatment of nonmutualist institutions, the capacity of authorities to implement the law, as well as some regulatory aspects such as the ceilings on interest rates, which may affect credit union performance (Lelart 1996; Berenbach and Churchill 1998).

The development of microfinance using these three models underscores two important points. First, the evidence suggests that new microfinance institutions are rarely the product of market forces. Most large and successful microfinance institutions reaching the poor in developing countries have relied on donor and government support, at least during their formative stage. Private research and development have contributed little to the microfinance revolution in the past 15 years (Zeller and Lapenu 2001). Second, a recent inventory of microfinance institutions (Lapenu and Zeller 2002) indicates extensive coverage in Asia, Africa, and Latin America. However, these institutions require stable macroeconomic and political environments to develop, and unstable countries remain out of reach of international microfinance initiatives.

The three divergent state roles result from different financial capacities and political will to support financial system development. Nevertheless, continued analysis is needed of how microfinance innovations can be broadly implemented, depending on whether the state can promote, directly develop, or impede microfinance initiatives.

Institutional Innovations for the Different Models

The three models presented above differ in the respective roles of the state, NGOs, and private commercial banks. The impact of the inner circle of institutional

---

8. Parmec stands for Projet d'Appui à la Réglementation des Mutuelles d'Epargne et de Crédit (Project to support the regulation of savings and credit cooperatives).

innovation presented in Figure 1.1 of this volume, mainly analyzed here in terms of outreach, depends in part on which model is considered. Analysis of the different country case studies provides some insights into the conditions that can enhance the impact of institutional innovations.

Adoption of Innovations

The three models of state intervention in microfinance contribute to the adoption of innovation in different ways. The model of integration, which includes microfinance within the public sector, can support innovations that act as public goods. In Indonesia, BRI-UD adopted a large range of innovations to address market failures, including an information system through local supervision and responsibilities, incentives for employees, borrowers, and savers, the establishment of market rules, and cost management. These credit and savings service innovations were successfully implemented and disseminated in other Indonesian microfinance programs (PHBK, P4K), the regional state-owned banks (KURK, BKK), and the rural private banks (BPR). Indonesian innovations could be replicated in other countries, and BRI-UD serves as an example of best practices.

Because NGOs receive some grants from donors and also have a deep knowledge of local characteristics and constraints, they may be well positioned to test new market niches, such as the poorer strata of the population or poorer areas, or to test new methodologies (Gulli 1998). The state may still need to invest in the implementation of innovations such as microfinance services to agriculture or insurance services. Many studies underscore the urgent need for rural household insurance to cope with individual and covariant risks (Zeller et al. 1997; Nguyen 1998). Insurance may also reinforce microfinance transactions to secure repayment. State-owned institutions with large networks can fulfill the conditions required for insurance systems—large and diversified participation that supports risk pooling. Some NGOs and local organizations, aware of insurance needs, have already sought to develop insurance schemes, but they have been hindered by the narrow range of their client portfolio.

On the other hand, the integration model may slow down microfinance innovation. In India, the slow pace of transformation of the Regional Rural Banks (Mahajan and Ramola 1996) constrained adoption of improved practices. Individuals as well as organizations with bargaining power have a crucial stake in perpetuating the system (North in Harriss, Hunter, and Lewis 1995). A balance of power must be created between the state, local politicians (modern and traditional authorities), and financial institutions to avoid political intrusion, while ensuring a dynamic adoption of innovation and sound financial practices. The balance of power can be created through external control, access to information, and participation in decisionmaking by all the actors.

Breadth of Outreach

EXISTENCE OF A BANKING STRUCTURE IN RURAL AREAS. The presence of a publicly owned banking structure can enhance the breadth of microfinance outreach. The models of state integration or complementarity in microfinance support broad coverage of the rural population. The success of Thailand's state-owned Bank for Agriculture and Agricultural Cooperatives (BAAC) in reaching 80 percent of the 5.6 million rural families is impressive and unprecedented in developing countries (Yaron, Benjamin, and Piprek 1997). BRI-UD's network in Indonesia underscores the positive role of a large initial state financial investment. In 1996, 95 percent of BRI-UD units were profitable, while reaching an estimated 16 million savers and 2.5 million borrowers. However, most BRI-UD borrowers are not the poorest among Indonesia's rural population. Nevertheless, BRI-UD's large and powerful network does support microfinance programs that reach around 200,000 poor families.[9] In countries such as India where 15,000–20,000 NGOs operate (Robinson cited in Kabeer and Murthy 1996), most NGOs work with hundreds, occasionally thousands, of members. However, this represents minuscule coverage when compared with the country's total number of poor and the government's coverage.

Microfinance institutions within the complementarity model use the banking structure to secure their activities and lower their transaction costs. Yet government and donor policymakers confront difficulties within public banking systems, such as low efficiency and low repayment rates, by considering three options: liquidation, privatization, or restructuring. The first two options often weaken rural banking system structures and may jeopardize further development of microfinance institutions dependent on the banking structure for their activities. The thinking and processes behind the successful transformation of BRI village units should be more widely disseminated, analyzed, and replicated in other contexts to maintain a rural banking structure. To cope with the risks of low repayment rates, BRI-UDs offer flexible services that fit local demand and strictly enforce repayment rules. Financial incentives for staff improve efficiency and reduce the constraints on change. Hulme and Mosley (1996) point out that the closure of nonprofitable institutions is relatively easy and facilitates the achievement of short-term public expenditure targets. However, the opportunity costs of not pursuing the "restructure" option may be very high.

ABSENCE OF A BANKING STRUCTURE IN RURAL AREAS. The alternative model increases the difficulty of developing microfinance institutions. In Madagascar, despite innovation within the microfinance network, MFIs operate within an inadequate banking structure and the total number of members

---

9. BRI supports the network of village units and a program of solidarity groups by supplying technical assistance (Lapenu 1996, 1998; Ravicz 1998).

reached is estimated at only 25,000. This corresponds to a national outreach of less than 2 percent of rural households after 5 to 10 years of operation.

The development of NGO-supported microfinance institutions as an alternative to government inadequacies faces serious constraints that may limit their outreach potential. Despite NGOs' growing importance in supporting microfinance development, they cannot be the only vehicle for microfinance services. Not all NGOs working in microfinance could be efficiently and sustainably transformed into regulated formal institutions—following the example of Bancosol and FIE (a finance company) in Bolivia or K-Rep (a bank) in Kenya. Many do not aim for transformation into a commercial bank and they often do not have sufficient capacity in banking skills, security, or human resources to manage such a transformation.

In the long term, commercial banks need to be more involved in supporting microfinance because of their physical infrastructure, well-established information systems, sound governance, available funds and established capacities for offering financial services. But their role and capacities for supporting microfinance need to be strengthened in terms of organizational structure, financial methodology, human resources, and cost effectiveness (Baydas, Graham, and Valenzuela 1997). Acting in a complementary role, the state and donors could facilitate capacity building within commercial banks to support microfinance innovations by investing in network building and compensating for the lack of a financial market. A minimum banking structure could facilitate the development of a rural financial system in which complementarity between institutions increases microfinance outreach and sustainability.

Depth of Outreach

All three models for supporting microfinance development face a trade-off between reaching the poorest and becoming financially sustainable. Despite the general objective of most microfinance institutions to alleviate poverty, and for some NGOs to fill gaps in the formal banking system, MFIs mostly locate in wealthier areas. Gupta (cited in Kabeer and Murthy 1996) argues that NGOs in India tend to follow the logic of the market and concentrate in areas where markets are well developed and people have started to articulate their needs as effective demand. The same observations are made about Madagascar and Bangladesh (Zeller 1993; Sharma and Zeller 1999). The choice of location may also be constrained by competition among networks and geographical areas; there are strong incentives for networks to be located in wealthier areas to secure better performance. In Indonesia, the central bank provides incentives to develop institutions on islands besides the more accessible Java and Bali, by giving easier access to operating licenses for the rural banks (BPRs).

Most impact analysis (for example, Hulme and Mosley 1996; Wampfler, Prifti, and Brajha 1996; Sharma and Buchenrieder in this volume) shows that neither NGOs, nor private commercial banks, nor state institutions seem to reach the poorest of the poor. Poverty means problems of access not only to financial services but also to other markets and services (such as labor, health, and education). Moreover, the very principles of some institutions are based on members' sharing the financial burden and risks between them, which often leads to the exclusion of the poorest of the poor.

Reaching poor households through financial services is likely to require some start-up subsidization, whose extent will depend on the expected social benefits compared with the costs (Zeller et al. 1997). It is widely recognized that achieving financial sustainability requires subsidies, which should support institution building and human capital formation rather than be used to reduce interest rates. Moreover, incentive structures that are conducive to an efficient use of subsidies must be elaborated through contracts between donors or state and the MFI, with the objectives and the use of subsidies clearly specified. Government institutions are often limited in their use of incentives (Stiglitz 1992) because of their susceptibility to rent-seeking pressure and a reluctance to enforce repayment in the face of adverse political consequences. In addition, the costs of mistakes made by one administration may be borne by later administrations. However, Stiglitz and Uy (1996) have highlighted the use of commercial, performance-based criteria by the public development banks in East Asia for allocating credit. These practices enhance the likelihood that funds will be allocated to sound ventures and reduce the likelihood of political abuse, and they should be replicated elsewhere.

The failure of integrated, complementary, or alternative models of microfinance to reach the poorest of the poor may arise from inherent limitations with microfinance as a tool to alleviate extreme poverty; financial interventions are just part of a range of choices for development assistance programs seeking to reduce poverty (Gulli 1998). In fact, the analysis of the failures and successes with public and private microfinance institutions highlights the importance of institutional governance structures, which goes beyond the distinction between private and public sectors. Stiglitz and Uy attribute the relative success of development banks and directed credit in East Asia to various factors, such as the ability to change poorly functioning credit policies rapidly, targeting credit mainly to private enterprises based on performance measures, limited use of subsidies and directed credit, and effective monitoring. Institutional governance structures have too often been downplayed or neglected. However, effective monitoring and performance measures, clear lines of accountability, feedback and sharing of responsibilities, access to information, organizational flexibility to adjust policies, a balance of power, and external and objective regulatory oversight can all lead to more efficient public microfinance institutions.

Clear rules in terms of responsibilities, power, control, and protection from political interference allow smooth functioning of public microfinance institutions, increased trust, more rapid resolution of conflicts, and better enforcement of the rules (Clarkson and Deck 1997). Even if ownership remains public, management's authority to implement best practices can vary within public institutions. The evolution of this authority can lead to large differences in performance. The socioeconomic environment also seems a more important factor than public versus private MFI ownership, and fair competition in particular can play a stimulating role (Sen, Stern, and Stiglitz 1990; Lapenu and Benoit-Cattin 1997).

The State and the Policy Framework

As microfinance institutions grow, issues concerning appropriate regulation become increasingly important. In theory the state has a major role to play in providing a regulatory framework and instilling confidence in it, but governments need to know whether microfinance threatens macroeconomic stability and whether regulators will be able to deliver effective oversight of a burgeoning number of diverse institutions. A minimum of macroeconomic and political stability is required for MFIs to fulfill their role. In the absence of macroeconomic stability, MFIs face excessive constraints, and very few can develop (Lapenu and Zeller 2002). This situation may represent a fourth model: "Absence of MFIs."

DIFFERENT MODES OF REGULATION.   The need to regulate microfinance is based on various arguments, the strongest being the need to protect savers. Recent experiences, such as the 1996 collapse of the Albanian "pyramids," underscore the risks associated with unregulated savings mobilization. To implement efficient intermediation, microfinance institutions need to leverage capital and mobilize external resources. This requires formalizing activities and following sound financial rules to gain the confidence of other financial institutions. Finally, MFIs may find that their official recognition gives them a competitive edge over informal competitors through increased client confidence and barriers to entry for informal institutions unable to meet regulatory requirements. However, in most cases, the low volume of microfinance transactions limits the threat to macroeconomic stability.

The regulation of microfinance institutions by external bodies requires specific skills and increased means to enforce rules. Traditional supervisory agencies in developing countries may already face difficulties regulating a small number of big banks. Moreover, they are unfamiliar with microfinance concepts and technologies and may lack training in effectively supervising new institutional types that deal with unconventional guarantees, have decentralized operations, and are large in number (Jansson and Wenner 1997; Berenbach and Churchill 1998). On the other hand, NGOs want the authority to collect deposits without incurring regulatory costs and restrictions. However, regulations without adequate authority and the capacity for supervision and enforcement usually end up being of little use.

The apex institutions are often claimed to be substitutes for an absent formal regulatory framework and enforcement bodies. However, as pointed out by

Chaves and Gonzalez-Vega (1994), even if apex institutions can perform important monitoring functions, they are not ideal frameworks for prudential regulation, particularly when their expertise is limited, supervision fails to be neutral, and supervisory activities and management tasks are not kept separate so as to deal with only a small number of clear rules.

Any institution involved in microfinance should define from its inception a proper governance and supervision system based on clear rules and sharing of responsibilities. Donors, governments, and operators should follow a professional code of ethics. For example, a clear distinction appears necessary between (1) microfinance activities that involve the strict enforcement of contract loans with commercial interest payments and capital reimbursement, and (2) rural subsidies channeled through health services, the food supply, education, and microenterprise technical support.

Effective regulation that avoids rigid rules and narrow microfinance definitions can strengthen the microfinance movement and spur innovation. Models of integration such as in China, India, and Viet Nam, where the state seeks narrow control of microfinance development, can impede institutions' financial viability[10] and curtail the rural poor's access to financial services. Madagascar and West Africa have opted for an orientation toward mutualist principles; however, even when conforming to rural socioeconomic conditions, innovative newcomers may encounter barriers to entry. Mutualist approaches can also constrain development capacities within existing networks that are unable to fulfill mutualist requirements, such as local savings mobilization or a member-based ownership structure. MFI involvement in the development of regulatory systems can be an important means of addressing their institutional needs.

THE SPECIFICITY OF MICROFINANCE.   Beyond the necessary internal control of MFIs, external regulation must be defined, taking into account the microfinance risks and constraints, which differ from those of commercial banks. Even if some general prudential rules are the same for both commercial banks and MFIs, such as transparency in ownership and financial accounting and the necessity of financial sustainability, some rules for MFIs need to be more flexible and others need to be stricter than those for commercial banks. The specific characteristics of microfinance institutions are presented in Table 14.2.

Because microfinance is a relatively new phenomenon, greater flexibility is required to encourage innovations in institutional forms, to motivate investors with diverse backgrounds and perspectives, to allow new types of collateral that do not require specific provisioning, or to accept some forms of subsidization for start-up capital or innovations. On the other hand, because of microfinance's short history, its sources of capital are less secure, and this requires stricter

---

10. In India, until recently, interest rates have been kept low and capped for loans up to Rs 25,000 (around US$1,000) (Mahajan and Ramola 1996).

TABLE 14.2 Recommended regulations for microfinance institutions compared with commercial banks

	Regulation for Microfinance Institutions Should Be . . .		
	More Flexible	More Strict	The Same
Institutional form	Microfinance is a relatively new phenomenon, so regulation should encourage innovation[a]		
Ownership	Regulations should encourage investors motivated by social objectives, from diverse backgrounds and perspectives, or local private investors (local governance)	Because MFI investors may have limited capacities to provide capital, stricter rules are needed for reserve and capital	Transparency, operational independence, and clarification of ownership ownership are all required
Documents from clients	Because of illiterate clients and in order to lower transaction costs, regulations should limit procedures for clients		
Financial services	Regulations should encourage cost-saving services (for example, mobile banking)	MFIs are providing new services on the market, which require more testing and prudent introduction. In general, there is no demand for deposits and no business in foreign exchange	
Financial accounting			Transparency is necessary
Limits on interest rates	MFIs' higher transaction costs require regulations that allow interest rates that tend to cover the costs		

Minimum capital requirement	Owing to the social importance of encouraging MFIs, regulations should limit the impact of this rationing device	
Capital adequacy		Because of MFIs' less diversified portfolio and the risks of capital shortage in the case of emergency, there is a need for stricter rationing
Provisioning	Most loans are uncollateralized, and repayment incentives and nontraditional collateral (such as a solidarity group) should be recognized; specific provisions are not necessary	Delinquency is often more volatile and MFIs are more subject to covariant risks, so there is a need for stricter rules on provisioning
Liquidity requirement	The small size of transactions means less concentration of risks on a small number of big borrowers	MFIs face a high level of risks from the seasonality of demand, dependency on donor funds, and short-term liabilities, which may require stricter rules on liquidity
Financial performance	Subsidies could be justified for (1) the initial stage of formation of MFIs, and (2) innovation to reach the poorest people or remote areas	In general, there is a necessity to reach financial sustainability

SOURCES: Lapenu (1996); Jansson and Wenner (1997); Rock and Otero (1997); Berenbach and Churchill (1998).

[a] In Latin America, new types of financial institutions have been created by laws to facilitate the development of microfinance, such as the Bolivian Private Financial Funds and the Peruvian Entities for the Development of Small and Micro Enterprises (Jansson and Wenner 1997).

rules in terms of ownership, provisioning, and capital adequacy. Moreover, MFIs provide new services in the market that require more testing and prudent introduction.

In addition to the novelty of MFIs, their differences from commercial banks derive from the specificity of the services provided. Because MFIs deal with poor or illiterate clients, they should have more flexibility in terms of the documents required from clients, cost-saving services offered, and the type of collateral accepted. On the other hand, they may have a less diversified portfolio and they can be subject to more volatile delinquency, which may require stricter rules on capital adequacy, provisioning, and liquidity requirement.

Table 14.2 demonstrates that MFIs need to be governed under specific regulations and not directly by traditional banking laws. The Indonesian banking law (McLeod 1992; Lapenu 1996) is a prime example. The law defines only two types of institution: commercial banks and the Bank Perkreditan Rakyat ("people's credit banks" or rural banks). The BPRs are much smaller than commercial banks, and they are required to follow specific prudential rules. These offer a flexible framework for rural banking that has been implemented, step by step, through various decrees. The 1992 banking law was enacted nearly 10 years after the first decree initiating financial liberalization in 1983. In 1998, new decrees were adopted to deal with the financial crisis that struck Indonesia, endangering its rural system.

Conclusions and Policy Implications

Both in spite and because of enthusiasm for microfinance, urgent questions regarding the role of the state in microfinance need to be addressed. Comparative analysis of MFIs in various developing countries brings out several points concerning an active role for the state.

As pointed out by Stiglitz (1998), lending responsibility belongs within the private sector. However, the countries examined in this chapter have also shown that, in the rural financial system, state-owned institutions may achieve considerable outreach compared with most NGOs and private commercial banks not yet involved in microfinance. The existence of a banking sector in rural areas can help MFIs develop by reducing their transaction costs as a result of the financial and technical links they can establish with the banking system.

Where an extensive network of financial institutions already exists, the state's responsibility is to strengthen the financial system's structure and, where appropriate, to transform and restructure public institutions to serve rural areas better, as was the case with Bank Rakyat Indonesia in 1983–86. The state must also offer a conducive regulatory and economic framework to allow private institutions, particularly microfinance institutions, to develop without unnecessary constraints. "Partnerships" should be established between the public and the private sector (Stiglitz 1998). The government can also change the "game" that private participants play in ways that are welfare enhancing.

Where no rural banking network exists, a public role is needed to create a minimum banking structure to address the failure of the private sector to respond to the financial demands of specific poorer segments of the population.[11] The state can develop public branches or provide incentives for commercial banks through performance-based subsidies or through investment in innovations. This minimum banking structure may be a precondition for microfinance institutions to move in.

Few MFIs are currently sustainable and they continue to rely on subsidies. The microfinance success stories indicate that subsidies are needed for (1) start-up investment and network building, and (2) the development of innovations as a public good, in particular to define insurance schemes or to compensate for missing financial markets.

Most impact analysis has shown that microfinance services do not reach or do not have a clear impact on the poorest of the poor; it is certainly an illusion to think that microfinance alone will draw this part of the population out of poverty. Extreme poverty requires complementary services (infrastructure, education, and health services), which can be offered, for example, through NGOs or state services, but independently from financial services. If a clear objective is to alleviate the poverty of the poorest households and remote areas, the public sector must invest in these operations, since sustainable MFIs will not be able to fulfill this role. Where no banking structure exists, this may also mean that the necessary conditions for development of the rural financial system are not yet fulfilled; in this case, the state must primarily invest in roads and market infrastructures, for example.

To protect clients and strengthen institutions, microfinance must have a clear juridical and regulatory framework. The monitoring framework should be defined decree by decree, in order to remain flexible and adaptable to changes and failures. Incentive structures should be established so that all the actors have a stake in a well-functioning microfinance system. The regulatory agencies need increased human and financial resources, which could be provided through donor and state support.

The regulatory complexity involved in microfinance requires that some "rules of the game" be established and implemented beyond the strict enforcement of the regulatory framework. At the level of financial institutions, efficiency in outreach and sustainability depend, above all, on practical and professional

---

11. Adequacy in meeting the demand by the poor necessitates client proximity, small transactions, and alternative forms of guarantees—not just a land certificate or a regular salary, etc.

governance with clear definitions of responsibilities, strict enforcement of rules, and widespread circulation of information. Efficient governance is the best determinant of MFI performance, whether owned by the public or the private sector.

Financial market efficiency can be enhanced when the functions of the state, for-profit financial service providers, and nonprofit institutions work in complementary or synergistic ways. The state is best placed, by virtue of its legitimate powers of coercion or rule-making authority, to foster a conducive environment. However, exercise of such power tends to attract rent seeking, and measures to discourage such behavior are required if the state is to succeed in its role of facilitating efficient commercial transactions and relationships (for example, with the involvement of a wide range of stakeholders in the discussion and clear definition of rules, commercial- and performance-based criteria for allocating credit, and improvement of the governance structure). Donor and government support may motivate commercial banks to offer microloans or to lend on a wholesale basis to specialized providers of microloans. Public policy should dissuade specialized providers, such as NGOs, from distorting financial markets through subsidized interest rates or low repayment rates. Those that do not wish to provide market-oriented financial services may be more suited to enhancing the microfinance impact on the poorest by providing training, group formation, screening, local supervision, and health and education services. Microfinance can be a powerful tool for rural economic development in developing countries. Yet the objectives must remain realistic.

References

Adams, D., and R. Vogel. 1986. Rural financial markets in developing countries: Recent controversies and lessons. *World Development* 14: 477–487.

Baydas, M., D. H. Graham, and L. Valenzuela, 1997. Commercial banks in microfinance: New actors in the microfinance world. Photocopy. Ohio State University, Columbus, Ohio, U.S.A.

Berenbach, S., and C. Churchill. 1998. *Regulation and supervision of microfinance institutions: Experience from Latin America, Asia, and Africa.* Occasional Paper No. 1. Washington, D.C.: Microfinance Network.

Besley, T. 1994. How do market failures justify interventions in rural credit markets? *World Bank Research Observer* 9 (1): 27–47.

Chavez, R., and C. Gonzalez-Vega. 1994. Principles of regulation and prudential supervision and their relevance for microenterprise finance organization. In *New world of microenterprise finance*, ed. M. Otero and E. Rhyne. West Hartford, Conn., U.S.A.: Kumarian Press.

Clarkson, M., and M. Deck. 1997. Effective governance for microfinance institutions. Focus Note No. 7. Consultative Group to Assist the Poorest, Washington, D.C.

Colliot, E., and H. V. Ngan. 1997. Le marché financier: Complémentarité entre une Banque d'Etat et un projet de crédit décentralisé (Plaine des Joncs, Viet Nam). *Agriculture et développement* (15): 59–65.

Creusot, A.-C., C. Klébert, L. Q. Tuan, and N. T. Bich Van. 1997. Le crédit rural décentralisé au Viet-Nam: Perspectives d'institutionnalisation. *Agriculture et développement* (15): 53–58.

Gulli, H. 1998. *Microfinance and poverty. Questioning the conventional wisdom.* Washington, D.C.: Inter-American Development Bank.

Harriss, J., J. Hunter, and C. M. Lewis. 1995. *The new institutional economics and Third World development.* London: Routledge.

Hulme, D., and P. Mosley. 1996. *Finance against poverty,* 2 vols. London: Routledge.

Jansson, T., and M. Wenner. 1997. *Financial regulation and its significance for microfinance in Latin America and the Caribbean.* Washington, D.C.: Inter-American Development Bank.

Johnson, A. 1996. *Microfinance in Viet Nam: A collaborative study based upon the experiences of NGOs, UN agencies and bilateral donors.* Hanoi: Consultative Group to Assist the Poorest and United Nations Development Programme.

Kabeer, N., and R. K. Murthy. 1996. *Compensating for institutional exclusion? Lessons from Indian government and non-government credit interventions for the poor.* IDS Discussion Paper No. 356. Brighton, U.K.: University of Sussex.

Krahnen, J. P., and R. H. Schmidt. 1994. *Development finance as institution building. A new approach to poverty-oriented banking.* Boulder, Colo., U.S.A.: Westview Press.

Lapenu, C. 1996. Vers un nouveau rôle pour l'Etat et les institutions privées dans le développement du système financier rural indonésien. Ph.D. dissertation. CIRAD, ENSA, Montpellier, France.

———. 1998. *Indonesia's rural financial system: The role of the State and the private institutions.* Asia Series on Sustainable Banking with the Poor. Washington, D.C.: World Bank.

Lapenu, C., and M. Benoit-Cattin. 1997. The restructuring of the Indonesian rural financial market: An interpretation using the framework of contestable market theory. Paper presented at the 23rd Conference of the International Association of the Agricultural Economists, Sacramento, Calif., U.S.A.

Lapenu, C., and M. Zeller. 2002. Distribution, growth, and performance of microfinance institutions in Africa, Asia, and Latin America: A recent inventory. *Savings and Development* 1 (26): 87–111.

Lelart, M. 1996. *La loi Parmec sur les mutuelles d'épargne et de crédit dans les pays de l'UEMOA.* Document de recherche No. 17–96. Orleans, France: Institut Orléanais de Finance.

McGuire P., and J. Conroy. 1998. Effects on microfinance of the 1997–1998 Asian financial crisis. Second Annual Seminar on New Development Finance, 21–25 September, Goethe University, Frankfurt, Germany.

McLeod, R. H. 1992. Indonesia's new banking law. *Bulletin of Indonesian Economic Studies* 28 (3): 107–129.

Mahajan, V., and B. G. Ramola. 1996. Financial services for the rural poor and women in India: Access and sustainability. *Journal of International Development* 8 (2): 211–224.

Mukherjee, J. 1997. State-owned development bank in microfinance (the BRI). Focus Note No. 10, Consultative Group to Assist the Poorest, Washington, D.C.

Nguyen, T. D. P. 1998. Food insecurity and the evolution of the endogenous risk-sharing in the Sahel. Ph.D. dissertation. Department of Agricultural Economics, Ohio State University, Columbus, Ohio, U.S.A.

Ravicz, R. M. 1998. *Searching for sustainable microfinance: A review of five Indonesian initiatives.* Policy Research Working Paper No. 1878. Washington, D.C.: World Bank.

Rock, R., and M. Otero. 1997. From margin to mainstream: The regulation and supervision of microfinance. Action International Monograph Series No. 11. Somerville, N.J.

Sen, A., N. Stern, and J. Stiglitz. 1990. Roundtable discussion: The role of the state and the private sector. In *Proceedings* of the World Bank Annual Conference on Development Economics 1990. Washington, D.C.: World Bank.

Sharma, M., and M. Zeller. 1999. Placement and outreach of group-based credit organizations: The cases of ASA, BRAC, and PROSHIKA in Bangladesh. *World Development* 27 (12): 2123–2136.

Srinivasan, G., and D. S. K. Rao. 1996. *Financing of self-help groups by banks: Some issues.* Working Paper No. 8. Lucknow, India: Bankers Institute of Rural Development.

Stiglitz, J. E. 1992. *The role of the state in financial markets.* Washington, D.C.: Institute for Policy Reform.

———. 1998. Redefining the role of the state, what should it do? How should it do it? And how should these decisions be made? Tenth Anniversary of MITI Research Institute, Tokyo, Japan, March 17. Available at <http://www.worldbank.org/html/extdr/extme/ jssp0.31798.htm>.

Stiglitz, J. E., and M. Uy. 1996. Financial markets, public policy, and the East Asian miracle. *World Bank Research Observer* 11 (2): 249–276.

Wampfler, B., L. Prifti, and M. Brajha. 1996. Etude des stratégies des ménages ruraux, de leurs activités et de la place du crédit ADF (Albanian Development Fund). Centre de Coopération Internationale en Recherche Agronomique pour le Développement, Montpellier, France.

World Bank. 1997. *World development report 1997. The state in a changing world.* New York: Oxford University Press.

Yaron, J., M. P. Benjamin, Jr., and G. L. Piprek. 1997. *Rural finance: Issues, design, and best practices.* Washington, D.C.: World Bank.

Zeller, M. 1993. Credit policies for food security in Sub-Saharan Africa: The case of Madagascar. Final report to GTZ. International Food Policy Research Institute, Washington, D.C.

Zeller, M., and C. Lapenu. 2001. Promoting institutional innovation in microfinance: Replicating best practices is not enough. *Development and Cooperation* 42 (1). Frankfurt am Main, Germany: Deutsche Stiftung für Internationale Entwicklung (DSE).

Zeller, M., G. Schrieder, J. von Braun, and F. Heidhues. 1997. *Rural finance for food security for the poor: Implications for research and policy.* Food Policy Review No. 4. Washington, D.C.: International Food Policy Research Institute.

15 Recent Developments in Rural Finance Markets

JACOB YARON AND McDONALD BENJAMIN

Rural financial markets have a pivotal role to play in promoting rural economic development and poverty reduction. They fulfill this role when they facilitate payments, risk, and liquidity management in rural areas and intermediate loanable funds to the most productive investments in response to price and profit signals. However, rural financial markets (RFMs) have frequently attracted few private for-profit formal financial intermediaries, owing to the high cost associated with serving rural clients in sparsely populated areas, the underdevelopment of complementary markets and related institutions, the meager availability or absence of reliable collateral, highly covariant risks, and large seasonal fluctuations in rural areas in the demand for and supply of short-term financial resources.

Recognizing the limitations of RFMs in developing countries, states pursuing both rural growth and more equitable income distribution have often considered interventions in RFMs to be inevitable. These interventions have taken many forms, but have focused in particular on augmenting the availability of agricultural credit and on reducing the interest payment burden on farmers. Consequently, agricultural credit programs, including the widespread establishment and support of specialized agricultural credit institutions, have been central to government interventions in rural financial markets. Donors have frequently supported these interventions by assisting in their design and by channeling substantial financial resources for on-lending to bolster growth in agricultural production and poverty reduction. The disappointing performance of countless donor-supported rural financial projects can be ascribed largely to (1) insufficient knowledge or misconceptions about the real problems afflicting rural financial markets (such as information asymmetry, segmented markets, and high transaction costs and covariant risks); (2) the effects of historically distorted, urban-biased macroeconomic and financial policies on the rural sector; (3) insufficient attention to the underlying legal and regulatory framework governing financial contracts, particularly as they relate to rural investments; and (4) poor management of rural financial institutions.

321

Since the early 1980s, governments and donors alike have increasingly recognized the importance of encouraging the development of healthy rural financial markets—involving savings mobilization and self-sustaining credit to a variety of rural enterprises—as opposed to intervening exclusively through targeted, subsidized agricultural credit programs. This new paradigm for expanding incomes and reducing poverty in rural areas has spread relatively slowly in many countries, owing in large measure to vested interests in the traditional model and to the challenges involved in selecting and implementing a sharply different set of policy alternatives and institutional designs. Nevertheless, a growing body of evidence from countries ranging from Mexico to Indonesia suggests that, by implementing what have become best practices in rural finance over the past decade and carefully adapting them to the local socioeconomic and cultural settings, it is possible not only to reduce or eliminate the heavy fiscal costs associated with inefficient or inequitable agricultural credit systems but also to promote efficient rural financial markets that vastly improve risk management, resource allocation, and economic development in rural areas.

This chapter identifies key challenges to efficient rural financial intermediation, and characterizes the traditional approach to addressing some of these challenges as well as the shortcomings of this approach. The chapter then presents a strategic framework for the new approach to rural finance that has emerged since the 1980s, including the types of interventions that might be warranted at a policy and institutional level. Next the chapter proposes performance criteria by which the merits of direct interventions in rural financial markets can be assessed, before describing the performance and operations of three rural financial intermediaries (RFIs) that have thus far proven to be highly successful, with a particular focus on the village banks of Bank Rakyat Indonesia.

The Challenge for Rural Financial Intermediation

Financial intermediaries face several challenges that prevent financial markets in general, and rural financial markets in particular, from operating efficiently. Most of the obstacles are related to the promissory nature of financial contracts. Because of the time component of financial contracts, financial intermediaries and their clients require affordable and reliable information to determine the riskiness of transactions, a reasonably stable political and economic environment in which to extend contract maturities, freedom to price perceived risks appropriately, and the ability to exercise remedies when contractual terms are not honored. These conditions are rarely met. The main problems are related to (1) the broader macroeconomic policy context; (2) the sectoral policy context; (3) the legal and regulatory framework; (4) shortcomings in financial markets in general; (5) systemic weaknesses of rural financial markets; and (6) poorly designed interventions.

FIGURE 15.1 Foreign exchange premia and economic rates of return on agricultural projects supported by the World Bank

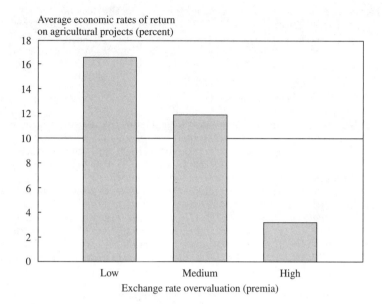

SOURCE: Isham and Kaufmann (1995).
NOTES: "Low" premia are overvaluations of less than 20 percent; "medium" premia are overvaluations of 20–200 percent; "high" premia are overvaluations greater than 200 percent.

The Macroeconomic Environment

Inappropriate macroeconomic policies have often undermined efforts to strengthen financial sectors. Macroeconomic instability affects RFMs directly through monetary variables such as real interest rates, or indirectly via shocks to clients of financial institutions. Persistent distortions in key macroeconomic variables (such as overvalued exchange rates) distort price signals, causing financial markets to channel excessive resources to inefficient sectors and products instead of to sectors and products with comparative advantage. Isham and Kaufmann (1995) found that countries with the highest degree of distortionary macroeconomic policies, as reflected in foreign exchange premia, have had the weakest experience with the performance of their agricultural sector projects (Figure 15.1). This clearly has adverse implications for the rural financial intermediaries that channel resources to such projects.

The Sectoral Policy Context

Government price controls, trade policy, and public investment priorities frequently distort the allocation of resources by financial intermediaries (Box 15.1).

BOX 15.1 The "eight pillars" of urban-biased policies

Past decades have been characterized by policies aimed at achieving accelerated industrial development. These policies have as a rule adversely affected rural areas, frequently to the point of undermining rural development (Schiff and Valdes 1992). Yaron, Benjamin, and Piprek (1997) identify the following "eight pillars" of urban-biased policies as typical of the strategies that have hampered the development of rural communities and the promotion of rural financial markets.

1. Overvalued exchange rates.
2. Excessive taxes on agricultural exports.
3. High effective rates of protection for domestic industry, the outputs of which are used as agricultural inputs.
4. Low, controlled, and seasonally invariant prices of agricultural products.
5. Disproportionately high budgetary allocations for urban, rather than rural, infrastructure (roads, electricity, and water supply).
6. Disproportionately high investment in human resources in urban, rather than rural, areas (health and education).
7. Underdeveloped legal and regulatory provisions regarding land titling and collateral for typical rural assets (land, crops, and farm implements) relative to urban assets (cars, homes, and other durables).
8. Usury laws that rule out the small, risky, and high-cost loans typical in rural areas.

The "eight pillars" of urban-biased policies include, for example, high effective rates of protection for industry, which both raise the costs of agricultural inputs and alter the domestic terms of trade in favor of the industrial sector. When states have intervened to support agriculture, it has often been through inefficient parastatals operating in areas that the private sector can manage better (such as input supply and marketing), while investment in essential public goods, such as rural roads, agricultural research, and public registries, has been neglected.

Legal and Regulatory Constraints

Problems with enforcing contracts increase uncertainty and reduce the expected returns to creditors from financial transactions. Increases in transaction costs reduce the supply of loan and deposit services. In many countries, deficiencies in laws, regulations, and institutions prevent the formal sector from delivering credit to farmers and rural businesses (Fleisig and de la Peña 1996). These impediments may make it difficult for the formal sector to lend to the informal sector and for banks and other financial institutions to lend to nonbank creditors (typically traders) who have many advantages in efficiently reaching poor rural borrowers. Creditors need a system through which claims against property can be created, perfected, and enforced. The more uncertain and expensive this process, the less willing are creditors to lend. Problems can arise in *creating* a mortgage or a claim on movable property because of untitled land, high registration costs, or the absence of legal provisions for future interests. When *perfecting* a claim, there may not be clearly designated, easily accessible registries, and search costs may be high. *Enforcement* of claims on mortgaged land or property can be extremely costly, lengthy, and uncertain. Other laws and regulations that constrain rural financial intermediation include exempting property provisions that prevent rural smallholders from using their smallholdings as collateral and usury laws that rule out small, high-interest loans from formal financial intermediaries.

Financial Market Constraints

Imperfect information and consequent incentive problems, together with financial market rigidities and social barriers to financial transactions, preclude an optimal allocation of resources. The high costs for depositors and other creditors of financial intermediaries to acquire sufficient information to monitor financial intermediaries adequately lead to major moral hazard problems for intermediaries using other people's money. These include over-leveraging, assumption of excessive risks, self-dealing, and fraudulent practices. Externality problems can arise when runs on weak banks spill over to sound ones or high-risk intermediaries draw depositors away from prudent ones. In addition, government policies frequently introduce financial market rigidities, risks, and repression in the form of directed bank lending to inefficient parastatals or to government-targeted sectors, typically at administratively fixed interest rates. Social barriers to financial intermediation include socioeconomic class, caste, ethnicity, and gender barriers, which frequently impede financial exchanges. They also include language, literacy, and numeracy constraints that aggravate information barriers.

Systemic Weaknesses of Rural Financial Markets

Whereas the above limitations affect both urban and rural financial markets, several variables particularly constrain rural financial intermediation. Poverty, low population density, isolated markets, high covariant risk, small-scale transactions, and seasonality often result in high transaction costs, lack of traditional collateral, high income fluctuations, and limited opportunities for risk diversification. These characteristics of rural financial markets often scare off traditional for-profit financial intermediaries. However, these challenges also underscore the benefits the rural poor can gain from access to efficient consumption-smoothing mechanisms and financial services that can help them out of poverty (Benjamin 1994; Zeller et al. 1997). To provide such services in a viable manner requires well-tailored financial products and operating procedures.

Poorly Designed Interventions

Governments have often attempted to address the lack of credit in rural areas through direct interventions. However, as argued in the following section, these well-intended rural financial interventions, involving subsidized credit targeted exclusively to agricultural production, have in practice generally impeded the development of rural financial markets (Von Pischke, Adams, and Donald 1983).

The Traditional Approach to Rural Finance

The "traditional" approach has usually implied a high level of direct government intervention in RFMs in the form of targeted credit, with government-owned and government-managed RFIs receiving concessional loans and on-lending to customers at below-market interest rates. The underlying logic is that agriculture is the mainstay of rural development, that increased food production is needed to feed growing urban populations, that this requires increased agricultural productivity through more advanced technology, and that subsidized interest rates on well-targeted loans would accelerate agricultural modernization and growth. The subsidies on credit and other agricultural inputs (such as fertilizers, pesticides, seeds, water, and electricity) have also been considered as a way of compensating the agricultural sector for the heavy implicit taxation involved in fostering industrial expansion through urban-biased policies.

Although there is some evidence of capital accumulation and agricultural production associated with subsidized credit (Khan 1977; World Bank 1993), the overall experience with the traditional approach has been bleak (Adams, Graham, and Von Pischke 1984; Yaron, Benjamin, and Piprek 1997). In particular, the poor still have inadequate access to credit, savings, and insurance services in most developing countries' rural areas. The disproportionate and often exclusive emphasis on RFIs disbursing agricultural credit has led to the general neglect of portfolio quality, nonfarm rural development, savings mobilization, and efficiency. This is because traditional interventions have typically been based on misconceptions about the real challenges facing rural communities and have been directed toward the symptoms rather than the causes of inadequate rural financial intermediation. For example, low participation in formal financial activities has wrongly been understood to be the result of the poor's inability to save or to pay market rates of interest.

These misconceptions have had several consequences:

- Because rural communities have been perceived as being too poor to save, efforts have concentrated almost exclusively on the provision of credit, ignoring the perhaps more crucial benefit of rural savings facilities.
- Subsidized interest rates have led to RFIs often being perceived as governmental credit disbursement windows rather than self-sustaining financial institutions, which has led to a poor loan repayment culture.

- Employees of state-owned credit institutions have often engaged in rent seeking, giving priority to borrowers willing to share the subsidy inherent in below-market interest rates with them through side-payments.
- The traditional approach has focused on lending for agricultural purposes while ignoring small nonagricultural rural enterprises and, therefore, has neglected opportunities for risk diversification and income growth.
- Subsidized agricultural credit has, at times, resulted in production inefficiencies by targeting the wrong products and by encouraging the adoption of excessively capital-intensive farming technologies (Khan 1977), with the result that low-interest loans have displaced agricultural laborers and have increased rural unemployment.
- The poor design and performance of most state-owned RFIs, and their access to concessional funds and frequent bailouts, have discouraged private for-profit financial intermediaries from engaging in rural financial intermediation.

Even the argument that these subsidies are justified as "compensation" for a poor policy environment fall apart upon closer examination. Schiff and Valdes (1992) found that, from 1960 to 1984, income transfers through all input subsidies averaged only 2 percent of agricultural gross domestic product (GDP) for the 18 countries in their study, whereas indirect interventions resulted in negative transfers of 15 percent of agricultural GDP. Policy distortions affect entire agricultural sectors, but compensation is usually captured by only a few farmers. For example, formal agricultural credit on concessional terms rarely reaches more than 30 percent of the farm sector. Moreover, wealthy, well-connected farmers have usually captured most of the subsidies; very few subsidies have reached the most needy farmers.

The New Approach to Rural Finance

Radical change has long been advocated by a few lone voices (Adams, Graham, and Von Pischke 1984; González-Vega 1984; Vogel 1984). The new approach is, however, gradually becoming mainstream thinking, particularly since the late 1980s, when evidence of "success stories" started becoming known (see section below). The new approach focuses on the primary goals of rural development: income expansion and poverty reduction. It recognizes that providing rural finance may not always be the most cost-effective way of reaching these goals and that effective rural financial intermediation should often be complemented by other government action-oriented policies, such as increased investment in rural infrastructure and in human development. The new approach proposes an active role for government in establishing a favorable policy environment and a sound legal and regulatory framework to facilitate the functioning of rural financial markets, but a more limited and carefully justified role in terms of direct interventions.

A Strategy for Expanding Rural Incomes

There is growing recognition that governments should first and foremost facilitate the workings of markets so that private participants can allocate resources efficiently in response to price and profit signals. This is a fundamental departure from the planning philosophy underlying the traditional approach to rural finance, which held that governments could and should steer agricultural investments in order to achieve more rapid economic growth. Under the new approach, there is no presumption from the outset that "government knows best." Before a case can be made for any interventions, the new approach calls for an analysis of the underlying causes of depressed rural growth. This requires an assessment of the efficiency of rural markets, including rural financial markets, and a determination of the causes of market inefficiencies. These inefficiencies are generally the result of some combination of poor macroeconomic and sectoral policies, a weak legal and regulatory framework, or market failures.

Once the causes of market inefficiencies are identified, governments can review the options available to them by using cost–benefit analyses to determine the most appropriate actions. Generally, addressing policy constraints and strengthening the legal and regulatory framework will create more opportunities and incentives for private participation in rural markets, including RFMs. In order to minimize potential distortions from government interventions, policy reforms and legal and regulatory reforms should take first priority. However, there may still be identifiable market failures, related, for example, to information barriers and unduly high-risk premia that preclude potentially lucrative economic activities, or to the inability of enterprising new entrants in a market to capture the full benefits of their investments. Addressing such market failures may require direct (that is, fiscal and/or institutional) intervention by governments. However, not all market failures can be removed cost-effectively via public interventions. Therefore, the most cost-effective methods of dealing with market failures should be identified and evaluated, taking into account governments' own potential for failures. If market failures cannot be removed cost-effectively, direct interventions aimed at increasing incomes are not justified.

Interventions Aimed at Poverty Reduction

Rapid growth in rural economies is often the most promising way to reduce rural poverty. However, raising average rural incomes may not be sufficient to reduce poverty if economic growth is not shared. Chronic poverty appears to be mainly due not to market failure in credit or other markets, but rather to low factor productivity or low endowments of nonlabor factors per person. Where such conditions persist, even perfect markets may coexist with substantial chronic poverty. To the extent that well-designed market-enhancing interventions can efficiently improve access to credit by those among the poor who are liquidity constrained, they should be welcomed.

Nevertheless, there may also be circumstances in which a program of targeted interventions for poverty reduction is justified, regardless of whether market failures (or cost-effective interventions to remove the market failures) have been identified. In these circumstances, the case for direct interventions is based on social norms and assessment of costs and benefits of alternative, nonfinancial intermediation interventions to reduce poverty. For example, the severity of poverty may compel immediate or short-term actions, such as food aid or financial assistance following natural disasters.

More generally, though, findings by Hulme and Mosley (1996) call into question the effectiveness of poverty-oriented credit schemes in benefiting or even in reaching "the poorest of the poor." In particular, there is evidence that the use of credit differs between the poor and the very poor, with the former applying loans to more risky and productive investments, including technological transformations that can lift them out of poverty, whereas the very poor apply credit to risk-reduction purposes (consumption or low-risk, low-yield production technologies) that generally fail to raise incomes substantially. Indeed it can be counterproductive if excessive peer pressure is applied to force repayments when borrowers face particularly adverse circumstances, so they are obliged to clear their formal debts through costly informal loans or reductions in assets. To sum up, it is hard to maintain that the solution to poverty reduction—beyond the poverty reduction achieved through general expansion in rural incomes—lies solely in targeted credit schemes. Valid alternatives may include targeted food support, employment generation via public works, investment in rural infrastructure, or increased human resource development.

Creating a Favorable Policy Environment

Weaknesses in the policy environment frequently reduce market efficiency and warrant priority in a strategy to promote growth in rural incomes. The main attributes of a favorable policy environment for rural financial intermediation are maintaining macroeconomic stability, removing urban-biased policies, and promoting integrated and resilient financial markets.

ESTABLISHING A FAVORABLE MACROECONOMIC ENVIRONMENT. Both external and internal factors may generate macroeconomic instability. External risks, such as terms of trade shocks, can be diversified by opening domestic markets to foreign investors, or they can be hedged in international options and futures markets. Internal factors include volatile fiscal and monetary policies, as well as political risk. The goals of prudent fiscal and monetary policies should be price stability and sound, well-aligned exchange rates, which foster macroeconomic stability and promote integrated and resilient financial markets.

REMOVING POLICY BIASES AGAINST AGRICULTURE AND RURAL DEVELOPMENT. Rural development in most developing countries has been slowed by policies that favor industry over agriculture and urban over rural sectors. Such policies reduce the profitability of agriculture and nonfarm rural enterprises and inhibit the development of rural financial markets. Working principles for creating an improved environment for agricultural and rural development include establishing a neutral trade regime between agricultural exportables and importables, removing nontariff barriers, realigning overvalued exchange rates, reducing excessive industrial protection, shifting public investment priorities toward rural areas, and increasing participation in community development.

PROMOTING EFFICIENT FINANCIAL MARKETS.   Like other financial intermediaries, RFIs are exposed to risks that can lead to crises. These risks are increased by financial repression, by inappropriate regulation and supervision, and by ill-designed direct interventions in financial markets. Governments can promote financial markets by strengthening the supervision and prudential regulation of financial intermediaries and by introducing measures supporting financial liberalization (including deregulating interest rates, reducing high reserve requirements, and relaxing credit controls). Governments can establish special prudential regulatory requirements for semi-formal institutions operating in rural financial markets that take into account the challenges of accumulating capital and intermediating resources locally. Inefficient policies, such as requiring banks to lend a large proportion of their funds to unremunerative sectors of the economy (such as agricultural parastatals), should be abolished.

Strengthening the Legal and Regulatory Framework

Reforms of systems of secured transactions are relatively new, and there is as yet no outstanding example of comprehensive, successful reform in developing countries. But reform efforts under way in different countries (for example, land titling in Thailand and regulatory reforms in Bolivia) show that, taken together, such reforms should have an impact in developing countries similar to the effect they have had in industrial countries (Fleisig and de la Peña 1996). The legal, regulatory, and institutional changes needed to increase access to credit in rural areas include titling and registering land; reforming the law on secured transactions; reforming legal registries and expanding the scope of private operation; lowering the costs of registration and foreclosure; drafting specific, clear, and limited homestead provisions; and removing interest rate ceilings.

Performance Criteria for Evaluating Rural Financial Institutions

Evaluations of the impact of agricultural credit projects on the farm level are fraught with methodological problems relating to the fungibility of money and the assessment of additionality: would a given agricultural investment simply have been undertaken with alternative resources if a credit program had not provided the investor with a loan? Rigorous econometric studies of these types of questions are often costly and highly specific, making generic application of their findings impossible. Yet attributing "production gains" to access to formal credit can be misleading unless inherent measurement difficulties are overcome. Indeed, production gains have often been attributed to formal credit in an exaggerated and unjustified manner.

A framework for evaluation of RFIs introduced by Yaron (1992) has gained wide acceptance among practitioners and academics. The framework proposes two primary criteria: outreach and self-sustainability (Figure 15.2). It is based on the assumption that RFIs that provide a broad range of services to the target clientele in an efficient manner are likely to have the desired impact of increasing incomes and reducing poverty. Although not constituting a full cost–benefit analysis, evaluating the performance of RFIs based on these criteria can often serve as a quantifiable proxy for the impact of RFIs.

Outreach is measured by several indicators, such as number of clients, average loan size (as a proxy for income level), and percentage of female clients (where it is observed that social norms discriminate against women). Self-sustainability is assessed by calculating an RFI's Subsidy Dependence Index (SDI), which indicates the percentage by which an RFI's average yield earned on its average loan portfolio would have to be increased to make it self-sustainable (that is, subsidy independent). The SDI also indicates the cost to society of subsidizing an RFI measured against the interest earned by the RFI in the marketplace, which is conceptually similar to estimating the matching grant an RFI is enjoying to remain in operation. The main factors that contribute to self-sustainability are adequate on-lending rates and interest rate spreads, high rates of loan collection, high levels of savings mobilization, and low administrative costs.

Examples of Successful Rural Financial Institutions

Three Asian RFIs are widely considered to be successful judged by the two primary performance criteria of outreach and self-sustainability (Table 15.1). They are the Bank for Agriculture and Agricultural Cooperatives (BAAC) in Thailand, the *unit desas* (village banks) of Bank Rakyat Indonesia (BRI-UD), and the Grameen Bank (GB) in Bangladesh. These RFIs have succeeded in providing financial services (credit, savings, and insurance against emergencies) to rural micro-entrepreneurs at unprecedented levels, serving over 20 million people in Thailand, Indonesia, and Bangladesh. Even as they have achieved unprecedented outreach, these institutions have decreased or eliminated their dependency on subsidies, contradicting the long-held presumption that the provision of financial services to rural micro-entrepreneurs can never become a financially viable proposition.

The first common characteristic contributing to the three RFIs' decreased reliance on subsidies is a consistently high rate of on-time loan collections

FIGURE 15.2 Outreach and sustainability

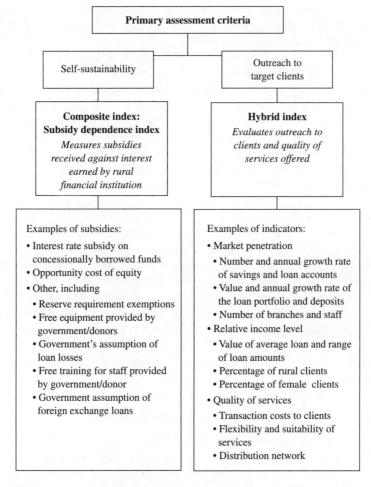

SOURCE: Yaron, Benjamin, and Piprek (1997).

(around 90 percent or more) over a long period of time, although the country-wide floods in Bangladesh in 1998 had a major negative impact on the Grameen Bank's recovery performance. This outcome compares with collection efficiencies of 50 percent or less for large traditional lending programs in several countries. The high on-time collection rate is the result of adhering to financial discipline and applying efficient operating procedures in screening, monitoring, and enforcing loan collection. Moreover, these RFIs have recognized that good loan repayment is essential to break free from dependence on public sources of

TABLE 15.1 Selected outreach and sustainability indicators for three successful rural finance intermediaries

Indicator	Bank Rakya Indonesia–Unit Desas, Indonesia	Bank for Agriculture and Agricultural Cooperatives, Thailand	Grameen Bank, Bangladesh
Outreach			
Target clientele	Rural, low- to middle income	Low- to middle-income farmers	Rural poor
Number of clients (millions of savers/borrowers)	14.5 / 2.3	3.1 / 4.3	2.1 / 2.1
Clients as share of target clientele	Loans: 5 percent Deposits: 20 percent	76 percent of farming population	Half of all villages
Outreach to women (percentage of clients)	25	n.a.	94
Average loan amount as per- centage of GDP/ capita	54	52	64
Sustainability (percent) Operating costs over average assets, 1989	10.90	3.00	9.30
Operating costs over average annual assets, 1995	5.30	2.90	7.00
Interest spread over average loan portfolio, 1995	21.80	4.10	8.00
Return on equity, 1995	136.00	7.10	10.40
Return on assets, 1995	6.10	0.55	0.14

SOURCE: Yaron, Benjamin, and Piprek (1997).

financing, since depositors will place their savings only in soundly managed financial institutions.

A second factor contributing to self-sustainability has been the application of "high" lending interest rates and maintaining relatively "high" financial spreads. Real lending rates in the vicinity of 20 percent and above have often been found necessary to cover costs, but these rates are still substantially lower than the interest rates charged by local moneylenders.

The third factor that explains the superior performance of these three RFIs is the ability to provide financial services while benefiting from economics of scale and substantially reducing their transaction costs (Table 15.1). This was achieved via profit-related incentives for staff (despite being partly or fully state-owned RFIs); strong management information systems that have allowed for improved management of operations and tracking of arrears; and a range of flexible operating procedures and techniques adapted to specific social, economic, and cultural circumstances. These procedures include peer monitoring, mobile banking, streamlined approval procedures for small initial loans (which limits exposure to new clients but rewards timely repayment with larger follow-on loans), and a range of substitutes for traditional collateral requirements and enforcement methods (notably reliance on peers or village chiefs to screen applicants, guarantee borrowers, or encourage repayment of loans).

A final common feature that is important to underscore is the fact that all three RFIs have had fairly high levels of autonomy in formulating operational policies, despite being fully or partially state owned (although both the BAAC and the GB have felt some pressure to contain interest rates below levels that would have allowed them to become fully self-sustaining). From a social point of view the high degree of management autonomy has paid off handsomely: instead of operating as highly subsidized RFIs that serve a limited, usually better-off clientele, the BAAC, the GB, and BRI-UD have reached a wider client base with less reliance on subsidies. This has enabled poor and small-scale entrepreneurs to benefit from diversified formal financial services that are significantly more affordable than those available from informal sources. In the case of BRI-UD, the need for subsidies to support rural financial intermediation has been eliminated completely, and BRI-UD has matured into an exceptionally profitable institution with particularly successful outreach in rural areas. This success warrants further analysis to identify replicable features of the BRI-UD methodology.

The Exceptional Experience of BRI-UD

BRI-UD was established in 1984, on the vestiges of the BIMAS (Mass Guidance) program of directed credit for rice intensification. The BIMAS credit program had essentially accomplished its goal of making Indonesia self-sufficient in rice production in the mid-1970s, but by the early 1980s the program was becoming increasingly unsustainable, owing to subsidized interest rates, poor loan repayment, and employee incentives directed toward credit disbursement rather than profits. Increasing expenses related to BIMAS credits and declining government revenues forced the Indonesian government radically to alter the mission of the BIMAS program. The BIMAS credit program was transformed into BRI-UD, which had to provide rural financial services on a self-sustaining basis or be disbanded. With a relatively small initial subsidy in 1984, BRI-UD became profitable in just over two years and became a world-leading rural financial intermediary. By the end of 1995, BRI-UD was serving around 2.3 million borrowers and 14.5 million savers. Sustained profitability was achieved through, among other things, substantial market penetration of the rural low-income clientele.

Governance and Institutional Strategy

The most fundamental change that occurred in moving from BIMAS to BRI-UD was to ensure appropriate governance, by granting management broad control over operational decisions and holding them accountable for BRI-UD's financial performance. Indeed, BRI-UD became an independent profit center within Bank Rakyat Indonesia in 1984. With external technical assistance, BRI-UD immediately established new strategies and objectives: namely, it set about engaging in genuine financial intermediation to the broader low-income rural population on a self-sustaining basis, rather than leaning on government to support targeted credit for agriculture.

New Products and Modes of Delivery

This change in strategy involved designing new loan and savings products tailored to the demands of the rural clientele, as well as low-cost delivery systems for providing these financial services. In particular, small one-year loans are provided for all viable income-generating activities on an individual basis, and collateral is strongly desired but not mandatory. The application process takes only about one week for a new borrower and less time for a repeat customer. On the deposits side, BRI-UD offers four choices of savings instruments, with generally positive real interest rates that depend on account size and liquidity. BRI-UD has over 3,500 unit offices and 430 village posts in rural areas; wherever the volume of business is relatively small, mobile offices are introduced that provide limited services, visiting clients once or twice a week.

Cost-Containment, Pricing, and Spreads

These techniques combined with a growing volume of business have allowed BRI-UD to cut operating costs (excluding loan loss provisions) as a percentage of average annual assets from 15.1 percent in 1985 to 5.3 percent in 1995 (Table 15.2), which is very low in the microfinance business. Loan loss expenses are also kept low: because the small loan amounts (US$512 per borrower in 1995) and relatively costly legal procedures make the cost of pursuing foreclosure prohibitive, clients are screened based on available information and are given incentives for repayment with interest rebates of 12 percent per annum and access to additional, larger loans. The client incentives, together with performance-related incentives for staff, have led to consistently high recovery rates (with around 95 percent on-time repayments) and thus to low loan losses.

TABLE 15.2 Outreach and financial self-sustainability of Bank Rakyat Indonesia–Unit Desas

Indicator	1985	1990	1995
Outreach			
Average annual loan volume (US$ million)	162.0	562.0	1,178.0
Number of outstanding loans (million)	1.0	1.9	2.3
Average outstanding loan amount per borrower (US$)	162.0	296.0	512.0
Average annual deposit volume (US$ million)	49.0	685.0	2,382.0
Number of deposit accounts (million)	n.a.	7.3	14.5
Average deposit amount per saver (US$)	n.a.	94.0	164.0
Financial self-sustainability (percent)			
Nominal average yield earned on the loan portfolio	27.4	31.5	31.6
Nominal average interest rate paid on deposits	10.5	11.3	9.7
Nominal interest rate spread	16.8	20.2	21.8
Inflation	4.7	7.4	9.4
Real average yield earned on the loan portfolio	21.7	22.4	20.2
Real average interest rate paid on deposits	5.6	3.6	0.3
Lowest nominal lending interest rate needed for financial self-sustainability	36.2	27.2	17.5
Lowest real lending interest rate needed for financial self-sustainability	30.1	18.4	7.3
Operating costs as a percentage of			
Average annual net loan portfolio	20.5	12.9	12.6
Half of the average annual net loan portfolio and deposits	31.5	11.6	8.3
Average annual total assets	15.1	8.0	5.3
Profits (US$ million)	–0.8	34.3	170.2
Percentage of profitable units	48.3	89.1	95.7
Average annual deposit volume / average annual loan portfolio volume	0.31	1.22	2.02
Subsidy Dependence Index	32.2	–13.7	–44.5

SOURCE: Yaron, Benjamin, and Piprek (1997).

FIGURE 15.3 Nominal lending and deposit interest rates of Bank Rakyat
Indonesia–Unit Desas

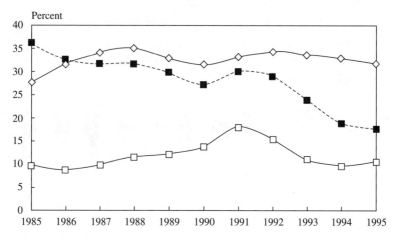

SOURCE: Charitonenko, Patten, and Yaron (1998).

BRI-UD applies relatively high loan and deposit interest rates while maintaining a lucrative interest rate spread to cover the costs of servicing small
loans and deposits. The interest rates charged on loans are designed to ensure
that the full financial, operational, and credit risk costs are covered. The average annual yield earned on loans has oscillated around 32 percent over recent
years while average annual financial costs have been about 10 percent. This has
resulted in a substantial average spread of slightly above 20 percent (Table 15.2
and Figure 15.3).

Systems and Staffing

BRI-UD has developed its own management tools, including an extremely
efficient management information system that allows management to assess the
performance of each unit and apply a sophisticated employee incentive system
that encourages profitability, loan recovery, and savings mobilization. In particular, BRI-UD's more than 21,000 employees and trainees are eligible to
receive 10 percent of their respective *unit desa*'s annual profits as a bonus compensation, up to 1.5 months' salary per employee. By replacing the inadequate
civil service pay scales with a performance-related incentive system, the focus

FIGURE 15.4 Subsidy Dependence Index of Bank Rakyat Indonesia–Unit Desas

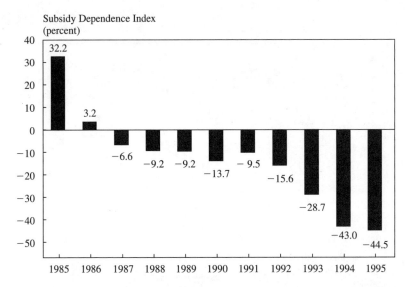

SOURCE: Charitonenko, Patten, and Yaron (1998).

of BRI-UD's staff and management has shifted from credit disbursement to motivating loan recovery and savings mobilization.

The Financial Bottom Line

Between 1985 and 1995 the share of BRI-UD units that was profitable doubled from 48 percent to 96 percent. In 1995, BRI-UD earned a net income of Rp 407 billion (US$170 million at the then prevailing exchange rate) on a beginning-of-year capital of Rp 99 billion—an astounding 407 percent return on start-of-year capital—which translated into an exceptionally high 6.1 percent return on assets. The Subsidy Dependence Index (SDI) of the BRI-UD turned negative in 1987 and the RFI has remained self-sufficient ever since (Figure 15.4). In 1995 BRI-UD could have reduced its on-lending rates by more than 40 percent (from 31.6 to 17.5 percent) and remained subsidy independent.

The outstanding performance of BRI-UD in Indonesia demonstrates that financial self-sufficiency can be achieved through the adoption of innovative operating policies that meet the demand for financial services from low-income, rural clients. BRI-UD has succeeded in reaching financial self-sustainability while providing credit and savings services to rural low-income families, the vast majority of which have never previously had access to formal financial intermediation services.

Conclusion

Considerable progress has been made over the past 20 years in developing cost-effective approaches to providing rural financial services. The underlying paradigm has begun to shift since the 1980s from a traditional approach based on subsidized lines of credit to targeted agricultural beneficiaries, toward the provision of genuine rural financial intermediation through both savings and credit services for rural populations. This paradigm shift has not occurred more completely owing to delays in transferring, adapting, and applying successful methodologies in new contexts, as well as to the lack of political visibility of or support for policy reforms that could in certain cases reduce returns for powerful vested interests. Thus, for example, BRI's village banks are run profitably, but BRI's traditional lines of agricultural credit, which are still extended through the broader banking network, continue to be unprofitable at current lending rates and still experience weak collection efficiency. Similarly, throughout East Asian and other emerging economies, reforms in prudential regulations and supervision, as well as in the legal and regulatory framework governing the creation, perfection, and enforcement of collateral pledged under credit contracts, have not been introduced as rapidly as is desirable. With hindsight, policy and regulatory shortcomings such as these contributed in large measure to creating the preconditions for the financial crisis in East Asia, and help to explain the delays in restructuring and recovery from the crisis.

At the institutional level, the experience of successful RFIs, especially the *unit desas* of BRI, suggests that rural and microfinancial services not only can be provided to low-income rural clients at lower costs than previously thought possible, but also can be provided in many instances while reducing or even eliminating the need for subsidies. Indeed, the simple, innovative, and largely replicable techniques adopted by BRI-UD have generated enormous returns for the bank, pointing the way for providers of rural financial services in other countries that wish to adapt and customize lessons from this new and promising approach to rural finance for their own socioeconomic and cultural environments. The key lesson from BRI-UD's experience is very clear: rural finance can be highly profitable, even when it serves low-income clients.

References

Adams, D. W., D. Graham, and J. D. Von Pischke. 1984. *Undermining rural development with cheap credit*. Boulder, Colo., U.S.A.: Westview Press.

Benjamin, M., Jr. 1994. Credit schemes for microenterprises: Motivation, design, and viability. Ph.D. dissertation, Georgetown University, Washington, D.C.

Charitonenko, S., R. Patten, and J. Yaron. 1998. Bank Rakyat Indonesia—Unit Desa 1970–1996. Draft Case Study for the Sustainable Banking with the Poor Project. Processed. Africa Technical Department, World Bank, Washington, D.C.

Fleisig, H., and N. de la Peña. 1996. *Creating a legal and regulatory framework to promote access to rural credit.* Washington, D.C.: Center for the Economic Analysis of Law.

González-Vega, C. 1984. Credit-rationing behavior of agricultural lenders: The iron law of interest rate restrictions. In *Undermining rural development with cheap credit*, ed. D. Adams, D. Graham, and J. D. Von Pischke. Boulder, Colo., U.S.A.: Westview Press.

Hulme, D., and P. Mosley. 1996. *Finance against poverty.* London: Routledge.

Isham, J., and D. Kaufmann. 1995. *The forgotten rationale for policy reform: The productivity of investment projects.* Policy Research Working Paper No. 1549. Washington, D.C.: European and Central Asian Country Department IV, World Bank.

Khan, A. R. 1977. *Poverty and landlessness in rural Asia.* Geneva: International Labour Organization.

Schiff, M., and A. Valdes. 1992. *The plundering of agriculture in developing countries.* Washington, D.C.: World Bank.

Vogel, R. 1984. Savings mobilization: The forgotten half of rural finance. In *Undermining rural development with cheap credit*, ed. D. W Adams, D. Graham, and J. D. Von Pischke. Boulder, Colo., U.S.A.: Westview Press.

Von Pischke, J. D., D. Adams, and G. Donald, eds. 1983. *Rural financial markets in developing countries: Their use and abuse.* Baltimore, Md., U.S.A.: Johns Hopkins University Press.

World Bank. 1993. *A review of bank lending for agricultural credit and rural finance (1948–1992).* Operations Evaluation Department Report No. 12143. Washington, D.C.: World Bank.

Yaron, J. 1992. *Assessing development finance institutions—A public interest analysis.* Discussion Paper No. 174. Washington, D.C.: World Bank.

Yaron, J., M. Benjamin, and G. Piprek. 1997. *Rural finance—Issues, design, and best practices.* Environmentally and Socially Sustainable Development Studies and Monograph Series No. 14. Washington, D.C.: World Bank.

Zeller, M., G. Schrieder, J. von Braun, and F. Heidhues. 1997. *Rural finance for food security for the poor: Implications for research and policy.* Food Policy Review No. 4. Washington, D.C.: International Food Policy Research Institute.

16 Credit Systems for the Rural Poor in the Economic Transition of China: Institutions, Outreach, and Policy Options

ZHU LING, JIANG ZHONGYI, AND JOACHIM VON BRAUN

Since undertaking market-oriented reforms in the late 1970s, China has enjoyed rapid economic growth and a substantial reduction in poverty. As a result the country's financial system is under increasing pressure to adjust to the new economic outlook. Rural China, for instance, lacks a comprehensive social security system (especially for farm households). The financial system can address this problem by providing access to credit and savings services that will help rural residents (especially the poor) fund production and consumption activities and overcome food and income crises. But the formal financial system has not extended its credit services to the rural poor, and low repayment rates have made credit programs designed to reduce poverty impossible to sustain. For this reason, one of the top priorities on China's current policy agenda is creating innovative microfinance programs. The government has already launched several experimental programs.

The growing interest in microfinance raises a number of issues important to understanding the current situation and to designing alternative policy options. These include

- the creation and operation of financial institutions in rural areas;
- the kinds of outreach these institutions offer rural groups, especially the poor;
- the determinants of access to credit for the rural poor, through either formal or informal institutions;
- the effects of new institutional arrangements promoting microfinance;
- recent experiences with microfinance pilot programs in rural China; and
- alternative policy options for reforming rural financial institutions and facilitating access to credit for the poorest groups.

This chapter addresses these issues and provides some policy conclusions.

This chapter is a revised version of one that appeared in Zeller and Sharma (2000) and is reproduced with permission from the German Foundation for International Development (DSE).

Rural Poverty in China

In China the poor are officially defined as those who were once able to work but have fallen into poverty. The country has a serious labor surplus. Against this background, poverty in rural areas is increasingly the result of unemployment and underemployment related to the structural adjustment and enterprise reforms that are part of the development process and economic transition. Another type of poverty, "transient poverty," is generally caused by natural disasters and failures of market competition. Poverty is also associated with inflation and personal misfortune.

China is unique among transition economies (including Russia and most East European countries) in that the rural poor are in the majority. The poorest citizens are concentrated in rural areas in the northwest and southwest. In 1995, after 10 years of large-scale poverty alleviation programs, the percentage of poor in these regions was more than 10 percent—at least 3 percentage points higher than the national average (IRD/CASS/SSB 1996).[1] Most of the poor work or have worked in the agricultural sector, and they are concentrated in regions with adverse living conditions (a lack of resources or an underdeveloped economic and social infrastructure).

Owing to the distribution of land (including usufruct) within rural villages, China has no landless poor. The profile of the rural poor in China is typical of developing countries and includes low literacy rates, poor health, and a lack of marketable skills. This profile is both the result of poverty and the reason the poor tend to become poorer.

Government Responses

Along with individual donations and international development assistance, significant public funding is being channeled into antipoverty initiatives. The resources committed by the central government to alleviate rural poverty at present total around 15.3 billion yuan annually (this is in addition to the conventional preferential policies favoring poor people and the areas where they live, such as fiscal transfers to local governments, income transfers to individuals, and tax reductions and exemptions).[2] Three types of funding are used to finance the three types of poverty alleviation policies and programs carried out in poor areas (Office of the State Council 1997):

- Budgetary funds for assisting less developed areas by investing in social infrastructure (18 percent of available resources).

---

1. In 1995, the rural poverty line was set at a per capita annual net income of 530 yuan, which was equivalent to one-fourth of the urban poverty line. In the same year the rural poor totaled about 6,500 million people.

2. One U.S. dollar was equal to about 8 yuan.

- Funding for public works programs to improve the economic infrastructure (26 percent of resources).
- Subsidized credits to stimulate local investment activities (56 percent).

The credit program is the largest antipoverty scheme in rural China. The loans have been distributed through and managed mainly by public financial institutions in rural areas.

Financial Systems in Rural Areas

The credit programs for poverty reduction were designed within the context of overall economic reforms. The reforms have affected the institutions that administer antipoverty programs as well as the programs themselves.

Reforms of the National Banking System

Unlike the Central and East European countries that underwent "shock therapy" during the transition, China has adopted gradualism. This policy has had at least two important advantages: fewer economic recessions and social disturbances. But it has also had disadvantages, including rent-seeking activities and irregularities in the operation of the part-market, part-planned economy of the transition.

In the initial stage of the reforms, economic decentralization and the growing interactions between the Chinese economy and the world market led to the dissolution of the existing mono-banking system. One of the components of the new central banking system was rural public financial institutions. During the 1980s and 1990s, the authorities also introduced a growing number of Western-style monetary policy instruments.

Since then the level of monetization (M2/GDP) of the Chinese economy has grown dramatically, increasing from 86.47 percent in 1990 to 106.06 percent in 1995 (Shi Wei 1998). Diversified financial markets (including insurance, portfolio, and foreign exchange markets) are gradually being developed. These developments have spurred further reorganization of the country's financial institutions. Since 1994 the central bank (the People's Bank of China) no longer provides loans, but instead focuses on stabilizing the Chinese currency and supervising other financial institutions. Three new banks have been established to deal with the credit business formerly handled by four sectoral banks, and these four banks are being transformed into state-owned commercial banks (Pei Chuanzhi 1996).

Despite these reforms, the efficiency of the Chinese financial system is far from what is required by a market economy: the autonomy of the central bank cannot be guaranteed; the various levels of government still exert tremendous influence on the way credit is distributed; interest rates are determined primarily by the central government; the financial system consists exclusively of public institutions; and state-owned banks still handle nearly 80 percent of China's savings and credit business. This scenario has developed because the reforms have aimed to combine market forces with a socialist framework that officially implies public ownership of the economy. Thus private domestic institutions cannot gain entry to the banking sector, although 139 foreign financial institutions are already doing limited business in a few cities. Top-level policymakers may also see the current institutional infrastructure as providing them with an easy means of intervening directly in the macroeconomic realm.

The monopolistic position of state-owned banks has segmented the financial markets, reduced the efficiency of the entire financial system, and impaired the effectiveness of macroeconomic management by the central bank. In addition, numerous state-owned industrial enterprises that incur large losses have impeded the transformation of sectoral banks into commercial banks. In the mid-1990s, at least 20 percent of sectoral banks' 2,400 billion yuan in outstanding loans were bad debts, mainly from loss-making state enterprises (He Dexu 1995). Furthermore, a number of banking and nonbanking financial institutions have violated laws and regulations, setting up risky businesses and speculating. Many have already incurred considerable losses (Dai Xianglong 1996). Because of the Asian financial crisis, the central government and the People's Bank have strengthened actions to regulate the financial market. But serious corruption and financial crimes are still being uncovered, revealing the weaknesses of the risk-control mechanisms and supervision systems. The Chinese financial system and its methods of operation must be changed further in line with the economic reforms.

Rural Financial Institutions

One of the outcomes of the rural reforms and economic development has been the formation and expansion of formal rural financial institutions. Following the abolition of the People's Communes in the early 1980s, some 230 million peasant farms emerged, creating enormous demand for financial services, especially credit. Because the farmers had land tenure and owned their produce, they had strong incentives to invest more, produce more, and sell more. Rural nonagricultural enterprises managed or supported directly by local governments developed rapidly. Against this background, the Agricultural Bank of China (ABC) and the Rural Credit Cooperative (RCC) were separated from the central bank. In late 1994 the Agricultural Development Bank of China (ADB) was set up as a rural policy bank. The three banks provide a framework for the formal financial system in rural areas (Figure 16.1).

These three institutions remain relatively stable, even as the reforms continue. The ADB is authorized to provide state agencies with low-interest, government-subsidized loans for purchasing, storing, distributing, marketing, and processing major agricultural products such as foodgrain, cotton, oil seeds, pork, and sugar. It is also authorized to distribute loans aimed at alleviating

FIGURE 16.1 Organizational structure of formal financing institutions in rural China, 1995–96

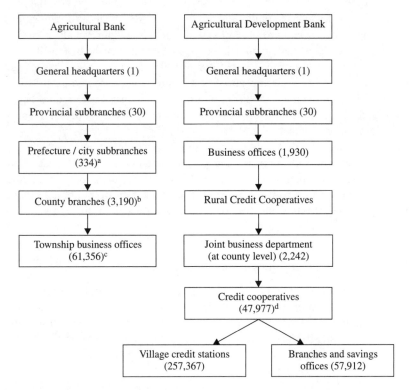

SOURCES: State Statistics Bureau (1996:613, 617); Editorial Office (1996:546); Agricultural Development Bank of China (1996:7).
a Includes 14 subbranches in cities, covered by a separate state plan.
b Includes 834 offices located on the outskirts of cities.
c Includes 26,960 savings offices.
d Includes 675 rural credit cooperatives in joint villages and 185 in villages.

poverty, promoting technological improvements, and capital construction. At present, however, the ABC distributes these kinds of loans, because the ADB is not yet fully operational.

The ABC, which was one of four state-owned sectoral banks, is now in the process of becoming a commercial bank. Its structure follows that of the national administration—that is, it is a hierarchy with headquarters in Beijing and branches in provinces, prefecture cities, counties, and big townships. The RCC is a public financial institution similar to the ABC. Though policymakers expect the branches of the RCC to become real cooperative organizations like those in other market economies, so far these transformations have not taken place (State Council 1996).

Both the ABC and RCC mobilize savings from rural households, but only the RCC provides loans to individual farmers. The ABC finances organizations belonging to the agricultural support system, including industrial and commercial enterprises. This fundamental division of labor between the two institutions is administratively stipulated (State Council 1996). Every township has at least one RCC. The RCC's savings and credit business is transacted by full-time credit officers or by village credit stations managed by part-time credit officers. Clearly, the RCC is the only formal financial institution penetrating to the grassroots level of rural society.

The system should be able to extend its services to farmers' households. However, because state agencies and government-supported enterprises have been given priority in providing credit, the formal financial system cannot meet farmers' demand for credit. As a result (and in addition to traditional private lending among families and friends), various informal credit organizations have emerged.

Participation in Credit Systems for the Rural Poor

The rationale for providing credit to poor people is to support their efforts to create new sources of income through investment activities and to facilitate consumption. Even under normal conditions, poor people's income flows fluctuate substantially from one season or year to another. Access to credit and savings services can help reduce both the magnitude of these fluctuations and the adverse effects on basic consumption levels (Zeller et al. 1997).

A sample survey of 1,920 rural households was conducted in 1993. The households were selected from 34 villages in 12 provinces with a fair amount of regional disaggregation (Zhu, Jiang, and von Braun 1997). The results distinguish between "poor households" and "nonpoor households." The poverty line for households is 600 yuan, and 30 percent of the households sampled fall below this poverty line. Comparisons of the mean values of key variables such as income and consumption of major food items suggest that the sample comes close to reflecting the average of the poor regions of rural China in the early 1990s.

A comparison of loan sources and patterns of utilization for poor and nonpoor households produces the following findings (Figures 16.2 and 16.3):

1. A slightly larger ratio of poor households obtained a loan (31 percent of poor households, compared with 27 percent of nonpoor households).
2. The pattern of loan sources did not differ much between poor and nonpoor households. Poor households received a slightly lower percentage from banks (29 percent) than nonpoor households (32 percent); in both groups,

FIGURE 16.2 Loan structure and use pattern among poor households in rural China

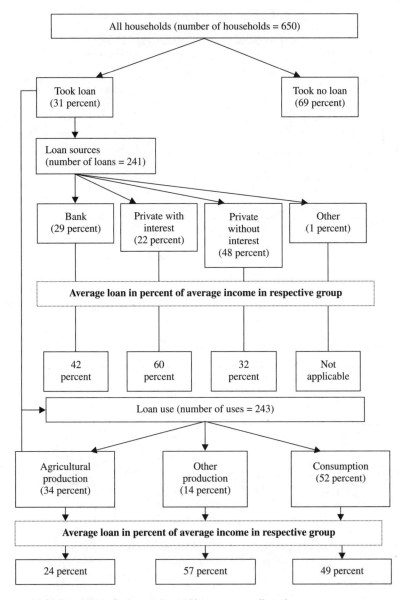

NOTE: Multiple responses for loan source and loan use were allowed.

348   *Zhu Ling, Jiang Zhongyi, and Joachim von Braun*

FIGURE 16.3 Loan structure and use pattern among nonpoor households in rural China

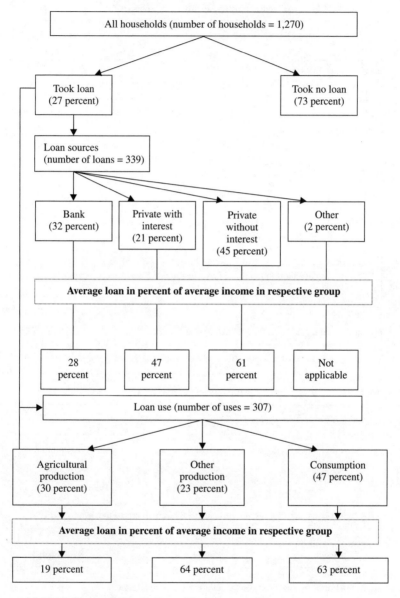

NOTE: Multiple responses for loan source and loan use were allowed.

private loans without interest were the most frequent source of credit (48 and 45 percent, respectively).
3. Private loans clearly are important sources of financing in poor areas of China, representing quite significant proportions of present annual income.
4. Bank loans tended to be smaller than loans from private sources, including private loans that accrue interest. Relative to income, bank loans were more prevalent among poor than among nonpoor households (42 percent versus 28 percent, respectively).

Anyone who obtained a loan from a formal source was considered to have participated in the formal segment of the credit system in the year under observation (1993). Similarly, anyone who obtained a loan from an informal or private source was considered to have participated in that sector of the rural finance system.[3] To present the determinants of participation briefly for each sector (formal and informal), a univariate probit approach was used, as follows:

Probability of participation = f(institutional environment,

infrastructure environment, asset base of household,

human resource situation of household),

where participation is a $(0,1)$ dummy variable (1 if the household obtained some credit, and 0 otherwise) (Table 16.1). Our analysis shows that institutional-level factors, especially the level of banking activity in the province, and infrastructure are significant determinants of participation in the formal sector. Household-level economic factors, including human resource factors, seem to play only a limited role in determining participation or nonparticipation.

Our analysis indicates, first, that the penetration of financial services in a province seems to have a favorable effect on the probability of obtaining loans from private sources in the same province. That is, wherever the formal sector is more active, the private informal sector also seems to be stimulated, with the effect of improving participation. The two sectors seem to move together to some extent.

To estimate the quantitative impact of the determinants identified in the probit model, the Heckmann procedure was employed for each of the formal and informal sectors, using the subsample of those households that actually obtained loans. The regression analysis showed that the size of the asset base is of similar significance for both formal and informal loans and is even more

---

3. Although the data set described above offers opportunities to address all these questions to some extent, certain limitations prevent a fully satisfactory analytical approach. These limitations apply, in particular, to distinguishing among the possibilities of access, especially a more specific separation of the determinants of willingness to borrow and the constraints on borrowing (Zeller et al. 1997). A comprehensive analysis of the frequency and consequences of being subject to credit constraints cannot be performed in this context. The analysis is therefore largely confined to the determinants and effects of participation in credit systems.

TABLE 16.1 Determinants of participation in credit systems in rural China

Variable	Regression Coefficient	*t*-Values
Formal credit sector (results of probit model estimates)		
HOUSIZE	0.0355	1.48
ASSETS	−0.00001	−0.85
LAND	0.0058	0.34
DISTANCE	−0.0204	−1.12
EDUCAT	0.0535	0.97
AGEHEAD	0.0096	0.22
PROVBANK	0.6814	6.88
Intercept	−2,004	−8,078
Informal credit sector (results of probit model estimates)		
HOUSIZE	0.0418	2.11
ASSETS	−0.00001	−1.03
LAND	−0.0403	−2.46
DISTANCE	0.0157	1.04
EDUCAT	−0.0743	−1.68
AGEHEAD	−0.0750	−2.18
PROVBANK	0.1661	2.31
Intercept	−0.635	−3.25

NOTES: $N = 1,797$. Description of variables (mean values in parentheses):

HOUSIZE (4.59)   = household size (persons)

ASSETS (2403.37) = household assets and deposits per capita (in yuan)

LAND (2.38)   = per capita land area (in mu)

DISTANCE (1.85) = distance of village from road (in kilometers)

EDUCAT (2.28)   = education level of household's main income earner (grade achieved)

AGEHEAD (2.69)   = age of head of household (1 = 20–30, 2 = 30–40)

PROVBANK (0.55) = intensity of banking in the province (1 if more than 10 percent of households obtained credit, 0 otherwise)

significant in the private informal sector. This result implies that asset-poor households may be largely excluded from participation in credit systems.

Additional information not presented suggests that, of the different types of property, a household's monetary deposits are most significantly correlated with the size of loan obtained (correlation coefficient = .53). The greater the deposits a household has made in the RCCs, the larger the amounts of money it borrows (or is allowed to borrow) from the institutions. This result was interpreted by the RCCs' credit officers in interviews. The RCCs prefer monetary deposits as loan guarantees, for two reasons. First, the institutions are not permitted to trade land in the market, and, second, the market for other assets in rural areas, especially in poor regions, is not well developed.

Credit Programs Designed to Reduce Poverty

Chinese policymakers considered the shortage of funds for poor areas an obstacle to development and a constraint on poor residents' ability to finance production and consumption activities and overcome food and income crises. Credit programs to reduce poverty were designed to solve these problems, but the designers always confronted a difficult policy issue: how to make financial service systems accessible to the poor while ensuring that financial institutions remain viable and sustainable.

Loans in these programs have interest rates at least 20 percent lower than normal official interest rates (2.88 percent in 1993 and 4.70 percent in 1995) and a term of one to three years. Initially these subsidized loans were to be granted to enterprises in poor areas by the ABC and to individual households through the RCCs. From 1986–87, direct loans to the poor accounted for 60 percent of the total volume of subsidized credits (ABC 1987). Unfortunately, a large number of the loan programs targeting households failed for three reasons. First, poor borrowers lacked the skills to manage investment projects and fulfill payment obligations. Second, technical assistance and marketing services were insufficient. Third, the RCCs, with relatively fewer credit officers, could not effectively supervise the volume of these loan programs within existing institutional frameworks.

In response to this lack of success, the share of lending to households declined to around 20 percent of the subsidized loans in the early 1990s. The programs targeted mainly the enterprises and service organizations involved in poverty reduction. These groups aimed to reduce poverty by providing jobs and services for the poor or by involving poor households in the enterprises themselves (Office of the Leading Group 1989). In fact, most enterprises and governmental institutions took advantage of the subsidized loans to implement their projects in locations with relatively favorable natural and economic conditions. Thus, poverty reduction loans have been used chiefly in comparatively rich areas located near the towns, public roads, and factories of poor counties. The beneficiaries of the projects have typically not been poor households but the projects' organizing units and the average nonpoor households participating in the projects.

Parallel to the change in the composition of the recipient group, the emphasis of credit use shifted from the agricultural to the nonagricultural sector. In 1986 and 1987, agricultural loans made up about 55 percent of subsidized credits (ABC 1988). By 1992–93, this share had declined to 30 percent. Repayments of loans by enterprises have remained at a disappointing 50 percent or less (Office of the Leading Group 1998). This level is much lower than the average rate of loan recovery on regular credits issued by the ABC and RCCs (around 88 and 84 percent, respectively) (Editorial Office 1996).

The bad debt was the result of several factors. First, because of direct intervention by local governments, banks cannot select the projects they want to finance. Many projects organized by governmental groups failed, and a number of the enterprises directly or indirectly established by the governments have incurred losses. As a result, project organizers and enterprises are not able to repay their loans. Second, the credit programs include so many welfare components (for instance, subsidies) that many borrowers try to keep the funds as long as possible. And, finally, in the current transition period the systems for enforcing legal agreements and social contracts have been far from effective. This has encouraged many borrowers to violate their contracts.

Institutional Experiments at the Grassroots Level

Subsidized credit programs have not made financial services any more accessible to the poor, nor have they generated higher efficiencies in the use of loans. For these reasons various new organizational forms of rural financing have been created.

Semi-Formal Organizations

Semi-formal organizations, supported by line ministries and recognized by the central bank, include cooperative foundations (initiated by the Ministry of Agriculture) and mutual assistance savings associations (MASAs, initiated by the Ministry of Civil Affairs). Cooperative foundations were established in one-third of the townships in rural China and compete with the RCCs for business. The foundations may lend only to those residents who hold shares in or have made deposits at the institution. MASAs were set up in 173,000 villages (more than one-fifth of China's villages), mainly in poor and disaster-prone regions. The major activities of these associations are food insecurity and emergencies, but well-managed MASAs have also provided production and consumer loans as well as relief measures for the poor. Credits are limited to a maximum loan size of 500 yuan, and the longest duration of a loan is one year. The MASAs' resources consist of members' savings, state relief, subsidies from village collectives, and donations. Typically, the resources are divided into three parts. One part is deposited in RCCs, banks, and insurance companies; the second part is used for loans to members; and the third part is loaned to nonmember enterprises.

Microlending Programs

Since the early 1990s, foreign financial assistance to China has increased, bringing with it new institutional forms and new methods of project management. One of the most vigorous institutional experiments with foreign aid is rural microfinance for the poor. The two most common approaches, used by the Grameen Bank of Bangladesh and the rural general loan project of Bank Rakyat of Indonesia, have been adapted to local conditions. In 1996 and 1997 eight provincial governments adopted the experiment, promoting microlending programs for the poor with local budget funds and subsidized loans. According to incomplete statistics, microfinance programs financed with either foreign aid or domestic resources can be found in 201 poor counties (representing 34 percent of the counties designated as poor by the state). The programs cover about 200,000 poor households and have a total volume of credit funds of approximately 200 million yuan (Morduch, Park, and Wang 1997; Zhu, Jiang, and von Braun 1997).

Small loans (averaging 1,000 yuan) have been channeled through the ABC, the RCCs, project management systems, or quasi-nongovernmental organizations (NGOs).[4] In most cases the member-based credit groups that are formed use the Grameen Bank's approach—lending with guarantees based on the "social capital" of the group and amortizing the loans at group meetings. Compared with MASAs, microlending programs that receive strong management assistance and offer noncredit services from project offices have extremely high rates of loan repayment—over 90 percent for most experiments (Wu Guobao 1998). Peer supervision and savings mobilization are largely responsible for these results.

Unlike traditional subsidized loan programs, the new microlending programs have reached the poor directly. The selection process is strict and the criteria for recipients clearly defined. Priority is given to women from poor households, who receive loans as group members but implement investment projects with their households. In this way, microlending programs not only help poor households create assets and opportunities for self-employment but also improve the status of women in rural society.

Microfinance programs in China differ from their counterparts in Asia. The Chinese model is characterized by external management assistance and often suffers from government interference. All the credit groups have been closely guided by project officers, most of whom are public servants temporarily seconded to lending programs. They are not specialists. Although they receive short-term training and in turn train members of the credit groups, they are still less skilled than employees of formal financial institutions. It is not clear whether these officers will continue working with the groups when the projects are over, or even if the groups can be sustained without continuing external management assistance.[5]

---

4. For example, the ABC channel has been used by the International Fund for Agricultural Development, the World Food Programme, and the Australian development agencies for the credit components of their projects. The UN Children's Fund (UNICEF), the UN Development Fund for Women (UNIFEM), and the World Bank have adopted the RCC channel. The Ford Foundation, the UN Development Programme, and OXFAM favor the project management systems. Programs financed only from domestic sources use all of the distribution channels.

5. In the past, MASAs found that a number of groups were paralyzed by the unfavorable legal framework, low literacy rates among people in poor areas, and a lack of credit management skills within the organizations. Leaders also abused their power, and individual members violated their contracts.

The government's power penetrates from the central administration to the grassroots level in rural areas through the administrative network. The few NGOs that operate in rural areas are very weak, and some areas have no NGO activity at all. One problem is trust: without an official introduction, local people are unlikely to accept outsiders with new projects. Credit programs that rely on foreign aid collaborate with governmental institutions or involve local officials as project officers. (In fact, the NGO leadership that implements microfinance programs consists mostly of such officials, and their organizations are thus called quasi-NGOs.) Local governments launch the domestically funded micro-lending programs. The advantage of involving local authorities is that governments at different levels can easily transfer information and technical services from existing rural economic support systems into the microfinance programs. The disadvantage is that government intervention may have rendered the poor only passive participants in the implementation process. The risk of investment failures (similar to those in earlier subsidized loan programs) is therefore very high.

Credit utilization is not linked to savings mobilization. Both quasi-NGOs and projects receiving foreign assistance are legally allowed to undertake financial dealings. They can distribute loans, as long as the interest rates are below the average official rates, but they are not allowed to take deposits. At present, interest on loans to members of credit groups is around 7 percent, a rate that barely lets quasi-NGOs cover their operating costs. Even though the direct costs of the projects are relatively low because project officers are paid by the government and subsidies are often provided by local budgets, the initial capital tends to shrink. The financial sustainability of many microlending programs is thus in doubt.

Policy Conclusions

MICROLENDING PROGRAMS ARE REACHING THE POOR.   Nonpoor and average households are often the first to benefit from official credit programs for poverty reduction. However, some informal financing organizations, for example MASAs, have integrated the poorest groups into credit service systems. These organizations have been able to link financing systems with social security systems at the village level. They also combine disaster mitigation with poverty reduction efforts by performing part of the relief functions of government institutions.

LINKING CREDIT UTILIZATION AND SAVINGS MOBILIZATION WORKS.   In the credit business, informal credit organizations must be allowed to link credit utilization effectively with savings mobilization. In this way groups can support their business operations primarily with their own resources. Rates of loan repayment improve as group members' responsibilities increase. Mem-

FIGURE 16.4 Design of the credit service network at the grassroots level in rural China

bers can also oversee credit utilization themselves, which is another useful way of increasing loan recovery rates.

NEW LINKAGES CAN IMPROVE ADMINISTRATION. Existing institutional capacities in China's rural financial system can and must be utilized effectively in any new institutional design for rural credit. The best means of utilizing these capacities is to create new linkages among financial institutions and to accord the institutions greater independence. Agriculture banks and credit cooperatives would do well to hook up with informal credit organizations. Where village credit stations exist, agriculture banks and credit cooperatives can use them to reach rural households. If such a link is impossible, the two formal financing institutions should release loans to informal credit organizations (Figure 16.4). These informal organizations are more efficient in providing small loans to the poor.

RURAL FINANCIAL MARKETS HAVE NOT BEEN SUFFICIENTLY LIBERALIZED. The liberalizing of markets for products, services, and labor is an essential element of China's economic reforms. But the important markets for credit and finance (especially in rural areas) have not been seriously affected. The need to activate financial markets and related services is particularly relevant in poor rural areas. In particular, flexible, open credit markets for the rural poor will facilitate economic growth and development in rural areas and allow these regions to catch up with the rest of the country.

ADMINISTRATIVE INTERFERENCE HAS AFFECTED PROGRAM OBJECTIVES. Administrative interference has gradually redirected microlending programs away from the initial target groups. Officially fixed low interest rates have caused banks to exclude a huge number of small customers from subsidized loan programs in order to keep transaction costs down. The substantial subsidies involved in credit programs have induced interest-seeking activities and allowed the various governments to interfere directly in the credit business. Credit risks have also increased as responsibility for loans becomes unclear.

FIXED INTEREST RATES HOLD BACK MICROLENDING OPERATIONS. As a precondition for maintaining a comprehensive microlending system, the state needs to authorize the agriculture banks and credit cooperatives to lend at market interest rates to informal organizations. Informal organizations must be allowed to make their own decisions regarding interest rates on savings deposits and loans. The state can thus indirectly help these informal groups become self-sustaining and increase their effectiveness in delivering needed development assistance to target groups.

THE RURAL BANKING SYSTEM DOES NOT MEET THE NEEDS OF THE POOR. The rural banking system does not cater appropriately to the market demand and needs of the poor. Comprehensive adjustments to the rural financial system have yet to be designed, but they will need to take into account the specific constraints, needs, and potential of the rural poor. Today's poor are not recipients but active partners in the development of new financial institutions.

LOCAL AGENTS LACK THE NECESSARY SKILLS TO IMPLEMENT CREDIT PROGRAMS. Local group agents are more effective than any other external organization's agents in training and helping the poor to make the best use of credit services. These local group agents themselves need training in banking and project appraisal in order to become effective partners both to the poor and to the banking institutions.

References

ABC (Agricultural Bank of China). 1987. *Report on improving the utilization of subsidized credits for poverty reduction.* Beijing.

———. 1988. Improving rural financial services to support economic development of poor areas. A working report. Beijing.

Agricultural Development Bank of China. 1996. *Annual report.* Beijing.

Dai Xianglong. 1996. The new development of the financial sector. *Almanac of China's finance and banking* (Beijing): 27–30.

Editorial Office. 1996. *Almanac of China's finance and banking.* Beijing.

He Dexu. 1995. Monetary reforms in China: A review of 1994 and a look forward to 1995. *Economic Information* 3.

IRD/CASS/SSB (Institute for Rural Development/Chinese Academy of Social Sciences/ General Team of the State Statistical Bureau for the Rural Socioeconomic Survey). 1996. *1995 Rural socioeconomic development report of China.* Beijing: Social Science Publisher of China.

Morduch, J., A. Park, and Wang Sangui. 1997. Microfinance in China. *Poverty and Development* 4: 8.

Office of the Leading Group of the State Council for Economic Development in Poor Areas. 1989. Regulations for managing economic entities for poverty reduction. Beijing.

———. 1998. Operation of microfinance with poverty reduction purpose. *Tribune of Economic Development*, No. 1. Beijing.

Office of the State Council. 1997. Stipulations on management of the state funds for poverty reduction, August 1. *China's Underdeveloped Regions* 4.

Pei Chuanzhi. 1996. The present situation of financial reform in the 1990s and its prospects. In *Credit for the rural poor in China*, ed. Zhu Ling, Jiang Zhongyi, and Joachim von Braun. Proceedings of a workshop held in Beibei, China. Beijing: Kiel (in Chinese and English).

State Council. 1996. Resolution on rural financial system reforms, August 22. Beijing.

State Statistics Bureau. 1996. *Statistical yearbook of China*. Beijing.

Shi Wei. 1998. Analyses on the depth of the financial market of China. *Research on Financial and Economic Issues* 8.

Wu Guobao. 1998. Experiments with rural microfinance for poverty reduction. *Reforms* 4.

Zeller, M., and M. Sharma, eds. 2000. *Innovations in rural microfinance for the rural poor: Exchange of knowledge and implications for policy*. Proceedings from an international conference organized by the German Foundation for International Development (DSE), the International Food Policy Research Institute (IFPRI), the International Fund for Agriculture (IFAD), and the Bank of Ghana. Feldafing, Germany: German Foundation for International Development (DSE).

Zeller, M., C. Schrieder, J. von Braun, and F. Heidhues. 1997. *Rural finance for food security for the poor: Implications for research and policy.* Food Policy Review No. 4. Washington, D.C.: International Food Policy Research Institute.

Zhu Ling, Jiang Zhongyi, and J. von Braun. 1997. *Credit systems for the rural poor in China*. New York: Nova Science Publishers.

PART V

Summary and Implications for Policy and Research

17 Summary and Implications for Policy and Research

RICHARD L. MEYER AND MANFRED ZELLER

The studies reported in this book contribute to many of the debates that have emerged in recent years about the policy objectives and role of microfinance in the development of low-income countries. The vision of the early microfinance pioneers has been achieved in important ways in several key programs. But the vast majority of microfinance institutions (MFIs) serve relatively few clients and depend on subsidies for their survival. Many offer only simple standardized products with little flexibility to adjust to the diverse demands of their clients. Many are making slow progress toward becoming more professionally operated and efficient financial institutions. But high levels of client dropout are reported by many MFIs, so new products and services are needed that are more attractive to clients. This situation is directing greater attention to issues of client demand and preferences, which are the focus of many studies in this book.

Important unresolved issues remain about the future of microfinance, especially in rural areas, but several implications emerge for microfinance policy from the studies reported here. Several of the book's chapters also raise important methodological and definitional issues that need to be addressed in future research. In this chapter, we summarize the key findings of the studies in the volume, report key policy implications, and identify areas for future research.

The Critical Triangle of Microfinance

A new paradigm emerged in the 1990s about the appropriate way to nurture the development of financial markets. The old paradigm, used to rationalize state intervention in small farmer credit programs, defined the financial problem largely as one of overcoming the supposed market imperfections that prevented creditworthy farmers from accessing formal loans. The financial system came to be viewed not as a market but rather as part of the input supply system to promote new technology, stimulate production, and raise incomes. Governments and donors provided large amounts of funds at subsidized rates to lenders that on-lent to targeted clients at cheap rates. The health of financial institutions was largely ignored, as was client demand. The new paradigm now employed widely in microfinance emphasizes the concept of financial sustainability. The costs and risks of lending are considered to be key factors that impede access to loans, and appropriate pricing is viewed as crucial for sustainability. Innovations are valued that reduce costs and risks and are designed to provide more demand-oriented financial products for the poor.

Financial sustainability is now one of the three principal objectives of public support. The second is to improve outreach to the poor, that is, the expansion of the financial frontier to people previously excluded from accessing banking services. Clearly, not all market failures that impede access to finance can be sustainably addressed by the state, but some can, for example through institutional and technological innovations that reduce the costs and risks of microfinance. The third policy objective is to improve the impact of microfinance; that is, to increase the benefits received by the poor. While financial sustainability is a necessary precondition for the stability and permanence of the financial system, outreach to and impact for the poor are important determinants of the economic sustainability of public support for microfinance. If outreach and impact were not public policy concerns, there would be little justification to invest public resources in microfinance institutions. In this context, subsidies may be a legitimate way to stimulate start-ups and speed innovation rather than create dependency and directly reduce interest rates for borrowers, as was done under the old paradigm.

The three objectives emphasized in the new paradigm of outreach, financial sustainability, and impact form what we term the "critical triangle of microfinance" represented in our conceptual framework schematically represented by Figure 1.1 on page 6. The inner circle within the triangle represents the many actions and innovations of financial institutions that contribute to meeting these three objectives. Microfinance policy can also contribute through targeted subsidies for institution building and institutional innovations. This circle focuses attention on what financial institutions can and should do. An important difference between the largely failed experience of small farmer agricultural credit and the recent microfinance revolution is the amount of experimentation conducted by MFIs leading to breakthroughs in methods to serve the poor. One of the most important developments is that group lending has been improved so that it works far better for many MFIs today than it ever did for agricultural credit. Moreover, a few flagship organizations, such as BancoSol in Bolivia, the Bank for Agriculture and Agricultural Cooperatives in Thailand, and Bank Rakyat Indonesia–Unit Desas (BRI–UD) in Indonesia, have demonstrated how to expand outreach and improve sustainability simultaneously. Their experience, as well as that of others, provides cautious optimism for a massive, sustained expansion of financial services to those outside the frontier of formal finance by financial institutions that couple microfinance best practices with a commitment to experiment with new approaches for different target groups in diverse socioeconomic and agroecological settings.

The outer circle in Figure 1.1 represents the equally important factors outside the direct control of financial institutions that affect attainment of the three objectives. These are mainly the policy framework, both macroeconomic and sectoral, and the socioeconomic, agroecological, and political conditions influencing the performance of financial institutions. The policy framework primarily includes macroeconomic and financial policies affecting economic growth and stability. It also includes financial infrastructure such as courts, land registries, and property rights, as well as sectoral policies that directly or indirectly influence the economic activities and opportunities of the clientele of MFIs and the demand for financial services. Moreover, the underlying conditions include factors such as population density, telecommunications and road infrastructure, human and social capital, and other determinants of growth and equity. These conditions are particularly relevant for determining the success and failure of agricultural finance. Repressive urban-oriented policies undermined agriculture and contributed to the failure of agricultural finance programs in the 1960s and 1970s. Recent policy reforms have reduced much of that urban bias, increased the demand for financial services, and improved the prospects for successful rural financial intermediation. Many countries, however, still lack an enabling environment and supportive institutions, so that financial market development in rural areas remains constrained.

Access to and Demand for Financial Services

Much of the earlier concern about financial services for small farmers, as well as the recent drive to expand lending to the poor, has been driven by the notion of a gap between demand and supply; that is, potential clients are willing and able to pay for services but suppliers are unwilling or unable to provide them. The research reported in this book demonstrates the complexity of these issues and how the typical MFI approach of providing short-term loans to the poor reflects a highly simplistic view of the role of financial services in the management of firms and households in low-income countries. Zeller and Sharma (Chapter 2) provide a more comprehensive understanding of the demand for and use of finance in a conceptual framework that distinguishes three pathways through which financial services affect households. The first is often the only one recognized by advocates for small farmers and the poor; it is the traditional rationale of providing loans to expand investment and generate income. Pathways two and three show how access to financial services affects the management of asset portfolios and smoothes household consumption. Using this framework, they demonstrate two important points. First, the demand for financial services is much greater and more complex than normally assumed. Second, estimating the impact of providing financial services to the poor is more complex than simply trying to attribute changes in production or income to receiving a loan, which has been the focus of much impact analysis.

The cross-country comparisons presented by Zeller and Sharma show that an overwhelming majority of the poor engage in some type of financial transaction. The fungibility of loans implies that loan demand and use are driven by the overall budgetary needs of the household. The poor often borrow from informal sources for consumption-related purposes. In comparison, the nonpoor report borrowing larger amounts for longer periods for investment and more frequently from formal sources. Because a relatively smaller proportion of their expenditures are on food, the nonpoor tend to use a greater share of their funds for consumption of other goods and for production purposes. The poorer the household, the more important precautionary savings and insurance services become. Understanding these patterns of financial management is essential for assessing the nature of the demand for financial products for the poor.

In Chapter 3 Nguyen et al. show that the nature of the local environment affects household demand for and use of financial services. In the highly risky and poor environment of Burkina Faso, true household demand for financial services is more diverse and complex than observed demand. In this environment population-induced changes in production have increased uncertainty, and savings play a major role in consumption smoothing. Observations of informal financial transactions provide clues about the nature of demand. Informal savings in particular have multiple roles and take many forms. The authors note that, independently from the household head, each economically active member of the household has his or her own specific demand for financial services. Women, in particular, are heavily constrained by lack of capital, which influences their choice of economic activities.

Most market transactions of households in Burkina Faso take place in local markets, where households with adequate resources can profitably exploit market niches. Microfinance projects have been created to provide targeted savings and credit services to help households exploit these niches. Because of risk aversion, however, funds borrowed from the four projects studied are rarely used to finance new activities. Borrowers know that using loans to expand economic activities can easily lead to market saturation. In-depth studies of the use of loans by women reveal complex patterns of short-term consumption smoothing and long-term wealth accumulation. Providing savings services to assist households to smooth consumption may be a more effective way to help the poor than the heavy emphasis on loans targeted for specific purposes. These findings contribute to our understanding of how the demand for financial services is shaped by gender and by economic opportunities.

In Chapter 4, Stanton analyzes client demand and relates it to the targeting efficiency of Mexican financial institutions. Her survey of clients reveals that private banks tend to serve wealthier clients. Considerable leakage has occurred of program funds in state-owned banks that target poor clients because these banks also serve many wealthier nontargeted clients. Wealthy clients frequently borrow from informal sources as well. Many analysts of such borrowing patterns elsewhere are quick to attribute them to lender credit rationing, but Stanton notes that demand factors are also important. Demand is affected by client perceptions of costs and benefits. The cost calculation includes the transaction costs of all procedures involved in applying for a loan and the probability of actually getting it when applying. Therefore, analyses that supposedly demonstrate lender credit rationing of the poor may underestimate the effect of the decisions by the poor to apply for loans. Lenders concerned about targeting efficiency in reaching the poor need to consider more carefully the design of their products and procedures, and the perceptions of potential clients about the probability of actually getting a loan. Complicated procedures increase borrower transaction costs, so some potential clients will choose not to apply while others will not apply because they believe their applications will be rejected. This self-selection process influences the composition of borrowers found in lenders' portfolios and reduces targeting efficiency.

The concept of borrowing limits used by Zeller and Sharma (Chapter 5) in their Bangladesh study advances the credit demand analysis for rural households and improves our understanding of credit rationing and borrowing behavior. The authors define access to credit as the maximum amount borrowers could borrow and compare this with the amounts actually borrowed. A borrower is said to have access to credit if the borrowing limit is positive. Some households may not borrow at all or borrow less than their borrowing limit. In contrast to the Stanton analysis, which focuses on transaction costs and the probability of getting a loan, this analysis suggests that the benefits of actually borrowing could be lower than the value of holding unused borrowing capacity as an asset for future use. The Bangladeshi MFIs studied were successful in reaching their poor target groups, especially women, irrespective of the finding that access to credit increased with the amount of land owned in both the formal and informal credit markets. However, the amount actually borrowed did not depend on the amount of land owned, suggesting that other factors, such as the lack of access to complementary inputs, may constrain borrower demand in land-rich households. The authors interpret the fact that most households do not retain unused borrowing capacity as evidence that credit constraint occurs in both the formal and informal sectors. Households' use of their full borrowing limit implies that present use of funds is valued more highly than future use. The simultaneous borrowing from both formal and informal sources suggests that they are not substitute sources of loans and that the expansion of MFIs does not crowd out informal sector lending. This finding is attributed to the different characteristics of formal and informal loans. The terms of MFI loans are conducive to investment purposes whereas informal loans are used more for consumption smoothing.

Little information exists about rural household demand for and capacity to repay long-term loans in developing countries. Because most MFIs provide only short-term working capital loans, there is little field experience to generate insights about demand. Land markets are thin in most developing countries and lending for land acquisition is rare. Yet access to loans to make long-term investments may be a crucial way to lift the poor out of poverty. Chapter 6 by Lyne and Darroch is important because it discusses the financing of land reform in South Africa. An important constraint in land reform projects is the inability of land recipients to amortize the full market costs of land acquired. A major part of the South African reform is market based, so successful implementation depends crucially on voluntary transactions between a seller and a buyer with adequate debt repayment capacity. A small sample of private land transactions involving disadvantaged farmers in KwaZulu-Natal reveals that they are relatively wealthy and were able to finance 70 percent of their purchases from equity capital. Even so, their loan installments were high relative to current farm earnings. An innovative scheme to finance transactions of sugar land employs an interest subsidy that increases the ability of the buyers to meet amortization costs successfully. This financial arrangement, largely funded from private sources, provides insights into how declining interest subsidies may make it possible to surmount borrower cash-flow problems so that market-based transactions become feasible. Unless farmers have large amounts of equity or other income, such as nonfarm sources, a special mechanism is needed to enable them to participate fully in the land reform. So far it appears that the poor have not yet been well served by the South African land reform.

Three major themes or conclusions emerge from these five chapters of Part I. First, access by the poor to savings, credit, and insurance services can be enhanced by institutional innovations. Second, whether improved access to a service is useful and, hence, whether the poor will demand it will depend on the characteristics of the product and the client's perception of the costs and benefits of using it. Here, the conclusion is that savings and insurance become relatively more important the poorer and the more risk averse are the clients. Third, further innovations are needed at the institutional level to improve access to those financial services for which the poor are willing to pay. Matching access (or supply) to demand is one of the major MFI challenges, and a precondition for successful outreach to the poor. Successful, demand-driven outreach, in turn, can contribute both to achieving MFI financial sustainability as well as to improving impact at the client level. Thus, these results emphasize the need for market research to evaluate the nature of market demand and for demand-oriented innovations in microfinance policy and operations.

Outreach and Sustainability

The four chapters in Part II provide insights into two issues in relation to the outreach and financial sustainability of MFIs. The first is the problem of how to measure the client profile of MFIs as one dimension of their outreach performance. The second concerns the technologies that MFIs use and their impact on financial sustainability. A major difficulty in analyzing the comparative performance of MFIs is the lack of a common method to describe the characteristics of clients served. This is a crucial problem because there may be a trade-off between depth of outreach and financial sustainability. One MFI may be more sustainable than another because it serves a richer clientele.

Paxton and Cuevas (Chapter 7), Navajas et al. (Chapter 8), and Zeller et al. (Chapter 9) use innovative techniques to measure the client profiles of selected MFIs. Whereas Chapters 8 and 9 use indices of absolute and relative poverty drawing on a range of poverty indicators, respectively, Chapter 7 by Paxton and Cuevas develops a simple depth of outreach indicator. The authors compare the average income of MFI clients in Latin America, the proportion of female clients, the proportion of rural clients, and the proportion of uneducated clients with country averages for these variables. MFIs that serve a clientele that is poorer, more female, more rural, and less educated than the national average generate a positive outreach index. The index is easy to create because only the average level of income is needed for the clients. The indicator is then compared with the Subsidy Dependence Index for five MFIs in Latin America. Credit unions scored higher on breadth of outreach (number of clients) and sustainability, whereas village banks scored higher on depth of outreach (their clients are poorer). This finding is consistent with the fact that village banks tend to target the poor whereas credit unions have a lower- and middle-class clientele. The authors believe that the potential trade-off between depth of outreach and sustainability could be reduced if the village banks achieved greater economies of scale available to them.

A limitation of the Paxton and Cuevas outreach index is that it considers only average client income, rather than the full distribution of client incomes in an MFI's portfolio, and it does not relate average income to absolute poverty indicators in a country. No information is provided to determine whether average income levels are above or below some absolute measure of poverty established for the country. Navajas et al. attempt to resolve these problems in Chapter 8 by analyzing the distribution of clients by poverty level in a study of five MFIs in Bolivia. They estimate the poverty levels of sampled clients using methods similar to those of the national poverty assessment. None of the five MFIs serve the very poor and most clients tend to be clustered just above or just below the national poverty line. The three MFIs that use a joint-liability group lending technology tend to reach a slightly larger proportion of poorer clients than the two that primarily lend to individuals. Since all five were making strides in achieving subsidy independence, it is difficult to argue that choice of technology is crucial to sustainability. Matching occurs between type of client and type of MFI: clients who can provide suitable collateral can access individual loans; those who cannot resort to group loans. Client preferences are revealed by the tendency for clients to switch from group to individual loans when the opportunity arises.

Zeller et al. (Chapter 9) present a method that uses qualitative and quantitative indicators reflecting different dimensions of poverty, such as food security, housing, ownership of assets, and human and social capital. Compared with the method of Navajas et al., which measures absolute poverty and is able to identify how many poor are reached by MFIs, Zeller et al. feature a method that measures the relative poverty of MFI clients compared with the general population living in the operational area of the MFI. Common to both methods is that poverty is seen as a multidimensional phenomenon and an index is created featuring different dimensions of poverty. In countries such as Bolivia where an index of absolute poverty exists, the method developed by Navajas et al. has clear advantages in being able to measure not only relative but also absolute poverty, which is an important concept in national and international dialogues. Yet most countries rely on comprehensive and costly household expenditure surveys for measuring absolute poverty through the poverty line method. In still other countries, data from recent national poverty studies are not available or are not made available, or only at a high cost.

In countries where national data for measuring absolute poverty are difficult and costly to access or to replicate through field surveys, the method presented in Chapter 9 may offer a cost-effective alternative. It allows relative poverty to be measured at comparatively low time and cost requirements, and can answer the simple, but important question: How poor are the clients in relation to the population living in the operational area of the MFI? The method is applicable not only for assessing the poverty outreach of MFIs but also in evaluating development policies and projects in general. The results from four country case studies show that MFIs reach diverse client groups, depending on their product design and delivery system. For example, and consistent with its declared business mission, 58 percent of the clients of the group-based MFI in South Asia belonged to the poorest third of the population in its operational area, and only 3.5 percent belonged to the wealthiest tercile. This MFI targets poor rural women, and it enforces strict targeting criteria by obtaining poverty-related information through a client entry interview. However, this targeting strategy creates additional costs for the MFI, which need to be weighed against the objective of reaching or maintaining financial sustainability. The MFI in Central America, which seeks to reach micro-, small-, and medium-scale enterprises through different types of financial products and technologies, served poorer as well as wealthier clients—again consistent with its mission.

Chapters 7–9 contribute to the discussion about the importance of different types of lending technologies in meeting the objectives of sustainability, outreach, and impact. So does the study by Heidhues, Belle-Sossoh, and Buchenrieder (Chapter 10), which compares the transaction costs of three lending programs in Cameroon. The first two programs use solidarity credit groups, whereas the third, a credit union, provides loans directly to individuals. The analysis distinguishes pure transaction costs from risk costs, which represent the costs of loan default. Both components contribute to total lending costs. The results indicate that group lending may not always have lower transactions costs, either for the lender or for the borrower. Individual lending may have lower default rates and, therefore, lower risk costs than group lending. In fact, the individual lending scheme of the Cameroonian Cooperative Credit Union League (CamCCUL) had the lowest total lending costs. CamCCUL's average lending transaction costs amounted to 15.5 percent of the loan amount compared with 64.0 percent for the group lending program of Fonds d'Investissement des Micro-réalisations Agricoles et Communautaires (FIMAC) and 82.9 percent for the group lending program of Crédit Agricole du Cameroun (CAC). FIMAC's costs were very high because of the transaction costs in forming, training, and monitoring the groups; in CAC, little time and effort are invested in forming viable groups, and the resulting dismal average loan default rate of 78 percent drives up lender transaction costs.

However, Heidhues et al. note that these stark differences among the three institutions are also due to three factors that raise issues about their comparability. First, whereas CamCCUL serves a wealthier clientele, the other two institutions seek to reach poorer people. Declining unit transaction costs for larger loan sizes tend to reduce the costs of lending to wealthier clients. Second, CamCCUL predominantly serves clients in cities and rural towns, whereas FIMAC and CAC serve rural villages, which tends to raise lending costs because of increased communication and travel costs, the sparser density of clients in rural areas, and the increased risks of loan default owing to climatic factors. Third, CamCCUL was formed in the 1960s, whereas the two group lending institutions began operations only in the early 1990s. As an institution matures and establishes a long-term client base, it can exploit economies of scope, scale, and risk. Hence, although the authors suggest that individual lending can achieve low transaction costs, the study is not conclusive about lending costs for group loans. Further research is needed to control for the characteristics of the clientele and the age and size of the institutions.

The chapters in Part II featured alternative methods for measuring the depth of outreach of MFIs that are suitable for operational evaluations in different socioeconomic contexts. One of the conclusions drawn from these chapters is that the two performance criteria of MFI outreach and financial sustainability must be analyzed simultaneously. Achieving excellent outreach to the poor may well imply weak financial sustainability, and vice versa. Logic suggests there is a crucial nexus between institutional and product design, type of clientele served, loan sizes, and sustainability of MFIs. Making and recovering small loans to the poor in an efficient manner requires appropriate design, and the design of products and institutions affects client demand, as noted in the previous section. The more efficient the design, the greater are the prospects for financial sustainability while at the same time reaching large numbers of poor people. These innovations are within the scope of financial institutions as represented by the inner circle of Figure 1.1. But the many external factors represented by the outer circle also affect performance, and microfinance policy has an important role to play in influencing progress in both the inner and outer circles.

Impact

Creating market-oriented products that are demanded by the poor affects outreach, which in turn influences financial sustainability. The design of MFI products and services may also affect the impact on clients, as noted in the chapters in Part III.

In their comprehensive review of impact studies in Chapter 11, Sharma and Buchenrieder distinguish investment-led benefits, which conceptually correspond to the first pathway distinguished by Zeller and Sharma (Chapter 2), from insurance-led benefits, which relate to the second and third pathways. Overall, the investment-led impact studies present very mixed results. Apart from methodological differences, the studies show that country- and program-specific conditions have a large bearing on whether the impact of credit is positive, negligible, or even negative. One important factor is the extent to which complementary production inputs are available to the borrowing farmer or entrepreneur. Loans received in the absence of complementary inputs will more likely be used for consumption smoothing and other insurance purposes that stimulate consumption in the short term but may even reduce it in the long term. However, it was difficult for Sharma and Buchenrieder to identify specific aspects of MFI institutional design that were associated with greater impact. Disentangling the impact of financial and nonfinancial services is extremely difficult, and the problem is compounded by the fact that MFIs offer different services, making it hard to compare them.

A number of studies reviewed by Sharma and Buchenrieder, as well as Chapter 12 by Diagne, point to the critical role of infrastructure, extension, and technology in determining whether or not credit access enhances income. Their review suggests that insurance-led impact studies reveal somewhat more positive and less ambiguous evidence of impact, and that this type of impact may be especially relevant for a poorer clientele. Product innovation with respect to savings and insurance services may therefore be particularly promising. The authors conclude that further rigorous research is required to improve our knowledge of if, when, and how much impact can be attributed to credit access and actual borrowing. However, with the exception of Diagne's chapter, recent research has failed to distinguish between the impact of actual borrowing and the impact that can arise from having access to credit. Diagne's innovative work points out a number of challenges in developing a satisfactory methodology for impact assessment. With the present state of knowledge, there appears to be no agreed-upon methodology for assessing impacts of credit programs. This lack limits our understanding about how best to improve impact through microfinance policy.

The issue of whether or not depth of poverty influences the impact of the financial services received remains unclear, and analysis is hampered by the lack of rigorous methods to compare the depth of poverty outreach across MFIs, as noted above. Although Part II in this book features innovative methods to measure depth of outreach and links this issue with sustainability, future research needs to link outreach with impact as well. Since the determinants of poverty are complex and go far beyond mere access to credit, simply granting loans to the poor is unlikely to release all the constraints that prevent them from escaping poverty. It is no coincidence that successful poverty-oriented MFIs have flourished better in urban or high-potential rural areas with above-average infrastructure and market access and where borrowers benefit from complementary public and private services that enhance the profitability of their loan-financed investment. Sharma and Buchenrieder find the relationship between financial sustainability and program impact on the poor to be less well developed in the literature and even more difficult to measure than other impact questions. The study by Mosley and Hulme, which they review, demonstrated a positive correlation between financial sustainability and impact, but its several methodological shortcomings and data limitations cloud the results. The study did not have sufficient controls for depth of poverty so the sustainability effects could not be easily disentangled from the poverty levels of the clients.

Diagne's study of the efficiency of smallholder production in Malawi (Chapter 12) reveals little or no credit impact on the technical efficiency and productivity of tobacco and maize production. His study is unique because he makes a distinction between access and participation in the credit market: access is measured by the credit limit, whereas participation is measured by the amount borrowed. This distinction is important for impact analysis because credit access influences household outcomes through two main channels. In the first channel, access can alleviate liquidity constraints, thereby enabling a farmer to acquire inputs and farm equipment to increase output. The second channel (equivalent to Zeller and Sharma's second and third pathways in Chapter 2) works through the positive effect of access on household risk-bearing capacity, which affects the adoption of new, riskier technologies. Moreover, the option to borrow, even if not exercised, helps avoid risk-reducing, inefficient production practices such as mixed cropping, late planting, and poor timing of input applications. The econometric analysis, however, finds no significant impact of credit access on technical efficiency and productivity, except for tobacco production in one survey region and for local maize. Although the drought during the two survey years may have influenced this result, the analysis highlights that credit access may not have a positive impact on income and agricultural productivity if complementary inputs, especially improved agricultural technology, are not available to farmers.

Kochar's study (Chapter 13) is also innovative in trying to assess how, in the absence of insurance markets, anticipated ill health affects the asset portfolios of households and, in turn, their poverty level. Households were found to use emergency loans and informal savings in advance of illnesses to deal with health problems. In this type of situation, the availability of formal loans for emergencies and health insurance could improve household welfare. The loan products of several key MFIs are already designed to serve this market because they lend for any purpose, whereas others lend only for productive purposes.

The literature review by Sharma and Buchenrieder reveals gaps in at least two areas of impact assessment. The first is the provision of savings facilities for the poor. Several analysts argue that providing secure methods to hold savings is a better way to help the poor than inducing them to borrow. The large amount of savings channeled by the poor into informal savings mechanisms is taken as evidence of the demand for savings. Savings may be accumulated for asset purchases and for insurance purposes; however, many MFIs do not accept savings and some others offer only compulsory savings that cannot be easily accessed, so their value to the saver for either purpose is limited. Therefore, impact studies need to deal with the difficult problem of assessing the specific features of the savings products as well as the amount of savings held by the household. The second gap in impact assessment concerns the concepts of credit limits and unused borrowing capacity. Diagne's study is unique because most impact studies focus on the household's actual use of a financial service (for example, the amount borrowed). Unused borrowing capacity represents an asset not used. But having this asset in reserve may induce households to use their other assets differently. For example, they might choose to allocate their own liquidity to more profitable or more risky projects, knowing they could borrow if the returns are not as good as expected. This concept is not well appreciated by either researchers or MFI managers. In fact, existing clients who do not continue to borrow are labeled "dropouts" and may even be considered to harm operations because they borrow less than projected amounts. It is difficult for microfinance advocates to appreciate that a reliable lender provides a valuable service simply by being available to make loans, but it is not easy to measure impact in this situation.

These methodological problems, plus several others identified by Sharma and Buchenrieder, demonstrate how difficult it is to study impact. Changes observed in clients may be due to a variety of factors besides participation in a microfinance project. These problems underscore the challenge that remains in deriving robust conclusions about impact and in assessing possible trade-offs and synergies between impact, outreach, and financial sustainability. In the absence of measurable estimates, the best indirect evidence of impact is when clients choose to continue to use financial services offered by MFIs at market prices, and when MFIs serve a poorer clientele on a financially sustainable basis without direct subsidies covering the costs of service provision. The fact that clients switch from established MFIs to alternative sources, as is occurring in the highly competitive urban markets of Bolivia, implies that the alternative products are more desirable and, in the eyes of the clients, have greater impact.

The studies of microfinance impact featured in this book lead to the conclusion that more rigorous research is required to improve our knowledge of if, when, and how much impact can be attributed to access to credit and other financial services. The evidence of impact available so far suggests promising returns from public and private investments in microfinance, but also raises valid concerns about the danger of overinvestment, particularly in areas where complementary investments are lacking. On the basis of current knowledge, it is obvious to conclude that microfinance is not a panacea for poverty alleviation. Sequencing of investments is important and microfinance may better follow rather than precede investments in other critical areas, such as infrastructure, technology, human capital investments, agricultural research, and extension.

Moreover, the appropriate role of research in assessing microfinance impact in order to guide policy needs to be reviewed because the research community is still developing cost-efficient and reliable tools for impact assessment. Currently the state-of-the-art methodologies for impact assessment require the use of large-scale household-level surveys that feature before-and-after or with-and-without comparisons and allow for measurement of short- and long-term impact through panel data. This type of research design can hardly be financed by an MFI. The limited budgets available for project monitoring, therefore, may be better used to assess customer satisfaction and preferences. Results from these market research studies can be directly fed into product design, and therefore may be more useful for practitioners and clients, and ultimately for policymakers. Having said that, research on impact assessment in the future should take the form of a few well-funded, carefully designed studies that can effectively grapple with the many methodological problems. If robust conclusions can be obtained from these careful studies, MFIs may be spared the burden of collecting impact data that cannot yield robust findings, but distract them from the important analysis of their operations and sustainability.

Public Policies for Finance

Part IV of the book concerns the outer circle in Figure 1.1, which deals with the policy and economic environment for microfinance. The widespread failures of small farmer credit projects have made many analysts skeptical about the role of public support for financial market development. The supposedly good results obtained from state intervention in East Asian financial markets are interpreted as an exception unlikely to be replicated in most developing countries. Lapenu in Chapter 14 analyzes the arguments for state intervention and concludes that the state can act effectively to nurture financial markets when the functions of the state, for-profit providers of finance services, and nonprofit institutions work in complementary or synergistic ways. The state is best placed, by virtue of its legitimate powers of coercion or rule-making authority, to provide a stabile macroeconomic and conducive regulatory environment. However, exercise of such power will attract rent seeking, and measures to discourage such behavior are required if the state is to succeed in its primary role as facilitator of financial systems development. Lapenu acknowledges that there is a role for the state in supporting institutional innovations, thus assisting MFIs to expand the inner circle in Figure 1.1. She further recognizes a role for the state in designing and implementing an appropriate legal and regulatory framework for microfinance that contributes to enlarging the outer circle by giving more flexibility to MFIs to innovate and to improve impact, outreach, and/or financial sustainability.

Inadequate regulation and supervision of the financial system were among the many problems contributing to the recent financial crises in Asia and the Soviet Union. They are also widely recognized as a potential problem for microfinance. Improving MFI sustainability often requires mobilization of savings, but protection for savers becomes an issue when unregulated MFIs begin to mobilize savings in large quantities. The fierce competition among financial institutions in places such as Bolivia may undermine the careful approach followed by the pioneer institutions, with negative consequences for the entire microfinance sector. The challenge in many countries is to develop a framework that regulates microfinance but does not strangle innovation. The need to strengthen the capacity of supervisory and regulatory bodies has become clear because of the many failures of formal financial systems. In most countries, however, adding a large number of MFIs to the responsibilities of regulators will likely overtax their limited capacity. Mixing self-regulation with limited external regulation is likely to be more consistent with the institutional capacity of most countries in the near future. Support from donors and government may encourage commercial banks to make microloans or to lend on a wholesale basis to specialized providers of microloans. Specialized providers, such as NGOs, should be encouraged by public policy not to distort financial markets by setting interest rates that do not cover their costs. Those that do not wish to provide financial services on this basis may be in a better position to enhance the impact of microfinance for the poorest by providing training, group formation, screening, local supervision, and health and education services, rather than by lending to them.

Yaron and Benjamin in Chapter 15 agree that the old agricultural credit paradigm, which focused on direct support for specific programs, largely failed, and they support the new paradigm that emphasizes financial sustainability of the MFIs. They acknowledge that rural financial intermediation faces several problems, including macroeconomic policies, sectoral policies, the legal and regulatory framework, general shortcomings in financial markets, systemic weaknesses of rural financial markets, and poorly designed interventions. They identify "eight pillars" of urban-based policies that distort the demand for financial services and resource allocation by financial intermediaries. Recognizing the bad experience with agricultural credit projects, they argue that the appropriate role of government in the new paradigm in support of financial markets is mostly indirect—creating a favorable policy environment and strengthening the legal and regulatory framework. They propose a framework comprising a multiple variable hybrid outreach index and the Subsidy Dependence Index as the primary assessment criteria for rural financial institutions. Using this two-part framework, they document the exceptional performance of the *unit desa* system of Bank Rakyat Indonesia (BRI-UD) to show what can be accomplished by innovative financial institutions when appropriate conditions have been created. Surprisingly, however, many rural financial institutions in Indonesia have not employed similar policies and procedures and, as a result, have not been as successful in achieving high levels of outreach and sustainability. Moreover, the recent financial crisis revealed the weaknesses of the country's regulatory and supervisory framework. Many financial institutions are failing and have to be recapitalized. The BRI-UD experience can be interpreted, therefore, as an example of how one institution with appropriate designs and policies can prosper in an environment in which others fail.

The microfinance experience in China, as described by Zhu, Zhongyi, and von Braun in Chapter 16, highlights the difficulties and challenges in transforming a financial system for a planned economy into one for a more market-oriented economy. The analysis shows that the old paradigm is alive and well in China's financial sector policies. Although policy reforms have provided greater scope for rural private enterprises in recent years, the Chinese government retains tight control over its rural financial system and the allocation of financial resources. The financial system is struggling under the burden of supporting loss-making state-owned industrial enterprises. The results of a rural survey conducted by the authors reveal that slightly less than one-third of poor and nonpoor households received a loan in the survey year. The level of banking activity in a province had a positive effect on the probability of a household obtaining a loan in either the formal or informal sectors. The size of the household asset base influenced the possibility of getting a loan from either source, so asset-poor households have more difficulty in accessing financial services. Subsidized rural funds designated for the poor have often been diverted to richer regions. Because of this problem, the Chinese authorities have pursued the old paradigm in designing special subsidized microlending programs targeted to the rural poor. Two of the microfinance experiments follow the Grameen Bank and BRI-UD models. They have managed to reach the poor more successfully than other rural programs but they suffer from government interference and donor dependency.

Implications for Policy and Research

Clearly, microfinance has achieved important successes and millions of poor people previously denied financial services from banks now receive loans from MFIs. Some have access to savings and other financial services. Many MFI programs are located in urban areas, but some are expanding into the rural hinterland, although they are mostly confined to areas with high population densities where loans are often used for nonagricultural purposes. The research reported in this book reveals that many fundamental micro and rural finance issues need much more study. MFI field operations have far surpassed the research capacity to analyze them, so excitement about the use of microfinance for poverty alleviation is not backed up with sound facts derived from rigorous research.

Given the current state of knowledge, it is difficult to allocate confidently public resources to microfinance development. There is little solid evidence on the important question of which institutions, products, and technologies are most appropriate for achieving success in particular situations. Institutional development of MFIs is still a major challenge in spite of the success of a few flagship institutions, and the very subsidies that sustain many MFIs may reduce the incentives in the short term for building self-sustaining institutions. Much more systematic comparative analysis of MFIs is needed to evaluate the alternatives of upgrading informal institutions, downscaling the outreach of formal institutions, and creating new institutions from scratch to serve the poor.

The techniques for measuring MFI financial sustainability are well advanced, but those for measuring depth of outreach—that is, the poverty level of the clients—are not developed to a point where they provide consistent information. Several chapters in this book feature new and innovative approaches, and further progress by future research in this field is needed in order to enhance our understanding of depth of outreach of MFIs. As of now, there is only sketchy evidence to show if one type of MFI consistently reaches a different poverty level than another. Because of this, we have very limited quantitative knowledge about the trade-offs between outreach and financial sustainability. Impact analysis has even more limitations. Therefore, one important research objective is to develop better methods to measure depth of outreach and impact. Better measurement is essential for improving our understanding of the trade-offs and synergies among the three objectives postulated in our critical triangle of microfinance. Practical tools for impact assessment are also needed for use by MFIs but, if sophisticated methods are not yet considered reliable, simple but robust approaches will not emerge soon. Meanwhile, research should also focus on market research to explore the preferences and demands of clients and nonclients of MFIs in different socioeconomic groups. These marketing studies will likely generate more immediate and operationally relevant information for use by policymakers, donors, and microfinance practitioners in the near future than will detailed impact assessment studies.

Given the state of the art, the chapters in this book have not attempted to answer the questions of how much, when, and where policies should support the formation and operations of MFIs for the poor. It is recognized that the state and NGOs played a critical role in generating recent successful innovations, and that role should be exploited in the future. Public investments and subsidies for the microfinance sector should be guided by the principal objective of generating new products or institutional prototypes for specific socioeconomic and agroecological settings that can be replicated and adapted by other financial institutions. These innovations become public goods, available for use by everyone, and one of the principal roles of the state is exactly to produce such goods. Microfinance policy, therefore, can play an important part in accelerating institutional innovation that ultimately meets client demands and is both growth and equity oriented.

This volume, as well as most microfinance research, has provided relatively little information to resolve the challenges of agricultural finance. Compared with urban microfinance, agricultural finance faces problems of a more dispersed clientele, higher communications and transportation costs, greater seasonality and lumpiness in household cash flows, larger loan amounts, more covariate income risks among potential clients, and an urban bias in governmental policies. The new paradigm of financial sector development offers general guidelines about how to approach this challenge and avoid past problems. But a vast amount of work is required to understand the market for rural finance and create the innovations necessary for successful financial intermediation. Pushing out the financial frontier in rural areas, plus consolidating the gains made in microfinance, will provide a full agenda for financial innovators, policymakers, and researchers well into the twenty-first century.

Contributors

Dieudonné Belle-Sossoh received a doctoral degree in agricultural economics from the University of Hohenheim, Germany, in 1997. The topic of his research was a comparative analysis of the transaction costs between group credit and individual credit in the rural financial sector of Cameroon. He has since returned to the Ministry of Agriculture in Yaoundé, Cameroon, as coordinator of the National Food Security Project.

McDonald Benjamin is the World Bank's resident representative in Ecuador. As a financial economist, he has worked for the World Bank on a broad range of financial sector issues, including micro and rural finance, banking system reform, housing finance, and pension system reforms. He holds a Ph.D. in economics from Georgetown University, Washington, D.C., and an M.A. in philosophy, politics, and economics from Oxford University, U.K.

Michel Benoit-Cattin is a development economist at the Scientific Division of the Centre de Coopération Internationale en Recherche Agronomique pour le Développement (CIRAD) in Montpellier, France. He currently is the leader of CIRAD's promotion program for international scientific exchanges. At CIRAD, he previously was the head of the research unit on microeconomic aspects of agricultural and rural development.

Joachim von Braun received his doctoral degree in agricultural economics from the University of Göttingen, Germany, in 1978. Before joining IFPRI as its director general in September 2002, he was a professor at the University of Bonn, director of the Center for Development Research, and head of the Center's Department for Economics and Technological Change. His research and policy advice focus on poverty reduction, food policy, and technological and institutional innovation. Von Braun serves on boards of international institutes and is president of the International Association of Agricultural Economists (2000–2003). His recent books address issues of poverty and famine in Africa, the future of villages, biotechnology in developing countries, and Russian agriculture in transition.

Gertrud Buchenrieder has been a junior professor in the Department of Development Theory and Agricultural Policy in the Tropics at the University of Hohenheim, Germany, since October 1996. She conducts research and holds lectures in development policy and economics, focusing on rural finance, agrarian reform, and food security. Although the geographical research focus of the department lies traditionally in Sub-Saharan Africa and Southeast Asia, she has extended the spectrum to Central and Eastern Europe in recent years. In autumn 2000, she accepted an invitation from the Tufts University School of Nutrition Science and Policy, U.S.A., as visiting scholar. Her graduate studies at Ohio State University, U.S.A., were funded by a Fulbright grant. Her doctoral thesis was awarded the J. G. Knoll Science Prize by the Father and Son Eiselen Foundation, Ulm, Germany, in 1996.

Carlos E. Cuevas is a lead financial economist at the World Bank, Financial Sector Development Department. A specialist in rural finance and microfinance, he manages or participates in World Bank lending operations, sector work, and technical assistance, primarily in Latin America and Africa. Before joining the World Bank, he was a senior microenterprise specialist at the Inter-American Development Bank (1993–95) and an assistant professor of agricultural economics and finance at Ohio State University, U.S.A. (1984–93). He holds a Masters degree in agricultural economics from the Catholic University of Chile and a Ph.D. in agricultural economics from Ohio State University. He has published extensively in the fields of rural finance and micro/small enterprise finance.

Mark Darroch is a senior lecturer in agricultural economics at the University of Natal, Republic of South Africa. His research interests are in land economics, agribusiness strategy, and agricultural finance. He has presented papers on his primary research interests at international conferences in Australia, Canada, England, Hungary, South Africa, the United States, and Zimbabwe. As a visiting lecturer at Purdue University, U.S.A., in 1998, he conducted research on supply chains for new "output" trait crops at the Center for Agricultural Business, and taught food and agricultural business strategy. He has also been a consultant on projects for engineering companies, development institutions such as the United States Agency for International Development (USAID) and the World Bank, producer associations, and commercial banks.

Aliou Diagne of Senegal is an impact assessment economist at the West Africa Rice Development Association (WARDA). Before joining WARDA, he was working at the International Food Policy Research Institute (IFPRI), Washington, D.C., conducting research on rural financial policies in developing countries, with a special focus on Malawi where he was posted from 1994 to 1996. He received a B.S. in applied mathematics from Cheikh Anta Diop University in Senegal. He earned an M.S. in agricultural economics, an M.A. in economics, and a Ph.D. in agricultural economics and economics, all from Michigan State University, U.S.A.

Claudio Gonzalez-Vega is a professor in the Department of Agricultural, Environmental and Development Economics and in the Department of Economics at Ohio State University, U.S.A., where he is also director of the Rural Finance Program. He has degrees in law and economics from the University of Costa Rica, a Masters degree from the London School of Economics, U.K., and a Ph.D. from Stanford University, U.S.A. He has been a consultant to many major international organizations and has written extensively on development finance, financial regulation, and policy reform.

Franz Heidhues has been professor for development theory and policy in the Department of Development Theory and Agricultural Policy in the Tropics at the University of Hohenheim, Germany, since 1982. His research areas include food policy, rural financial market development, innovation and agricultural productivity, and natural resource management in developing countries. Since 2000 he has been head of the interdisciplinary Special Research Programme (SFB 564) on "Sustainable land use and rural development in mountainous regions of Southeast Asia" at the University of Hohenheim. He also serves on the board of Deutsche Welthungerhilfe (German Agro Action) and on the board of the German Israel Fund for Research and International Development (GIFRID), and he is a member of the Scientific Advisory Council of the Federal Ministry for Economic Cooperation and Development (BMZ).

Carla Henry currently works for the International Labour Organization of the United Nations (ILO). She holds an M.B.A. from Virginia Polytechnic University, U.S.A., and an M.S. in agricultural economics from Michigan State University, U.S.A. She has extensive experience working with government, nongovernment, and private sector institutions in the areas of association and enterprise development, agribusiness marketing, rural and microfinance development, and quantitative market research.

Anjini Kochar received her Ph.D. in 1991 from the University of Chicago, U.S.A., where she also attained an M.A. in international relations. Prior to her current position as senior research scholar at the Center for Research on Economic Development and Policy Reform at Stanford University, she was assistant professor of economics at Stanford (1991–2002). Her primary area of research is microempirical analysis of household behavior in developing economies, focusing on savings, health, and educational outcomes.

Cécile Lapenu works with the Comité d'Echange, de Réflexion et d'Information sur les Systèmes d'Epargne-crédit (CERISE). CERISE is sponsored by
four French organizations supporting microfinance institutions in Africa, Asia,
and Latin America, and its aim is to promote knowledge exchange for improving microfinance practices. From 1997 to 2000, she joined the International
Food Policy Research Institute, Washington, D.C., as a postdoctoral fellow, and
conducted research on the performance of microfinance institutions and the role
of the state in financial markets. Before joining IFPRI, she was with the Centre
de Coopération Internationale en Recherche Agronomique pour le Développement (CIRAD). She received her doctoral degree in agricultural economics from
the Ecole Nationale Supérieure Agronomique de Montpellier, France.

Michael Lyne is a professor of agricultural economics at the University of
Natal, Republic of South Africa. He has pursued his interests in land policy,
finance, and institutions with colleagues at the Land Tenure Center, University
of Wisconsin-Madison, U.S.A.; Lincoln University, New Zealand; and the Rural
Finance Program at Ohio State University, U.S.A. Eight of his papers have won
prizes, and he has refereed papers for the journals *Agrekon, Development
Southern Africa*, and *Agricultural Economics*. He was a founding director of
LIMA Rural Development Foundation, a local nongovernmental organization
involved in agricultural and rural development.

Richard L. Meyer is emeritus professor and senior research specialist in the
Department of Agricultural, Environmental, and Development Economics at
Ohio State University, U.S.A. He is a former director of the Rural Finance Program in the department and the university's Director of International Programs.
His publications have concentrated on the area of developing agricultural and
microfinancial systems. His most recent publication is *Rural Financial Markets
in Asia: Policies, Paradigms, and Performance*, published in 2000 by the Oxford University Press and the Asian Development Bank. He received his M.S.
and Ph.D. degrees from Cornell University, U.S.A.

Sergio Navajas, a native of Bolivia, is senior economist at USAID/Bolivia.
Before he joined USAID, he was senior researcher in the Rural Finance Program at Ohio State University, U.S.A. His research has focused on microfinance, rural finance, and poverty and more recently on trade in Latin America
(Paraguay, El Salvador, and Bolivia).

Geneviève Nguyen is assistant professor in rural economics in the Research
Unit Dynamiques Rurales at the Institut National Polytechnique, Ecole Nationale
Supérieure d'Agronomie, Toulouse (INP-ENSAT), France. Her research areas
include household economics, the supply and organization of rural services,
and territorial development in various countries in Africa, Asia, and Europe.

She received her Ph.D. from the Department of Agricultural, Environmental, and Development Economics of Ohio State University, U.S.A.

Julia Paxton is an assistant professor of economics at Ohio University, U.S.A., where she teaches development economics. Her research interests include group lending, outreach measures, and savings by the poor. She has worked on microfinance research with the World Bank Sustainable Banking with the Poor Project (SBP), the Consultative Group to Assist the Poorest (CGAP), and Ohio State University Department of Agricultural, Environmental, and Development Economics, where she obtained her doctorate in agricultural economics.

Jorge Rodriguez-Meza is a senior research associate with the Rural Finance Program in the Department of Agricultural, Environmental, and Development Economics at Ohio State University. He works on rural poverty and microfinance issues and holds a Ph.D. from Ohio State University and a Masters degree from the University of London.

Kimseyinga Savadogo is an associate professor in the School of Economics (UFR/SEG) at the University of Ouagadougou, Burkina Faso, where he teaches microeconomics and econometrics and works on rural livelihood issues relevant for Burkina Faso. He holds a Bachelors degree in Economics from the University of Yaoundé (Cameroon) and Masters and Ph.D. degrees in agricultural economics from Purdue University, U.S.A.

Mark Schreiner is a senior scholar with the Center for Social Development at Washington University in St. Louis, U.S.A. He is also a consultant with Microfinance Risk Management. He studies practical ways to help the poor to build assets through both savings and loans. In the United States, his work focuses on development-based welfare policy. In developing countries, he works on microfinance, and especially credit scoring.

Manohar Sharma joined IFPRI in 1993. He has an M.S. degree in agricultural economics from the University of New England, Australia, and attended Cornell University, U.S.A., for a Ph.D. in the same field. Sharma is a research fellow in the Food Consumption and Nutrition Division.

Julie Stanton is assistant professor in the Department of Food Marketing at the Haub School of Business, St. Joseph's University, U.S.A. She was previously on the faculty of the Morrison School of Agribusiness and Resource Management at Arizona State University, and received her Ph.D. in agricultural economics from the University of Maryland in 1996. During 1986–96, she worked with the World Bank in its research departments, including field work studying the agricultural supply response in Mexico. Current research efforts include studying the difficulties small producers face in the new global market (particularly Mexican producers wanting access to the U.S. market; the economic and financial viability of alternative crops on fragile lands, focusing on mesquite pods; the implications of different views on "organic" food for domestic and trade policy; and the practical issues facing food exporters wanting to do business with emerging market countries.

Betty Wampfler works as a researcher at the Centre de Coopération Internationale en Recherche Agronomique pour le Développement, France. She received her Ph.D. in rural economics from the Ecole Nationale Supérieure d'Agronomie de Montpellier, France. In CIRAD, she is in charge of the research and development activities on rural financial institutions.

Jacob Yaron, now retired, was the senior rural finance advisor at the World Bank at the time of contributing to this work. He is the author of many articles on the issues of rural and microfinance, providing advice on the design and monitoring of Bank projects related to financial intermediation and the revitalization of banks. Prior to joining the Bank he was chief financial officer of one of the largest Israeli corporations, AIPM, and senior vice president of finance, accounting, and management information systems for the company, whose stock was traded through daily arbitrage in the American and Tel Aviv stock exchanges.

Manfred Zeller is a professor at the University of Göttingen, Germany, and director of the Institute of Rural Development. His recent research includes impact assessment of agricultural and rural development policies, strategies to promote pro-poor agribusiness and microenterprises, measurement of poverty, and spatial econometric models of land use change and deforestation. He received his doctoral degree in agricultural economics from the University of Bonn, Germany, where he taught as senior lecturer at the Institute of Agricultural Policy before joining IFPRI in 1991. Until 1999, he led IFPRI's multicountry research program on rural financial policies and food security.

Jiang Zhongyi received a Masters degree in agricultural economics from Beijing Agricultural University, China. He is a senior research fellow at the Research Center for Rural Economic Policy under the Ministry of Agriculture of China. His main research interests are policies on land tenure, poverty reduction, and rural social services.

Zhu Ling received a doctoral degree in agricultural economics from the University of Hohenheim, Germany. She is the deputy director in charge of research and education at the Institute of Economics, Chinese Academy of Social Sciences, Beijing. Her main research interests are income distribution, rural development, and poverty issues.

Index

Page numbers for entries occurring in boxes are followed by a *b;* those for entries occurring in figures, by an *f;* those for entries occurring in notes, by an *n;* and those for entries occurring in tables, by a *t.*